Get the Guests

Psychoanalysis, Modern American Drama, and the Audience

Walter A. Davis

THE UNIVERSITY OF WISCONSIN PRESS

The University of Wisconsin Press
114 North Murray Street
Madison, Wisconsin 53715

3 Henrietta Street
London WC2E 8LU, England

1   2   3   4   5

Printed in the United States of America

Library of Congress Cataloging-in-Publication Data

Davis, Walter A. (Walter Albert), 1942–
Get the guests: psychoanalysis, modern American drama, and the
audience / Walter A. Davis.
308 p.   cm. — (The Wisconsin project on American writers)
Includes bibliographical references and index.
ISBN 0-299-14150-0 (cl).   ISBN 0-299-14154-3 (pb)
1. American drama—20th century—History and criticism.
2. Psychoanalysis and literature.   3. Subjectivity in literature.
4. Theater audiences—Psychological aspects.   5. American
drama—20th century—History and criticism—Theory, etc.   I. Title.
II. Series.
PS350.D38   1994
812'.509353—dc20   93-38608

To Chris and Steve
in abiding love

I have heard
That guilty creatures sitting at a play
Have by the very cunning of the scene
Been struck so to the soul, that presently
They have proclaim'd their malefactions.
—*Hamlet* II.ii.588–92

A book must be an ice ax to break the sea frozen inside us.
—Kafka

Claudius: What do you call the play?
Hamlet: "The Mouse-trap." . . . 'Tis a knavish piece of work, but
           what of that? . . . we that have free souls, it touches us not.
           Let the galled jade winch, our withers are unwrung.
           —*Hamlet* III.ii.236–43

for here there is no place
that does not see you. You must change your life.
—Rilke

Contents

Contents

Acknowledgments

We live and act on many stages, each with a drama appropriate to it. And in all, with luck, gratitude rises and awaits its occasion. And thus genuine thanksgiving—

In the academic theatre: two colleagues who aided mightily in its completion, Mary Wagner and Gareth Euridge; two who did not live to see its final form, Henry Schmidt and Richard Bjornson; and one, Timothy Wiles, who on two separate occasions interrogated every word of it.

In the theatre itself, where the generosity of other players makes acting an existential endeavor: Edward Albee, Dick Casey, Brian Dennehy, Harold Eisenstein, Carter Lewis, Geoff Nelson, Gena Rowlands, Judy van Kirk, and Ionia Zelenka.

In the theatre of psychoanalysis, where the great discontents wait to grieve themselves toward a new humanity: Nathan Adler, L. Brooks McCutcheon, and my analyst and beloved inner presence, the late Marjorie Rowe.

In the theatre of the Dojo, where self-respect finds its true discipline in the body: sensei Bill Evans and sampei Rob Andre.

And, in the theatre of lasting affections: Allen Fitchen, Gary Heim, Stephen Lacey, Tom Quinn, and Lois Tyson.

The word beyond speech is attempted in the dedication.

A Methodological Note

This book constructs a new theory of the psyche through an act of literary interpretation. A double heresy, since such a project disrupts two disciplines, psychoanalysis and literary criticism, by radically altering the terms of their relationship. To these heresies I add a third: I develop the theory by submitting five plays to close interpretation in an effort to show that, contrary to popular opinion, close reading is not the secure achievement of our profession but remains largely its undiscovered country. For the most part, when texts are analyzed to illustrate the interpretive power of critical theories, little happens beyond the subsumption of selected data under categories that remain fixed a priori, unable to find in the text anything but the terms of their verification. Genuine close reading subverts that operation: the text is allowed to complicate, test, and subvert frameworks, because patient attention to its concrete complexity becomes a movement of surpassing that opens on the discovery of the new.

Prologue: In the Theatre

The purpose of acting is to drip acid on the nerves.
  —Jack Nicholson

Audiences know what to expect and that is all they can believe.
  —The Player-King, in Stoppard's
    Rosencrantz and Guildenstern Are Dead

The director's first job is to cast the audience.
  —Grotowski

. . . the power of the text to claw.
  —Beckett

The theatre will never find itself again except by furnishing the spectator
with the truthful precipitates of dreams.
An image is true insofar as it is violent.
  —Artaud

Reducing complexity is a ruse.
My goal is to create images that will sit in the Unconscious.
  —R. B. Kitaj

The priest is the guardian of the mysteries. The artist is driven to expose
them.
Criticism is the art we need most today.
  —William Gaddis, *The Recognitions*

Theatre is the public airing of secrets.
We don't need censorship; we have interpretation.
Literature is the Medusa; criticism, the shield.
Representation always exceeds intention.
  —Author's aphorisms

Theatres should be built next to grave-yards.
  —Jean Genet

Get the Guests

Introduction: The Medusa and the Shield

The Being of the Critic

Here is a chain of supplements which give us one way to look at the current situation of criticism:

The self is a system of consensual validations and reflected appraisals.

The Profession is the way one goes about constructing such an identity by engaging in the rule-directed activity of whatever "theoretical" group within the profession one has decided to put one's money on. Pluralism, as currently conceived, provides the final line of defense for this arrangement.

Most professional students of literature are technicians who, like Thomas Kuhn's "normal scientists," prove their membership in the community by putting reigning paradigms into practice.

Every practice depends upon an implicit set of theoretical assumptions. To prevent that condition from becoming a source of critical reflection and interrogation, a way must be found for theory and practice to reinforce one another.

That way is the activity we call interpretation. Through it, approaches justify themselves by showing their power to illuminate texts.

Interpretation thus provides the capstone that completes the identity that the critic and the community fashion for themselves. The literary work has become the occasion for this process to grow and prosper.

As a result of these practices, a curious "world in the head" is constructed. We live, as professionals, at several safe removes from ourselves. The power of the literary work to disrupt us at the deeper levels of our psyche is contained.

Get the Guests is an attempt to reverse this situation in order to get the patient back on the table. In attempting to expose the psyche of the critic, my goal is to restore our contact with it—and with that which measures it. One reason why critics are reluctant to discuss motives is that they have difficulty seeing that they have motives. The fortress called mind marginalizes such considerations. It is hard to find the motives underlying one's investment in a given theory because motives are carefully hidden within the cloak of reasons; and resistance to their discovery is so strong that raising the possibility that psychological forces shape our activity opens one to the charge of motivism—and immediate dismissal. As a result, the discussion of theories remains, by and large, an exercise in hyperrationality and abstract gymnastics confined to the discussion of arguments and methods, assumptions and rationales within a logical space that cannot be violated. We move in a circle which remains dedicated to the underlying assumption that whatever one's theoretical approach, rational considerations are what led to it and what alone may someday lead to a change of mind. Ours is an enterprise conducted in the mind by agents who have transcended other motives—save one, the career imperative, where everything we don't let ourselves know about ourselves gets channeled.

A hermeneutics of engagement violates the social contract on which the discipline, as currently constituted, depends.[1] Its founding assumption is that we remain, in all our activities, deeply conflicted beings who have taken care to know ourselves only in the most protected ways. The text is the great threat to this edifice. And because it can disrupt it from within, the text must be conquered. Literature is the Medusa because there is no way beings constructed such as we are can fail to be threatened by an activity which has as its subject all that we have banished in order to construct the shields that protect us from ourselves. We don't need censorship; we have interpretation. We use it to make safe the fortress, reinforcing the defenses that protect us from our inner reality by projecting them upon external sources of anxiety. As Freud noted, even though defenses remain largely unconscious, the ego always enjoys the opportunity to employ them. Each time it successfully does so its security grows as the threat from reality recedes. Interpretation is the activity whereby we make the world safe—for ourselves. (The best example of all this, for reasons that will become apparent, is psychoanalytic criticism.)

We will regain contact with ourselves and with the text only when we shatter the shields and enter the text, realizing that it is, at the least, an Other with the power to force us to confront things we don't want to know about ourselves. What we need is a criticism that will use the text to pry open the crypt wherein we have buried our psyche, making the anxiety thereby set loose the force that can lead us most deeply into the text. Once we do so we may even find that our theoretical systems are far more conflicted than we care to admit and far more dense with underlying motives than we had imagined. We might then begin to discern beneath the previous chain of supplements another chain:

Theory is the intellectual defense mechanism that enables us, in mastering the text, to protect and reinforce our ego-identity by displacing the motives that control our psyche into a "rational" hyperspace. This displacement constructs a split between the rational, "objective" self and the rest of the psyche.

Reason becomes the defense that keeps all else repressed.

It thereby produces an ego for itself: the identity of the critic.

That ego is a system of defenses designed to deliver us from anxiety.

It derives its force from underlying motives and conflicts which we do not want to face.

The circle thereby established is one of projection and denial. The split-off psyche expresses itself through the process of denying itself.

But once we grasp the primacy of the psyche, we have just begun. The psyche must be driven back to deracinate its hiding places. The appeal of a theory is often that it offers us mastery in precisely the area of our psyche where we have the least control and the greatest need to assert the contrary. This need is now confronted with the necessity of reversal. Thus, for example, the theory of emotion we use to control our emotional participation in a work is delivered over to the emotions we cannot control. The text's effort to bring us to them becomes the object of interpretation. Psychoanalytic approaches, in turn, reveal the defensive nature of their constructs. The trouble with most theories of the Unconscious is that they have made little acquaintance with that power and its ability to disrupt the systems of defense we keep constructing to protect ourselves from it. And so it goes. Once we take this step, the mastery we claim for our approach reveals the anxiety that made mastery in this particular area so important to us. We may even come to discover the suspicious similarity our most exalted theoretical accomplishments bear to the system of sustaining lies they were meant to make foolproof.

We might then attain a new insight into the being of the critic—the void within and the pit beneath. Literature is what we don't want to know because of the demand it makes on us. We find ourselves instead in a situation similar to Karenin's upon the discovery of his wife's adultery. It troubles him for a few minutes, but once he gets his rational identity back in place, it appears in its proper light and he knows how to deal with it. That "dealing" is a model of the critic's position with respect to the literary work. And as Tolstoy shows us, Karenin's rational stance is the perfect way to carry out a system of resentment and revenge.

The Being of the Text

The being of the text derives from a radically different condition. A hyperrationalism might be appropriate if we were dealing with something like pure geometry, but its inadequacy becomes apparent when we reflect on the vast distance between it and the subject it claims to master. Literature represents human beings caught up in vital passions, engaged with one another in conflicts that go to the depths of the psyche, with one's existence—and not merely one's rational identity—at stake. Literature moves in the broadest and most concrete of hermeneutic circles—an existential circle of subjects' engagement with themselves and one another at a depth that strips away all complacencies. The discrepancy between that fact and the identity we have constructed for ourselves as critics should give us pause. For we move in the narrowest of hermeneutic circles, one based on the refusal to ever let ourselves become genuinely engaged.

If we approach it in the right way, literature has the power to shatter that paralysis. Given its experiential density, the text engages all that we bring—and refuse to bring—to it in a process of discovery which forces us to expand our concepts beyond their present state so that they can articulate an awareness that extends our being. What Freud said of poetry's implications for psychoanalysis is here made the working principle of interpretation: the poets knew the Unconscious first and continue to know it best because they immerse themselves in the process. Our task is to develop a theory of the psyche that will more closely approximate that effort. Thus, although the orientation of this inquiry is psychoanalytic, my effort is to advance psychoanalytic concepts—and an understanding of the psyche—that cannot be found in Freud or in any of the current schools of psychoanalysis. It constitutes, instead, their immanent critique and a liberation of their repressed. The effort throughout is to tunnel to a deeper psychic register than most analysts have been willing to plumb. Literature, and specifically drama, is central to that effort. We go wrong from the start, therefore, whenever we impose fixed psychoanalytic concepts on a literary work, because we thereby invert the proper relationship and sever the sovereign possibility: that of learning from art radically new things about the psyche.

As long as we stay stuck, as critics generally are, in the epistemological bind of all neo-Kantianisms (i.e., the one-way movement from concepts to percepts, the superimposition of fixed a priori theoretical frameworks on texts), there is no way we can reverse this situation and engage the experiential depths that literary works probe.[2] For in order to create the possibility of such an engagement, we must find ways for the literary work to exceed our concepts and shock us toward a knowledge beyond them. Instead, unfortunately, criticism remains trapped in a situation similar to that of those analysts who are incapable of recognizing or learning from countertransference and who, to protect their unexamined psyches, silence the most eloquent witness who is also the source of all new developments in psychoanalytic knowledge, the patient. Unwittingly perhaps, we perform a similar act to keep the greatest patients barred from the room. Works of art are the most meaningful and challenging patient-analysts available, but they speak only to those who are ready to probe the wounds they open up within us. To create such an encounter, I employ concepts derived from a number of competing analysts to move toward a position none of them attained. Hoping its metaphoric connotations will point the way, I use throughout the book the word *Crypt* (and cognate terms) to designate the alternative theory of the psyche I am constructing. The crypt is the place or psychic register of those primordial anxieties and affects that we build other psychological theories in order to repress and deny.

Because a new understanding of the literary work is the condition for its genesis, the Crypt is here presented as process *in statu nascendi*. To pry it open I follow throughout each chapter this procedure: I offer introductory formulations of psychoanalytic concepts. Interpretation of the particular drama under discussion then generates a richer and more complicated understanding, leading to the new conceptual formulations requird to proceed deeper into the drama. The dramatic structure of each play thus becomes the force producing the theory constructed in order to articulate the psychological knowledge contained not only in this particular series of works but also in the larger drama that is created by bringing these five plays together in a single dialectical movement. That movement is not chronological, but dialectical. Thus, for example, discussion of Eugene O'Neill's *Long Day's Journey into Night* follows the chapter on Arthur Miller's *Death of a Salesman* because O'Neill's examination of the family goes to those places where Miller's drama fears to tread. The architectonic of the entire book thus resembles the process Hegel designated by the term *Aufhebung*: a partial understanding is situated and corrected by a new examination, which extends a single order of concepts until the full awareness implicit in the initial problematic has been completely worked out.[3]

Current psychoanalytic theories and concepts are thus used not as fists but as probes which the literary work drives beyond themselves toward a new understanding. That understanding is defined by the only connection that makes intersubjectivity—and the literary experience of same—worth having: the risking of myself in a situation in which the action of another psyche puts the in-depth relationship I have to my own psyche at issue and at stake. When literary experience moves in this medium, it becomes a unique way of knowing: a cocreated intersubjective transaction in which one subjectivity intends and is intended by another subjectivity, with the discovery of what both psyches resist knowing being the goal and moving principle of the engagement. Only when we engage in such a process will "subjective criticism"—and by now it should be clear that all critical theories are, ultimately, based on an implicit theory of subjectivity, which they reify—become what it should be: an attempt to recover the power and value of literature as a uniquely revelatory experience and of critical theory/interpretation as an existential act. If we begin to move in this direction, we will no longer have to fear that the desire—and the wound—which originally bound us to literature is the thing we must sacrifice in the classroom, in graduate education, and in our careers. We will have made criticism the one thing it should be—the "most dangerous game" in which we are both the hunter and the hunted. If we cannot follow the ethical implications of Nietzsche's call to construct lives that will bear aesthetic scrutiny, we should at least stop disguising the fact by imposing our resentment on the phenomena. The issue we face isn't a choice between objectivity and subjectivity, but the question of how deeply we must go into our subjectivity. Unfortunately, most theories of subjective criticism are a travesty of this dynamic. Perhaps the best one can say of them is that they illustrate how defenses operate and thus constitute an inadvertent contribution to psychology.

Authentic subjectivity is finally a discipline of courage, not of self-indulgence. Its primary requirement is a willingness to drive the text into the deepest places of our inauthenticity, there to breed its force as an achieved discontent or disgust with ourselves. Literature offers the possibility of the most radical ethic of reading because it asks us to risk and transform ourselves in depth and to learn from the anxiety it produces the nature of the struggle that is alone proper to self-overcoming. Other theories can then be known in terms of the anxiety they repress, the psychological disorders they serve, and the emotions they protect by holding the real emotions at a safe distance. Perhaps their greatest value is in showing us what we do not want to know and feel and, in so instructing us, help us summon the courage to negate them.[4]

The Being of Drama

The two previous sections draw out the terms of a contradiction. Drama constitutes its dialectic. Through that process the false relationship is exposed and the proper one established.

Drama contains this power because everything in it derives from a single circumstance—the relationship to the audience. Grotowski says that the director's first job is to cast the audience. It is also the playwright's and the ensemble's work and the key that offers critical theory the most radical entry into the theatrical event. For in casting the audience one engages in a complex inquiry into the nature of group psychology in order to create a pulic space that is unique—and that is rapidly disappearing in modern American society.

In modern America the public sphere is by and large the place where we gather to hear the big lies so that everyone in attendance can celebrate the ideological commonplaces that protect us from ourselves. As the privileged space for the operation of ideology, the public sphere interpellates subjects by constructing selves filled to bursting with all the requisite ideas, beliefs, symbolic fetishes, and emotions. In public space, social institutions stand forth and legitimate themselves by offering rituals of pseudodeliberation and pseudocommunication. Sunday worship, the political address, televised congressional hearings, the daily news "bite," are so many rituals which, like the ads they ape, tell us who we are and what we value. And, like good consumers, we glut ourselves upon the Symbolic. If we go to church, listen to the state of the union address, or watch the news expecting to hear the truth, we are sure to be gulled. Public space addresses one and all to put us collectively to sleep.

Drama is the exception. It creates a unique public sphere in which an audience gathers to hear, witness, and suffer the public airing of secrets— about themselves. Implicit in every drama, by reason of its form and the concreteness of the experience it represents, are the conditions of a group psychology in which the audience is exposed and put on trial. When that process works, the audience finds itself in a mousetrap in which the supposedly "pathological" characters on the stage reveal, even as they undergo, the conflicts which the audience wants to keep hidden from itself. Theatre is dangerous because it publicly stages the truths about society which that society wants to conceal.

Theatre contains this possibility because drama represents the process whereby the subtext of our life catches up with us as a direct result of the accumulated efforts we have made to escape it. Those efforts constitute the true content of our character and the continuity of our life. No matter what we say or believe about ourselves, we are what we have done. Drama brings that reality home to roost. It thus represents the occasion most of us have found ways to indefinitely defer. Perhaps the real difference between art and life, between us and the agents on the stage, is that they are more complex and potentially more honest because drama deprives them of the exits we have contrived to protect us from ourselves. The ego is the bastion of that enterprise, its system of defenses the rich panoply we have elaborated to arrest and dissolve the conflicts that fester in our psychic depths. It is also the identity we bring to the theatre, hoping the evening's entertainment will be no harder to digest than the dinner we just ate in preparation for the after-dinner sleep in which we will dream on both. We thus come to the theatre as mirror images of the critics who will later make foolproof our escape routes by providing the train of intellectualizing defenses we call interpretations. But if we enter the theatre in bad faith, we also come uneasy, at some level of our consciousness, about that fact, even when our uneasiness takes the form of sadistic pleasure in watching the spectacle of agents who suffer because they have failed to achieve the harmonious adjustments that confer the substantial identity from which we safely view their plight. Or perhaps we're just interested, willing to learn a thing or two about human nature if the proper rhetoric of "fiction" is preserved so that "essential human verities" can police the drama when it goes too far or fails to restore the values and emotions the audience needs—and demands.

If we let the text of the drama cut through the various rational identities we have constructed for ourselves and impinge directly on our psyche, drama becomes one of the most dangerous acts of discovery because it engages everything we don't want to know about ourselves by exposing the phantom status of everything we do. Through that process, the psyche of the audience becomes one with what is enacted on the stage. The supposedly psychopathological characters become active representatives of the buried truths about the audience brought to light—and inflicted upon them. Drama thereby enacts a group psychological process in which the operations that protect the audience from themselves are exposed by the action of characters who are caught up in a process in which those defenses no longer work because the conflicts they were meant to avoid have finally come home to roost.

Drama thus contains the possibility of irreversible psychological discoveries, because its structure delivers us over to ourselves in a way that leaves us with no way to reassert our defenses except as desperate lies. In showing us what it means to be a dramatic agent, drama forces us to relate to ourselves in depth. Every great drama puts the audience on trial because it forces them to confront the real conflicts in which their being as agents resides. When we truly enter a drama, we become one with the characters on the stage as we suffer together the movement toward recognitions that can no longer be escaped.

Aesthetic and ideological distance is thus precisely the enemy drama undermines from within. Its purpose is to shrink the space between us and the stage, to abolish the fourth wall and bar the exits. In this effort, drama finds itself at odds with most of the theories that have been developed to account for it. Once a drama begins, there is no way to limit where it may go and no way to impose the guarantees required to give things a "proper" cathartic outcome. Drama takes our ideological needs and submits them to our existential situatedness. When drama remains honest to its situatedness, everything arises out of an immanent logic of experience that is radically existential. This logic makes drama an inaugural and uniquely revelatory way of knowing the world in which all the comforting explanations we would impose upon experience are given over to a more concrete and immediate process.

The antitheatrical prejudice is poorly understood when we confine it to thinkers such as Plato. The real prejudice is prosecuted by thinkers from Aristotle to Girard, who praise and "interpret" drama the better to protect us from it. The purpose of drama is not to create rituals that cleanse the collective psyche of tensions in order to protect the *socius* by catharting disruptive emotions so that we can leave the theatre "calm of mind all passion spent," ethics and jurisprudence confidently restored, but to offer places where these needs, and the structures they superimpose upon experience, are exposed to critique.

The Actor's Being

The actor's art is the final link in the chain and the most intimate way in which the audience is cast. Acting is the process in which an ensemble works upon one another in an effort to root out everything inauthentic in one another's being. When actors come to their task with the proper readiness to probe their psyche, they discover together subtexts and through-lines by inflicting them upon one another. They tear at one another's psyches in order to get at the depths of the characters they play. Rehearsal is the search to discover the shared secrets about the audience they will later stage before them. When it is authentic, acting is an attempt to represent the audience to itself in precisely the way it never wants to be seen. The special insight good actors have into the emotions is the knowledge that few of us really know how we feel, since that burden is what we are most concerned to escape. As Robert De Niro notes, people don't express their emotions; they disguise their emotions—and it is only in the process of disguising our emotions that our true emotions come out. The actor's task is to actualize that process so that our innermost secrets can be staged before us in order to reveal that the mask is never more starkly exposed than when it is held most rigidly in place. When we unravel, most of us do so through reification. Habit, as Beckett says, is a great deadener—and it finally presents the corpse. A great performance springs a mousetrap in which we are revealed to ourselves reified, arrested, and held up to public view.

That is why a play develops its deepest dramatic possibility when the audience is present. Rehearsal then grows to the event, as the ensemble senses and plays off the responses the audience gives them in order to lead the audience where they don't want to go. Performance is the effort to activate a group psychology in order to unravel and transform it. Onstage the one thing one is constantly aware of is the audience's response. It is the process which one constantly adjusts and builds upon, for it alone is the process by which the play, as public space, is realized. One knows what the nervous laughter signifies, the hushed silence, the inappropriate guffaw readily seized on by others who seek the escape it offers, the anxiety and outrage that greet the descent into fundamental conflicts, the straw clutched at for comic relief, the applause that often signifies no more than the plea to be reassured through the bow that says it's all been a game. When things go badly, the audience successfully resists. On those grand nights when everything goes right, we get the guests at a level that, at least momentarily, transforms their relationship to their very being. Articulating this possibility is the task of dramatic interpretation. It must chart, meticulously, what would happen in the ideal performance that would get the guests by catching them up in the psychic structure scored in the text.

Incipit tragœdia

In studying the theatre event, the chapters that follow attempt to enact and thereby retrieve the hidden drama that is at the heart of all dramas: the relationship of the psyche to itself as it projects and denies the conflicts that constitute its innermost core. As we will see, the assiduous avoidance of that drama is the source of the theoretical impasses of contemporary theory and of the cognate disciplines on which it depends for its interpretive frameworks. As Freud said, the poets knew "it" first, and they continue to know it best. They offer us a chance to expose the limitations of the frameworks we impose upon their work in order to protect ourselves from what we might know when those frameworks come crashing down upon us.

My earlier book *Inwardness and Existence* constructed the terms for a hermeneutics of engagement that would make it possible for us to risk ourselves in the act of interpretation. *Get the Guests* provides the example which illustrates and concretizes that process. It attempts to engage the being of the critic by showing how drama subjects its audience to a process which exposes the arrested drama of their own psyche. The effort thereby is to reconstitute dialectic as a critical method by revealing how dialectic inhabits the structures that rule—with an eventual and tragic necessity—at the innermost resources of our being as dramatic agents.[5] If, as Arthur Miller argues, every drama is a jurisprudence, then we have barely begun to understand the true operations of the law.

1

Souls on Ice:
The Iceman Cometh

The Iceman Cometh has a metapsychological status for a study of how drama casts the audience, because it attains an in-depth analysis of group psychology by dramatizing the process whereby the repressed truths of group behavior come to light. That process requires four acts which have the structure of a single and irreversible process. In each act the group tries to abolish conflict by coalescing around a shared need which offers a shared identity. But as each identity crumbles—as a result of Hickey's action—the defenses and the root disorder that motivate the collectivity surface. The defenses no longer work, but the disorder, stripped of evasions, announces its true terms, as in each act the group regresses to a more primitive psychological state in an effort to achieve the collective ego required to discharge conflict. In tracing that process Eugene O'Neill develops an understanding of group psychology that constitutes a major contribution to a branch of psychoanalysis much in need of its example.[1]

If in *Waiting for Godot* the same thing happens twice, in *Iceman* the same thing happens, with a difference, four times. Each act dramatizes an identical process in order to cut deeper, each time, into the heart of the disorder. The group is caught in a repetition-compulsion; Hickey is caught in the need to expose their repressed. Each act accordingly constitutes for the group a regression to earlier modes of psychic functioning, an attempt to resolve a collective disorder which only succeeds in bringing its most archaic sources to the surface. In O'Neill's hands repetition thus produces that kind of reversal that is uniquely revelatory: a structure of tunneling from one apparently coherent psychic structure to the more primitive one underlying it in a progressive descent which pries open the deepest psychic crypts.

In studying the lengths to which a group will go to discharge a threat to its existence, the play exposes the ultimate motive behind group psychology. That reality, as we'll see, is the working of death as the force that unites the group from within and to which all its labors are finally dedicated. In forcing us to confront death as the true force binding groups, O'Neill develops a vision that extends to far more than the behavior of drunks in bars. The setting in fact constitutes a brilliant estrangement effect, since it relaxes the censorship that would prevent the audience from realizing too quickly that the collective processes staged in Harry's saloon represent what human beings necessarily conceal about the needs that inform group behavior in general. For once this connection clicks, the audience becomes the subject of the play. What is enacted onstage mirrors what takes place in the audience as it responds. The fourth wall is shattered. The theatre event has become a struggle in which our response implicates us in a dialectic that will reveal everything we don't want to know about the psychodynamics informing our "nature" as social beings.

Group Psychology: An Introductory Sketch

Once we get beyond the myth of an autonomous individuality prior to all relations with others, group psychology becomes interesting and dangerous. Groups aren't simply something we need. We are inconceivable without them. Two canonical concepts in social psychology set the basic orientation: the self is a product of reflected appraisals, and consensual validation is the process of identity formation. In an ironic inversion of Nietzsche, we become who we are by internalizing the attributions of others. We maintain and "change" our identity by adapting ourselves to the legitimation rituals that structure the groups to which we belong.

To feel the full bite of these reflections, we need to focus on those primary groups we cannot be without (church, polis, profession) and to which our allegiance is so total that group and self are inseparable extensions of one another. Primary groups give life a purpose by offering explanations of realities that would otherwise prove unintelligible or unacceptable. Faith in the group's beliefs delivers one from the anguish of individuality. Groups make a space where one can go for acceptance and for deliverance from existential contingency and social impersonality. The group delivers the goods; it fulfills needs so totally, in fact, that its collapse alone enables us to see the motives underlying our steadfast devotion to it. One who would destabilize any group must alienate it, must perform a *Verfremdungseffekt*, by exposing the rituals through which the group creates and maintains a shared identity. To do so one must block those rituals and turn them back against themselves.

We might then begin to see that delivering us from certain realities is the group's primary reason for being and the source of its constitutive operation—the act of exclusion that banishes the source of disruption. Groups achieve solidity through acts of exorcism. Invariably group membership requires the sacrifice of something psychologically threatening within the self that must be made to seem worthless and contemptible. Groups rid us of inner conflict, and when they work the observance of group practices eventually obliterates any memory of the prior disorder. In this sense all groups require an Other within the order of the psyche that must fill the role of scapegoat, victim, or enemy and a leader who embodies the identity that will keep the repressed image from surfacing.[2]

The leader produces group coalescence by theatricalizing the self-image the group requires, thereby becoming an ideal representative of the group's defining desire. Groups coalesce around the "presence" of the leader because that identifiction forges from the dispersed, fractured, and insecure "identity" of the members a single will which becomes, through allegiance, a unified power of action. Groups must enact rituals which proclaim and solidify identity, because until the theatrical moment is attained, the group floats endangered by dissolution. The leader's task is to create symbolic actions that ratify a collective identity centered around his status as master of ceremonies celebrating the group's ideology. To perform his functions the leader must be an ideal representative of the group's ideology. The corollary: any weakness or failure in the leader reintroduces into the group the specter that is being exorcised. As we'll see, the irony of this circle lies in the hollowness of its terms.

Whenever one tries to disrupt a group, one naturally encounters strenuous resistance because one has reactivated the primary anxieties that motivate group identification. Groups are like Heidegger's broken hammer.[3] We only know the purpose they serve and the world they conceal when they break apart. When a group dissolves, the "repressed" returns as the members regress once again to their basic fears. To understand any group, one must therefore activate its suppressed drama. Such, in any case, would be the role undertaken by the Socratic actor who entered a group intent on exposing its psychodynamics. It is unlikely that Theodore Hickman would understand the concepts outlined above. But he knows something more important: how to enact them—in a bar.

Why do drunks drink? Because there is something even more self-destructive that they want to forget. Every bar is a stage, and the drunk's tale, a cover-up which disguises a deeper disorder. Drunks have patiently waited for the one event they can use as the excuse to give up their lives. In "waiting" for it, of course, they've structured their lives in order to bring it about, but this is the consciousness they must deny. The tale they tell thus resembles a psychoanalytic narrative, in which the "real story" constantly oozes out in the subtext. Through endless talk about their lives, drunks incessantly flee their origins. The psychology of victimage requires that one keep retelling one's tale in order to displace the self-consciousness that reemerges whenever the telling stops.

Such an effort requires reinforcement. Drunks are inveterate social beings; telling demands a sympathetic audience of fellow sufferers. We need to be relieved of anxiety together. Getting the right codependents is the act necessary to prevent self-knowledge. Everyone in *Iceman* lives in terror of confinement. A steady supply of reflected appraisals is needed to tranquilize consciousness. In these ways drunks provide perhaps a privileged insight into the psychology of groups in general and the actual function that being with one another performs in groups which have more successfully disguised the ties that bind them.

Act I: Catharsis Through Comedy

Returning to Consciousness: The Renewal of Death-Work

Act I of *Iceman* represents the consciousness we rush to the group in order to escape and to which we return whenever the group breaks down. A calm of death prevails, as each drunk wakes to resume the burden of consciousness. But with consciousness comes the communal need to restore illusions and defenses. To escape reality, individuals conspire to tranquilize one another by sharing their stories. The narrative projection of one's being is here based on a sympathetic contract which sacrifices, for the greater good of the community, any questioning of these narratives. Each member tries to become the right audience—for the others.

The basic fear that consciousness brings is of being left alone in a room, with no listener, assaulted by the repressed story that one escapes only by fabricating other stories. The naked consciousness that erupts in each agent as the day begins establishes anxiety as that experience which, however momentarily, brings the psyche before itself. The proper name, accordingly, for the shared effort to extinguish it is *death-work*.[4]

O'Neill's primary task in preparing Hickey's entrance is to establish death-work as the core rationale of group behavior. Waiting for Hickey also reveals the difficulty of that labor. Lacking a figurehead, the work of discharging consciousness remains tenuous. Fellowship is pumped up to keep the group from collapsing back into anxious isolation or erupting in an aggression that simmers in the knowledge each has of the other's lies. In love with easeful death, the group longs for Hickey, who will enact the ritual whereby all tension is released in saturnalia and carnival. The group awaits the comic actor who promises a comic catharsis. Larry's role doesn't disrupt but solidifies this process: as "phoolosopher" he is the exception into whom the group projects the consciousness Hickey will banish for good.

Group Psychology and the Estrangement Effect

The estrangement effect Hickey introduces is that of an actor who refuses to play his customary role. That refusal doubles his audience back upon itself. From his entry, Hickey destroys habitual expectations. While his customary role was that of a master of ceremonies celebrating the collective dream of release, he now represents the principle of reversal, which inaugurates drama because it challenges collective needs in a way that makes change or the extinction of consciousness inescapable alternatives. Like Hamlet, Hickey warns his audience that he is preparing a mousetrap for them by exploring the functions his former role played in their psychic economy. A preacher's son and a successful salesman, Hickey knows that the art of rhetoric depends on this: to sell anything one must sell the self-image the customer will gain by buying the product. The hard Brechtian task of the actor playing Hickey is thus to represent this character in a new way while recalling the appeal of all the old ways. Otherwise the mousetrap will remain empty. The group wants a leader who will discharge collective tensions through actions that will be expulsive, manic, and underterred by irony. To get the guests, Hickey's initial task is to replay the old games while taking the pleasure out of them. "If that's what you want to believe . . ." has become the question mark he adds to all interactions. Hickey's statements are all implicit interrogations designed to put his audience on the hook. His repeated refrain takes the kick out of everyone's champagne: "If anyone wants to get drunk, if that's the only way they can be happy, and feel at peace with themselves, why the hell shouldn't they?" (79).[5]

The challenge set, the group now performs habitual actions under a strain that starts to expose the underlying motives those actions serve. Hickey has established new terms for narrative self-presentation. He claims that unlike them he has had the guts to face himself and banish illusion, thereby attaining the ability to act on the group in a way that will bring about "the happiness of all concerned" (79). He also knows that these assertions stir up group defenses that must be fully activated before he can get at what haunts the "private" psyche of each member. In seeking sleep, he leaves the group with the countervailing need to find the mechanism that will exorcise his presence and reestablish its collective identity. Mosher's story of Doc performs that function and, in doing so, exemplifies the kind of humor drunks require. Drunks know that they are dedicated to self-destruction, but they can only face that fact by turning the common death drive into a joke shared at the expense of life. Doc's story is a monument to that need, because it abolishes the difference upon which life depends. Like the Hickey of old, Doc preaches the gospel that "staying sober and working" is what "cuts men off in their prime" (88). Doc's messianic purpose is to extend his "miraculous cure" so that there won't be "a single vacant cemetery lot left in this glorious country" (90). He predictably becomes the butt of his own joke when he perishes because he's so busy administering the gospel that one night he forgets to get drunk. The group dissolves in laughter at the punch line, because wit here liberates an aggression that feeds on life. In this joke death wins by dissolving any difference. As Freud shows, wit is always contentious: the outsider here mocked is life itself. The goal, in leveling all distinctions, is to unbind psychic tensions. The energy needed to sustain conflict, upon which life depends, is reduced to absurdity. At the end of act I the group achieves collective discharge in what we may call a comic culture of the death instinct.

That new collective unconscious reveals that the true function Hickey previously performed was to salve the psychological state to which the group must regress in order to discharge his changed presence. But the joke only gives momentary relief, because they have not been able to die. Death-work requires a more complex agon. It is hard work, as Beckett says, but they are now committed to it because the mousetrap has sprung. Group fusion through the joke is only momentary; the act ends appropriately with the group again dissolving, as each member stares at Hickey, "puzzled, resentful and uneasy" (90).

System, Structure, and Dramatic Process

We now have the categories we need to grasp the dialectical structure of the play. Each act begins with a new mode of existential individuality which the group must discharge by finding a new mode of bonding. Hickey's function as actor is to shatter that effort, producing in reaction the collective regression whereby the group descends to a more primitive identity. The psychodynamic structure of the play is contained in the transformation these categories undergo in each act, in an irreversible structure of devolution which makes explicit the true meaning of the subtext that is present from the opening moves. In repeating an identical process at a new depth, each act constitutes the analysis of a distinct group psychology in an ongoing process that aims to expose the ultimate "foundations" of group behavior.

Thus, act I represents individuality as an anxiety over the return of inner voices that is so overwhelming one will do anything to obliterate consciousness. Accordingly, group psychology strives to sustain a low-level passivity while awaiting the leader who will provide the positive libidinal charge needed to solidify the group "ego" in a ritual celebrating their lowest common identity, the drunken orgy that extinguishes consciousness. In challenging that drive, Hickey introduces the possibility of an individuation that purges the psyche of the needs that bind individuals to groups. As its representative, he becomes the outsider who blocks projection, thereby threatening the psychological economy on which the group identity depends. In regression they take on the first form death-work must assume to discharge that threat. The new psychological condition they thereby attain becomes the subject of act II.

You, lecteur: *O'Neill's Audience*

We now add the category that announces our darker purpose. *Iceman* engages its audience by forcing us to take up a series of positions that are analogous to the responses of the group onstage and that, like them, we resist with all the "devices" at our disposal. Ours, of course, are intellectualizing defenses, which lack the immediacy of a drunk's methods but may finally amount to the same thing. One thing is sure: the double position act I puts us in challenges ordinary responses.

We begin, like Larry, in the grandstand, because we naturally want to sustain a distance from the "low," naturalistic characters onstage. But identifying with Hickey as critical consciousness is a hard move to make. While the group reacts defensively to Hickey, we suspect he's covering up a great deal. To solidify our psychological superiority, we become masters before the fact, ready to fill in the gaps in his character by discovering his motives. We all love to find the flaw in anyone who claims to have *the* solution. In presenting himself as the Lacanian "subject supposed to know," Hickey activates an aggressive suspicion that grows in proportion to whatever anxiety his questions awaken in us. In such matters the best defense, of course, is to invoke whatever psychological commonplaces we need to assassinate the character of whoever threatens us.

But in positioning us between Hickey and the group, act I blocks such operations by making us become an audience that is internally split. The comic discharge of pity, which is perhaps the first desire most audiences bring to the theatre, is made impossible by the awareness we gain of why the group onstage adopts that response. However, Hickey's unqualified attack on groups in general and his single-minded focus on their "neurotic" foundations make us long for the constitution of a collective psychology that would not be subject to such a critique. On a deeper level, we necessarily distance ourselves from both the group and Hickey because their conflict entails a rift between self-preservation and self-knowledge. If we laugh with the group at the end of the act, we perhaps find during the intermission that it is an uneasy laughter which dissolves the moment we reflect on its terms. Identifying with Hickey offers no relief, however, for unlike the comic actor who asks us to join him in general mirth, often at his own expense, Hickey is enigmatic and, like Hamlet, withdraws behind knavish speeches that, we fear, may sleep in a foolish ear. We would like to discharge this tension by getting a secure handle on his motives, but we suspect that any premature, reductive explanations will shortly leave us in a position where we will look too much like the characters onstage. So, unlike the group, we find ourselves less together at the end of the act than at the beginning, because the working of its structure has transformed us from an audience confidently together seeking discharge and the reaffirmation of common values to anxious agents who have begun to reflect apart. Drama has begun to affect us in a new way. We suspect that the purpose of some dramas may be to destroy audience solidarity rather than celebrate it.

In opposition to Wayne Booth's notion that we read from and to a fixed identity from which we can be persuaded to consider certain troubling things if the author assures us that a secure scheme of publicly recognized values will keep things from getting out of hand, act I catches us up in a process in which we begin to suspect that O'Neill may have a darker, more disruptive purpose.[6] Free-floating anxiety has begun to circulate throughout the theatre, threatening to reexistentialize us in a privacy in which we will find ourselves, though surrounded by others, alone, bereft of communal contexts of explanation and response.

In so positioning us, act I has set a mousetrap for the intellectualizing defense of the ego. Whether we realize it or not, a negative countertransference has been formed.[7] The play has begun to work on an anxiety that will open up our psychic basement. Act I takes the voyeurism we bring to the theatre and confronts us with the possibility, sure to activate vigorous resistance, that theatre's authentic purpose may be to subject us to a dread that comes only when all our foundations begin to collapse.

In its conclusion act I poses this challenge by staging it. Like the group onstage, we face a dilemma. If we join the group in its laughter, we do so to expel the threat of individuation. Laughter offers release from the greater expenditure of energy that is required whenever one refuses conventionalized roles and responses. Refusing laughter, on the other hand, implies the need to differentiate ourselves from the group onstage by assuming the task of unmasking defenses and lies. Either choice situates us in O'Neill's mouse-trap. The story of Doc first activates a recurrent structure in which the difference between life and death is dissolved. The choice we make in re-sponding to it situates us for a subsequent discovery that the joke has been on us. In working on us, act I subjects the attitudes that most audiences bring to theatre to a critique which suggests that the traditional ways we respond to drama (i.e., "the universal principles of human response") actu-ally constitute so many ways of protecting ourselves from it.

Act II: Aggression, Anxiety, and Collective Death-Work

Silent Spring: The Dialectic within the Psyche

In act II the comic carnival of release becomes an aggressive culture of the death drive. Aggression emerges as the motive that has controlled the group from its inception. It now surfaces because it provides the only means whereby the group can re-form in a way that excludes the threat in its midst. The first effect of Hickey's mousetrap is to force the group to repeat its founding need from the regressed state to which he has driven them. That reaction is a watershed moment because it reveals anxiety and aggression as the basic dialectic at work within the psyche.

Psychic conflict must be projected, or it festers within, forcing us to confront repressed motives that must be denied. Projection is that mode of aggression that rids one of inner conflict by investing it in others. When a group hits on this possibility, mutual cruelty becomes the complicitous pro-cess that forges a new collective ego capable of banishing the threat of psychological knowledge. The true effect of Hickey's action, once the joke passes, is to bring each agent, however momentarily, before the choice that defines the psyche: the effort to change by taking action within oneself or regression to a new mode of group deliverance. Not surprisingly, the "patho-logical characters on stage" enact the latter alternative, thereby giving us a systematic insight into how projection functions as the glue of a collectivity.[8]

Projection is necessarily an aggressive act, because its purpose is to exorcise inner anxiety, to externalize one's disorder by putting it on someone else's back. That is the reason why most relations with others are disguised dramas of mutual aggression which flourish through displacement and denial. Change, in contrast, derives its possibility from two things: one sustains discontent with oneself and then uses that feeling to probe one's psyche. Taking action within oneself requires reversing the direction of aggression. Aggression turned inward must wage a direct attack on the system of lies that controls one's inner psychic economy. Through that act, anxiety finds its proper target, the self, and with it the possibility of sustaining the only state that can produce change within the psyche.

Anxiety offers three options. We can displace it by projecting its cause outside ourselves. Depriving ourselves of this operation, we can try to sustain anxiety in its free-floating state, knowing that flight from it simply traps us in our initial condition. Or we can modify the direction of anxiety by making it the force we direct inward in an attempt to articulate the repressed conflicts it derives from. Aggression toward oneself is the sine qua non for this effort; a direct attack on one's defenses is the target. To engage that possibility, however, a striking reversal of function is required. We must overcome the traditional view of anxiety's signal function as that affect that alerts the ego to employ defenses.[9] Rejecting that mechanism is the act that inaugurates the possibility of taking action within oneself. Anxiety is "changed utterly." It now alerts us to an unresolved conflict in our psyche that must be probed by making aggression the force we use to root out the disorders within.

Anxiety and Herding

Such a use of anxiety is the rare act. Generally we choose, instead, to lay our anxiety off on others, which is why most social arrangements become policing operations in which aggression is always in danger of erupting. This is especially the case whenever a group has been forced to reflect, however momentarily, on the disorders it harbors. For then the happiness and the "good of all concerned" are secured only when all are brought to one standard, low and mean.

That psychodynamic constitutes the activity of the group in act II. They are now a dissolved "group" that must rebuild itself from the ground up, but with aggression now serving as the basis and organizing motive. Deprived of a flattering group identity, individuals return to a self-loathing that projects itself in undifferentiated spite as it seeks the suitable object onto which self-consciousness can be discharged. Bereft of illusions, each individual regresses to a self-contempt which makes all concrete relations with others theatres of an aggression which constantly erupts and circulates freely, threatening the possibility of any group solidarity. Yet since this process generates the search for a common enemy or victim, it becomes the basis whereby a new group comes into being. Aggression in its metonymy stands forth as the true epigenesis of group formation. In the circle that is now being drawn, aggression is the ruling principle that brings the group back into being and that controls its restored functioning. It does so by using the power of exposure and exclusion to bind the members around a group image that is derived from what is weakest in each psyche (97). Thereby the true nature and function of pity are revealed.

As act II begins, the simmering resentment that was kept comically in check in act I through a shared, teasing recognition of human weakness erupts in violent psychological attacks on one another. Once individuated and placed on the hook, weak individuals must put down others in order to project the very self-image that must be denied. But given individual weakness, projection requires support: it must be supplemented by other voices. The recurrent structure early in act II is thus one in which two or more individuals band together to expose or exclude another. And in an easily shifting play of allegiances, most find themselves at different times in each position, as is reequired for the proper effect. The initial round, between Chuck, Cora, Margie, Pearl, and Rocky, and its eventual discharge onto Larry (100–103) exemplifies the process, since Larry's laughter at everyone's expense awakens a "unanimous hostility" that enables Rocky to "transfer his anger" in a way that gets everyone off the hook. The psychodynamics underlying two clichés about group psychology—the best defense is an offense, and there is safety in numbers—are thereby exposed as mechanisms dependent on a regression to infantile behavior. The objective correlative of that move is the preoccupation everyone has in act II with name-calling (whore, pimp, etc.) and its defensive mirror, the euphemism ("We're tarts, that's all"). The first puts the other on the hook; the latter protects the self from awareness. Anxiety is discharged by identifying the potential outsider as "wimp," while an acceptable self-image is restored by getting others to enhance it with the appropriate language games. The goal of both processes is the creation of the outsider, since aggression will continue to circulate freely until a large enough group is created and the one who withholds assent is found. Such an agent must be a perfect receptacle for the anxiety at the foundation. Whether they know it or not, the group is now "waiting for Hickey" in a new way and needs his presence to solidify the new collectivity.

While this dynamic takes form, Hickey plays his role by playing a waiting game. He knows that his medicine/poison (*pharmakon*) must be given time to work.[10] Nothing is slain in absentia. The group must activate the true terms of its togetherness so that the truth about pipe dreams and the pity that has heretofore bound them together can be exposed. By forcing the group to find the collective psychology that will exclude the threat he represents, Hickey sets them up for a new exposure of collective motives.

In springing that mousetrap, O'Neill will bring about a change in our understanding of the nature and function of pity. The play is full of abstract, quasi-Nietzschean discussions of pity, but it is the context in which act II places that emotion—and our attitude toward it—that exposes its basement. While act I revealed pity as the soft basis of group identification, act II reveals the mutual aggression underlying pity. Appeals to pity rest on this contract: I'll give you the lie you need so that I can rest assured I'll get the same from you. Aggression is the subtext. The threat of exclusion binds those who share pity to a fear that must be projected. Pity and fear thus supplement one another in a relationship that is decidedly nontragic. Flight from knowledge is pity's foundation, while extinguishing fear requires placing that burden on someone else. As they circle through the group, these emotions produce nothing stable because the real truth they give forth is that everyone sees through everyone else's lies. The truth of each person's character is on the surface, known by all, requiring no deep analysis. That is why puncturing and then restoring illusions becomes the game everyone plays in order to forge a new identity. Groups unite not because the members don't know who they are, but precisely because they do. Projective aggression fuels the effort to restore one another's defenses. Bluster and bravado sustain a manic identity for each member. To solidify, however, the group must take common action and defeat the force that threatens it. Projection must cleanse the psyche by making that threat an object of ridicule so that the group can transfer its impotence onto the outsider. Castration has found its true purpose.

Hickey does his best to provoke this reaction. As a Socrates who sets mousetraps and then dares his audience to take the bait by refuting the doubts he has planted in their psyches, he forces the group to act out the very motives they want to deny. Brought to the surface and made the new bases of group identity, repressed motives ripen toward the trap he will spring in act III, when he cares each person to disprove him and reclaim their pipe dream, knowing that the action required to do so will, in its collapse, make the truth inescapable. If nothing is slain in absentia, then act II is the necessary step through which Hickey's guests make their psyches fully present.

Nothing illustrates that condition better than the new exercise of humor that brings act II to a close. Joking no longer celebrates group unity or brings collective relief through the unbinding power of the death drive. Instead, humor sustains and focuses aggression in a sexual attack on the excluded individual. Mocking Hickey as castrated male completes a negative transference whereby Hickey becomes the reservoir of the sexual fears and conflicts of the group. In porojecting those conflicts onto Hickey, the group has unwittingly revealed the psychic disorder that act III will get at. A collective panic to deny the psychological significance of sex is upon them, because sex exposes the deepest wound in each psyche. Death-work now has a new reality that must become the tendentious object of humor. The group has a

new purpose in retelling a joke they never tire of—that Hickey's wife is
sleeping with the iceman. The motive for Hickey's aggression is thereby
identified as the need to project his castration onto them. His charge that
they are cowards is reversed. The joke dangles a new possibility before them,
the chance to share their castration by laughing about it. Just as act I
abolished the difference between life and death, so humor now reduces sex
to insignificance. The explosive laughter thereby released expels the psychosexual conflicts that have formed the ill wind blowing through the aggressive and euphemistic operations that have occupied so much of the act. The
group needs to deprive sex of danger and of psychological significance
because sex tears open the crypt. At the depth of each psyche, core conflicts
have been reawakened. Aggression has not been discharged; it has, rather,
found in psychosexual conflict its source and target. For the group, libido
and aggression (Eros and Thanatos) are not opposed drives, but handmaid-
ens, with the repressed conflicts of the former informing the violent operations of the latter. If sexual conflict is the anxiety that individuates the
psyche, then the lesson of act II is that the repression of sex, and its
pseudomastery, are the deepest source of group psychology.

Hickey welcomes the laugh at his expense because he knows that it
exposes a condition he will turn back against each of them in act III. On
previous visits, Hickey enjoyed making himself the butt of the iceman joke
for the mirth of all. Now picturing him this way only underscores a meta-
phorics in which he is the phallic aggressor who penetrates their shields to
mock their impotence. And they know as much, because this time the joke
does not discharge the underlying resentment that binds them, or the anxiety
that erupts at act's end with the news of Evelyn's death.

In Us, Before Us: The Group and the Audience

Does the group's transparency confirm our difference, or does it suggest a
possibility we must hide through the belief that our psyche is so deep and so
encrusted, in any case, by defenses which have become ego-syntonic that
neither exposure nor self-knowledge are to be feared? We like to think of
ourselves as radically different from these characters, but insofar as we
respond in similar ways whenever someone challenges one of our communal
beliefs or our professional identity, we give ourselves the lie. Act II creates
this tension in us in order to trap us, at its conclusion, in a dilemma that is
the dialectical *Aufhebung* of the one we faced at the end of act I.

For the group onstage, defenses crumble quickly. Self-knowledge is constantly present to each agent and just as constantly denied. All that is required to activate a massive collective resentment is a simple challenge to the

group's self-image. By introducing suspicion, Hickey offends the community, raising the specter of questions it insists must remain suppressed. In response, it employs the traditional device used to banish the Socratic threat: the effort to assassinate the character of the aggressor by finding the neurotic motives behind his actions.

In studying this operation, *Iceman* gives a new twist to the dogma of traditional rhetoric that you can't persuade people by offending them. This truth may hold, but it does so in the hollowness of a tautology, since persuasion without offense usually amounts to simply telling people what they want to hear. Offense, in contrast, is the risk required for vital communication to begin. Defenses must be activated, the sores of discontent rubbed raw, and projection turned back against itself. Communication then becomes a genuine drama in which both parties are engaged. Like the group onstage, we may not go to the theatre looking for such an experience, and we can always find ways to dismiss works that offend us, but we should perhaps become aware of what such a reaction often signifies.

In act II pity and fear are revealed as counterfeit emotions: they do not produce an agon of reversal and recognition, but a displacement of aggression that feeds on projection and denial. In seeing this as Hickey's goal, the group is ahead of him. Hickey hides such motives from himself behind a messianic conception of his mission. By act's end, though, he has begun to suspect that he may be engaged, despite his intentions, in reenacting a crime for motives that will expose everyone to far more than he intends. Having made the analytic turn, he is caught in the dilemma Socrates deftly avoids. He can't arbitrarily stop questioning the motives behind his actions. The dialectic of anxiety and inwardness has become his destiny. The kind of self-knowledge and deliverance he wants to bring the group may be no more than a defense against self-discoveries he can only displace and deny by controlling the content and results of everyone's self-knowledge. But dialectically he is caught in a process whereby each action he takes leads to a deeper insight into his motives, which undercuts the project he has erected in an attempt to keep them repressed.

We are trapped in a similar dilemma. Insofar as we identify with Hickey's activity—by assuming that the truth should be told even if it doesn't produce the good of all concerned—we are committed to probing his unconscious motives. This stance is a far cry from the reductive schemes of explanation we were tempted to apply to Hickey at the beginning. Interpretation now turns on the uncovering of complex psychological motives.

In other words, Hickey offers us the role of analysts only to uncover in that activity motives which challenge the comforting reassurances required to protect the ego-identity of the analyst. In Hickey's case, every action exposes the repressed. Applying this recognition implicates us in a process in which "Know thyself" has become an imperative we must apply not only to our interpretations but to the repressed conflicts displaced through them as well. Analytic honesty demands no less of those who use it. We have no way to protect our psyche from the kinds of things Hickey discovers about his. Dogmatic psychoanalysis has given way to a hermeneutics of engagement.

But sustaining such a position involves immense difficulties for those who would become the audience required by the work. The reservoirs of pity are drying up. Drunks are not pitiful but malevolent. When properly tuned, they may strike a sympathetic chord. But they become uncanny representatives who stir up deeper anxieties about the human condition once they start acting out their founding anger. And that reaction cuts deeply into us once we see that a self-knowledge, always just beneath the surface, is what fuels the cruelty. Perhaps the "deep" truth about the psyche is our refusal to admit or attend to what we know we're doing. Constituting this recognition opens up tragic possibilities most audiences are quick to expel. If people know what they're doing and keep doing it anyway, sacrificing anyone, however close, in order to maintain the lies required for their peace of mind, and if such are the motives made avid by group psychology, then we have no choice but to refrain from that felicity.

In doing so, we become, like Hickey, strangers to ourselves, bereft of the protection collectivities supply, the identities they confer, and the self-discoveries they obviate. The malevolence of the group is such, however, that it deserves the cleansing brand of a violent honesty. Aggression is Hickey's proper role and the most wakeful attitude we can take toward our reactions. Our purpose as audience can no longer be to restore the ego and its defenses, since doing so amounts to endorsing the circle of violence which well-functioning defenses beget. Perhaps there is no basis for group identity that isn't worthy of contempt and no analytic process that doesn't entail its own feast of aggression, the goal being not to restore collective values but to destroy them. But that's a possibility few can face, especially those, such as analysts, priests, and literary critics, who are dedicated by profession to finding out the truth about themselves and sharing that experience with others.

Once all this clicks, we have attained the proper analytic position: anxiety floods the stage. If we rush to extinguish that anxiety by projecting it into a rich anticipation of Hickey's exposure, we should also realize that what is uncovered in that process will necessarily expose us to further discoveries about our resistances and repressions. Our "identification" with Hickey's analytic activity has backed us into this psychological space. In reaction, splitting rises up as the primitive defense that offers the best way to separate ourselves from Hickey. But Hickey may be the cracked mirror which heals the split by presenting us with the self-knowledge we flee.

As we move between Hickey and the group, seeking a place to invest our anxiety, we find ourselves trapped in a dilemma. The group regresses further, while its critic moves toward a tragic agency that will expose an order of psychic conflict which will destroy any hope we may retain of recovering the psychological identity we had at the beginning of the play.

Act III: Acting Out One's Paralysis: Death-Work as Comedy of the Absurd

The Mother of All Groups: The Internalized Other and Super-Ego Pathology

To kill a pipe dream one must kill the internalized other who enforces it as the fundamental terms of one's self-paralysis.

The drunk's problem is one of superego pathology. In that economy, drink provides an externalized system analogous to the hysteric's object. It is Janus-faced, because drink regressively restores two things: an infantile object-relation to which one is tied by bonds of "love," and the self-punishment this object exacted as the price of its "affection."[11] Drunks are haunted by that (m)Other who reduced them to insignificance. Through drink one regresses to an infantile state of paralyzed dependency which condemns any attempt at separation and individuation to perpetual failure. The introject controlling the psyche is an internal saboteur, a persecutor disguised as a loving presence.[12] That voice bequeaths the contradictory burden of a double message: You must make me proud of you, and you will always fail, which is why I love you best when you come back not with your shield but on it.

This is the genesis of pity and the basis of its appeal: *in illo tempore* a (m)Other's overweening love expended itself on an unworthy object. Once that internalization is set, self-pity becomes one's self-reference. We judge ourselves through the eyes of one who gave us a love we didn't really deserve. If the Other sacrificed themselves in the process, so much the better for the installation of that voice as one's internal regulator. Having destroyed the Other, we must repeat that act within by drowning every effort to "realize" ourselves in a tidal wave of guilt, which is also the source of the anxiety that arises whenever we do something that offends this inner voice. Individuation equals transgression: to restore the sacred presence to the throne, we must undo our act. Self-unraveling has become our fundamental project. Its power derives from the underlying condition we refuse to face. The (m)Other's project was soul-murder, and love the perfect method, since it is the best way to plant death-work within a psyche.[13] To really control anyone, you must first convince them that you love them. Prohibition organizes an opposition. Overt hatred creates resistance: the hardened heart resists the condemning voice. Love, however, insinuates. The basic trust it creates empowers attributions—You're chaste, you're ambitious, you're a good boy, you won't disappoint me—which form an "identity" that is infected with every repressed conflict the (m)Other needs to project and deny.[14]

Parenting creates for many the irresistible temptation, the chance finally to reverse things, to assume the superior position and project onto a pristine psyche the disorder that was once inflicted on us. Cruelty rises to its sabbath, having found its deepest motive. We do unto the other what was done unto us. We take our resentment, and we pass it on. In the spontaneity and vulnerability of the child, we see ourselves as we once were: the repressed rises to the bait. Sadly, few parents resist this temptation.

The inner world that results from such regimes of cruelty has this structure. One needs to take on as guilt the aggression of the internal saboteur by sustaining low-level depressions which constitute a slow process of living death—of life as suicide. Psychic undoing is the inner imperative that regulates the psyche. It ties one to rituals of endless mourning which have as their object oneself. Failure is the endless pursuit, because any attempt to get free of the parental introject, to be happy or independent, is experienced as a transgression one must pay for by depriving oneself of inner peace. That creative aggression toward oneself, in which we earlier located the possibility of change and freedom, is thereby blocked. Every effort to strike inward at the object in order to free oneself by undoing the bonds of false love must turn into an act of aggression toward oneself. The psyche is trapped because freedom requires a psychic murder one cannot commit. Some internalizations need—and deserve—to be destroyed. Unable to do so, one repeatedly acts out the inner paralysis. Drunks share the fate of those "wrecked by success": they simply forestall the day in which achievement turns to ashes in the mouth by living out its sequel.

Drunks are poets of sorts because they've found a way to externalize what Gregory Bateson terms the double-bind in a way that foregrounds the punishing superego at its foundations.[15] Drink externalizes an intrapsychic economy in which we forever sit paralyzed before a superego which casts on us the Sartrean look that tells us we are *nada*. The failure to mount a significant battle with that attribution derives from this condition: one cannot liberate one's aggression toward the inner object in any constructive way, because the object remains the inner voice one keeps endeavoring to please or, since it amounts to the same thing, the voice one offends through the passive-aggressive activity of drinking. Intrapsychically, the drunk is caught in an arrested, frozen drama: the name of action is always lost, because the (m)Other is always watching before the fact, prepared to annihilate every effort. To avoid facing this situation, the drunk must sustain an illusory game. One is always getting ready for the day in which one will take action, or, during recovery, the day one will prove strong enough to handle an occasional drink. Through such folly, self-redemption and the externalization of temptation alternate in what act III of *Iceman* reveals as the subtlest operation whereby the saboteur sustains its power.

This is the presence Hickey brings center stage in act III by forcing group members to take the "pipe dream" action required both to redeem themselves and to justify the (m)Other's continued faith in them. Failure will bring out the true terms of their inner condition. In the process, the sexual subtext that was extinguished through laughter in act II reemerges as the core conflict controlling the intrapsychic economy outlined above. Sex leads, as always, to the deepest layer. To succeed, soul-murder must plant itself in the genitals, because sex is the experience that necessarily puts one at odds with the saboteur since it brings repressed conflicts into the open as sources of self-frustration.[16] We first discover the saboteur's power when desire and the experience of an other who violates the (m)Other's programming awaken that voice as it rises up to reclaim us by turning the possibility of our liberation into a scene of frustration and paralysis. We then discover, often after repeated failure, that the (m)Other's sexual conflicts are at the core of the repressed system we must reverse if our life is to be anything more than the repetition of a fixation.

What the drunks will discover in act III is that their relationships have never been anything else. In finding a new object, they merely found the person perfectly suited to repeating their frustrations with the original object. As Freud noted, neurotics either find someone like the frustrating parent or force someone different to become so. O'Neill's encyclopedic concern is to show all the ways this can operate. For some drunks the problem is with the wife; for others it is the mistress, the buddy, the boss, the white man, the pimp, the whores. But all variants are so many incarnations of the (m)Other. In dissolving pseudodifferences, act III forces the group to recognize that they are bound together because they share an identical psychological condition. Once that recognition clicks, no catharting joke about sex can intervene, for all now know the joke has been on them.

To reverse its sting, one impossible thing is needed: the recognition that the relationship to the internalized (m)Other is one of hate, not of love. This is the repressed truth that cannot be said and that is broadcast in every action. That condition holds because repression doesn't bury a wish or an idea; it buries a duplicity in which both parties are implicated. The psyche is trapped in ambivalence by the complicity of two lies: the claim by the (m)Other to have acted out of love and the subject's claim that the deepest feeling is reciprocal. The pipe dream is the delay of action needed to sustain both lies. It functions as an externalization of the fear that, according to Donald Winnicott, controls the depressive psyche: the fear that hate will prove stronger than love.[17] Depressives refrain from action while staging richly emotional internal dramas—which invariably constitute passive-aggressive assaults on themselves—because they fear that if they ever let their real emotions out they will drown the stage in retributive aggression. Heroes of sorts, they endlessly perform punitive action on themselves to forestall the crisis of ambivalence. Acting out is the only mode of action possible, because the purpose of action is to unravel one's project in order to sustain one's inner psychic condition. Experience must be deprived of existential possibility; deeds that would outstrip the (m)Other's control must be endlessly rehearsed, then blocked. The pipe dream creates the temporality needed to sustain that process, while acting out is the attempted reversal of our condition which exposes its repressed terms. Dialectic here works by an inversion which reveals the truth ambivalence disclaims. Failure alone delivers one from confronting the buried feelings that a clarifying deed would bring to light.

Drama is the study of what happens to conflicts when the terms of their possible reversal are activated. Digging into the core paralysis of agents, its concern is to see if conflict can be lived through toward genuine change. Its task is to strip away everything else in order to get at those points where people are blocked, to see if possibility can force its entry *there*—in the *Da* of *Da-sein*. When a dramatist confronts that question honestly, failure is one of the richest possibilities. One possibility implicit in any drama is its dissolution in Bergsonian comedy: the control of the mechanical where we had hoped to find the flexibility of the human.

Act III takes that comic principle and moves it into a tragic context. Action here becomes a parody of itself—of freedom, independence, and self-reliance—as O'Neill's characters come to resemble Beckett's. Harry Hope's paralysis halfway across the street, unable to move either way, represents in tableau the process each character enacts, proceeding toward a goal only to freeze and then turn back. Action traps them in the "recognition" that for them reversal is impossible. They will deny this recognition when they return to the bar, but they cannot re-repress it. As such, they have become ripe for another kind of reversal—the movement in act IV whereby death will finally cancel the burden of life.

The Psychodynamic Structure of Act III

To get there, the collective psyche needs the movement of reversal of act III. The sexual humor that produced the catharis of act II has come home to roost. Humor may discharge tension; it also activates a memory that can only be repressed by putting the "horns" on the other. A sexual wound now floats, metonymically, throughout the group. When we meet them in act III, the group has become a theatre of henpecked men and nagging women. Because their sexual conflicts have surfaced, group regression requires a new mode of aggression. All relations collapse into a master-slave dialectics of dominance and submission, in which a general uxoriousness is projected in taunting challenges to disprove the impotence everyone sees in everyone else. Murderous desires break loose and take delight in anticipating the other's failure. The controlling projection is to demonstrate that the other is the slave to a dominant Other in order to deny that this condition is the truth of one's own inner world. Each character knows they've been dared to take an action that will force them to confront their innermost fears. The anxiety now circulating freely among them is the horror of psychological self-knowledge.

The irony, of course, is that this condition will become the basis for forging a new group identity. We attain the quick of the ulcer. The psychological condition groups exist to obviate will now be shown in its naked functioning. Each character stands alone, before the founding terms of a paralysis. The contradiction at the center of each character's core conflict is exposed. Character interpretation has found its proper focus. In Harry Hope, we have a whining wimp who met his perfect match in a castrating bitch who pushed him into the world and whom he now spites by claiming that grief over her death is the cause that makes it impossible for him to leave the bar; in Jimmy, we have one who manipulated his wife into adultery so that he could sanctify his castration/impotence; in Willie, we see his endless efort to redeem himself in the eyes of a duplicitous father whose expectations he deliberately frustrated; in Parritt, we observe the need to confess to the surrogate father their shared hatred of the mother who dominates and castrates both of them; in Larry, we see his refusal to admit female sexuality as the real source of his cynicism; in Chuck and Cora, we have a couple dedicated to mutual sexual debasement disguised as an affectionate haven in the storm. And so on. The characters' lives have caught up with them. The cover stories have unraveled. A world of hatred erupts from long concealment.

Because everything that rages within has broken loose, the characters project murderous aggression in an attempt to keep aggression from turning inward. That is the reversal that must be prevented, or the self-hatred consuming them will expose its tie to the internalized (m)Other. The only way to deny the terms of that conflict is by inflicting them on others. The basic fault becomes the target everyone goes after.

In act III aggression becomes the search for the victim and for supporters in the kill. As a group, they are starting to take on the characteristics of the Crowd, herd animals seeking the prey that will enable them to bind together in the blood-feast.[18] Hickey's challenge intervenes, momentarily displacing that drive, only to make it imperative. In daring each of them to take action, Hickey has set the perfect mousetrap, for the action each proposes to take can only be performed by killing the internalized Other. He has gotten them in the position where they either have to take action in themselves, by acting in the world, or admit their paralysis and internalize its content.

The latter is the state they attain when in resentment and defeat they find themselves at act's end together again but lacking the power to discharge their discontents. Group identity and deliverance will have to come from somewhere else. They will not have to pine for that principle long or in vain. For in their failure another agent experiences another kind of reversal. Hickey is a salesman who sells himself a bill of goods by selling it to others. When the goods prove rotten, one intention, identified as the motive behind his action, collapses, and another comes forth. Act III teaches Hickey that he is implicated in his own mousetrap, caught up in a drama in which the layers of his Unconscious are being progressively uncovered. The need invested in his project is to convince himself that he is one kind of person in order to deny the nagging suspicion that he is another. He can only put his doubts to rest by bringing the group to a state that will constitute, in effect, a collective attestation of his benign motives. In daring them to face themselves, he is asking them to prove his theory of the "cure" and the messianic self-conception that underlies it.

For all the conflict it generates, Hickey's official purpose is not to destroy the group but to save it by bringing the gospel that unites all in a solidarity that confers lasting peace, because it is based on a correct understanding of human nature. By act III he has begun to suspect that he may have other intentions, that his entire project may in fact constitute a massive defense against self-knowledge. To vanquish that prospect, Hickey now goads his audience. He must put his theory to the proof because he finds that it is faltering within. He has begun to suspect that his real purpose is to displace a tragic order of self-knowledge by "persuading" others to accept a less exacting self-knowledge, which has the added charm of releasing everyone from further internal probing. What Hickey fails to anticipate is the abyss of interminable self-analysis his project generates. The death of the pipe dream forces each individual to confront a deeper and more disruptive truth. Rather than stimulating cathartic release, it quickens depression by identifying its source.

That fact brings Hickey back to the thing he most fears. He has undertaken his project to gain a double assurance: that Evelyn and he acted out of love for one another and that, by memorializing that action, he will bring its consolations to the group. Should that purpose fail to produce the necessary results, however, enlightenment will become mass deception. The group must lie to Hickey, and he to them, coercing one another's "happy" responses in order to blow the whole thing away. The peace of all concerned can then only be purchased by embracing some new and more desperate illusion.

Harry's paralysis in the street is the structural turning point of the play, for Hickey as well as for the group. In Harry's paralysis, Hickey's project collapses. All the ideals he projected into it begin to reverse themselves. The group is worse off than before. Forcing people to see the truth does not set them free; it delivers them over to an awareness they are unable to bear. A manic effort at denial surfaces in Hickey as his plan unravels, because he is now tormented by the possibility that aggression, not love, is the basis of his activity and accounts both for what he did prior to his arrival and for the messianic project he has formed in order to conceal the motives behind that act.

Like the group, Hickey has been acting out. And like theirs, his acting out exposes his core paralysis. In him, however, that event erupts inward, engendering the true dialectic of the psyche. To get rid of a pipe dream one must deracinate the motives it conceals. Acting out one's paralysis is but prelude to that task. Taking action in oneself requires that transforming vicissitude of anger in which aggression turned back inward wages a direct attack on what was projected outward. Acting out exposes a frozen inner drama which can be reversed only by rooting out the poison within.

In act IV Hickey will prove himself worthy of this recognition through a self-examination that is of central importance to my larger purpose, since it offers a systematic—and tragic—understanding of the dialectical structure of the psyche. Unlocking that structure requires a rigorous internalization of this basic condition: the motive we give for our actions usually conceals another motive which is its opposite. Intention is part of a truly insidious cover-up. If we really strip the layers of the onion, we don't move from one positive motive to another that may not be quite as nice but that only gives a slight blow to our self-esteem. We descend instead into the basement of our mendacity. This is the position Hickey now finds himself in. Insofar as we move with him into this domain, we face the possibility that the truth of our character may be the exact opposite of what we proclaim. In its psychodynamic structure, act III creates the movement necessary for such an audience to come into being.

Negating the Negation: Three Audiences

Ritual Theatre: Theory and Practice

Act III constitutes a ritual which exposes the psychological disorder that informs the traditional view of theatre's ritual function. Hickey's conscious project exemplifies the concept of psychological cleansing through drama on which this theory prides itself. Collective ills are identified. Action purges them. The crisis of escalating violence is halted. The messianic leader, through his action, relieves collective guilt. The good of all, and the health of the restored community, is assured through a collective unburdening of malign motives. The sacrifice of the pipe dream becomes the common sacrifice which brings lasting peace.[19]

Insofar as we have invested ourselves in this theory, act III constitutes the mousetrap that prepares us as audience to suffer in act IV the exposure of the hidden motives that inform it. O'Neill positions us for this discovery by withholding the grand term that caps ritual—the scapegoat—until its true psychological function emerges, when the group rushes to that mechanism in order to discharge the burden Hickey's self-revelation places on each of them. In so doing they offer us the possibility of constituting a response which exposes ritual as the last and most cunning resistance to the internalization of tragedy.

Act III positions us for this experience by showing that cleansing rituals are really self-paralyzing rituals. Acting out inner conflicts doesn't remove them; it makes it harder to re-repress them. Most theories of catharsis inadvertently exemplify the view of hysteria Freud rejected in founding psychoanalysis; that is, the notion that a simple recovery of the repressed removes the frustration it created. The failure of the drunks to reverse themselves through "action" brings forth a radically different intrapsychic condition. The wound festers within, discharge is blocked, and projection is denied. They have finally become infected with themselves. Resentment no longer provides a way of bonding and binding, for resentment now strikes inward. Such is the human condition at the end of act III. The group may still long for the big love feast, but they know that Hickey has brought death into their midst by establishing it as the power that has always presided over them. It now rages within, seeking a final release from consciousness. The ritual they now require will expose the secret that ritual keeps about its psychological foundation.

The Action Affected by Psychoanalysis

Act III positions psychoanalytic theory for an equally troubling experience. In act III Hickey activates the group's negative transference in order to put his positive countertransference on trial. Forcing the transference is the last-ditch effort in a blocked analysis to get the patient to confront his or her psyche. Two assumptions inform the act. Until the repressed is faced, it will continue to rule. Once it is confronted, and worked through, real change becomes possible. Action is the necessary alembic. Acting out in the transference brings forth the repressed; working through resolves it.

Comic and ironic theories of the therapeutic results of psychoanalysis rest on this economy. As comic process, therapy purges folly and restores healthful living: it moves ineluctably to the "marriage" in which, thanks to analysis, one finally is able to form healthy relationships and take up a productive life in the community. American ego psychology celebrates this position.[20] The ironic concept of therapy, typified by Lacan, undercuts these claims without unseating them. An ironic attitude toward oneself deprives the narcissistic *moi* of the illusion of ego-integrity: recognizing desire as a source of unavoidable disorder produces an internal distancing that enables us to avoid repetition or to laugh at ourselves when we find we haven't.[21]

The tragic drives both positions to a deeper self-confrontation. Psychoanalysis, however, continues to resist this issue, because the tragic submits its ruling concepts and practices—as well as its messianic social role—to a fundamental challenge. Nietzsche was perhaps the last great thinker to affirm the value of a tragic culture and to understand the resentment it breeds in those incapable of the imperatives it places on the psyche. As he knew, those who regard the tragic as that woeful prospect we must avoid or overcome have never understood it from within. Though most analysts have conveniently forgotten it, Freud's Spinozistic concept of "recognized necessity" implicates psychoanalysis in this issue, but only by exemplifying a more general problem.[22] The tragic has been poorly served by the theories that have been developed to explain it. Most theories of tragedy—since, and including, Aristotle—may be most significant when seen as defenses against the tragic, as exorcisms, prayers for deliverance. As critique, act III positions us for the experience through which act IV will rethink the tragic by exposing, from within, the interpretations used to defend against it.

In the Seats: The Actual Audience

As act III builds, we find ourselves anxiously desiring relief from an accelerating tension while questioning the motives behind that desire. Pity is gone, replaced by fear of what will happen when the group finds no escape. What group psychology will they perforce regress to in search of deliverance? We are beginning to experience both the conditions whereby the Crowd comes into being and the internal violence it necessarily projects as the basis of its fusion. The effect of depth analysis on subjects who cannot endure self-knowledge is truly horrifying.

Shifting to Hickey only intensifies this anxiety, for we can no longer project and discharge the burden of knowledge onto him. We anticipate instead that failure will force him to keep the date with his unconscious. Interpreting Hickey's motives no longer discharges tensions; it binds them to a new anxiety over the depths to which analysis may lead and the tragic results it may bring.

This anxious probing of Hickey's motives necessarily forces us to question our own, since any attempt to short-circuit that issue or intervene prematurely with an explanation that assures our difference from Hickey requires the use of defenses that may very well be exposed within the self-analysis Hickey will carry out in act IV. We cannot resist engaging our own psyches in the analysis of Hickey's without convicting ourselves of deliberate psychological blindness. The obvious qualification is that nothing compels us to take up this challenge except the psychodynamic movement that has structured the play. If we have "honored" it, our position is no longer antianalytic, since that would align us with the group, or reductive, since Hickey's complex agency has outstripped the simple motives we were inclined to posit at the beginning. This is not to say that such responses can't control an audience, but rather that we don't want to be discovered belonging to such a group. For that audience is no longer present in the theatre except in the intricate evasions whereby shame assumes the pose of detachment. The irony is that reaction alone can discharge the play, because the power of its psychodynamic structure leaves such beings with no other way to come together.

Those who try to remain present face a sterner, more exacting master. Group protection has been shattered. The core conflict that defines each psyche and the action that exposes its paralysis have been found out. To internalize the play, we must perforce seek out what would constitute a similar situation for ourselves and what we would have to do to pass the test they fail. And we face that question existentialized by Hickey, delivered by his agency and example to an anxiety that isolates us from the possibility of any collective unburdening. Once we have begun to interrogate our motives, without ego defenses and "redemptive" guarantees, what will we uncover about the actual structures on which our psyche depends for identity maintenance?

I have offered three ways of formulating what act III does to the audience. Combined in a single concept, they indicate that its target is the deepest source of resistance: the refusal to internalize depressive anxiety and to undergo an experience in which every projection is driven inward with no release and no way to halt a descent to the repressed. This has now become the theatrical space.

Confronted by it, regression has started to feed on the desire for collective unbinding. For those onstage, the death-work controlling each psyche has now broken loose. The only way they can regroup is by projecting murderous desires in an effort to stave off a suicidal implosion. Acting out has created a new theatre of the absurd. Each agent stands frozen in a pose of comic mechanization which is merely the last defense against the knowledge to which failure has finally brought them—that hatred is the inner knot that binds each of them both to the (m)Other and to one another.

Act III thus constitutes a process in which the theatre of the absurd is referred *avant la lettre* to the deeper logic of tragedy. Fearing that closure, the absurd attempts to arrest drama in a purely formal, aesthetic realization of paralysis. As such, it constitutes a defense against the deeper probing of that paralysis, a refusal to mourn which turns what Beckett calls "the inability to be born properly" into a permanent condition. The group at Harry's is frozen in perpetual mourning because they have never mourned properly: lying to oneself about one's relationship to the internal object is the source of that paralysis. As long as hate, and not ambivalence, remains the inner truth one refuses to face, self-unraveling and collective hatred are the necessary acts that hold the knot in place. Our "love" of the inner object gives death dominion over life: we murder ourselves in order to escape having to commit a necessary murder within.

The true dialectical connection thereby eludes us. Hate and love aren't dualistically separate categories but products of a single psychogenesis. Dualism is resistance, an intellectual defense based on a splitting mechanism which is used not only to guarantee "the bonds of love" but also to keep aggression from moving to the necessary embrace with its proper target. In the dialectic that informs the psyche, hate may not prove stronger than love, but it is invariably prior, with love the modification which emerges only through the active reversal of its power.

Hickey prompts such considerations because this is the mousetrap disclaimed aggression has landed him in. He can only forestall the mass destruction that he now suspects has been his true aim by turning his aggression back against himself. But he faces a new dilemma: he now knows that he has become a stranger to himself and doesn't know what he's done or why. He does, however, know this: as a result of his action, the bar is now a place of endless suffering without relief. All defenses have been shattered, yet consciousness cannot be discharged. Each agent sits alone, confined to the room each has done everything to escape. The group will pine for collective release. Act IV will show what must happen for them to achieve it.

Act IV: Death-Work In and For Itself

Toward Narrative: Ontological Guilt and the Rhetoric of Fiction

Everything in *Iceman* happens contrary to expectation because the play is reversal throughout. Act IV will drive that process to its foundations. The dialectical structure of the entire play will stand forth as a series of mousetraps sprung. In stripping away the layers of his own deceit, an actor (Hickey) will constitute a theatrical space in which everyone is brought before their guilty secret. The ultimate bases of group psychology will be exposed as the group members struggle to escape the inexorable terms of their common tragedy.

The collapse of Hickey's project has activated a subtext he must try to purge by offering a full account of his motives. The narrative moment is at hand, and the group is situated for a maximum impact, because everyone has just acted out the contradiction that will come to define it. This is perhaps the nature of narrative: we construct one story to exorcise another story which lives on as the subtext that eventually catches up with us. Unbeknownst to the teller, all narratives may constitute a structure of reversals that will eventually bring the truth to light. Manic projection has heretofore saved Hickey from such a prospect. His messianic mission has been to bring to others the gospel that will deliver him from himself. Like all discourses addressed to the other, Hickey's effort is grounded in the Hegelian struggle for recognition: by accepting his theory of life and the cure it brings, the group will give back to him the self-conception he needs to sustain.

When that project breaks down, the aggression that informs it erupts within his psyche. Socratic methods crumble. Mania now reveals itself as a defense against depression, a refusal to probe the repressed. This is the trap Hickey has set for himself. He can only hold his unconscious at bay by offering a narrative account of his life that will produce conviction and compel collective assent by establishing, with Cartesian clarity, the benign motives he needs to claim for everything he's done. The narrative will thereby redeem his project, for once they understand his story, the group will renounce their resistance and respond in the right way.

That narrative is riven from the start, however, by a recognition with the power to overturn everything. Hickey now sees that aggression has formed the basis of his activity. That fact suggests that the peace-giving rationale is a cover-up. The only way he can reaffirm it is by arguing that his aggression is "the right kind of pity." Its product is self-knowledge as the basis for right action toward oneself and others. Its target is guilt as the force that traps everyone in a vicious circle of self-pity. Its necessary result is peace and loving regard for the agent who brings its benefits. The actual result— everyone is worse off than before, with resentment general—undercuts the fine logic of this quasi-Aristotelian sequence. Aggression has broken loose from every *ratio* and stalks the stage. The group hates Hickey and firmly believes that he hates them. Hickey's narrative must exorcise that specter by demonstrating his benign motives in a way that will reverse the aggression he sees in the group's refusal to accept the peace he offers. Recontextualized, aggression will be admitted, the better to be denied. It is a desperate and magical project, a massive rhetorical undertaking. But it will produce its opposite at every turn, bring to light the recognition that now haunts everyone: aggression is that ground phenomenon which can't be recontextualized. It shatters every attempt to deny or mitigate its force.

The problem of guilt is readied for the final dialectical turn. Hickey's project is based on a profound insight into the nature of guilt. He knows that everyone is ruled by a guilt that reaches down into the innermost hiding places of the psyche. The kind of guilt to which he constantly refers is not a consciousness of faults tied to particular deeds, but a self-reference that defines and regulates our very inwardness.[23] Guilt is the ultimate term of self-mediation, the engine that drives all the behaviors that make up one's relationship to oneself and others. As group psychologist, Hickey sees the bar as a huge pool of guilt, which is why nothing but self-undoing can issue from it. Guilt informs the temporality of the pipe dream, making it a vicious circle whereby any attempt to project beyond one's condition necessarily collapses.

But a new insight has begun to eat away at Hickey. He now suspects that guilt may be the secret agent behind the kind of peace he offers. Peace for Hickey requires the abolition of consciousness in a timeless state of not caring, because its purpose is to extinguish the consciousness that arises whenever he stops talking. He needs collective release more than anyone, because he can't find peace until he has everyone "feeling the same way." Guilt for him can only be "extinguished" by a collective act of denial. But if that is so, then Hickey's project constitutes massive, extended death-work projected as an act of love. Guilt ties one to repeated aggression, both inner and outer. What Aristotle called the self-movement of pity may be no more than an attempt to deny that awareness by producing weakened subjects who will herd together, craving "peace" in order to hide their shame. Hickey has begun to suspect that there may be no right exercise of pity. Confronting guilt points to a more exacting knowledge of one's relationship to the other. What kind of recognition would constitute it, and what lies would that recognition expose? These are the questions that will drive Hickey's narrative.

Hickey and the group now stand at cross-purposes, in mutual resentment, with Hickey on the hook since he must offer a narrative that will transform their response. Just as the group has brought him to this pass, so its members' reactions to his tale will form an integral part of it. Faced with the horror he is driven to expose, the group, regressing to its foundations, will become a chorus embodying, in the interpretations it imposes to escape Hickey's tale, the root mechanisms we all use when self-knowledge must be denied. In exploiting them, the group will achieve a new and final solidarity through a collective regression to the real tie that binds them. As they echo and complete one another's lines, they will come to find in revenge the motive that will enable them to fuse together under the reduction that blows their entire experience away—the proclamation that Hickey is insane.

But Hickey's madness is of a tragic order. As his narrative progresses, Hickey reverses himself and assumes the burden of the unconscious as it arises to destroy the tale he tries to tell by bringing forth another. Such "madness" derives from a systematic awareness of the repressed as the principle that organizes one's entire life. It thus reveals precisely what the group must deny: and that dialectical connection makes Hickey's tale a mirror of what they would have to face if they attempted a similar reflection on their tale. Since they cannot, the revelation of Hickey's unconscious activates their flight to a new collective unconscious. Group psychopathology is thereby revealed in its foundations as the need to collectively deny and discharge the kind of awareness Hickey suffers.

Act IV is dominated by Hickey's narrative and punctuated by the group's reaction to its disclosures. That interaction forms a structure of reversal and recognition that dialectically reinterprets and transforms everything that has happened by revealing the core disorder that has been displaced and delayed during the first three acts. Hickey will reveal his true motives. The group will regress to its true foundations. And as the two structures split, the play will reveal their abiding connection—and situate us firmly within that space.

The Nature of Storytelling: Hickey's Narrative

He doesn't know it, but in striving to construct a narrative that will save his project, Hickey has become a dialectical agent faced with the labor of the negative. His resistance is such, however, that he begins not with the negative, but with its opposite—negation, the explicit denial of unacceptable motives wherever they surface. As Freud notes, negation is a primitive defense mechanism which gives forth a clear index of the truth—but as in a peep show. Unconscious motives are expressed so that they can be explicitly denied, yet they continue to erupt, unraveling the discourse constructed to expunge them.[24]

The setting is ripe with an atmosphere that reinforces that mechanism. Group hostility must be extinguished because it mirrors the inner consciousness that eats on Hickey—the growing fear that hate presides over everything that has happened. Hickey is caught in the return of the projections. He resorts accordingly to projection as his first line of defense. He accuses the group of "putting on this rotten half-dead act just to get back at me! Because you hate my guts!" (225). The possibility displaced by that mechanism then enters through the negative, as a statement he must make in order to deny: "It makes me feel you suspect I must have hated you. But that's a lie!" (226).

In beginning his narrative, Hickey inadvertently underscores the dynamic that will drive it. It is in the gaps, the breaks, the ruptures in a narrative that the unconscious streams forth. A tale told to "repress" the truth continually gives forth the very thing that must be denied. Negation then tries to fill the breach. But it can only do so by offering, as explanation, further narrative. As that process develops, new and richer mechanisms of denial will be required, because the truth keeps erupting, each time exposing a deeper psychic register. In spite of himself, Hickey is in the process of creating a theatrical space in which a knowledge of one's true relationship to the Other will be staged. The theatre has become the place of the shared secret, the space of maximum anxiety. Aware of that fact, Hickey's audience is present, for the first time, in the appropriate mood, that of "awakening dread" (227). Hickey is going to tell them a bedtime story, a love story. As chorus, they are defined by the refrain that reveals their entanglement in a similar mechanism of negation: "We don't give a damn." They shrink from Hickey's tale because they know it mirrors their own. Thus, the interaction staged before us represents a single psyche revealed simultaneously in the two directions that ground all of its operations. The group and Hickey split at precisely the place in the psyche where their identity is joined. Such dialectical precision leaves no exit.

Like all romantics, Hickey rests his case on "the law of the heart" (227). We judge actions by their motives, and Hickey would claim the purity of Kant's categorical imperative for the act of murder. He is convinced that the group will see "how damned grateful" they "ought to be" (228) once they realize that the same motive informs what he did for Evelyn and what he has tried to do for them.

In a sense Hickey's narrative is a speech made over a dead body in an attempt to create in the corpse the consciousness that will enable both departed and mourner to rest in peace. If Hickey can get his audience to confirm his motives and return the right emotions, he can create Evelyn's consciousness and have it come back to him as a collective avowal. By the same token, their refusal to comply represents the consciousness within the dearly departed which he must exorcise. Thus do the dead live on in the imaginary conversations we stage within and then repress by getting their surrogate representatives to accept that "sympathetic" contract which falsifies the mourning process, making it endless: Don't speak ill of the dead, especially to others.

Hickey as Ancient Mariner tells his tale in an attempt to put nagging doubts to rest. Those doubts reach back to his beginnings, suggesting connections he can only fathom by establishing the narrative continuity of his entire life.

Folie à deux

He begins by noting his similarity to his father, the preacher who sold Hoosier hicks "nothing for something." He omits any information about his mother. But he quickly fills in this gap by showing how that absence was supplemented from his earliest days by Evelyn. They were, indeed, made for each other—the eternal adolescent negative attention seeker and the (m)Other as martyr and engulfing presence to whom the son must forever return for forgiveness. Hickey's piety is such that he will try to tell his story from Evelyn's point of view as a "sentimental reminiscence" (232). Only by holding this note can he sustain the illusion that, following her example, he acted out of love.

Perfectly suited to each other's disorders, Hickey and Evelyn form a *folie à deux*. Awareness of conflict is ignored and change prevented through the erection of a hyperconsciousness which reaffirms on all occasions a single idealizing interpretation of the relationship. So joined, both participants ooze betrayal. Fragmentation of relatedness is the only way to sustain each role. Hickey acts out, then begs forgiveness, so that Evelyn can enhance her long-suffering role by making excuses for him. Joined in mutual deceit, the relationship must proceed to the stage of the promise, which is made, as both know, so that it will be broken. "Even when I'd admit things and ask her forgiveness, she'd make excuses for me and defend me against myself. She'd kiss me and say she knew I didn't mean it and I wouldn't do it again. So I'd promise I wouldn't. I'd have to promise, she was so sweet and good, though I knew darned well—" (233).

Hickey's narrative first ruptures here—"No, sir, you couldn't stop Evelyn" (233)—in the momentary suspicion that everything he does serves Evelyn's master plot, casting him in the Sartrean bind of acting for another's ends. Evelyn demands his drunkenness as token to her power to forgive and thereby become the good mother who defends sonny against the world with a boundless faith that will be rewarded when he finally proves everyone wrong. The small-town atmosphere, where virtue and vice are publicly staged and recognized by all, contributes mightily to the process. Evelyn is a great actress who will never leave the town because she can't relinquish the stage. Hickey is merely her favorite prop.

The *folie* therefore takes this form. Hickey must devise new acts to increase his unworthiness so that Evelyn can display her power to forgive. As in Sartre, loser wins either way: once sonny grows up, he will see that she alone can make him happy; when he fails, her martyrdom is assured. Evelyn's language betrays her scenario with striking clarity: " 'I know I can make you happy, Teddy, and once you're happy you won't want to do any of the bad things you've done any more' " (234).

Such baby talk compels Hickey's assent because he has internalized the true structure of the relationship. Guilt has become his internal regulator. Hickey contantly sees and judges himself under the eyes of the (m)Other. Projecting guilt accordingly becomes the basis of all social relations which take the form of kidding people along in whatever illusion they need to sustain a similar paralysis. Drunken fellowship is false fellowship because it's really a displacement of the aggression one can't act at home. In comforting one another, drunks trap one another in a cyclical guilt in which they are always in effect returning home with the proof of their unworthiness.

Once such a pattern is established, it can only feed the disorder in spiraling repetition. Evelyn's sabbath of forgiveness increases the guilt that inhabits her "victim." "I'd want to reform and mean it. I'd promise Evelyn, and I'd promise myself, and I'd believe it. I'd tell her, it's the last time. And she'd say, 'I know it's the last time, Teddy. You'll never do it again.' That's what made it so hard. That's what made me feel such a rotten skunk—her always forgiving me." To advance the process, a new transgression is required. "Playing around" with other women fills the bill, but only if it is a "harmless good time" that doesn't "mean anything," because its meaninglessness confirms its meaning for Evelyn (235). Sin and pleasure, let alone a genuine relationship with another woman, can't exist, because transgression is undertaken only so that one can unravel oneself in guilt before the Other. Displaced aggression has created the perfect double-bind. Hickey has now internalized the superego proper to his condition. Evelyn is always present internally, watching Hickey fail and then taking him back into her arms.

With tarts Hickey feels shameless and "free" to "tell a dirty joke" knowing he'll get a "laugh." But to complete the act he must bring it all home by finding some way to confess to Evelyn so that he can experience in her sufferance the proper judgment: "Sometimes I'd try some joke I thought was a corker on Evelyn. She'd always make herself laugh. But I could tell she thought it was dirty, not funny" (236). Hickey need say no more to tell us all we need to know about the nature of their sex life. Hickey and Evelyn are a necrophiliac couple: both sleep with the iceman.

The Turning Point

The nail in Altoona is inevitable, the turning point in which aggression starts to turn back on its source. The split between the hyperconsciousness and the repressed—which this marriage has labored to reify—has begun to reverse itself. The old structures will continue to operate, but with their underside now rising to claim them. It takes no master psychologist to see that Hickey has been deliberately careless in getting and "curing" his infection: "The quack I went to got all my dough and then told me I was cured and I took his word." Even more transparent is the explanation he gives Evelyn: "But I wasn't [cured], and poor Evelyn— But she did her best to make me believe she fell for my lie about how traveling men get things from drinking cups on trains." But none of that matters. What really matters is getting the right feelings about the "event." Hickey can no longer be just a bad boy. He must internalize a new superego: self-loathing must become his self-reference. Only thus can Evelyn be freed for the play of pure spectacle, the exhibitionism of a martyr cleansed of inwardness by the eyes of the generalized Other, the town full of "neighbors shaking their heads and feeling sorry for her out loud" (237).

Both actors are ready for a pure enactment of their roles. Hickey has to "take the pledge" so that both can watch Evelyn's face, transfixed in achieved bliss: "I could see disgust having a battle in her eyes with love. Love always won" (237). Hickey wants punishment. What he fails to see is that he's being given the worst kind—the slow torture of a passive-aggressive martyrdom enacted with relish before his eyes.

Retelling breaks down here, however, in the second significant rupture.

Hickey sees the desired effect Evelyn's action has on its victim: "(*He bursts out in a tone of anguish that has anger and hatred beneath it*) Christ, can you imagine what a guilty skunk she made me feel!" To preserve her holiness, he must now undo this awareness. This struggle, between awareness and denial, is enacted in Hickey's next speech, which narrates the battle between his suspicion that "it isn't human for any woman to be so pitying and forgiving" and his inability to get her to react in kind to his transgressions. What he fails to see is that she's devised the perfect revenge. Her martyrdom has become the end result and purpose of everything that both of them do. Guilt, as repetition-compulsion, condemns Hickey to the ceaseless act of unraveling himself under the eyes of the Other. The more he confesses, the more she forgives. The more he asks her to repay him in kind, the more she does by refusing to do so. The possibility of communication— or of probing together the shared disorder that has brought the marriage to this pass—is abolished. Hickey must pretend to be kidding when, in effect, he begs her to commit adultery, because "she'd have been so hurt if I'd said it seriously. She'd have thought I'd stopped loving her" (238).

Love has become pure unbound death-work, exacting its price because there is now no action that will not advance the lock it has on both of them. Since pity is its mode of expression, they regress, as couple, to pity's pietà: "It got so every night I'd wind up hiding my face in her lap, bawling and begging her forgiveness. And, of course, she'd always comfort me and say, 'Never mind, Teddy, I know you won't ever again' " (239). Negation is a nice mechanism for dealing with a paraphraxis, a slip of the tongue, but it has its true feast when it becomes the principle structuring an entire relationship. Sex holds no candle to such delights.

The Space of Tragedy

But the truth will out. Hickey has backed himself into that corner where emotions reverse themselves and one's true feelings surface. Negation now requires the assertion—"Christ, I loved her so"—but that mechanism of denial will collapse as such "love" moves to its final dialectic. Everything now gets doubled back upon itself, with pity caught in its own toils. Three voices haunt Hickey's consciousness: sometimes he finds he can't forgive Evelyn for forgiving him; at times he catches himself hating her for making him loathe himself, and that feeling starts seeking someone else to blame. He is in that situation in which insight into the other *and* the labor to undo that awareness will generate the final and most malignant structuration of the superego. Humiliation will become the internal force regulating the psyche. He now sees that "sometimes when she'd kiss me it was like she did it on purpose to humiliate me" (239). What Hickey fails to see is that humiliation strikes the deepest chord in his psyche because it alone enables him to undo his awareness by turning all of his hatred back upon himself. It is, in short, the only way he can cleanse and regain his object/abject.

He has attained the intrapsychic position of Hamlet—that state of depression in which, as Winnicott suggests, one keeps everything inside, in ceaseless failed mourning, because one fears that hate will prove stronger than love. Such a psyche moves toward endgame. Suicide or murder are the only ways the structure can fulfill its telos. Once aggression is turned inward it becomes the Kafkan ice ax that strikes at two conditions: the internalized (m)Other who is both the source of one's frustrated love and the object of one's justifiable but deeply unconscious rage; and "the bonds of love," the deeply knotted, convoluted affections that tie one to this object. The only genuine alternative to murder is to kill within oneself everything that binds one to the (m)Other in endless self-frustration. A neurotic system is sustained by the desire that empowers the voice of the (m)Other: that's the marrow one must deracinate.

Everything has conspired to bring Hickey and Evelyn to what I will term the justice of human relationships. The first time they related to each other as bad boy and forgiving mother, they set down a pattern in which death, engendered, became the desire that blows through every facet of the relationship. Habitual behaviors and tragic reckoning are end points in an inexorable structure which gives life a seamless continuity. There is never an innocent moment in any relationship. Things are always taking on direction. Nothing in the psyche stays in place: all structures grow as the repressed evolves new forms and behaviors in moving to some inevitable event. Time, defined by the promise and its necessary violation, has now become the pure movement toward catastrophe. That imperative informs the "final test" the couple constructs as Harry's birthday approaches. The night before, Evelyn can sleep in peace because she knows there's no way she can lose. Hickey, with lidless eyes, is left in isolation to face the truth of their relationship.

When murder then outs, it activates the structure of reversals that will bring Hickey fully before himself. In death Evelyn is supposedly freed from "the misery of loving" Hickey. But Hickey can't repress the feeling that "a ton of guilt" has been lifted from his mind, because the deed has, in fact, reversed the inner structure of his psyche. Guilt was for Hickey hatred from the Other internalized as identification with the aggressor. Directing that aggression outward on its source liberates, however fitfully, a consciousness that names the true motive of the murder and discerns the appalling nature of the forgiveness that would be bestowed even on this deed. "I remember I stood by the bed and suddenly I had to laugh. I couldn't help it, and I knew

Evelyn would forgive me. I remember I heard myself speaking to her, as if it was something I'd always wanted to say: 'Well, you know what you can do with your pipe dream now, you damned bitch!' " (241).

It is a moment of complex significance. In uttering the truth, Hickey addresses a final word to the psyche of the person he has just delivered from consciousness. The hatred that erupts is rage over the recognition that in whatever afterlife one cares to imagine, Evelyn will forever refuse any alteration of her role. Murder is the act that momentarily reverses pity and guilt by liberating that recognition. It must, however, be immediately denied, lest tragic knowledge annihilate Hickey's entire narrative and the purpose he still hopes to realize through it. "No! I never—! . . . No! That's a lie! I never said—! Good God, I couldn't have said that! If I did, I'd gone insane. Why, I loved Evelyn better than anything in life!" Negation now requires the annihilation of the psyche: "You know I must have been insane, don't you, Governor?" (242).

Tragic Inwardness: The Last Reversal

Hickey finally "knows" what he wants from his audience. He sees that he has acted in bad faith from the beginning. His real purpose, he now fears, is what drunks always want: to be relieved of existence together, to have illusions restored, delivered, as a group, from the awareness that gnaws at one's psyche whenever one is sober and alone. Caught in his own mouse-trap, he must get that response or face a more horrifying possibility: that everything he's done since his arrival has been a reenactment of the motive that has just been disclosed. The space of tragedy looms as endless claustrophobia: when one's tale is a tragic one, one forever reenacts the crime in an effort to escape it. Faced with this new eruption of the unconscious—and of the necessary connection between his attitude toward the group and his speech over the dead Evelyn—Hickey retreats, proving himself, for the moment, incapable of tragic individuation. He begs the group to deliver him, because he now knows that he has, in the name of love, brought into their midst the aggression he first unleashed in killing Evelyn. He has repeated that deed by destroying the collective psychology on which the group depends. He begs the group to undo that act in order to protect him from himself. He needs them to declare his insanity, for the alternative is a tragic awareness that would leave everyone fixated on the omnipresence of death-work in all the ways of love. How do you get rid of hate? Perhaps you don't. Perhaps it alone is endless, unconquerable. In going into the nether regions of death, Hickey hasn't found a "womb" of fear and regeneration but a reservoir of rage. In trying to mitigate its force, he ripens toward the final reversal.

Continuing to repreat rituals in which death-work is both enacted and delayed will no longer work. Murder removed that possibility. One can act death only as long as one remains frozen before action, the way Harry was when he stopped halfway across the street. One either acts death passively or attains an active awareness of how death structures human relationships. Hickey's action commits him to the latter awareness.

In seizing on insanity as the explanation that will let the group off the hook, Hickey gives way to a final pull of pity, but it is grounded in an awareness that nothing could ever change them because they are already dead. In offering himself as scapegoat, Hickey undoes his project without negating the tragic understanding it has brought him. In sacrificing that awareness for their collective release, he exposes the true motives that drive groups to embrace the scapegoat mechanism. In letting them go, he does not cancel his deed but accepts the recognition of its purpose: he has come to bring death, to force the dead to see that they are dead and to take away all protective shields. In a first internalization of that knowledge, Hickey takes on tragic stature by affirming madness as the content he must constitute, the undiscovered country he must fathom. For in confessing madness, he simultaneously performs and negates his speech act. He lets them off the hook in order to put himself on it.

He is left, accordingly, with this impossible task: "I've got to explain to Evelyn" (245). He will in inner reality forever address that Other in an unending wake, an endless obsessional circle of awareness and its undoing. In its response the group give him a first taste of the interpretation Evelyn will endlessly proclaim. Her certitude—that Hickey was insane when he killed her—is the abyss he enters with the knowledge that he wasn't. In living on, he will forever unravel himself before the Other, because he now knows that the Other is the consciousness that undid every effort he made to express the true terms of their relationship. Evelyn's love is infinite, because her blindness to herself is endless. Hickey is trapped in the tragic duty to become the consciousness that probes their relationship in depth without ever gaining release from it. He must forever retell their story—but from a subtext become more cruel with each probing. Because he has merely attained the first stage of that knowledge, he leaves the stage proclaiming the lie which shows that his psyche has attained the condition we call hell: "All I want you to see is I was out of my mind afterwards, when I laughed at her! I was a raving rotten lunatic or I couldn't have said— Why, Evelyn was the only thing on God's earth I ever loved! I'd have killed myself before I'd ever hurt her!" (246). Negation is now confirmation—and Hickey knows it. It will be up to Parritt and Larry to fathom the content of that consciousness.

For the Group: Reversal and Recognition as Death-Work

The group seizes the other opportunity. Listening in silence, they've heard, and know they have their work cut out for them. When act IV began, the group had again collapsed into tortured isolation, but this time with no way to forge a new group coalescence. Acting out delivered each member to an unbearable self-knowledge. Each sits alone regressed to the one defense that remains—a stagnation in which living on equals waiting for the end. Collective energies collapse in the repeated refrain: "Who cares?" That condition is a complete reversal of the state we found them in in act I and a regression to its foundation. In act I anxiety and the struggle to discharge tension united them, whereas they now sit like cadavers without the energy either to project aggression or to seek comic deliverance. The bar has become a tomb.

But it is an uneasy resting place. Death remains hard work, easily disrupted. Everyone cringes when Hickey reappears, because they know he will now take the step they fear. Having made them act out their paralysis, he will force each to confront its terms. As he begins, the burden of that collective Unconscious erupts in one of the most staggering moments in the play: Jimmy Tomorrow's confession that he manipulated his wife into adultery to give himself the excuse he needed to drink his life away. I have held back discussion of it until now so that we can see its structural function. A collective trauma bursts loose in Jimmy's confession. It is an utterance that comes straight from the Unconscious, setting forth the awareness that will click in each psyche as Hickey's narrative drives its message home. Jimmy Tomorrow sees, for a moment, the hidden continuity of his life and the true terms of his relationship to the Other. But of necessity "no one gives any sign of having heard him" (230). And having made the speech, he unwinds like "a mechanical doll." The truth hasn't set him free; it's left him expended without reserve. O'Neill will never compromise a naturalistic understanding of human behavior: for most of us recognition is no more than a fitful consciousness. Insight is but prologue to negation and implosion. The first response that erupts from a regressed psyche is invariably the most revealing, especially when, as with Jimmy, the truth must be uttered right away so that unburdening can commence. But such a mechanism can only be used once. Deprived of it, the group can only stage its protest by listening in a stunned silence, punctuated only by pathetic protests begging Hickey to stop.

When, much later, Hickey exits, still talking, the group finds itself trapped in the position that erupted in Jimmy at the beginning. But confession won't unburden them, because Hickey's narrative has exposed all the hiding places that give life the continuity of the repressed. None of them can any longer tell their story, because every episode is now poisoned with the truth. The only way they can escape is by making death-work the shared process that will enable them to achieve as a group an unburdening that must be total. For that to happen, collective regression must descend to the ultimate basis of group pscyhology.

The simplicity of the operations they use to exorcise Hickey stands in striking contrast to the complex freight thereby discharged. The dialectic of that connection reveals the true nature of group psychology as collective death-work. Hickey's audience has found itself in the theatrical space where the guests are got—the space of theatre as the public disclosure of shared secrets. They have listened, appalled by connections. Hickey's story is their own, and it forces them to recognize an identity that exists at the level of psychic structure. The only way they can escape that recognition is by annihilating all connections. Once defenses have been destroyed and the enabling lie on which the psyche is grounded exposed, the only way to discharge conflict is by taking the path of infantile regression toward the final solution. The negative transference is all that remains, and it must be resolved by the most primitive defenses—undoing and blowing away.[25] Mania supersedes all other operations in a drive for collective release. The unconscious motives informing ritual theatre thereby stand forth for all to see. Guilty creatures sitting at a play now find the true value and function of the scapegoat mechanism. It is the projection that enables death-work unbound to attain its long-deferred and ghostly saturnalia.

Mania is the elation that arises when a threat that has struck an inward chord has finally been expelled. In celebrating its triad—triumph, contempt, and denial—mania voids the psyche.[26] Hickey is disposed of, and any reference his narrative could have to the group is obliterated. Certitude is thereby assured. Hickey is insane. Reductionism triumphant unleashes a chorus of glee in which there are many tunes but no real differences, as all voices dissolve in sheer noise and Hugo's bitter refrain. Stoppard's Player-King says you can't act death. The ending of *Iceman* gives that belief the lie.

In act IV the group reveals infantile regression followed by death-work as the glue that holds them together. Tragedy creates in them the necessity of a movement that inverts its shaping principles. Tragic revelation becomes the occasion for the exercise of communal blindness. The two choices determining the psyche's dialectic stand in sharp relief. If, at the end, the group catharts pity and fear, it does so through a stark reversal of function: the libido binding them together discharges conflict by making absolute the refusal to connect.

Hickey has brought them to this final regression by enacting the opposite movement. In act IV Hickey performs the rarest of acts. He takes his projections back inside himself and drives them to the source from which they proceed. Everyone projects, but for most denial cleanses us of the deed. So reinforced projection externalizes aggression, making the psyche safe from itself. When the grand project meant to conceal that fact fails, Hickey turns the whole thing back upon himself. He thereby attains the proper direction of aggression. Aggression turned inward probes the layers of the repressed, issuing in a narrative which, despite considerable resistance, has discovery of the repressed as its structure and through-line. For what Hickey learns is that hate is stronger than love, and its intricate modes of operation are the force that gives his life the continuity of a drama which evolves, at each stage of its development, the new psychic formation required for its prosecution.

In driving the projections back inside, one thus comes at last to one's true condition: authentic depression, the realization that life is a process in which we inflict our conflicts on others to avoid facing them. Hickey, as salesman and actor, has always fled depression, only to learn that it has controlled his life by trapping him in the double-bind known as reparation.[27] Away from home, he pines in false mourning, bearing the guilt he confesses on his return so that he can be absolved by the other. He now learns the folly of that act: reparation seems to cleanse the psyche but actually restores the power of the internalized (m)Other to enforce yet another cycle of self-unraveling.

Depression for Hickey has never been more than an occasion for self-undoing. Whether depression can be worked through in another way remains a question we will return to in subsequent chapters. Thanks to Hickey, we now know its direction. Depression remains endless, unresolved mourning as long as one refuses to take up the proper task of aggression: the act of committing within the murder of the internal saboteur who controls and harms the psyche most when operating in the guise of beloved object. True depression begins when, without defenses, one is prepared to face the most violent feelings about self and other, without seeking some way, at the end, to undo one's experience and thereby resume the process.

Played properly, Hickey in act IV becomes the actor Artaud and Grotowski dreamt of. All masks are shattered from within. The unraveling of mania produces an eruption of the unconscious. Before he gives the group the escape hatch he knows they will seize, Hickey offends his audience to the quick. Theatre has become a place of total exposure, and on that note he leaves, "still signalling, through the flames."

The group's response thereby becomes the final, cruelest revelation of the unconscious. The last joke may be on Hickey, but in it the group regresses to the source underlying previous uses of humor as defense and discharge. In labeling Hickey insane, reductionism and denial release an orgiastic discharge of death-work celebrated as such. The group gets what audiences come together to share. In the process, they reveal its foundation: successful discharge of conflict requires the mass psychology of fascism.[28] Disorder is located in an external agent. Labeling that agent mad, sinful, sexual, banishes the threat to the community. Naming is the supreme speech act because it extinguishes consciousness. The group thereby becomes a collective body seeking its pleasure in a total unbinding of psychological conflicts. Mass orgasm produces the peace that passeth understanding. Thanks to ritual, the group is finally one with itself and stands before us in tableau as a paradigm of the operations audiences employ to protect themselves from drama.

To join them, all we need do is follow the yellow brick road. The real question is whether one can resist the temptation. That is, what psychological act must one undertake to constitute the inwardness of an audience that would overcome the operations on which this group depends? In forcing us to confront this question, O'Neill has made us an offer we can't refuse. *Iceman* reveals group psychology as a pathological process in which we band together in mass deception to sustain a collective neurosis. Challenged, groups only regress; they will apparently descend to any pit to expel a disruptive presence, and they attain peace only when everyone employs the most reductive mechanisms. By laying bare the structure of regressions whereby the group achieves its purpose and pleasure, O'Neill offers a shattering mirror to all humanistic accounts of the rhetoric of assent. In giving us a systematic understanding of death-work as the psychodynamic of group psychology, O'Neill brings to the groups where we will find our deepest investments the brand of a cleansing honesty.

One application of that lesson is to traditional interpretations of this play. Even a critic as acute as Susan Sontag sees Hickey's insanity as a simple reversal; a complex plot is thereby reduced to manageable proportions. A similar need informs the search by others for the tragic flaw that will free us from having to internalize an agent like Hickey. In eloquent commentary on such operations, the tenants of Harry's saloon give us perhaps the deepest insight into the motives behind the quest for critical mastery: panic anxiety, the abject need to kill the work in order to save ourselves.

When you kill someone, you have to become that person. That's the fate of Hickey. It is also the final piece to the puzzle. Once we see Hickey's project as both reparation and an unconscious attempt to do to the group what Evelyn did to him, the entire play becomes an intricate structure of reversals, spiraling inward, to end not in De Manian undecidables—Is Hickey mad or isn't he? Does pity finally win out?—but in the arrival of something that is radically determinate. The opposition at the end of the play is no longer between life and death, but between two different forms of death. All human relationships, especially "loving" ones, are revealed as acts of aggression in which we try to do unto others what was done to us. The bonds of love, fellowship, and community are resolved into the aggression which informs them. To supplement Heidegger, we aren't tranquilized together; we are deadened, "corpsed," as Beckett puts it. O'Neill's meticulous naturalism serves an ontological concern: to reveal Being-with (*Mit-sein*) as death-work. The habits and behaviors that structure everyday life constitute so many ways in which we sacrifice inwardness to the herd instinct. Death works in every behavior whereby pity and fear, the counterfeits of anxiety, are projected as the terms of human relationships. Social interactions so dedicated form a vast theatre of what "mental health professionals" now proudly refer to as support groups, that is, social contracts based on finding modes of reinforcement whereby we extinguish our burdens by relieving others of theirs. Bad faith is of necessity an interpersonal, shared phenomenon: the group is its priest. Its purpose is to deaden any consciousness that could infect us with ourselves.

Iceman is a controlled laboratory experiment which uses the estrangement effect of the bar to highlight processes that characterize groups in general. The bar, as paradigmatic theatrical space for such operations, is the womb to which we return to be absolved together of the sin of existence. It is the place where one incessantly reenacts one's drama so that it will never take place, a theatre of desire where the shared goal is to be delivered from desire. In a sense drunks are the true ontological actors because they bring the subtext close to the surface. In them the disorders of the psyche and the role of the group in offering deliverance stand forth with a clarity that is carefully concealed in groups that have devised subtler protocols and more exalted rituals.

Hickey's failure signals a crisis in what we may term the effort of "the good analyst," the one for whom the goal of therapy is to remove whatever makes people sad and guilty in order to help them accept reality and find a healthy, productive role in the larger social community. The repressed, once known, is discharged; the ego thereby strengthens its defenses; adaptation to consensual reality testing assures everyone a piece of the rock. Hickey exposes the underside of these commonplaces. When the need is to make people happy and free them of conflict, the real desire is to sustain a warm illusion about oneself in order to deny unconscious motives and the aggressiveness of an activity which depends for its success on convincing others in order to escape oneself. Insofar as analysts refuse to probe such motives by undertaking the kind of exploration Hickey enacts in act IV, their activity can only make their patients worse—even if neither party ever knows it. The irony is that the message such analysts conceal is the only one they actually communicate: all participants in such a process are left with no real insight and nothing to work through. When conformity to the social order—masquerading as the achievement of identity in a conflict-free ego sphere—is the goal, all that's really going on is death-work made sure of itself through the construction of a realm of rigidified defenses and reified emotions.

O'Neill concludes *Iceman* by staging at the level of the primary process what such operations really affect in the psyche. In doing so he shows that the hallowed idea of "regression in the service of the ego" may be a cover for one of the primary ways in which death-work operates.[29] The therapeutic bond in which a healthy or emerging part of the personality joins the therapist in controlled regression into the repressed sounds good but may finally amount to mutual deceit, because in such a drama regression is never allowed its proper direction—the fathoming out of everything which the ego is set up to defend against and deny. When the repressed personality is carefully handled to preserve and restore the "healthy part of the personality," therapy becomes a sleight of hand played with gloves on.

For regression has within itself its own terms and principles of operation. Regression is the riving of close pent-up guilts and the riveting of oneself within them. It serves no ego because it knows there is no ego to serve. As long as the ego controls regression, the regressed psyche is never allowed to activate its inherent dialectic. That movement is the struggle to tear something out of one's heart at the level of the primary process by sticking to the emotions that emerge only when one is able to operate within that psychic space. Regression, so understood, inaugurates the possibility of turning oneself inside out by reversing the very structure of one's psyche. When the ego controls the analytic process, one remains instead trapped in yet another act of aggression against oneself. The attempt is invariably to hold the inner world at bay and keep its fixed terms on ice. The true splitting and fragmentation of the personality necessarily results. The defense ego is yet another avatar of the internal saboteur—intellectualization as extended analytic play, lacking the terms and urgencies of drama.

Toward an Authentic Audience: Parritt and Larry

Four interdependent structures converge at the end of the play. Together they define the mousetrap wherein *Iceman* gets the guests. One structure defines Hickey as tragic figure. A second defines the group's abolition of knowledge. Two lonely figures try to mediate the difference.

From the beginning, Hickey and Parritt know they are secret sharers who want to deny the connection that makes each the mirror of the other's repressed. As audience Parritt sees from the start the analogy the others struggle to deny. He is positioned for this knowledge because he has already acted and is living the awareness Hickey will come to. If maximum distance characterizes the group's response, maximum engagement characterizes Parritt's. He is an ideal audience because he knows that his story and Hickey's are variants of the "oedipal" crime, as are the suppressed tales of everyone in the bar: with wife, lover, son, friend, or rival, we reenact conflicts that have their origin in the family. Parritt adds the dimension that takes this complex to a new depth. He knows that his crime is greater than Hickey's because he has devised the perfect revenge. Hamlet is paralyzed by the recognition that the one thing you can't do when you kill someone is kill that person. Parritt has found the solution. His mother will be left alive, in prison, with the knowledge that her son's hatred put her there. Thus she already inhabits the psychic space Hickey will find himself in when, locked in unending dialogue, he will forever ask Evelyn to "renounce" her eternal forgiveness so that he may gain peace from its true text: the unbearable reality of ceaseless hate lurking in the abyssal deceptions of love.

For both Hickey and Parritt there is no exit. Hickey's narrative thus drives home for Parritt the only "shock of recognition" worthy of the name: the ethical imperative to make recognition the basis for self-judgment. Recognition is wonderful when it leaves us calm of mind, all passion spent. Parritt's inwardness exposes that commonplace. Finding in suicide the only appropriate justice, Parritt challenges the audience in a way that strikes deeper than Hickey.

To escape it, we distance ourselves from him, only to meet in Larry a space of reflection which doubles that act of interpretation back upon itself. Larry could have been a great literary critic, for he's always been sitting in the grandstand, finding in intellectualization the surest means of defense. The structure of the play, however, exposes both his brand of pity and his nihilism as reinforcing shields that hide him from himself. In recognizing this, Larry sees that he is the one convert to death Hickey has made. Constituting that knowledge has become for him the task of interpretation. Tragic knowledge begins when the grandstand collapses and one finds oneself onstage with the duty to constitute a consciousness that will comprehend the systematic structure of reversals and recognitions that Hickey's agency has enacted. Horatio has finally found his proper task. Drama can no longer be resolved into an affair of meaning, an ascent to thematics. Instead, the typical operations we perform to make interpretations must be blocked so that we can begin to suffer what they hide. Our task, with Larry, is to internalize the change affected by the work's structure and thereby attain its true content. For, as Larry now knows, pity is that discharge of responsibility that makes you feel good about yourself; nihilism is that abstract paralysis in which there is great comfort, since discovering the abyssal structure of undecidables finally renders insignificant any difference between life and death.

In rejecting both operations, Larry points us toward what I will term concrete reflection. Its task is to fathom the tragic theory of the psyche developed in *Iceman* and bring the disruptive implications of that knowledge directly to bear upon cherished assumptions of literary and psychoanalytic theory. Its imperative is the refusal to seek catharsis. In leaving us with Larry's singular consciousness, the play casts on us—as we flee together toward whatever shared comfort we can clutch to deliver ourselves from individuation—a final act of interrogation which reminds us that in leaving the theatre we carry death with us as the guilty secret we either inflict or are now prepared to expose in the primary place of its residence.

The Audience Engaged

If we become that audience, we are at the end existentially individualized, isolated from any group deliverance, and sent home to concretize the anxiety the work has driven into us. Home is where the heart is. It is the primary place where the disorders staged in the bar have their origin and where they proceed apace. The mousetrap created by situating us, as audience, between the group and Hickey has sprung. In act IV we, like the group, are positioned as guilty listeners, but their attempt to deny the truth delivers us to it. As we watch them live on, regressed in that final solidarity which exposes the root psychopathology behind ritual herding, the needs we invest in groups receive the final blow. In their "joy," we see a spectacle of utter futility—unrelieved, but endless and lacking pathos. Pity and fear are withdrawn as possible responses.. They can't be catharted because nothing has changed. Repetition and reification dissolve drama without resolving conflict. Insofar as we understand the regressive drive that has brought the group to its foundation, the possibility of joining any group becomes problematic. As audience we become instead individuals defined by an anxiety that can't be discharged but must be directed in isolation upon the layers of our inwardness—and their exposure. Regression in the service of the ego, and the group identity on which every ego depends for its maintenance, have been destroyed. Regression now moves in a new direction: progressive descent in an effort to annihilate the ego by discovering all that it hides. The play's effort has been to awaken this possibility in us and bar all exits that would relieve us from it. The space of theatre has been totally transformed. It is a hall of mirrors, reflecting the labyrinthine duplicity of everyone in attendance.

In Hickey's narrative the Unconscious becomes the subject of drama. The Unconscious that is staged, however, is that of the audience. In act IV Hickey becomes the agent who speaks to us at the most secret places of our psyche. He is no longer beneath us, and no tidy neo-Aristotelian judgments will restore the ethical and emotional norms needed to put him in his place. For Hickey has become a representative figure who performs the sovereign act: he has collected his entire life around its trauma and has discovered the continuity that brings the horror of the entire thing to light. He has centered himself in a way that gets at our deepest anxieties. Could our life, properly told, bring us to a similar awareness? Is everything we do to delay that recognition but a vicious circle that produces ever more insidious developments of the disease? Is love the way we prosecute and make a haven for our hate? Is the story we tell to escape that recognition no more than the big lie avid in its interstices? Hickey's narrative brings us before the most frightful idea—that hate is stronger than love and love the most perfect exercise of hate. The ego cringes, because the deepest motive for defenses has been exposed: ego-identity is the intellectualized world we construct in order to escape authentic depression.

So situated, we may discover, as we struggle in the infinite resources of our mendacity for some intellectualizing way to master the play, that we are not really different from the group onstage. To reverse that condition, the best antidote is a hermeneutics of engagement, since it strives to shatter the concepts and practices that prevent the literary work from becoming a situation of risk in which we may lose ourselves irretrievably. Such a hermeneutics strikes many critics as an unwarranted act of aggression toward them. From within, however, the issue is one of possibility. What kind of change in the structure of the psyche can be achieved by living out, as one's self-reference, the agon which *Iceman* has dramatized? This is, of course, the grand question of pscyhoanalysis, but O'Neill gives it a radically new direction. What is the proper use and direction of aggression? Is there a work other than death that can inform the self-mediation of the psyche? The greatness of *Iceman* lies in activating a possible reversal of function, whereby death-work can be turned back upon itself. Aggression now has its target and its dignity. It must be directed within to root out the core disorder that weds us to death.

In delivering us to that task, *Iceman* gets the guests by liberating the possibility that in retelling our story we will discover, like Hickey, that we have practiced systematic violence toward one another in that great exercise of our being we call love. Delivering that blow, *Iceman* reveals "calm of mind" as the ultimate pipe dream. The desire for catharsis is resentment toward the tragic and the task of internalizing its imperatives.

The group was cleansed by exploiting the negative transference as a principle of collective discharge. The authentic audience, in contrast, sustains a negative therapeutic reaction and turns it back on itself. There is nothing O'Neill could say at the end to comfort us, because comfort has been revealed as a trap. As a structure of reversals, the play uncovers the massive presence of death in those activities we confidently subsume under the concept of life in order to quicken in us a possibility that can only exist and be constituted in the teeth of death. All dualisms between life and death, love and hate—and the guarantees they assure—are abolished. We are set naked in a far different kingdom—that of concrete dialectics. Life can now have only one meaning: the redirecting of death-work inside, as aggression turned against the internal saboteur in an effort to reverse all the ways in which one's life has been a protracted soul-murder.

Iceman is one of the clearest examples of why thematic interpretation is such an invidious process. This play doesn't give us a message; it brings us before a possibility. As in the ideal Socratic situation, teaching here is not a process whereby a content is communicated but the space in which a certain action is performed. That action is reversal, the subjecting of the audience to the process through which alone they might become subjects opposed to death. Its true "message" is this: if you want to create possibilities, make structures. That is the only way to get at an audience, because it alone addresses the psychic place where the terms of resistance and discovery reside. Psychoanalysis and drama are identical processes because they have the same subject and follow the same method. But drama communicates by driving a nail into the deepest psychic register. In so doing, it establishes the ontological power of death as the "suffering and labor" of the negative within the psyche.[30] Life is the dialectical turning of death back upon itself, but contra Hegel, its only *situs* in reality is in the innermost recesses of the psyche. For psychological change to take place, active reversal as a dialectic, working with and within the experience of one's soul murder, must become the presiding force in one's inner world.

The greatness of *Iceman* resides in the intricate and inexorable logic of reversal and recognition that forms its structure. That logic is not one of aporia or deconstruction but of concrete dialectics. *Iceman* reveals death-work as a fundamental structure of the psyche in order to give us the possibility of internalizing that knowledge as the basis of our self-reference. As such, it forms the overture to the act we will attempt, in progressively more concrete ways, in succeeding chapters, as we explore wounds that strike closer to home.

The Perfect Couple:
A Streetcar Named Desire

Role-Playing . . . and Identity

"We've had this date with each other from the beginning!" (162). Stanley speaks the key line in the play.[1] Blanche and Stanley are made for each other. The "roles" they play are perfectly matched, mutually defining. Each meets in the other the one perfectly fitted to stripping away the masks and bringing basic anxieties to a head. In a sense, the play is about the clash of incompatible "acting styles," which perpetually mirror one another because they are designed to master identical psychosexual conflicts.

Roles are "identities" constructed to avoid interpersonal anxiety. When they work, they give us control in an area where we aren't in control. They are social identities constructed with reference to particular "significant others" who are objects of intense concern. We always prepare a face to meet the faces that we meet. Sitting before the mirror, putting on the mask, I gaze not into a bottomless pit or a perfected narcissism but into the face of the Other who will look upon my offering with the Sartrean power, through rejection, to turn me into a thing. Woman is that power for Stanley; man provides a similar occasion for Blanche. A role is always fashioned with a view toward conflict; it makes no sense apart from something we anticipate running up against in the world.

Roles are also products of shared, group identities. That is where they are learned, practiced, and inflicted, in the name of group solidarity, on those who would be different. Woman is perhaps never more central than when the guys are sitting around by themselves, talking. As Tennessee Williams shows, such scenes are agons in which men test one another's machismo—the constant need to prove that "I'm a real man"—with someone like Mitch present as constant reminder of what it looks like to fail at this ritual. No genuine feelings can be shared by males in such a society because the constant subtext of "conversation" is the testing of one another in terms of the male role.

The significant other to any role is the one who activates the conflicts it was meant to resolve. This is the role Blanche and Stanley play for one another. Blanche stirs his "character" from its phantom substantiality into dramatic agency, because she represents both the threat before which he must again prove himself and the rich opportunity to wage a truly significant battle and gain a famous victory. Stanley exacerbates Blanche's conflicts because he represents the male image that stands at the core of the disorder which haunts her consciousness and which, as we'll see, she struggles both to flee and to embrace.

Drama represents what happens to conflicts when they are activated and drawn to their inevitable conclusion. It begins whenever a role is made peremptory through contact with that Other toward whom it was defined in anxious reference. Under strain, the subtext keeps seeping through. The mask starts to fall, and each attempt to put it back on constitutes a further step in its shattering. Such is the structure of Blanche and Stanley's interaction and the task for the actors playing them. Even Stanley's apparent triumphs, like Blanche's "escapes," leave a residue of insecurity, a need to disrupt the peace, renew the battle, and bring it to a definitive end. The secret of both characters is that they are desperately wedded to their roles because for both, role-playing conceals and displaces a pit of insecurity and unconscious conflict.

Blanche is the obvious performer, the grand dame who weaves a theatrical web around herself in order to transform each situation into a magical act whereby everyone will stand transfixed, compelled by her performance. Stanley would like to convince us that he's the antithesis of such theatrics. He enters, one with his role: the mighty hunter, bearing meat. In machismo he has brought off the impossible Hegelian project: he coincides with himself and is always fully at home in his world. Williams' description of Stanley is not simply an act of erotic longing. It is also, as in Joyce's narrative method, a vision of Stanley as he would describe himself, had he the language, to his male friends: a dream of male self-presence, centered in the confident mastery of "pleasure with women." Walking across the stage, Stanley enacts a complex drama. Everything in the way he moves is fashioned to give the world the assurance of a man. Stanley is as theatrical as Blanche and has carefully tailored his body language so that every movement proclaims his phallic status.

Anyone who is this at home in the world is living in a world that is full of things he does not want to know. Stanley desires to represent Being, fullness, the absolute identity of "the gaudy seed-bearer" with his body and his environment in a relationship of comfort where sloppiness is of the essence. Stanley must represent solidity, substantiality, because beneath the posturing there is a pit of infantile anxiety, the state he's in whenever he fears abandonment, the loss of Stella. That fear is the true "center" of Stanley's being, the dependency his machismo is set up to deny. When loss threatens—as on the poker night when phallic posturing erupts in violence against Stella— Stanley's "identity" collapses back into need and demand. Stanley cries out for Stella, concentrating his whole being in a cry addressed to the body of the other. As with the child, Stanley's naked act is also a calculated act. In uttering his cry of helplessness and intense longing, Stanley knows where Stella hears it. She hears it between her legs. Whenever anxiety erupts, Stanley is lost until he regains a "substantial identity" he can have only when his woman is present as a sexual and maternal source of bodily reassurance. Falling to his knees and burying his head in her womb is a perfect iconic representation of her multiple function. Fear of maternal abandonment is the anxiety underlying Stanley's machismo. He is trapped in the psychic position of the child: when loss threatens, panic ensues, and nothing else exists until the object returns. For Stanley, the female body is the place where the male restores his "identity" whenever he is flooded by aggression and loss of control. His perpetual fear is that he may not be able to keep the woman in such a relationship.

Enter Blanche and the return of that fear and the memory of the famous victory in which he vanquished it. Blanche reminds him of what Stella was like before he pulled her "down off them columns" (137) so that the phallus could crow. Stanley must bring sex into any relationship with a woman, because every woman poses a threat. Women, especially those of "class," have the Sartrean power to make him feel like a thing—unless he can use his very physicality to reverse the relationship and compel a "refined" consciousness to recognize the real and substantial truth of human behavior.

Stanley is defined by the contradiction between his need to attract women who represent something "above" him and his need to bring them "down." This is the Hegelian dimension of his consciousness: "love" is a struggle for recognition and an effort to achieve a substantial identity. Stella is a profoundly ambivalent and perfect object-choice. Stanley stakes his existence on the notion that his sexual power is such that the refined woman will eventually bow before it.

Sex, accordingly, is the a priori category that defines his perception of women. For Stanley, everything women do, especially refined behavior, is part of a mating ritual—and he relishes every chance to strike through the masks. Stanley and Blanche are perfectly matched because Stanley's need gives him an acute insight into the sexual subtext of everything Blanche does.

Contra Treat Williams, Stanley is no dumb ape. As scene i shows, he is a man of keen if vicious psychological insight and of considerable mordant wit. He sizes Blanche up immediately. He knows who's been drinking his liquor, and he knows how to strip away Blanche's pretenses and get directly at her underlying anxieties. He is also an expert at putting all relations with women on a sexual basis of a particular kind, in which the sexual moves from the beginning within the register of aggression. In love with his fantasy of himself as walking phallus, he can't resist an opportunity to advertise the goods (by removing his shirt) and prove once again that sex is the only reality between men and women.

By the end of the scene, Stanley has acted out what he will assert repeatedly, with increased anger, frustration, and insecurity, throughout the play. All that women really want is to be overpowered by the force of a male sexuality that puts an end to all pretense. Stanley can't see anything women do as anything but a come-on, and he is powerless to resist the bait. There is even something religious in his obsession. Stanley can never laugh at "women's games"; for him this is a deadly serious business. Women's "airs" suggest a superiority before which he feels like the Hegelian slave denied recognition. He needs to render the interpretation that will reverse the situation by identifying the sexual subtext. He is the knight of a single idea who must strike through all masks so that the truth may stand forth for public inspection. Women are guilty of a terrible crime. Teasing, they produce sexual confusion in men, introducing nagging doubts about the sacred myth of male sexual identity and its primacy. As its incarnate representative, Stanley must bring them before the altar of judgment by using sex to restore the "truth" while exacting vengeance and punishment on those who breed confusion. No woman is going to pull the wool over Stanley's eyes. And he will not be content until those who try realize that being bedded by him is all they know on earth and all they need to know. Stanley repeatedly calls attention to his role—taking off his shirt, commenting on his sweat, and so on—because he isn't at home in it. He is rehearsing it, trying to get down all the right gestures and body language. He plays at his existence like a self-conscious actor seeking to perfect a role. He wants to naturalize himself in perfect imitation of all the tough-guy movies he's seen. This is the role he chooses, because it is the one that is perfectly designed to eliminate the anxieties inwardness always entails for him. Like Sylvester Stallone, he would like to be in a movie without dialogue, safe in a role defined solely by gestures and the sheer force of his physical presence as he grunts and frets his hour upon the stage. Inwardness is the enemy because it is feminine, and the feelings it brings are all connected with loss of control in the face of women. Iago keeps hunting himself, stripping away masks. Stanley, in contrast, would be pure self-presence in perfect coincidence at all times with the image of himself as phallus.

When everything must be externalized in this way, it is a sure sign of a massive internal conflict which cannot be addressed. That state is the inverse mirror image of the role, and it keeps breaking through as a direct outgrowth of the way Stanley uses the role to suppress it. De Niro's notion that emotions come out through the process in which they are disguised is especially relevant to the task of playing Stanley. Ironically, the Stanislavski "method" via Lee Strasberg was perfectly suited to the part. Marlon Brando was right for Stanley because he had a wonderful insight into the conflict between Stanley's insecurities and his faltering sensitivity, especially around Stella. Stanley is capable of great tenderness and is a man easily and deeply injured. He wants nothing more than to melt in gentle union with Stella; the moment when Brando carefully removes the lint from her dress (in some performances he didn't) speaks the measure of Stanley's need and of his twisted desire. Stanley, not Mitch, lacks the courage of his tenderness. It becomes the enemy whenever his abiding anxiety returns. Whenever Stanley is sexually threatened, everything disappears but his brute insistence on his role. Mechanization takes command; he becomes a terrifying incarnation of the Bergsonian comic condition. The key to Stanley Kowalski is not his sexual confidence but his sexual insecurity.

That is what Blanche brings out in a tension which progressively reveals the sexual instability that defines each character. Stanley's sexuality isn't the fixed identity that finally says, I've had enough, but the identity of a man on trial. The acting styles adopted by Blanche and Stanley are perfectly matched to a Brechtian task: they unmask one another.

Sex for her is also the conflict at the center of consciousness that must be expressed on all occasions, and the particular spin she gives it expresses the very thing he fears and abhors. While Stanley can't stand women's games, Blanche is the consummate game-player. Stanley must put an end to games to halt his anxiety; Blanche needs to play them to halt hers. On both sides the match is perfect, because sexual anxiety is at the root of both processes. Like Stanley, Blanche turns all relationships with the opposite sex into sexual encounters. In directing the first production, Elia Kazan noted that in each scene Blanche plays one of the roles traditionally characterizing southern womanhood. What he didn't see clearly enough is that she uses each role as a counter in a sexual game. Like Stanley, Blanche isn't secure until she has put things on a sexual basis. Stanley's first act in scene i is to remove his shirt; Blanche's first act in scene ii is to show her back. It is the opening move in the extended flirtation which the scene becomes. And the purpose of flirting for Blanche is not simply to deflect Stanley's inquiries. The most revealing moment in the scene comes when she sprays perfume in his face. The action is excessive, too overt, gratuitous, provocative, the expression of a surplus need. "If I didn't know that you was my wife's sister I'd get ideas about you!" says Stanley, already full of them (41). Blanche is after more than a compliment; the perfume functions as aggressive provocation. She is even more insistent than Stanley on making the sexual tension between them overt, to up the ante of aggression and reverse the advantage he gained in scene i. Whenever he fails to take the bait, she goads him, thereby assuring that he will file the message away for future reference.

Blanche and Stanley are perfectly adequated to one another at the deepest register of their psyches. Their clash is certain to bring forth the unconscious of both characters and through it the general problematic of sexuality in which, for Williams, everyone onstage—and in the audience—is implicated. To get inside that hermeneutic circle, however, various escape hatches must be closed.

In *Streetcar,* Williams constructs a mousetrap that gets at the sexual "identity"—and the theoretical guarantees girding that confidence—of a true plurality of audiences, many of whom have offered interpretations to escape its clutches. Blanche is a sex hysteric, Stanley a rapist; the play shows how the patriarchy works to enslave and punish women, it's not really rape given the sexual provocation she's subjected him to for months, and so on. Such interpretations aren't false, but they are parts of a much larger truth which is suppressed when they are offered as complete interpretations. Different audiences thus escape the hook the play has them on and miss the great wound in our sexuality and our identity that it tries to engage. To defend against that prospect, we impose partial views in order to rupture a complex dialectic. But the beauty of the play is that it challenges virtually every current theory of sexuality, of gender, of sexual identity, of "who's to blame."[2] Because that is the case, audiences struggle to find a way to escape: they limit the impact of the complex being dramatized by choosing sides or by finding an alternative which offers a sexual and/or psychological identity that escapes the disorder of the main characters. In doing so, however, one falls into the very trap Williams has carefully constructed. Stanley and Blanche are mighty opposites because they bring out the sexual conflict which no character in Williams' world escapes. One of his primary efforts, in fact, is to construct a total system in which all variants are manifestations of the same problem. Shifting to Stella or Mitch for relief only serves to bring us back with a vengeance to Stanley and Blanche, once we discover their complicity—and ours—in the sexual malaise which the mighty opposites drive to the event.

Four Characters, One Complex: A Hermeneutic Circle

Streetcar dramatizes a psychological complex which shows that the dominant male and female roles in our culture are perfectly matched to one another—and that the nature of that match is a pattern of mutual cruelty and sexual aggression. The beauty of the play is that it moves us beyond current ideological assurances to a recognition of how the two dominant roles create, sustain, and torture one another, allowing no exit from the complex they establish. All characters in the play mirror the same problem; none provide a solution. In undermining that possibility, the play implicates its audience in a structure that tries to make it impossible for any of us to deny our complicity in the psychological complex being dramatized. Because interpretation is the primary way in which we limit the impact of "texts" upon us, however, any work hoping to spring such a trap has its work cut out for it, since it must undermine, from within its drama, the different positions it knows audiences will assume in order to extricate themselves from what it represents.

The four characters form a single complex, in which the lesser characters complement the mighty opposites. As a totality, this system operates to deny us any exit from the complex dramatized by the play. This is the primary way Williams casts the net in which he traps the sexuality of an audience that he understands at a level that cuts through the possibility of any protected or privileged space (biological or Utopian) that either gender might use to escape. Roles are parts of a system, and until we know the whole set—and the psychology determining it—we can't understand any of the terms. Character is complicity, and the issue of sex appeal may have a good deal more to do with its "foundations" than we imagine.

The Phallic Principle

It's a hard truth for many, but sex appeal per se is a myth. Attraction—or its opposite—derives by and large from the conflicts that lure us into fascination with someone else's desire. To be "sexy," all one really has to do is become the screen for an other's projections. *Streetcar* maps a veritable system of such relationships, thereby offering the guests a mousetrap aimed at the psyche that is rooted in the organ.

Stanley has a certain sex appeal. This fact, once taken for granted, now has to be established, and against strong objections. One must argue the point nonetheless, for unless it is established one can't enter into the psychodynamics of *Streetcar*—or see the mousetrap it sets for its audience.

The basis of Stanley's attractiveness is the projection of sexual confidence. It may be a sham, but that does not lessen its power. Stanley affirms the sexual—directly, if bluntly, but with pride and respect for its power. He is a sexual being and proudly affirms that women are also. Confidence in his sexual identity makes him a perfect player in those elaborate social mating rituals that men and women in our culture use to enact their "noble selectiveness of sensuality." Mating games are ways of answering a number of unarticulated questions. Answer them right, and you get the prize. One of the things any woman worthy of the name wants to gauge is the extent of a man's potential uxoriousness. Will he stand up for himself, or is he really a "mama's boy" afraid to express feelings "proper" women might find objectionable? The instinct behind this question is a valuable one and justifies a number of nasty games. The appeal of Stanley is that of the man who sees through games and knows how to call them by their right names. Most game-players want to be seen through: challenging men is part of the search for a man who won't have the wool pulled over his eyes. Refusing uxoriousness requires a certain security in the face of possible rejection. Testing the other is one of the legitimate functions of game-playing. Stanley is the rude health that calls the tune in convoluted sexual games. Stanley knows when a woman is interested in him and has the sexual confidence to say so. One desiring to seduce him need not fear that he'll miss or fail to act on the message. That is the ground of his appeal, and of the sexual insecurities he acts on like a Rorschach. He has one more thing going for him: he looks like the young Marlon Brando. The audience this paragraph offended is, as we'll see, one of the primary ones that the play snares in a mousetrap that refers its ideological imperatives to their repressed.

Mitch is the foil that establishes the claims of Stanley's frank sexuality by giving us an insight into the psychodynamics of the opposite. The suspicion about Mitch is that intimacy with him will open the Pandora's box of sexual confusions, inhibitions, and resentments. Mitch's tortuous indirection and deliberate naïveté stem from the fear that if he expresses himself he'll be rejected. He is a gentleman because he fears to be otherwise; he knows that his courtly manners come from weakness, not strength. His exaggerated respect for women and his deliberate timidity make him an object of contempt and humor. His is the comedy of one unwilling—not unable—to see through "feminine" games. He never picks up on any of Blanche's suggestive remarks, and he never responds with more than a pathetic wince to the most obvious sexual put-downs.

Virtuosity is the chain he will fashion to bring the source of his anxiety into line. A woman senses that the question always hanging in the back of his mind is the one that finally proves decisive: Is this the kind of woman I can take home to meet my mother? Sex for him is something women don't want, something broached only with the greatest delicacy. Mitch wants to deny female sexuality in order to escape the question it raises for him—the question of whether he's a man. In Mitch's exaggerated respect lurks the double standard waiting another chance to imprison woman on that pedestal which is no more than a monument to the male anxiety, the fear that men will always fall short unless they find a way to harness female sexuality. Mitch's respectful, considerate sexuality is a greater threat to women than Stanley's frank come-on. For if a woman internalizes this view, male resentment becomes the norm whereby she regulates herself. Sexual ethics is the grand name for this disease. Mitch plays the lowest card in its deck: once a woman loses her reputation, she is no better than a bitch for rutting. Stanley claims adequacy to any form of feminine sexuality and is willing to risk himself in performance. Mitch would have women internalize his fear and police their sexuality accordingly. His complaint is like Othello's—"O why do we call these cunning creatures ours / and not their appetites"—but he has found the solution. Blanche is "disposed of" for Mitch once her past is known, while for Stanley her past is proof of a "suspicion" that makes her desirable. Both men debase Blanche for being a sexual being, but Mitch's dismissal is the truly insidious one. Stanley never claims to be ethical.

Stanley may be a fantasy, but he's a collective one created by both sexes. Weak men like Mitch see in him the fantasy which acts out the anger toward women which they refuse to admit, except vicariously. Mitch and Stanley are, indeed, brothers, and the phallic display of the one mirrors the phallic protest of the other. But Stanley is also a fantasy women perpetuate, for motives well worth specifying. He is a weathervane for activating two complexes that actually have much in common: the sense of guilt which can attach desire only to a debasing object, and that repression of sexual fears which masks itself as virtuous denial of sexual power. In both, the unconscious doth protest too much. The erosion of Stanley's sex appeal is this: the less repressed one is, the less attractive he becomes.

Sisterhood Is Powerful: The Woman's Part

Sisterhood is powerful, especially when it is defined by competition over men. This is the barely concealed subtext of everything that happens in the initial scene between Stella and Blanche. Like so many women, the two sisters define their relationship to one another in terms of their relationship to men. Their reunion is a series of maneuvers structured around an omnipresent but unuttered statement: One of us has a man, and one of us doesn't. Stella wants to care for Blanche, seeks her approval, feels guilty toward her, and is still disposed to viewing the world through Blanche's aristocratic eyes, as Stanley will learn at dinnertime tomorrow. She feels the need to justify her choice of Stanley. But beyond all this, she wants to crow, to savor her moment of sexual superiority in a series of well-aimed barbs—beginning with the line "I can hardly stand it when he is away for a night" (19)—that repeat a single message: I, not you, am the real woman who's got me a real man. I had the courage to reject the aristocratic pretense, and you cultured types won't intimidate me any longer. Because she wants to avoid conflict, Stella underplays everything, but that does not mean she lacks desire. Her deepest need is to convince herself that she's not like Blanche. What men did to her sister won't happen to her. Stella's desire is to avoid the disorders of female sexuality which she sees epitomized in Blanche. That is why sex for her is essentially a way of alleviating anxieties in quest of that bovine complacency that keeps her in a state of torpor. Kazan was right to insist that Kim Hunter retard all her movements and reactions. Stella uses sex to signify her "psychological" health and with it her victory over those things in their heritage that ruined her sister. Stella may have been the quiet one, but she wasn't inattentive. She saw Belle Reve as a no-win situation and took the first chance to escape. But escape is never enough. She craves justification, especially when the specter of the family disorder returns in that voice of haughty disapproval that has haunted and motivated her erotic choices. Stanley isn't escape; he's triumph, a clean exit and a new beginning. Stella wants to arise from his bed cleansed of the past. "What does a woman want?" In Stella's case, the desire is to avoid desire and its disruptions. Like Stanley, her quest is for Being, to coincide with her body in a release from anxiety.

Stella's overweening need to take care of Blanche falls into place. Knowing that bad relationships with men brought Blanche to her door, Stella wants to "nurse" Blanche's dependency while displaying her victory, thereby reassuring herself that she has escaped her sister's "fate." Blanche wants privacy, hydrotherapy, and lanterns; Stanley wants easy access to the bathroom; but Stella is relatively undisturbed by the living arrangements because she wants her sister to hear and to play the voyeur to her chance to shine as happily married pregnant sexual exhibitionist.

It's another perfect match. From her entrance, Blanche needs to look down her aristocratic nose at the Kowalskis' living arrangements precisely because everything in the house functions like a Rorschach rubbing raw her sexual anxieties. The Kowalski household flashes the red flag of her own sexuality in Blanche's face. Seeking a refuge from sex, she runs into the very room she desperately wants to escape because she knows how thoroughly she inhabits it. It is, indeed, a homecoming, and the repeated references to Belle Reve and the past are an attempt both to regain control and to take flight through hysterical posturing. Long before Stanley enters, Blanche's sexual imagination is primed, and her "cultured" coping mechanisms have already started to crack under the strain. When Stanley walks through the door, reality and Blanche's projections meet. As in a dream or an allegory, the male sexuality that has ruled her life now comes back at her from outside, fitted with the uncanny ability to see right through her.

> Stanley: Have a shot?
> Blanche: No, I—rarely touch it.
> Stanley: Some people rarely touch it, but it touches them often. (26)

The Necessary Supplement: All Men Are Brothers

Male solidarity is an equally compelling force in creating the sexual complex which the play dramatizes. Just as Blanche and Stella are more than sisters, Stanley and Mitch are true brothers wedded to a single vision. Stan acts it out; Mitch obsesses about it. Each needs the other to sustain his role. Contra Kazan, in representing them Williams is not offering us an alternative but a lesson in the absence of difference. Stan needs Mitch around as a foil to reassure himself—before the "macho" group of men—about his male virility and his vast knowledge of women. ("Hurry back and we'll fix you a sugar-tit" [48].) Mitch needs the same group, to sustain a vicarious identification while keeping himself safely ensconced in the slot of virtue. He can have the pleasure of hearing Stanley degrade women while congratulating himself that he's different. He might like to prove Stanley wrong, but in his heart he knows he's right. The voice ticking away in his head tells him one thing: You're a wimp. Women have pulled the wool over your eyes. When are you going to wise up and give them what they deserve?

When Stanley later plays Iago, he finds in Mitch a ready Othello full of similar suspicions about "these cunning creatures" and their appetites. Mitch puts women on a pedestal to deny female sexuality and his fear of its power. The collapse of this project proves that Stanley is what they really want—and deserve. Mitch plays a particularly insidious variant on Sartre's notion that "loser wins." Mitch wants to find a woman he can bring home to his mother, which is why he never really goes out with anyone else. All of his gentility is really a way of preventing woman from showing him anything that would threaten him. And where women are concerned, the world is full of things Mitch doesn't want to know because he's already convinced of them. He "keeps Stan around" to externalize his suspicions. The uxorious man who has the stud as his best friend is invariably a man who harbors deep resentments toward women but is afraid to admit or act on them. His love for Blanche is as false as hers for him and more in need of illusion. Mitch needs to prove that good guys don't finish last, because his fixed belief is that they do. His fear isn't that Stanley is what a woman wants, but that if he tried to be like Stanley he'd fail miserably.

Gentility is the game he plays to disguise his utter inability to get a handle on the games women play. Blanche spots this immediately and has great fun with it. Because everything Mitch does is defense and denial, he can only delay his conflicts, not resolve them. By the same logic, when they surface they must return in all their archaic fixation and accumulated fury. The pedestal is the device men like Mitch use to control women, to exorcise the threat of female sexuality, and, above all, to displace massive sexual insecurities by worshiping at the altar of their fears. Mitch doesn't simply believe that there are only two kinds of women—mother/virgins and whores. He programs every woman he meets to conform to the binary. He is considerate with women so that they won't inflict their sexuality on him. Of necessity, women have become experts at intuiting this message. They know that Mitch, not macho man, is the true representative of the "patriarchy," of resentment masked as morality. "Survival" demands mastering the psychology of this kind of man and tailoring one's behavior accordingly.[3] "Female" deception is always in part a recognition of what honesty would cost. Women learn to act chaste and speak very carefully around men like Mitch, who neither make nor tolerate off-color remarks. Harassment is child's play compared with the psychological torture Mitch inculcates.

Mitch is as tied to the assertion of phallic privilege as is Stanley, and given his inexperience, more bound to the fear that underlies it. Mitch lives in fear of the anger and self-contempt that erupts when the pedestal collapses, for then he can no longer deny kinship with Stanley in a brotherhood dedicated to hatred of women. His relationship to women is as aggressive as is Stanley's. The pedestal is the haven for a permanent insecurity that takes the form of anger displaced as control onto an object that externalizes his rage at himself. Unlike D. H. Lawrence's Mellors, Mitch doesn't have the courage of his tenderness because he knows his tenderness is a lie. He knows he is a weak, manipulated man whose sensitivity is a role played to deny his inability to act like Stanley. He is also a Stanley in the making. Wised up, the truth he secretly loves finally confirmed, he delights in righteous rage. (The true target of Mitch's anger—his mother—is thereby cleansed and protected from having anyone brought into her home.) This is a play about a rape following a near rape. That connection establishes the identity of Mitch and Stanley in the psychological economy of the play. The secret of their brotherhood is that in relationships with women, aggression always triumphs. (Blanche will show us that it also does in the relationship women have to men.)

In their interrelated roles, the four characters thus constitute the structural permutations necessary to the construction of a total system of mutual cruelty. Its focus is sexual wounding—the one opportunity no one ever turns down. Mitch's insecurity reinforces Stanley's machismo. They are opposite sides of an identical male fear. As mirrors, they show us that male sexual identity is a myth and that all attempts to fix it by assuming the phallic, as quasi-biological imperative, displace an unquenchable insecurity which derives from a single fear: that male sexuality is itself but a derivative response to the "greater" sexuality of women. Analogously, the specter of Blanche's neuroticism informs Stella's desire to accommodate at all costs. Her "healthy sexuality" derives from her need to assure herself that what "men" did to Blanche won't happen to her. This fear, however, assures her appropriation by the very male "order" that Blanche engages in dubious battle, knowing the price of victory will be the loss of what Stella receives. Blanche is the example that keeps Stella in line; Stella, the accommodation that inflames Blanche. Feminine sexuality in this system is either the bovine appendage to the pride of the male peacock or the self-torture of a sexuality that refuses to conform to that model.

To bar easy exits, I have focused this introductory sketch of the complex that *Streetcar* dramatizes on how the minor characters sustain it. To get at the psychic roots of sexual cruelty, however, and the aggression that drives it, we must probe the unconscious of the mighty opposites. That's where the date was made.

The Unholy Trinity: Sex Appeal, Flirting, Rape

To call it rape and say they've had this date from the beginning doesn't mean that every woman adores a fascist or that a smart lawyer (or critic) could get Stanley off the hook. But fear of ideologically correct reactions must not blind us to what is perhaps the greatest achievement of the play. In Blanche and Stanley, Williams charts with meticulous precision the structure of sexual interactions that so often issue in rape. We hate rape best if we listen to all that Williams tells us about it that we don't want to hear. *Streetcar* studies how the sexual tensions that make up the dominant pattern of relationships between men and women in our society form a vast system of mutual cruelty which no one in this play transcends. Sexual cruelty is the primary thing men and women do unto one another; rape, for all its horror, is part of a larger horror.

From their first meeting, Blanche and Stanley are locked in a sexual battle in which each tries to strip the other bare. Both tear at every shred of dignity in the other—and the target of attack is invariably the genitals. The play is in many ways an extended mutual assault, that is, a rape. And as we know, sexual pleasure is the last thing in the rapist's mind. Forced invasion of privacy for the sake of inflicting a destructive psychological wound—that is the target. The rapist's desire is to destroy the psyche by violating the body. These considerations increase the final horror of Stanley's act, but they also help us focus attention on the entire psychological complex that seeks "resolution," or the dissolution of drama, through that act. Blanche asks for it. That is the unsayable that must be said so that we can begin to know what it might mean.

The struggle between Blanche and Stanley ends in rape. That fact offers critics a neat way to dissolve ambiguities and achieve interpretive closure by isolating a fact and making it the sole term of feeling and judgment. The reductive charm of the fact is the retrospective power it gives of keeping the text in control. Stanley's act says it all: the play is about the violence of men against women. But to use an obvious metaphor, when we so reduce the complexities of a play which demonstrates that psychological reality is the primary reality, we rape it. In *Streetcar* everything makes sense only within a context in which psychological reality remains, in its complexity, the only basis of explanation. To understand what happens in scene x—and I may have many colleagues, among them women, who argue that the term *rape* is inappropriate for what happens there—we have to construct this larger context.

Flirting is still the grace note in the tedium of the day, the necessary overture in that noble selectiveness of sensuality that Nietzsche calls love. Or if you want a safer definition, it's the introduction of the possibility of sex into the interaction between two people. Such is its Platonic essence. But like sex, flirting's plasticity derives from its ability to take on new and different meanings. For Blanche and Stanley it has become the first move in the drama of aggression, round one in a master-slave dialectic void of any possibility of recognition. As with all games, the reason one plays is the important thing. Social games harbor a number of subtexts which become activated when the right players meet. *Streetcar* brings out the cruelest one that is, sadly, too often present in flirting.

Flirting for Blanche is the way one toys with men in order to provoke, then frustrate, them. Through flirtation one establishes one's superiority and takes delight in the exquisite pleasure of the put-down. Blanche isn't after a compliment, as she claims; she's after an advantage. Throughout the play she delights in the power to mock which successful flirting confers. Stanley gets angry, Mitch gets confused, the newsboy gets scared—and Blanche gets even. In flirting one twists the broken glass in their faces, but slowly, in a provocative yet castrating game which must continue indefinitely because it has come to serve ends that have nothing to do with sexual pleasure, save the pleasure of its indefinite delay. Only an "artist" of infinite wiles can win by keeping the opponent so confused that a frank assertion that puts an end to the game never comes. The thrill of the game is to run the risk of sex yet successfully elude the threat. Its purpose is to produce sexual frustration in men. Blanche's gambit is that she can produce so much confusion that men will be reduced to a state of chaos, their interpretive powers utterly jammed. (Mitch is a continual source of delight because he's the perfect audience: enthralled, paralyzed, and duped by every performance.) Blanche wants to do to men's minds what they've done to women's bodies. Flirting is the art one masters to adjust the odds, so that one can then show men to be the beasts and morons that they are. The glass must be finely ground and injected slowly into their systems, so that when it ulcerates, Blanche can have the pleasure of watching them squirm or rage.

If Blanche can provoke Stanley's anger yet keep it festering so that Stanley will turn it back against himself, she will have found a perfect way station on the route of the streetcar named desire. She can then play every variation on the game of the damsel in distress, savoring its aggressive resonances without the game ever having to end. Each role can then be played out as she creates a theatre in which the head of the house loses his props and is displaced while she watches the spectacle of his impotent rage.

Blanche knows that the insult is flirting carried on under another name. In it the aggressive side of sexuality becomes ascendant as dare, come-on. After Blanche finds she can't charm Stanley, she takes every available opportunity to insult him. All her insults are sexual provocations with a single text: Stanley is a vulgarian whom no self-respecting woman could ever find attractive. They also have a single aim: to undermine Stanley's sexual confidence. They are goads to sexual combat, certain to stir him into the one battle where Stanley is always at "issue," ready to offer the proof. Stanley's pride is his ability to put all relations with women on a sexual basis, where his sexual power will dominate. Blanche knows how to play every note on this pipe. He doesn't know it, but in scene ii Stanley gives Blanche all the information she needs. He may not compliment women on their looks, but he needs to think that his refusal to do so makes him irresistible. Everything Blanche does leaves Stanley in a frustration that can only increase his desire for the moment of phallic recognition and phallic assertion, because for Stanley flirting is the red flag that both attracts and enrages the bull. He claims he doesn't "go in for that stuff" (38). But he can't resist a flirt, because he sees exposing flirts as his "holy" duty. He always takes the bait because the flirt primes his own form of flirting—the open display of his sexuality as the force that puts an end to all "arguments." Women keep throwing come-ons followed by disclaimers at him. He then shows them

what "it" all really means and what they really want. Stanley is an inter-
preter whose hermeneutic possesses magical power: it never ends the relationship; it merely ends the conversation. Stanley is all *noumena*, the *ding an
sich* who loves to strip away the veils of illusion and lay bare the one true
interpretation. His investment in the game is thus as deep as that of the
subtlest flirt or the randiest whore, because exposing them confirms and
justifies his deepest need.

For Blanche such a match is perfect, because she flirts to put men down
and stir them into aggression. Stanley welcomes the game because it liberates and justifies an equal aggression. Both players thus activate the game's
major instability. Stanley is a quickly frustrated player in need of clear
victories to allay his underlying sexual anxieties. He believes in making
interpretive closure as soon as possible, and he also believes that the force of
his interpretations is such that they should compel assent. But he is easily
frustrated, because there is something in women's games that exceeds the
ability of his interpretive frame to control the game and bring things back to
basics. He also needs to add notches on his belt. Stella was an easy victory,
but Blanche is a real challenge.

Blanche's need is of a deeper order. Flirting for her is a way of rubbing
raw the sores of her own discontent—by bringing the other to a point of
maximum confusion, frustration, and anger. That is why she can never stop
when she has the advantage. The real flirtation is with danger; her bet is that
she can keep provoking male rage yet escape disaster. What she doesn't
know is that, in the process, desire has become, for her, not the opposite of
self-destruction but its primary mode. It is the way she savors her inner pain
and draws it out through what looks like aggression but is really a feast of
self-contempt. The constant payoff for Blanche is that everything she does
makes her feel worse about herself. When she sees in Stanley the man who
will destroy her and then uses every occasion to provoke him in precisely the
way certain to bring about that result, she has seized on sexuality for a
payoff so complex that only a long and patient detour can position us to
know what this woman "wants."

Sexuality as Mutual Cruelty

Beckett's pride in *Endgame* was in what he termed "the power of the text to
claw." *Streetcar* develops its sexual tension to a similar end. Sex in this play
is represented as a constant and oppressive presence craving release through
an accumulating violence. There is nothing that isn't sexual: sex is claustrophobic, hysteric, obsessional, a open wound oozing out into every situation.

Every gesture stages it; every interaction turns on it. Like the "Unconscious," it always craves release, and it is always on the verge of discharge through open violence. The first glance between men and women engages this harsh reality in inescapable struggle. This, and not rape, is the reality the play assaults us with, in an effort to strip away every illusion we use to hide from the conflicts implicit in human sexuality. The Hegelian dialectic of master-slave finds in sex one of its richest battlegrounds, because sex brings into play possibilities of psychological injury which transcend gender and extant power relations. Sex offers numerous ways of wounding and of triumphing, from every position. Sex here is not a melting flow toward Lawrentian union but a competitive tension which sets our teeth on edge as it builds toward rituals of open aggression.

All this is so because sexual identity is the precarious outcome of a complex process. Our sexuality first takes form as we struggle to mediate the conflicts of our family. Throughout life it remains one of the primary ways we experience and deal with repressed conflicts, usually at the expense of the other. Sex is the way we secrete the message we dare not speak, settle accounts, keep a terrible fear at bay. Pleasure, sadly, is often the least of our concerns. To such burdens *Streetcar* adds the recognition that there is no end to this strife and no one who escapes it. Avoiding the problem is but a momentary and illusory haven. Because sex and identity are so closely intertwined, this is an area of life where we remain subject to unexpected and striking reversals which have the power to bring the psyche to that knowledge of itself we have spent our whole life fleeing. Perhaps we all ride the streetcar without knowing it. There is a fundamental disorder at work in human sexuality, and this is the marrow the play wants to get at.

For those willing to think against the grain, *Streetcar* can be used to wrest back the exploration of psychosexual conflict from a feminism which often provides the equivalent in theory of the psychological operation known as denial. *Streetcar* is far more than yet another study of patriarchy, of what happens to women who live for men, of the psychology of the incipient wife-beater, and so on. For it places these problems in a larger structure in which the mutual cruelty between men and women is the prior reality from which sexual ideologies derive, especially those which use the defense mechanism of splitting to locate all problems in one gender. There are no pure origins, isolated phenomena, or privileged interpretive standpoints from which sexuality can be viewed. The sexes are in it together from the "beginning."

Stanley's phallic assertiveness is a counter to the castrating games women like Blanche devise to take revenge for what men have done to them. Psychosexual identity derives from a circle of entanglements in which no one is on top, nor is there any privileged origin. Mother's milk is full of mother's bile and of her justified resentment which the son passes on, doubly displaced as aggression toward women. In this vast circle of cruelties, there is no commanding position or any readily available exit. Those who think to find a solution through a leap to the logic of language—and the point applies both to Lacan and to those feminists who constitute their superior position by simply inverting him—perhaps reveal little more than the desire, endemic to theory, to use reified and a priori interpretations to arrest and foreclose the complexities of lived experience. For it is at the latter level that *Streetcar* sets forth the terms of their refutation.

For example, the notion that patriarchy creates the "disorder" of female sexuality is shown by *Streetcar* to be at best a one-sided distortion. The sexes create one another out of an insecurity that characterizes both positions in a dialectic that makes aggression the underlying and informing term of desire. The currently fashionable notion that male sexuality is a fixed quasi-biological identity while all the disorders of sexual identity devolve to the female is a rather preposterous act of psychological blindness serving a desperate wish-fulfillment, whether his, to establish a secure male identity by fiat, or hers, to deny that the male, the enemy, can have any psychological inwardness.[4] *Streetcar* implicates such operations in a mousetrap that exposes the typical attitudes and stances we adopt toward both our own and the other's sexuality as untenable efforts to escape a problem that cannot be laid to the fault of one sex or the other but must refer all such ideologies to that prior order of cruelty which they are fashioned in order to escape.

The key to such a discovery is an understanding of the sexual tension between Blanche and Stanley as the psychodynamic force that illuminates everything and everyone in the play. The sexual chemistry between Blanche and Stanley has nothing tender, romantic, or lilting about it. Sex is an ugly ritual of dominance and submission. It builds through an aggression which informs every mode of verbal and interpersonal behavior. In sexual attraction of this kind, hurting the other—who must be an object both of challenge and of contempt—is arousing. The turn-on is the threat the other represents. The other must possess that power which could be crushing and yet with which one must do battle. Sex promises a true clash of wills, a significant chance to assert one's superiority and to attain, through the other's defeat, the manic triad—triumph, control, and contempt—which puts the psyche's conflicts to rest.

In *Streetcar,* even when one is moved by the beauty or the power of sex, such a position is merely a way station within a larger process in which sex always returns to the struggle for psychological power. All the characters in the play are sexually on guard at all times because they know they are permanently at risk in their sexual being, threatened by receiving or reopening a wound that goes to the depth of their psyche. Blanche's life has been the agonized living of that awareness; Stanley's, the attempt to vanquish its very possibility. It is hard to imagine either character doing anything without giving it a sexual reference. Both are fixated on the image in a mirror they constantly hold up before themselves and before everyone else. They embody the general disorder we all know might someday catch up with us, acted out in a deliberate push to the end of the line. The other characters are, like us, the contradiction deferred or denied. What the play shows, however, is that in all cases the disorder rules. Ironically, the only one who puts up a struggle against it is Stanley Kowalski.

Stanley's Desire—And Its Reifications

Williams always thought himself a follower of D. H. Lawrence, a liberator and celebrator of the erotic. And one does not want to omit a good word on behalf of the colored lights. Stanley wants sex to be a liberating, playful overcoming of repressions, a renewal of primitive energies. For him, it is not a sad, guilty thing or an act one has to approach with a bundle of obsessional anxieties disguised as inhibition, refinement, or foreplay. Sex isn't what we collapse into after all the escapes, avoidances, and games have been played out. For in Stanley we give ourselves over to it, together, in a proud and powerful celebration of "things that happen between a man and a woman in the dark" (81). One doesn't feel empty afterward, nor does one justify sex in terms of something else. It is an end in itself. This, at any rate, is what Stanley and Stella would have us believe.

But even the great eroticism of the scene in which Stanley falls on his knees and buries his head in Stella is not without psychodynamics which on scrutiny have little to do with Rilke's "river-god of the blood." Stanley has lost "his baby, his girl," his source of a comfort and assurance that is finally maternal. Without it he is trapped in the only kind of existential anxiety of which he is capable—the feeling of abandonment—and like the child, he deals with his anxiety at a primary process level. Stella is the spool in his perpetual *fort/da*.[5] Losing the object, he is reduced to a state in which he can do nothing but cry until the object returns. Then there is bliss and forgetfulness—as after a good feed. The night of erotic renewal Stella and Stanley share is the triumph of the child who breaks things and then waves his pajamas as a flag of victory. Stanley's triumph is that of the eternal infant whose need brings the woman back to a state of womblike symbiosis in which all adult conflicts and transgressions—including his violence toward her—are dissolved, blown away, forgotten. Veneration—of Stanley's erotic energy—then becomes the primary object of sex, but infantile aggression is the initial turn-on. Sex for Stanley is pentecost, because it gives him a chance to crow narcissistically, in egocentric celebration of his phallus, to cry like a baby safely back in the arms of a mother who forgives and forever welcomes him home. Such is Stanley's version of paradise regained, a performance in which the woman is always the applauding adjunct.

Stella's sexuality is equally limited. Stella's affirmation of sex may be a welcome thing for a DuBois, but that should not blind us to the fact that sex for her is not really a matter of mutuality, psychological growth, or even of "tearing our pleasures with rough strife." Apart from a sort of bovine complacency, Stella doesn't appear to have a capacity for pleasure. She is the receptacle for her man's "gaudy seed," the breast upon which he cries and reposes, the "good mother" who lets sonny act out his aggressive fantasies and then presents her body as reward. Sex for Stella has nothing to do with an expanding subjectivity. It is, in fact, the antidote to that threat. Sex is valuable for Stella because it reassures her that she is not like her sister. But that is also why it locks her in a bind. It must remain in the order of the natural, a drive-discharge mechanism, a drug which extinguishes consciousness. Because her goal is to avoid the confusions of sexual identity, sex cannot be experienced psychologically or leave any residue of inwardness. It must remain the natural function which leaves one a supremely contented thing. Sex is the drug that keeps Stella in a state of torpor.

Because that is so, she has started to use sex for another kind of payoff. As she proudly tells Blanche: "This morning he gave me ten dollars to smooth things over." Stella is in the process of becoming one of the primary products of capitalism, the domestic hooker. Sexual favors are exchangeable for material goods. Permitting, even provoking, male aggression is part of the game one plays to keep hubby productive. Like the alcoholic's wife who prefers him drunk, Stella doesn't object to Stanley's violence because she knows how to use it to her own ends. Every situation can turn a profit. Stanley will soon have to provide far more than "meat," for the mighty hunter act will lose its appeal as the holy family grows. Nothing in the sexuality between Stanley and Stella opens them to a deepened intersubjective relationship; it leaves Stanley instead locked in a state of infantile dependency and Stella fostering that dependency for economic ends.

If Stella's sexuality harbors a telos in which human possibilities vanish as the exchange principle takes over, Stanley's harbors other vipers. Beneath the pose of sexual virility lie massive insecurities over women and unbridled aggression toward them. The phallus for Stanley is ultimately a weapon that forces women into line. Sex is always connected with taking women down from the marble columns to prove he isn't as common as dirt while suggesting that they are. Stanley may "love" Stella, but he only comes alive when confronting woman as threat. That's why he's constantly on the lookout for any "uppity" behavior in Stella and why he must do battle with Blanche, since her presence shows that his most famous victory is far from complete. What horrifies Stanley is the fear that the sisters may look on him with the same eyes. The connection he first spots in scene ii ("I'm not going to no Galatoire's" [29]) is precisely the one that pushes him over the edge months later in the birthday dinner scene (viii), when the sisters' statements have become virtually interchangeable, with Stella taking the lead in mocking his vulgarity.

Blanche is the specter of what will return in Stella when the colored lights fail. Stanley's deepest fear will be confirmed: he has been unable to satisfy his woman. His need to belittle Stella, especially in front of his male friends; his violence whenever she gets out of line; and his constant attention to the slightest sign of independence on her part show how uneasy is the head that wears the crown. Like all men who try to define desire in purely physical terms, Stanley is a hater of women. Victory necessarily breeds contempt. The prize must be belittled. Once he has won her, Stella must become a docile servant. Yet Stanley must repeatedly restage his victories, because he fears he's never won. That is also why he constantly seeks out new targets for his aggressions, from Mitch to the bowling alley proprietor. Blanche is a perfect target, however, because she provides an outlet that deflects Stanley's aggression from Stella while enabling him to attack the very things that upset him in Stella. Blanche thereby serves as the perfect object lesson for completing Stella's education.

Stanley's psychological economy stands in permanent readiness to vanquish, by whatever means, anything that threatens to deprive him of the recognition he needs in order to assure himself he has a secure male identity. His dream is that everything can be made to bow before the power of his penis to command submission. Like all fascists, he seeks a symbolic identity that will guarantee victory over all challengers. Like all children of magical thinking, his desire is to locate the solution to all problems in an organ—the magic wand with the power to compel the mother's love.

Peeling the Layers of an Onion: The Desire That Is Blanche DuBois

The First Layer: The Striptease, Southern Style

> *(He takes another step. She smashes a bottle on the table and faces him, clutching the broken top.)*
> Stanley: What did you do that for?
> Blanche: So I could twist the broken end in your face! (162)

Such is the desire of Blanche DuBois, the project defining her relationship to what is always at the center of her consciousness—men. Blanche has been described as a victim, an exhausted neurotic seeking refuge, a person without cruelty who has always been dependent on the kindness of strangers and who is still searching for "the one right man" (Mitch, according to Elia Kazan). Such readings identify some of Blanche's favorite roles, but the passivity they imply is foreign to her character. The key to Blanche DuBois is that she knowingly brings it all upon herself. Her deliberate activity is the force that drives the play. Blanche seizes every opportunity to express that which sickens her about herself. Kazan saw the search for refuge as her through-line, but the truth is that she destroys every possible haven.

Blanche is the unquiet consciousness of the contradictions that define her world, and all her actions serve to bring those contradictions into the open. The focus on intentions, explicit statements, and conscious motives always provides inaccurate accounts of such a dramatic agency. Blanche says she wants a man like Mitch, yet she can't resist every opportunity to make fun of him and mock his bungling sexuality. She fears Stanley yet seizes every chance to provoke him in ways calculated to undermine his sexual confidence. She can no more feel desire for "good guy" Mitch than she can deny the sexual attraction posed by Stanley. She is utterly dependent on men—and hates herself for it. She sees men as weak creatures ruled by vulgar lusts (epic fornications), yet she remains dependent on their kindness to rescue her from the very situations she creates in order to get them to abandon her. Blanche is not a bundle of contradictions but a system of contradictions with a consistent logic that can be formulated. As Derrida learned from Hegel, consistency in contradiction must equal the force of a desire.[6]

In Blanche's agency, Williams dramatizes the insight that unconscious conflict organizes our experience, by giving our actions the doubleness of a plot which brings about the very thing we fear. What has become the reductive commonplace of a certain vulgar Freudianism—the notion that what one deeply fears one also deeply desires—is revealed in *Streetcar* as a principle of dramatic agency which structures the dialectical connection between psyche and experience.

In Blanche character and action are processes that cut between conscious intentions and the myth of a dormant, substantialized Unconscious. The key to the Unconscious is that it is always active—with an activity that has the form of drama. This is the way in which Blanche's unconscious organizes her experience, not as a substance buried deep in her mind but as the constant a priori of perception and activity. It always hovers on the edge of her awareness because it throws off sparks, lighting up the field in which she finds herself compelled to act.

Dramatic agency transcends the conscious-unconscious opposition because it is the putting into motion of a contradiction. Conflicted beings are neither conscious nor unconscious of the terms of their struggle. They are caught up in something which requires "action," and it is only through the results of one's actions that one discovers one's motives. When we are caught up in intense conflict, the motives our actions incarnate are never transparent to us; their discovery can only follow upon action, because action is the existential attempt to mediate what otherwise remains both indeterminate and agonizing.

Everything Blanche does illustrates this doubleness. She is both a character trapped in roles and an ironic player who gives a Brechtian twist to the roles she performs. She has contempt for roles yet clings to them. She is lost without them and doomed with them. She dons them to avoid psychic dissolution yet plays them in a way that brings about that very result. Like the hysteric's symptom, roles for Blanche always point away from themselves toward something else. Conscious intentions have little to do with such a process, because the reality of a role lies in its unraveling. Blanche is the discontent of all roles, and that is why she plays them desperately but with a certain end-of-the-line, run-down quality, so that they will crack under the strain, revealing their underside. Knowledge for Blanche lies in exposing the bitter truth hidden beneath postures and traditions: it is sweetest when it reveals a motive sharply opposed to the values a role appears to serve. Unlike her interpreters, Blanche is a true master of roles who is never taken in by her ruses. When she plays the victim, for example, she does so to expose victimage and the convenient psychological functions it plays when we use it to discharge our pity for poor crushed neurotics like her.

The Second Layer: Desire as Being-Toward-Death

The deep desire that has always been at work in Blanche's effort to twist the glass in their faces is the desire to bottom out. Blanche isn't simply at the end of the line. She wants to be there, to force everything to its bitter conclusion. That is why she disrupts all possible havens. Bottoming out has become a positive desire, the one release from psychic pain. Then the worst will have happened, and she can't be hurt anymore. Blanche keeps seeking havens— Stella, Mitch, Shep Huntleigh—then destroying them because she knows that the first moment is merely a desperate choice meant to delay the inevitable process of self-dissolution.

The game with men is all there is, but Blanche plays it in a spirit of contempt for both the object of her longing and her own dependency. Despite her love of illusion, Blanche has few illusions about desire. Sex for her is that attempt to allay and avoid anxiety that only brings it back with redoubled force. Yet one must play this game, for apart from it there is nothing. Blanche is a victim of bored restlessness because she knows that all roles are attempts to ward off death. She stakes her existence on the notion that desire is the opposite of death, but all of her actions will bring her to the recognition that they are finally one and the same.

Masochism is a poor concept for describing such a structuring of experience. One payoff of games is that they lower self-esteem and increase desperation. But this happens because Blanche is that unquiet consciousness that disrupts every presence by seeing the underlying lie. (Her real soul mate is *Iceman*'s Hickey.) Her futility is that of one who keeps playing hollow games without being able to achieve the cynicism of Joan Didion's Maria Wyeth. Blanche remains devoted, with passion, to exposing the bitterest truths.

She structures experience accordingly. Every one of Blanche's actions delays yet expresses a meaning she flees yet runs to embrace. Flirting with Stanley is irresistible. Blanche may deny her intentions, but she is never taken in by her actions. She breathes the spirit of death into every role and game she plays, in order to inflict that awareness on the other characters by showing them how deeply they are already implicated in it. An understanding of how death works is the awareness she refuses to relinquish and through which she will attain the tragic.

The Third Layer: Culture and/as Resentment

Blanche has "tragic stature" because she takes a central and inescapable contradiction of desire to the end of the line. Most of us are wracked by superfluous, unsatisfied desire. Blanche draws out that contradiction to savor its bitterest fruit. As such, one of her most disruptive functions is as critic rather than representative of Culture. Culture for Blanche is not an alternative to sexual battle, but just another counter in the game. Her purpose in fact is to expose it as the system of lies that contributed most powerfully to her initial enslavement. It may be the high horse she gets on to deny her sexual conflict with Stanley, but it is also the ploy she uses to attract, control, and laugh at Mitch. The split function given by Blanche to culture reveals the underlying spite. Culture is what enfeebles us; it attaches us to weaklings like Allan and Mitch. Blanche can't invoke it without contempt. What once seemed a refuge from the brutal world of her family has become for Blanche the site of her bitterest reflections, which rise to a special pitch whenever Blanche refers to her students.

As teacher, she discovered that culture was not the possibility of liberation but one of the key formations holding the system of her enslavement in place. Culture is the cage in which fine little southern ladies are kept, the storehouse of romantic illusions that set them up for bitter disillusionment. Its only value, finally, is as a self-conscious piece of theatrical posturing one can use seductively to play with men. Blanche's purpose is to show, with contempt, that culture never was anything but a prop in the brutal business of desire. The socialization of women as male property through the repression of female sexuality is the one grand function Culture played in Blanche's literary heritage. Blanche would now take this insight and turn it back against the aggressor by using the texts her "fathers" taught her to ensnare men in a play of "illusion" that will eventually bring them not to Tara but to the Tarantula Arms. Culture properly inverted becomes seduction leading men into the spider's web of a voracious sexuality. Blanche can use culture to mock the naïveté of her students or to poke fun at Mitch. Or she can use it as a counter to provoke men like Stanley to sexual combat.

In her great set speech on Stanley's animality (scene iv), the lady doth indeed protest too much, with the pleasure of prolonged erotic contrast overcoming the pose of aristocratic nostalgia. Blanche desperately wants the culture-barbarism distinction to function dualistically here, with herself unambiguously on one side of that divided line because the events of the previous night have brought the need for a repression of desire to a panic state of hypertheatricality dedicated to the desperate hope that culture provides a principle of difference. But she already knows this is a lie, and it is the only time she uses culture in this way. Her desire isn't to flee the brutes but to do battle with them.

Culture is the gift her fathers used to make her weak. She will now return the favor by twisting the broken end of it in their faces. This is not active reversal but active *resentiment*. One of the main sources of Blanche's anger is her awareness of how completely she has internalized the "system" that sickens her and how powerless she is to break out of its confines. One can sin, but one can't escape that concept and the ways, as guilt, it haunts and unravels one's consciousness. Blanche is both a prisoner of the "feminine mystique" and an angry player of its game. That is why so much of her behavior is undecidable in terms of the activity-passivity binary. Her dialectical agency drives experience beyond the protective illusions and defenses of dualism.

The Fourth Layer: The Sins of the Fathers

As thoroughly as Stanley, Blanche has incorporated the dominant ideology. Women are sensitive, frail, refined, cultured. Sexuality for them is a complex psychological phenomenon, whereas for men it is merely a natural biological function. Men are strong, aggressive, bold, unromantic. Sensitivity is a feminine trait. Present in men, it is a sign of weakness, gullibility, or, as with Allan, of a deeper disorder. Sensitivity doesn't make men attractive; it makes them objects of manipulation or scorn. Such men can be sheltered (Allan) or can provide shelter (Mitch), but they cannot be loved erotically. From the beginning, Blanche can't help finding Mitch ridiculous. Blanche may want kindness, but she associates it with weakness. Like Stanley, she believes that men like Mitch are kind because they are afraid to assert their male prerogative. (Ironically, as she will discover, Mitch agrees.) Contra Kazan, Mitch can't be the one man who is perfect for Blanche, because try as she may, Blanche can't pass up any opportunity to make fun of him. Nor can she help finding him erotically repugnant. The scene with the newsboy illustrates this in a double way: the boy is both a way out of the sexual lethargy Mitch induces and a way of Blanche's priming herself for Mitch by acting out a stimulating fantasy.

When Blanche meets Stanley, she knows she has met her destroyer, because Stanley is the only kind of man her psyche finds stimulating. As the end of a long line, he is also the fruition of the complex that has been Blanche's proudest creation. In Stanley, projection and reality meet in such a way that in relating to him Blanche can recapitulate—in the purity of its essential psychological structure—the pattern that has given her life its narrative and dramatic continuity.

Mick Jagger was wrong. In one way or another we always get what we want and what we think we deserve. For we either find the person who suits our illness or we turn the other into that person. Blanche's relationship to men is a monument to these psychological aphorisms. Her primary fascination is with men of "epic fornications" (44), those who buy, use, and abuse women. Shaw, Kiefaber, and other pillars of the community are the kind of men you shack up with in the certainty that they'll hold it against you in the morning. Blanche is always being disposed of. It's a brutal game, and lust has little to do with its underlying motives, as Blanche has known for years. Yet she keeps playing. Why? Because playing the game is for her a tortured attempt at active reversal.[7]

Male epic fornications lost Belle Reve while leaving the women with all the pain, death, and responsibility. Blanche will enact the proper revenge by bringing the men who scared her to the room they think they control and turning it into the Tarantula Arms. She will mirror the epic fornications of the fathers by acting out the spectacle of a ravenous, unbridled female sexuality which corrupts all it comes into contact with. As the spider who inflicts a sexual wound on the psyche of her victims, she balances the scales of justice. Blanche will give men an unforgettable experience of their awkwardness, their vulgarity, and then of their inability to satisfy her sexual hunger. In her night she alone casts the Sartrean glance that makes the other feel like a petty, disposable thing. In Blanche the Southern belle liberates its repressed as sexual revenge on those who created the role. Playing Circe, she will make them all feel like swine. ("Swine, huh?" [156].) Blanche's deepest attraction to men like Stanley is the prospect of destroying their psychosexual indentity.

But twisting the broken bottle in their faces is finally motivated at a deeper level by Blanche's need to inflict pain on herself. Their spite assures her defeat and testifies to her fixation: the need repeatedly to do battle with this kind of man in a game that must be progressively lost because each round activates, as its necessary reaction, the growth of a group of men dedicated to male solidarity and revenge. Blanche's victims sully her name—and pass her around. She forces men to reveal the true terms of their solidarity, but at her own expense. Active reversal is blocked: Blanche's agency is doomed to a repetition in which she can only bring humiliation on herself. Rather than getting beyond her conflicts, she has assured their progressive worsening.

Blanche so thoroughly hates the object of her hate that she remains fixated on it. Repeating the frustrating relationship to her original object—the epic fornicators—remains the project she never surmounts. Her hatred is so thorough, in fact, that she must become identical to the object of her hatred so that she can then, as the figure of its scorn, bring that hatred down upon herself. Her psyche thus incarnates one of the most intricate ways in which inwardness can be constituted by identification with the aggressor. When, following Kazan, one sees Blanche as a character desperately seeking a man who is outside the dominant system, she becomes pathetic. But Blanche's quest is for no such man. She knows that all men are the same. All her actions are designed to expose the stark nature of that truth.

It is in Stanley, not Mitch, that Blanche meets the man who is "perfect for her," because he represents to perfection the male sexuality she's been doing battle with her entire life. If she knows immediately that he is her destroyer, she also knows that he is a fatal attraction, because he embodies to perfection the image that has dominated her entire erotic life. The relationship is sexual from the beginning—and virtually everything Blanche does advances that tension. Victimage is a false abstraction. What *Streetcar* dramatizes is the richer truth that the destroyer is the only person anyone ever meets. The conditions of object-choice, loving, and erotic attraction are grounded in the core conflict that stirs one's psyche into action whenever one finds that other who can advance the drama.[8] Such a meeting is as much an eruption from within as an assault from outside. Thus if Blanche is overwhelmed in scene i (or so plays it), scene ii finds her risen to the bait, relishing the battle.

The Fifth Layer: Guilt, The Facilitating Other, and the Conditions of Loving

Once they get the "facts" about Allan, many interpreters think they've hit pay dirt. Blanche is disposed of as a tidy neurotic case history: the repetitive acting out of guilt, derived from a single privileged event, establishes a strict causal chain along the streetcar of desire. We can now ride to and fro with no fear of losing our way. Such interpretations are reassuring because they pin guilt down. Even the most horrible revelation is comforting because it domesticates guilt by attaching it to a specific occurrence. The threat of its wider applicability and its deeper psychological roots is stilled. Heidegger's notion of guilt as an ontologically revelatory experience-force is exorcized. The betrayal of Allan, the loss of Belle Reve, the sins of the fathers—such localizations of guilt domesticate the deeper fear that guilt does not originate from such events but is prior to them. The psychological vertigo threatened by that possibility is precisely what returns with a vengeance once we see that the business with Allan is not an origin but is itself in medias res.

Guilt is the key to a character like Blanche, but causal, naturalistic explanation of her deliberate debasements is an inadequate mode of interpretation, as is a mechanistic understanding of the repetition-compulsion. Blanche requires and creates a particular situation: she repeatedly puts herself in positions that force others to do to her what she did to Allan, because she knows that what she did to him was not an isolated event but the whole pattern of her life. That pattern is the source of her guilt and of the repetitive action that brings to fruition her need to inflict that guilt upon herself. The relationship to men in general—and not to a single boy—is the cause and focus of that drama, because male aggression has created the problematic that is the core of Blanche's psyche. Blanche's project is to enact a dialetic in which desire—the force which produces death—will somehow overcome and defeat death. When she tells Mitch that desire is all-important, the only opposite to death, she exposes her deepest fear—the absence of that difference.

Blanche's family made the consciousness of desire-as-death her baptism. She has never been able to arrest its destructiveness, nor to put love in its place. The self-waste of her own spirit, the desperateness of her commitment to desire even as it tears away at the fabric of her character, is what disgusts her. Blanche sees death and guilt as the dominant facts of existence. But perhaps desire only implicates us further. Action may only bring more guilt on ourselves, not because we are marked forever by an original crime, but because desire itself is a product of the disorder it would allay. Blanche opposes desire and death in an attempt to deny a dialectical complicity she suffers repeatedly.

Concepts of origin, causality, and the single traumatic event that "explains" a life are attractive because they protect us from this broader and harsher possibility: the original object-choice of Allan, and the way Blanche structured their relationship, were already part of the psychological complex Blanche needed to bring to completion in order to know herself for the first time. We choose a lover to avoid a conflict and end up creating the very thing we fear. Both acts form part of a pattern that it may take our entire lives to complete or unravel. Experience is not a continuous chronological process, nor do its conflicts derive from a multiplicity of discrete, privileged events. The life of the psyche is primarily a matter of moving toward and away from core conflicts that only slowly reveal their terms. Experience is so fashioned that we simultaneously flee and pursue ourselves, so that the consequences of our earliest deeds might finally make themselves present. In place of causal chains and discrete events, a new idea presents itself: there are no accidents. We are always ahead of ourselves, incarnating conflicts we rush to catch up with, even when we contrive to make the reckonings look like a catastrophe that assaults us from outside.

Why did Blanche choose Allan? Romantic considerations aside, the soundest hypothesis we can establish derives from the doubleness implicit in Blanche's desire to reverse death. The moment she met Allan, she knew something was wrong with him. The stage was set. If I can make him okay, then I'm okay; rescuing him from his sexual problems delivers me from my own. Who is more assured of her sexuality than the woman who succeeds where all others failed? On the other hand, if he fails me, I win anyway, because I liberate my rage at that weak "feminine" sensitivity that makes both of us such poor citizens in a world of "epic fornications" and brutal desire. When Blanche "accidentally" enters a room and later "spontaneously" blurts out her disgust at what she saw, the truth she thereby carefully hides is that this is the date she and Allan have had from the beginning. Blanche's discovery of Allan's homosexuality externalizes and disguises the more disruptive sexual problematic that has structured their relationship.

Blanche chose Allan because she knew something was "wrong" with him. The question that prys open the lower layer behind her generosity is this: Why did failure breed such contempt? For such a result, the effort to help the other must involve a displaced and safe way to deal with something "wrong" in oneself. When we are implicated in the other's fault, a healing act promises to make us both whole. To understand such a project, however, conscious intentionality and the substantialistic unconscious provide equally inadequate conceptualizations. Blanche didn't know what she was doing because the whole thing with Allan was an effort to prevent that knowledge. But whenever one acts in order to avoid a conflict—or to gain a quick victory—one sows the seeds of the future conflicts that will bring forth the truth. The tragic irony of experience is that the desire to avoid self-knowledge is precisely what eventually brings us to it.

This is the sense in which Allan is a beginning. Blanche is neither conscious nor unconscious of the conflicts and motives that inform her relationship to Allan. Dramatic agency is lived in a more concrete realm and cuts through such conceptual alternatives. To be a dramatic agent means to act on the basis of conflicts and desires that structure one's experience without necessarily passing through one's consciousness. Our "whys" only become clear in the retrospective light of later events. We prize intentionality because it protects us from a recognition of our true agency, thereby limiting our ethical responsibility and providing a quasi-legalistic way of defending that limit. But to understand ourselves, we all need to catch up with our subtext.

This is the date, after Allan, that Blanche always insists on keeping with herself. After Allan, she can no longer suppress awareness of the unconscious dimensions of her agency. Her subsequent acts are an attempt to fit the punishment to the crime. Sex is the necessary field for that endeavor. Through it alone can she "repeat" the experience with Allan so as to bring out all the terms that were implicit in it—with herself in both positions. Men will now be the way to memorialize what happened to Allan, but with the roles reversed: Blanche is now the object of the deliberate cruelty she then inflicted. The purpose served by her project, however, is neither mourning nor active reversal. What Blanche wants to attain is the position of maximum inwardness. By making others do onto her what she did onto Allan, she can gauge the full effects of cruelty while keeping the victim alive. She is both the actor who brings it on herself and the victim who suffers its effects. The "tragic" dimension of Blanche's character is her drive to comprehend and suffer the nature of cruelty. Guilt for her is the attic process of internalizing and inflicting on one's psyche the consequences of one's crime, with no appeal made to innocence, ignorance, or intentionality to attenuate one's responsibility. Blanche DuBois is that rare being who accepts responsibility for her unconscious.

The secret Blanche and Allan had to hide was that of their identity. In helping him Blanche was nurturing her sensitivity against the brutal world of her family, but she was also displacing her sexual anxieties by turning them into an "ethical" act. The cruelest irony of such a project is that it's a blueprint for sexual dysfunctions or an asexual relationship. There is no way Blanche and Allan can really help one another, because their sympathetic contract forbids any exploration of the sexual reality that is the source of their anxieties.

Allan is thus the ticket to the streetcar, because this experience leaves Blanche with the bitter recognition that there is no term or haven that can be set up as an alternative to brutal desire. All such idealistic dialectics are flights from conflict and must be replaced by the only possible dialectic—that of desire. She must mock everything she once loved because she sees it now as no more than a false refuge against what it actually concealed and brought about—the onset of brutal desire. Stanley doesn't have to tell her that "there isn't a goddam thing but imagination" (158). Blanche already acts that recognition. Culture, refinement, poetry, are, after Allan, but a facade and a tool in the game of desire. Blanche delights in watching her students make their first discovery of love, not in nostalgia but in the cynical recognition that they are doomed to frustration. She must corrupt the innocence she once loved (the schoolboy, the newsboy) in order to rub raw the sores of her own discontent. No matter how much she may try to assert the opposite, the recognition Blanche lives is the Shakespearean one: that "Desire is death" (sonnet 147). All choices are "desperate" ones she can't "hold for long," because all are but delays, transfer tickets on the streetcar that leads directly to Stanley's cave, where the aggression that defines Blanche's sexuality will meet its perfect match. In the broken world of Blanche DuBois, there is no "visionary company of love."[9]

Guilt for Blanche is the key to the ultimate equation. Everything she does is an attempt to punish herself. Even in the midst of actions with a different aim or possibility, Blanche finds herself flooded with guilt. She thus organizes every experience so that guilt is the payoff. (We can, perhaps, probe this condition only after repeating the necessary caveat: this does not mean she wants Stanley to rape her.) Through Blanche, guilt is revealed as far more than a psychological burden. Its real power is as a principle of action that structures one's interpersonal relations. As such, guilt is the subtlest agent. Its proper tense is not the past but the future. The insidious thing about guilt is the comprehensiveness of its agency. The hypochondriac is lucky: his guilt assaults him, localized in the body. But like the ulcer that inward breaks, the primary way guilt operates in most of us is subterranean: a pervasive sadness, a gradual running down of psychic energies, a pattern of unhappiness we seem powerless to alter. The death of the spirit is guilt's proudest product. Guilt works best, in fact, when it never presents itself directly. For direct confrontation leaves it open to defeat, whereas indirect operation leaves it in a position to bow only at the end, when it presents the bill.

To meet this process head on and savor guilt, one must make it the principle that structures and overtakes actions which appear to rise out of a progressively diminishing yet still active desire for happiness or refuge. Then guilt can prepare a genuine feast for itself as it sets about to sabotage the last efforts such an agent makes to find a release from self-torture. Such is the way guilt operates for Blanche. In the course of the play she works all the variations on this theme in order to bring upon herself the catastrophe that alone expresses the truth and fulfillment of her desire.

Williams' Mousetrap: To Get Guests, Create Structures

The purpose of interpretation should be to open and sustain the wounds inflicted by the text. Plays are interrogative acts, the public airing of collective secrets which put the audience on trial. Rather than rushing to a play's thematic meaning, we should discover its question, then deepen its claim on us.

The question *Streetcar* asks is that of our sexual identity. It does so by constructing a vast circle of reciprocal determinations from which few of us can escape. It's easy to claim one isn't like Blanche and Stanley, but that misses the point. If Blanche and Stanley are not representative figures who bring out the basic disorder that defines the dominant relationships between men and women, who is? Can one escape that disorder, and how? Do women really want someone like Mitch, or is he merely the respite one seeks on the defeated side of one's attraction to men like Stanley? Is this not, in any case, the suspicion men like Mitch harbor as permanent rage at their uxoriousness? What man can assure himself he isn't, in the secret recesses of his psyche, like Stanley? Ideological correctness aside, how often is respect toward women a displacement of fear and aggression or the counter in a game of manipulation, seething with discontents? Similar questions undercut Stella's solution. How much of her sexual "health" is really pragmatic accommodation to becoming an object? In what ways is her sexual identity a quick fix and a permanent refuge, a "flight into health" in order to escape sexual confusion? Is there any sexual identity that doesn't mask deep-seated anxieties which apparently can only be dealt with by laying them off on the other? Is mutual cruelty the one unavoidable truth of sexual relations, the condition we must face as our common beginning if we would overcome it? *Streetcar* offers us this possibility by depriving us of a way to deny a disorder we must perforce take upon ourselves.

The key to this play's creative aggression toward its audience is that it offers no exit and no release. Sexual identity is put on trial. Each role we adopt to try to avoid the problem is unmasked. No solution to the basic conflicts between men and women is offered, and even the possibility of a solution is put in doubt. The play opens up desire not to offer us Lawrentian possibility but to show us all the ways in which desire is death. The beauty of the play is the revelation that no compromises are possible; all choices are desperate, riddled with the identical set of contradictions. The desire of the play is to inflict this truth upon us. Its purpose is to open up a great wound in our sexuality by showing us that it is already there.

Every good play is a mousetrap, and this is the source of its deepest affect on the audience. *Streetcar* implicates its audience through a play of shifting sympathies in which it is often impossible to establish who is the aggressor and who is being attacked. For example, unqualified sympathy for Blanche ignores this compelling fact. Stanley's home is invaded by a woman who seems intent on doing everything she can to displace him. In a sense, the wonder is that Stanley waits so long before he launches his "counterattack." While he then draws out his revenge slowly, with unexampled cruelty, his behavior is also a deeply wounded attempt to reassert his dignity in the face of four months of insults. *Streetcar* is neither the portrait of a neurotic woman nor a study of the sexist male. It is impossible to establish a single line of sympathy and use it to structure our emotional response to the play. The equations of neo-Aristotelian criticism break down, releasing the force of a reality they are meant to and cannot contain. To make that system work, we have to respond to the play in terms of the development of our desires and expectations for a protagonist about whom we are made to care as a result of our estimation of her moral character and her responsibility for the actions she takes in the situation in which she finds herself.[10] The only way to make that system work, however, is to short-circuit the emotional ambivalence the play strives to establish as an integral part of its effort to get us to see our implication in a psychosexual conflict that cannot be resolved or interpreted along such lines. The ethical framework that is required to render the kind of interpretations that would fix and resolve our responses is thereby put in question. On a less sophisticated level, the issue of melodrama, of whether hysteric Blanche is a tragic figure, conveniently displaces attention from the conflict structuring the work, while recent attempts to secure a feminist reading of the play offer an overtly ideological way to ignore or surmount its ambiguities.

The value of such interpretations is that they so clearly foreground their function as defense mechanisms. *Streetcar* opens up the great sexual disorder that is at work in our social interactions and then watches us scurry for the exits, seeking to limit the scope of the psychosexual anxiety which the work unleashes. Williams toys with interpretive frameworks in order to reveal their inadequacy by showing how the explanation they seize on is implicated in a larger web of connections which is the subject of the play. The concepts and frameworks of explanation we bring to the play don't work. That failure emerges as the most significant thing about them. The persistence of certain readings and the staying power of certain theories, despite their inadequacies, reveals the true function they perform. Interpretation is the act we perform to relieve ourselves of anxiety. By what token, discovering the nature of one's psychological implication in the play is largely a matter of identifying the way one places oneself outside it. Called on to present that evidence, both critics and those of lesser state invariably appeal not to "theory" but to the sovereign testimony of their experience. That act ironically completes the circle. For *Streetcar* represents the psychological roots of sexuality in an way that activates the desire of every audience to find a way to say it isn't so. Thus recent feminist critics, through denial, simply blow the whole matter away: Stanley's sexual attraction is dismissed, and/or Blanche's fatal attraction to it is seen as a sign of how the patriarchical order has imposed itself upon women. The uncanny truth thereby revealed is that the Utopian and not-yet-existent psyche of true feminist consciousness can't have anything to do with either Stanley or Blanche. For such an audience, the play can only be received as disavowed materials that cannot be experienced with the shock of recognition, except, that is, a recognition that one must disown it.

Williams' drama is far from the whole story of psychosexual conflict. But as an undeniable and central part of that story, it shows us that the blame can't be laid on a single cause—patriarchy, capitalism, hysteria—or purged by embracing one of the corresponding ideologies whereby we wash our hands of it. The play asks of us an engagement that allows no externalization and no minimalizing of our complicity. We cannot limit the problem, nor can we discharge our responsibility by identifying its origin and propagation as the activity of one sex. The play asks us, instead, as gendered audience, to see all the ways men and women are in it together. That is its greatest achievement—and its enduring scandal. For the right audience, everything the play does performs a Brechtian function on our sexuality, stripping masks to stimulate questions.

It's comforting to isolate the disorder and lay it all on Blanche as neurotic or discharge it all by seeing Blanche as victim. The audience can then enjoy, from the safe perspective of their normalcy, the spectacle in which she suffers her difference. But rather than letting us savor the pleasure of victimage, the play tries to get us to see the ways we avail ourselves of the structure of response in order to distance and protect ourselves from another response, which finds us implicated in conflicts that reveal most emotional reactions to the play to be guilt or resentment, because their unmistakable function is to protect us from things about ourselves we don't want to consider. Pity and fear are fine because they let us off the hook. But the truth of such responses is that they protect us from the tragic rather than opening us to it. Kazan had little idea how right he was when he titled the last scene "Blanche is disposed of," since that has invariably been the result of interpretations, including his. It is, in fact, the hidden purpose of all interpretations that make Blanche neurotic in order to preserve and protect "normalcy" from inspection. Kenneth Burke's notion of victimage perfectly describes the operations of this audience: it is cleansed, thanks to Blanche's "overstating of its case." So served, the audience can resume the position of Stella, the healthy pragmatist who knows it's not a good idea to look too deeply into things. For like Stella's reaction to Stanley's deed, such an audience can't retain anything that will disrupt its complacency. Theatre offers spectacles—the "fallen" or promiscuous woman, the woman destroyed by men. As spectacle, however, the object lesson it offers is useful because it enables us to rid ourselves of any doubts about ourselves. Blanche is valuable to this audience because she can't be internalized—only disposed of.

The Psychodynamic Structure of *A Streetcar Named Desire*

> Plot is the soul of tragedy.
> —Aristotle

Elia Kazan has left us a valuable legacy in his director's notes to the first production of *Streetcar*.[11] He there offers an illuminating analysis of the structure of the play focused on Blanche as a victim defeated by a brutal world in her quest to realize her defining need—to find refuge.

Here is Kazan's outline of the work's structure:

1. Blanche comes to the last stop at the end of the line.
2. Blanche tries to make a place for herself.
3. Blanche breaks them apart, but when they come together, Blanche is more alone than ever!
4. Blanche, more desperate because more excluded, tries the direct attack and makes the enemy who will finish her.
5. Blanche finds that she is being tracked down for the kill. She must work fast.
6. Blanche suddenly finds, suddenly makes for herself, the only possible, perfect man for her.
7. Blanche comes out of the happy bathroom to find that her doom has caught up with her.
8. Blanche fights her last fight. Breaks down. Even Stella deserts her.
9. Blanche's last desperate effort to save herself by telling the whole truth. *The truth dooms her.*
10. Blanche escapes out of this world. She is brought back by Stanley and destroyed.
11. Blanche is disposed of.

The problem with Kazan's "plot" is that it abstracts from the conflict that gives dramatic structure to the play.

To complete my interpretation, I will offer a contrasting scheme which opens up the harsher conflicts that Kazan's examination covers over. The structure of this play is defined not by the search for refuge but by the dynamics of sexual struggle. The focus of its plot, moreover, is not on a single character, Blanche, but on the interaction between Blanche and Stanley. That focus alone offers a complete and symmetrical reading of the play's structure. To establish it, we will schematize each scene, defining the dominant question it raises and the subtext it develops. These are the two key categories of inference that enable us to uncover the psychodynamics of a drama. Drama is that form where everything is in some way externalized, out in the open, present in action. But as drama teaches, action is never simple. The briefest human encounters often contain texts of the greatest complexity. This is one of the reasons why we so often contrive to avoid certain people. Drama is the art form that won't let that happen. Its unity is based on taking an interaction from its simplest beginning and drawing it out to its final fruition. Such is the rigor of *Streetcar,* the date Blanche and Stanley have from the beginning.

What follows is an attempt to schematize—in its necessary dramatic progression—the *dynamis* and telos of the psychological conflict that structures the play, through a summary of what each scene contributes to its development. Each summary concludes with an italicized statement which formulates, as explicit counter to Kazan's scheme, the depth psychology of the action. These formulations constitute a dialectical series: read in sequence they reveal the crypt pried open as the play descends into that deeply repressed psychological space in which it situates and traps it audience.

Scene i. Blanche and Stella: The question What does a woman want? is staged as the sisterly bond. In Blanche, Look what men have done to me, who has so much more experience of them than you. In Stella, You won then, but I'm the victor now because I've got a real man. The return of the repressed—Blanche as sister superior—is met by Stella's need to crow and to provoke the hysteric reactions that she can anticipate, given her knowledge of her sister's sexual instability. (As scene viii shows, Stella already knows all about Blanche's sexual history.) Stanley and Blanche: The mighty hunter meets the damsel in distress. Sizing up an opponent activates the feint/faint, with sexual battle thereby joined in the first incarnation of the dominant roles whereby men and women get the game going. Together, the two interactions represented in the scene establish, at a deeper psychic register, a recognition of unconscious envy as the center of sexuality, with mutual cruelty the mode of relating whereby all agents scratch at one another's wounds.[12] This superordinate need operates irrespective of gender and of other principles of familial and marital solidarity.

The competition of women over men activates the male need to seek out each woman's sexual insecurity in order to defend his sexual "identity" by putting relations on a secure sexual basis.

Scene ii.   This scene comprises the first attempts to strip the other, to use sex to play cat and mouse and to wound. Stella and Blanche: Sisterhood, as bonding, entails an effort to provoke and put down the male. Eating out at Galatoire's is the first dethronement and abandoning of the male. In reaction, the male need to expose the deceptiveness of women is activated. Flirting ensues. Women's way is Let's get uppity together and frustrate the male. His way is Let's strip away some of their airs and unpack their suitcase. For Blanche, flirting is rich opportunity, since the deepest sexual lure is cast by "the lady with a tragic secret." For Stanley, it's the return of the threat and the memory of his most famous victory. The pampered queen thus again meets the man who knows how to show a woman what she really wants.

Aggression rises, as the pleasure of stripping away the dominant masks each sex uses in order to provoke the other by stirring up underlying sexual anxieties.

Scene iii.   The need of the male group is to celebrate sexual aggression both toward women and toward other men. Stanley and Mitch: The brute needs the weak sidekick he can sissify in order to secure his reign over the group. The female response: If I can humiliate him in his temple, I'll prime the connection in which anger, frustration, and sexuality meet. One irony— Blanche and Stella aim at the same target, but for different reasons—begets a deeper irony: in Stanley's consciousness they are becoming indistinguishable.

Blanche and Mitch: The schoolmarm, offering a glimpse of stocking, hums "Rescue Me" to the man who thinks the way to a woman's heart, and to victory over his rival, is to prove he's different. Mitch: If I convince her I'm not a sexual being, will she love me? Blanche: When I finally meet a nice man, do I have to hold it against him? Stanley and Stella: The naked ape, the needy child, and the call of the wild. Payday: If I provoke him, will he explode, then rut unbound, leaving a ten-spot in my garter?

For Blanche, aggression is displaced into "romance," delayed and savored through literary allusions and linguistic foreplay. This is how the spider spins the web that entices the dupe to the Tarantula Arms. For Stanley and Stella, overt aggression is love play which builds to an orgiastic culmination in the return of the primal scream—"Stella!"—followed by a night of infantile regression.

Aggression toward women is the force that brings men together and through which they bond by feeding the aggression of the leader until it explodes in an explicit attack on the female object. The aggressive response of the woman who fathoms this dynamic: an attempt to separate out the weakest member and play with him in order to disrupt the group and taunt its strongest member.

Scene iv.   The turning point: Primed by sex, the mirroring relationship of the women splits apart. Stella, the sex object, crows, while the "lady" doth protest too much. The sexual competition of the sisters in scene i is repeated for the first big payoffs. The horrified southern lady, fulsome in the role and fixated on the beast, the destroyer, exhorts her double to a flight into ethics. The double, in turn, seizes the day to say one thing loud and clear: After a night in bed with Stanley, I find it hard to attend to long speeches. Stella's psyche has achieved its bliss and its reification: she will always return to the state this scene finds her in. In Blanche's psyche, however, the denial of sexuality has taken on a new desperateness. Repressed desire has broken through into consciousness and is only displaced through hysterical hyperconsciousness.

Stanley, the offstage listener, welcomes the return of the marble columns. Blanche's disavowal of sexual attraction inflames Stanley's rage because it confirms his suspicions about the seductive nature of her games. It also identifies her "refinements" as the mask that must be stripped away to get at her sexual insecurities, a counterattack Stanley sees as his holy duty.

The two main characters converge at the deepest psychic register. Blanche must project and deny what can no longer be repressed. Stanley resolves to go after the core of her psychosexual identity. Male desire is fully out in the open. In response, the female psyche splits. It either collapses to the status of a sheerly physical "thing," or it is torn in half by a contradiction that carries the unleashed force of a desire—that protest against sexuality that is both defense and fascination, girding itself for battle.

Scene v.   From this point on, the nature and function of games and roles change radically. What was earlier subtext is now on the surface. Stanley and Blanche use every occasion to provoke and taunt each other with sexual jabs and innuendos. The goal is to prime the other for sexual battle by debasing the other as a sexual object. Blanche's way: I'm a sophisticated southern lady with many gentleman admirers. That is, You're a pig, and sex with you would be the ultimate debasement. Stanley's way is cat and mouse foreplay, to torture the woman's mind so that the eventual discharge of sperm will be the good-housekeeping seal of contempt. The ironic connection: Sex for both is debasing, but its goal for one is self-debasement and for the other, self-aggrandizement.

Blanche's psyche, now trapped in its reliance on the defense of splitting, begins to fragment as she finds herself compelled to act out, in series, three connected roles: with Stanley, the Southern lady as the flirt who provokes sexually powerful men only to withdraw, deliberately leaving them frustrated; in conversation with Stella about Mitch, The Southern lady as the prim and proper role used to deceive gullible men, leaving them confused objects of amusement and ridicule; and with the newsboy, the Southern lady as the seductress, the corrupter of youth, turned on by the prospect of the first near rape.

Both Stanley and Blanche have committed themselves to acting out their hatreds. Sex is now nothing but aggression. All games and roles are played for that purpose. As a result, they unravel, because nothing can contain that drive. Seeking its objective correlative, it craves ever more overt, more violent expression.

Scene vi.   Blanche engages in a series of delays and displacements, but such operations no longer relieve an inner pressure which craves chances to wound the other. Blanche and Mitch: Teasing the oaf and laughing in his face are the backdrop to the long-delayed narrative and the key to its darker purpose. Blanche uses her story/secret as the lure to catch the man who knows his only appeal is the role of rescuer, protector. Because he thinks that's the only way he can get a woman, Mitch deliberately dummies up when she insults him and flashes her sexual past. Mitch knows he's playing the part of the castrata. For both, Stanley thus remains the power that is present in its absence, the controlling backdrop to the "perfect moment" in which they come together. Mitch is not the one right man for Blanche but the chance for respite, recuperation, and displaced aggression. She lands deliberately cruel blows on a weak male to get back into practice: laughing in one man's face as prologue to grinding the broken glass in another's.

The aggression at the core of Blanche's desire has fully surfaced. She tries to delay and displace it, but all under Stanley's shadow and in anticipation of battle with him. Relations with different "kinds" of men are all finally relations with the one man who is the sole object of psychic fascination and horror. Blanche thus reveals the basic condition of the psyche: until one works out one's conflict with the frustration object, that Other who is at the center of one's inner world, all other relationships will mirror its terms.

Scene vii.   Four months pass, raising two inescapable questions. Why does Stanley delay? Aggression is the sweetmeat one must age and savor by storing up grievances so that later, justified, its unbound power can destroy the opponent. It is also the pleasure of delay, of foreplay, of bringing the opponent slowly to the point of great confidence in her ascendance so that the sexual assault will strike deep into her psyche. Cruelty becomes deliberate when it patiently prepares a trap that will put the opponent in a position of maximum vulnerability so that one can deliver a devastating blow. Stanley is not alone in this. Such cruelty is one of the primary ways in which subjects create their inwardness, by hollowing out a space within their own aggression for its perfected exercise.

Why does Blanche stay? Aggression is also her meat. Her desire is to displace Stanley in his own home and to do so by rubbing his face in the role that maddens him—hydrotherapy, the paper moon, the flight into make-believe. Like Stanley, Blanche wants to imprint her psyche on the other psyche in order to destroy its phantom substantiality. This is the way she deepens her inwardness. The only real difference between them is that Blanche can't stop projecting, because aggression for her is also an act of self-contempt whereby she achieves satisfaction only by setting herself up for disaster.

At its psychological depths, the clash of the two psyches has now assumed this form: Both are killers out to drive the other person crazy.[13] *Sex as aggression is an attempt to destroy the psyche of the other by getting at the basis of his or her psychosexual identity and driving a stake in the heart. Delay primes that psychic register so that when the trap springs and the sexual comes to explicit assertion, genital wounding will carry the force of a death blow.*

Both Blanche and Stanley share Hamlet's knowledge: The one thing you can't do when you kill someone is kill them. The only true murder is the torture you plant in the core of the other's psyche so that he or she can live it in perpetuity.

Scene viii. The home has become a purely psychological space, with every "prop" in it a token in the battle where each sees in the other's action only provocation. Stanley's home, as male den in which he's Huey Long, has been usurped by the culture of manners. Sisterhood is now women banding together in open aggression to taunt the male as a nonsexual object of disgust: table manners as deliberate cruelty. The aim is humiliation, meant to drive the other into an impotent rage. Stella knows how to use Blanche to express her aggression toward Stanley, then retreat so the other will receive the blow. The columns never were tore down, and Stanley now sees this. Stanley's aggression has likewise become deliberate cruelty, drawn out for the pleasure of hystericizing one object as a scene of instruction for another, its displaced target. The surplus pleasure of destroying Blanche is an object lesson for Stella.

The stage of deliberate cruelty is reached. The goal now is to compel submission through humiliation. Aggression as deliberate cruelty takes as its target the seeking out and reopening of the basic wound that will bring about the dissolution of the other's psyche. Humiliation has become the basic term of interaction, because it alone gets at that psychic marrow, thus positioning the other for a blow that will be destructive.

Scene ix. This scene sees the second near rape. Mitch: The sexual rage of the weak, frustrated male is experienced, by him, as the long-awaited, deeply satisfying opportunity to play Stanley. Tenderness was always a ruse. The male flight from inwardness secures itself through the privileged act. For Blanche, the perfect match: Mitch's rage is experienced, by her, as the delightful, long-awaited opportunity to reveal feminine sexuality as the spiderweb spun to trap, torture, then engulf the male psyche.

The contradiction at the heart of Blanche's two conflicting roles—chaste vamp—is brought into the open as the two ways she plays out her sexual "desire." The desire for magic and the claim that one is really good at heart are the props whereby the spider woman inflicts her curse. The unity of the contradiction is the secret Blanche has kept from herself: Desire is death.

The rage of the humiliated male psyche erupts in sex-as-aggression, giving the woman her first chance to grind the broken glass in their faces. The tragic irony of Blanche's project—as an attempt to invert her origins—thereby becomes explicit. An overt attack aimed at humiliating the other's sexuality in order to destroy his psyche is the necessary prelude to asking that other to become the daddy-protector. The desire to be rescued and to find a haven is asserted only when she is certain it is already lost. In its wake, the possibility of perfect coupling arises in the fantasy of desire unbound, in love with easeful death, which Blanche enacts in soliloquy at the beginning of the next scene.

Scene x: The Perfect Couple. Both subjects have recently fulfilled the desire that gives them "identity." They are thus ready to unlock the desire beneath that myth. Mitch disposed of, Blanche's internal condition becomes explicit. Blanche's desire is to become the broken glass and grind that fragmentation in their faces in order to inflict it on herself. Her need is to play out the role that will bring things to a climax so that she can suffer the destruction that comes with the unmasking of that role—feminine desire fulfilled. Having acted out her basic psychodrama, Blanche can assume her greatest role: delusional regression into magical thinking as deliverance from the self-fragmentation she has brought upon her psyche. The object of deliverance lost, Blanche's psyche regresses to an autoerotic desire for death through flight into a world of pure fantasy where all she can do is rehearse scenes in which desire and death are one—either in the midnight swim and plunge toward the bottom of the pool of her psyche or on the cold white deck of Shep Huntleigh's yacht.

Stanley: Male desire fulfilled in the child/phallus liberates a festival of aggression as homecoming. That force floats free until it again finds the object which has just been vanquished by the phallic birth—those cultured women who regard "gaudy, seed-bearing" men as inferiors. Stanley's baby has put Stella in her place. But her former image rises up to spoil his celebration. That specter must be destroyed—by the proof made weapon.

The irony: Stanley wants Blanche out of his home and doesn't know she has already taken leave. "Swine," a literary allusion, provides her "hamartia." Stanley, the apostle of the literal, abhors imagination and poetry. It must be brought down to the world of brutal fact, reduced to the one thing Stanley can see: poetry is just another prop in the game of seduction, which will now suffer interpretive closure through the act, rape, that frees and focuses the aggression that has been building from the beginning. Blanche is already defeated, but Stanley can't see her frail attempt to sustain a shred of dignity and psychic integrity as anything but the last role that justifies the definitive, final response. And in this he is not entirely wrong. Blanche rises to the occasion, matching his role with what has been the truth of hers: she is the agent who breaks the shattered mirror of her psyche in order to get the glass to grind in their faces.

With the surface desire fulfilled, the underlying core fantasy that empowered it is unleashed and craves celebration. For the woman, the object (Mitch) must always be lost so that the dissolution of the psyche can be assured. For the man, the phallic proof provided by the child banishes the threat of castration and resolves all anxieties connected with women's otherness through the exercise of what can now be regarded as justice.

Stanley fulfills the core desire of the rapist: to use the phallus as the avenging weapon that destroys the woman's psyche. Properly provoked, penises produce psychoses. The Kowalski home has finally had the sacred installed on the throne.

Scene xi: How All Subjects Attain Their Bliss. (Some weeks later.) Stanley: Male identity attained must celebrate its victory in gratuitous violence toward everyone and surplus violence toward the defeated object. Crushing the lampshade is a displaced representation of the final act of contempt most rapists perform. Blanche: The quest for nondifferentiation is attained in the role beyond all roles—schizoid withdrawal from her own experience. Aesthetically one with herself, in *della robbia* blue, having etherealized herself out of existence, Blanche proclaims the saving contradiction: I was never here; I'm just passing through. Blanche's desire is thus fulfilled in reification, in the assumption of the role that forever banishes any further conflict with reality. Likewise reified in their roles, Mitch and Stella offer themselves and the audience pseudodeliverance. The guilt-wracked Mitch can only utter to Stanley the word that defines both—*brag* (164)—while Stella-for-stupor provides a degraded replica of her sister's need to banish consciousness. Unlike the Hollywood version, in Williams' text she offers Stanley the perfect happy ending: Stanley, not Mitch, gets the "sugar-tit" from a woman who now knows that her true role is to be his Mother. Her ironic future beckons: to juggle two babies who are sure to clash over the possession of the maternal object.

Bliss is aggression unbound. For the male, its free expression liberates the manic triad—triumph, contempt, dismissal—and dares anyone to object. For the female, its expression provokes a psychotic regression in which complete identification with the aggressor brings about the peace which passeth understanding—that of one's total psychic dissolution. Desire has always been death: in Blanche it now stands forth as such.

The (Gendered) Audience

In working out its structure, *Streetcar* plants a depth charge in the psyche of the audience. Each scene stalks and exposes a quarry which the next scene takes to a deeper psychic register. The through-line of that process is a systematic discovery of the way in which aggression forms the truth of sex. The work's purpose is to dissolve the difference between desire and death, libido and destruction. Every struggle to locate or sustain a principle of difference collapses. No way is found to halt a descent which brings to a crisis traditional dualistic attempts to oppose libido and aggression, sexuality and the death drive. In that crisis every confidence we have about our sexual identity and its alignment with "life" is put in question. The play practices a scorched-earth policy in showing how sexual aggression flourishes in every relation between the sexes. Sexuality in *Streetcar* is an escalating violence enhanced by "rituals" that build to a climax that gives neither party any real relief or any stable identity that will halt brutalizing repetition and the even more deadly need to find new turf on which to enact the process. Lacan says there is no sexual relation: Williams reveals the tragic content of that pun.[14]

The dialectical schema of the play's structure formulated above attempts to reinforce Williams' depth charge by articulating the wound that the play opens up within and for the right audience. It does so by identifying the basic fault at work in sexuality and the Crypt we must pry open if we are to reclaim desire from death. For to reverse the hold death has on sexuality, we need a complete knowledge of the ways it operates and the core conflicts from which they derive. To regain sex as Eros, we must win back our existence by confronting all the ways we deprive one another of it. This is the possibility Blanche DuBois gives us, by taking its opposite to the end of the line. *Streetcar* takes the inescapable, dialectical "connection" between our identity and our sexuality and rubs it raw.

All in the Family:
Death of a Salesman

Representation, Intention, and Ideology

Representation exceeds intention. That is why art remains a process of discovery in which the best-laid thematic plans fall prey to the emergence of a dynamic of human conflict that has a way and will of its own. In this sense all writers are existential, with their materials frequently surpassing and contradicting the limits they try to impose upon them. This is especially the case when a writer has certain fairly well-defined thematic and ideological ends, for in such cases the themes imposed on the materials inadvertently become parts of the process they would contain, revealing therein a function quite different from that the artist would give them. In such cases the task of interpretation is to produce the drama which the work resists by showing how the ideology the artist tries to impose on the materials is exposed by their inherent dynamic. The ideology of form is thereby revealed as the inability of a form to subsume the connections which the drama establishes.[1]

Death of a Salesman has a unique place in this study because it is such a work. It derives from a clearly defined intention and ideology which its author has been at pains to articulate in a number of essays that constitute one of the most complete records we have of how an essentialistic humanism conceives the nature and purpose of tragedy.[2] Those essays are a storehouse of humanistic commonplaces, replete with all the traditional pieties about human nature, the family, love, the workings of justice, the order of things, and the uplifting effects of tragedy. Miller leaps from Aristotle to the present in a single bound, reaffirming what we fear the common man may have lost in the modern world. The basic thrust of those essays is Miller's effort to preserve certain essentialistic values he associates with the family from a *socius* that encroaches upon it. The effort to split the two produces a series of contradictions which Miller circles around, without resolving, throughout his essays. Fortunately, the play he wrote is wiser and constitutes their dialectic, establishing connections that reveal the family and the *socius* as one in sustaining a disorder which exposes all the humanistic guarantees Miller would assert to protect us from it. Thus brought back into the world, those guarantees are revealed as integral props in sustaining what thereby emerges as a truly horrifying situation.

Death of a Salesman is about efforts at transcendence that fail because the values on which the efforts are based actually function to advance the disorder from which they promise deliverance by blinding characters to their situations, and specifically to what they are doing to one another. Everyone in this play, including the playwright, constantly strives to move from the situation to some ideological space of reassurance. But the guarantees thereby invoked play radically different function in the drama. A vast space of abstractions looms over the heads of all the protagonists. Each seeks therein the guarantee needed to prop up a collective illusion and the self-conception each agent needs in order to maintain a place in that collectivity.

As we will see, that ideology is neither an ideology of the individual nor of the *socius* but of their connection in sustaining a vast emptiness through a constant flight into abstraction. Much of the play is given over to a kind of obsessional cheerleading in which the characters try to convince one another that they can locate certain values in their lives and realize them in their world. The drama is wiser because it takes these operations and drives them back into the relationships, revealing the family as a manic system dedicated to sustaining a delusional process.

Shared delusion is the truth of the family as a social system. No member escapes it. Every attempt to transcend merely exacerbates the disorder. "We never told the truth for ten minutes in this house!"(131). Biff's recognition states the truth that the play makes concrete in ways he will never know, and that includes his paltry effort, toward the end, to formulate a saving recognition. *Death of a Salesman* is about how in lying to one another the truth gets told, without anyone ever becoming aware of it. The truth that emerges is a collective one about the family as a single "unified" psyche that is bound together in a complicity which each member struggles to escape by shifting its burdens onto the others. A circle of reinforcements is thereby created that sustains a common delusion, with each member playing an assigned part whenever the others waver. In invoking what comforts and renews, each agent reveals what traps the others. In invoking the needed guarantees, each inadvertently exposes the true function of those guarantees. The family is a vast mechanism for sustaining an illusion, and the identity of each member is determined by the role each plays in this process. In that system Willy may finally function as the ideal scapegoat for all concerned—including Miller and the audience—but the contribution each member makes to Willy's fate reveals the repressed truth about each and all.

In their incessant cheerleading, the Lomans always try to reassure themselves about two things that are finally indistinguishable—themselves and their eventual success, given their "moral" qualities, in American society. That connection exposes both terms. The hermeneutic circle of capitalism is thereby revealed as the need to mediate every experience by reference to its logic. When the Lomans talk, the reference constantly slips back and forth between the family and the *socius*, because the two realities are dialectically indistinguishable moments in a single process in which the characters "persuade" one another to reinvest their capital in the very beliefs that destroy them by inflicting those beliefs on one another in a zero-sum game. One cannot split family and society in order to protect one, but must see how they reinforce and determine one another.

That dialectical connection reveals the family as that social institution with a uniquely privileged ideological function. It is the place where we inflict the society upon one another. We do so, to invert Miller, because the family isn't an eternal verity with love, recognition, and mutual concern guaranteed immediately and a priori, but the place where the deepest psychosocial disorders are nurtured, because closeness to one another is the condition that breeds them. The family is the necessary site of ideological interpellation because it fosters and sustains the internalizations whereby subjects police one another at the deepest psychic register.[3] Unless a society can create the kind of psyche it needs, it can't sustain itself. The family is where it performs this essential operation. And it does so, of necessity, by forming a single collective psyche of mutually reinforcing roles.

We thus attain a properly dialectical understanding of the connection of the family and the *socius*. The family is the group psychology that mirrors and sustains the larger social process. The *socius* is its symbolic referent, the absent presence whose logic and ideology familial life replicates. "They behave like apes," a shocked Thomas Mann remarked on seeing the play. They do so because they incessantly ape the larger totality. The logic of capitalism is thereby revealed in a way that goes deeper than economics or the discovery of particular flaws in the system that can be corrected by social engineering or family therapy. The system itself is the hyperlogic that binds the characters in a group psychology which interpellates them as empty subjects who are filled by that which is itself empty of any real value or content. Willy Loman remains one of the true way stations of a capitalism rushing on a one-way track to its implosion.[4]

The ideology of society and of the family are one and inseparable. The former is the glue that gives the family a phantom sense of itself. Together they mutually reinforce the grand illusion which we call the American Dream, by making the inability to modify or transcend that illusion the inner voice that controls everyone's consciousness. Deliberation is a constant in the Loman household, yet all deliberations end where they began. The American Dream is this immanent process of reciprocal determination in which family and *socius* are indistinguishable components. The subject of *Death of a Salesman* is neither the familial unconscious nor the social unconscious but their complicity. Every attempt to separate them or to place something outside the process becomes a paradigm of abstract thinking. This knife cuts both ways, exposing the myth of the family as enclave in a dehumanizing society and the equally mythical notion that the family is the disorder which socialization heals. The concept of History is another way of formulating this connection, for history is the reality in which both terms are wholly engaged and determine one another. Every essentialistic value we would affirm in order to limit that process is caught up in it, irreversibly and without guarantees. The beauty of Miller's play is that in trying to find a saving presence in the family, he exposes and situates it within a larger process which he cannot control. In doing so he gives us the Real not as absent cause, as Jameson would have it, but as constant, albeit empty, presence.[5]

In *Death of a Salesman* Miller, who loves the family, exposes every value he finds in it as hollow to the core. This is the play he writes in spite of himself, and which we will produce by showing how every value he and his critics want to claim as inherent to the structure of the play is concretely situated and exposed within it. Among the key examples: Linda as a concerned, humanistic voice; Biff's redemptive self-discovery; Willy as scapegoat; and, above all, Miller's attempt to limit the social critique by shifting at key points to a "psychological" explanation of Willy's unique flaws.

Miller wants to protect and reassure his audience by offering them numerous exits. But each exit constitutes an ideological operation which violates what is concretely dramatized in the play. By liberating the latter, we deprive the audience of the experience they want to have when they interpret and respond to the play along the lines Miller indicates. Their needs, and Miller's, are thereby turned back against them. We thus unlock, through interpretation, the drama Miller tries to arrest but cannot: the audience as family is thereby delivered over to an understanding of how the group psychology it celebrates in the theatre actually works in the place of its origin.

The greatness of *Death of a Salesman* is that it constantly unleashes a subtext which its author cannot control. That subtext annihilates the humanistic ideology he tries to impose on his materials. The audience Miller wants to protect is thereby unmasked. Their needs are exposed in the most revealing way—as beliefs that cannot be earned dramatically. The failure of the characters in the play to realize those values concretely situates and mirrors the inability of anyone in the audience to do so. We can talk forever about humanism and the conventional pieties. The beauty of Miller's play is the concrete revelation that these beliefs have no ontological status; they function as forces within the drama rather than as terms of order for its explanation. Rather than sublimely rising above Willy's tragedy or embodying themselves concretely in it, these beliefs thereby stand forth as among the most powerful internal forces producing its inevitability.

For Miller the audience is a family. This is the dimension of the psyche the play addresses with every reassurance Miller can muster. By turning that process back against itself, we will create a new group psychology for that audience: depriving them of the consolations Miller offers in order to confront them with a historical reality in which the family is situated and from which there is no readily forseeable exit.[6] I should add that such an interpretation is not deconstruction but concrete dialectics, since the reading produced does not dissolve the drama of the play but reveals it.[7]

As we'll see, another way of formulating the problem is in terms of the aesthetic incompatibility or contradiction between bourgeois tragedy and the expressive dramaturgy Miller employs in this play. This will be the through-line of our interpretation: the attempt to show how the ideology of one form is disrupted from within by the force of another which uncovers a reality that outstrips every guarantee the former has traditionally used to contain it.

Act I: Come Back With Your Shield—and On It

Man and Wife Are One Flesh

Because it situates itself from the beginning within the family, exposition here is not dreary but sharp for those who have an ear tuned to the subtext. Willy's long day's journey begins with his exhausted return at night to his "foundation and support" to receive succor after yet another failure. What follows is hardly a scene of domestic renewal, however. Cheering each other up really amounts to driving the ideological stake into the other's psyche. Willy can only thrash out in accumulated frustration freely projected onto whatever object catches his attention. The question that haunts the scene and lights up its subtext: Is this displacement or the incipient perception of the dialectical connection Willy can't sustain? Linda's part advances that question: she deflects each blow by diffusing an air of sympathy, which, however, reveals her as the Spartan mother disguised as the passive wife. Willy has come back on his shield rather than with it. Yet all of Linda's attempts to cheer him up have one aim: to restore the "identity" that will force him to reassume the role that defeats him. Marriage is here a collusion dedicated to restoring a shared delusion. The apparent naturalism of the opening dialogue establishes the psychodynamics of this mutually frustrating process. Something is wrong, yet "nothing happened"(12). Willy "came back" because he "couldn't make it." But lest the Beckett-like dialogue flood the stage in questions thrown at absences, both characters quickly seize on externalization as the mechanism of denial. It must have been the coffee . . . "maybe it's your glasses." Together they thus attain the pseudo-solution of admitting a disorder while depriving it of psychological locus. Willy's mind needs a "rest cure." "Your mind is overactive and the mind is what counts, dear" (13). But since that reference weighs like a nightmare, it must be deflected through further displacement. Willy's feet ache. He needs an aspirin. Pain must be localized in the body, then discharged by blocking any route to consciousness.

Reversing the true relation brings it forth, but under the sign of nostalgia. Consciousness can only be extinguished by consciousness. Willy evokes the natural beauty seen during the previous day's drive in order to shift from the present into the past, from reality to dream. But then and now that process completes itself as Willy "awakes" to find his suicidal drift completing itself in highway carnage void of insight into its real object: "I might've killed somebody." The image of the crack-up presented here contains all that the play will drawn forth: past and present indistinguishable in the prefigurement of death. But for Willy, externalization severs that connection and exorcises the "strange thoughts" that kept surfacing while he was on the road (14). What Willy refuses to see in the total image he evokes is the absence of difference in the scene that defines dreaming. Willy is Melville's water-gazer updated, staring at America. He has looked too long into the sea and can never return except to find himself horribly awakened, though only for a moment, by that plunge where dreaming ends in death.

Significantly, Linda is so taken in by Willy's speech that she takes no note of a paraphraxis—the open windshield—that will shortly come a cropper. As we'll see, she is even more threatened than Willy by his "strange thoughts" but knows that safety depends on exorcising them by shifting Willy's attention back to the field of battle. Cleansing Willy's consciousness requires the renewal of pragmatics. Linda's need is to get Willy recommitted to the workplace, and the force of her rhetoric is such that he shortly starts to put his suit jacket back on, an absurd act deriving its rationale from the fact that Linda's subtext is full of barbs. "You're too accommodating, dear" (14). Willy has to be back on his feet fighting, but Linda can't be the target of the blows, nor can anger disrupt Willy's role in their dream. In effect, Willy is here first identified as scapegoat for the collective disorder of the family. For beneath the apparent agreement, the two characters diverge in a way that will become progressively significant, in showing that Linda's psyche is not a healthy alternative to Willy's but a flight to humanistic abstractions designed to protect herself from awareness of their shared disorder. Whenever Willy becomes the knight of the negative—"Work a lifetime to pay off a house. You finally own it, and there's nobody to live in it"—and is in danger of casting off his role, Linda flees into abstraction to deliver herself from his possible defeat. "Dear, life is a casting off" (15). When Willy, in response, reinvests his "capital" in the house, she gains a double assurance. He's back on his feet, and she's safely ensconced in transcendental commonplaces.

The threat of consciousness has not been exorcised, however, but shifted to the son. Both characters know that Biff already resembles, at an early age, the disorder that is now announcing itself catastrophically in the father. Moreover, a new inwardness has reared its head in the family. Willy's need to project and deny his condition makes him an aggressive critic of family values. Linda must deflect that anger, not to keep family harmony, but to sustain the familial delusion. She does so by leading Willy through a new round of delusional projection, whereby his anger surfaces only to be discharged. Biff moves from being a "bum" to one who's "not lazy." Thereby the voice of the internalized Other, who keeps the capitalist game in charge of "character" by defining financial success or failure as the one theatre in which one's worth is attested, regains command. "Never" is the only proper reply to the question of Biff's laziness. Linda thus caps Willy's train of thought with its categorical imperative, thereby revealing that she has even more at stake in the game than Willy. The assertion also reveals her previous "life as leave-taking" sentiments as no more than a posture which here unveils its true Spartan visage—"Never"—before retreating into pseudonurturing.

I'm being particularly hard on Linda at this point so that we can later see what's easily missed. The trouble with most accounts of Linda is that they begin too late in the game—"Attention must be finally paid to such a person" (56), and so forth—after she's got everyone properly positioned and has put her operations into hyperspace, with herself identified as the perfect, loving object beyond criticism and outside Willy's problems.

With the shared delusion made categorical, Linda and Willy can now work in tandem to exorcise inwardness. When Biff "finds himself," everything will be great. That "lure" in place, Linda can say he's "lost" so that Willy can reaffirm the one arena in which they will all be found. With such "personal attractiveness" and a "job selling," "he could be big in no time." "Remember . . ." Willy again "loses himself in reminiscences," as the contradictions of the present give way to the phantom past (16).

Conflict remains, and a third round will be required to purge Willy's aggression. The displaced focus is again Willy's body and Linda's nurturing. She's eaten up by desire for the new commodity "whipped cheese"; he, by his imperiled desire for the eternal verities. "I don't want a change!" (17). Every remark Willy makes derives from associations that show him projecting his inner conflicts into the scene as onto a Rorschach. There's no air; they're boxed in. We are always "inside his head," engulfed in the claustrophobic threat of being engulfed in an imploding consciousness, and nothing escapes it.

To exorcise that threat, Linda must insert the barb—"We should've bought the land next door"—that will restore the dream by tying its defeat to Willy's tail. They never had the money to make that purchase, but reality testing isn't what either is after. The line functions as a call to delusional reminiscence as the necessary escape route from conciousness. Willy can then project his frustration onto a new object—the budding capitalist builders who "massacred the neighborhood"—only to flee the implications by making the object of his rage perform a quick disappearing act. Willy momentarily gazes on what constitutes real progress in the system he idealizes, but he can't perceive what is before his eyes. If, as Marguerite Duras says, perception must be learned, Willy can't grasp Malthus except through a rhetoric of disgust in which he sees himself locked with his neighbors in "maddening" competition for diminishing space. But he must take this image downstairs to exorcise alone. Linda has better blinders, a positivism that openly contradicts itself in a jumble of factoids: "People" have "to move somewhere," and yet "I don't think there's more people [today]. I think—"(17). She can't complete her last line because the comic possibilities would stagger even Edith Bunker.

Willy is left to articulate the question opened by the dash, guiltily to an auditor who has already in effect left, her work done: "You're not worried about me, are you, sweetheart? . . . You've got too much on the ball to worry about." Further reassurance will have to come from the Big Other so that Willy can reinvest his capital in himself by putting his money on Biff. The possibility of insight is extinguished through the invocation of capitalist mythology: "Certain men just don't get started till later in life. Like Thomas Edison, I think. Or B. F. Goodrich" (18).

It is enough to tip Linda over the line into a celebration in which she repeats the paraphraxis that Willy now detects:

Linda: And Willy—if it's warm Sunday we'll drive in the country. And we'll open the windshield, and take lunch.
Willy: No, the windshields don't open on the new cars.
Linda: But you opened it today.
Willy: Me? I didn't. (18)

His confusion between past and present becomes hers, but when the contradiction surfaces she knows how to banish the threat of psychological reality by inadvertently parodying the terms of depth psychology in order to deny any way of pursuing the matter: "Something must've reminded you" (19). Memory for Linda is a momentary curiosity, as is everything else. Odd things occur; we note them to be done with them. They leave no residue in consciousness.

Linda's function in sustaining the familial disorder is now fully before us. She must bring Willy back to reality, and reality, whenever disruptive, must become unintelligible curiosity, so labeled and thereby dismissed. Linda's reality principle is the hegemony of the positivistic superimposed on all situations. A purely internal operation makes the structure psychologically foolproof: whenever failure threatens, one outruns it by affirming its inevitability. One thereby banishes any chance of its implications being driven back into the system. These three mechanisms constitute and exhaust Linda's inwardness. As the shared paraphraxis indicates, Linda and Willy are haunted by the same memories and dreams. They only arise in her consciousness, however, when they've first disrupted his. She then exorcises them by reducing a psychological text to a "factual" one. This operation is impossible for Willy, since it's all, thanks in part to her ministrations, firmly "inside his head," constantly triggered by facts which awaken associations he must flee by repressing a "historical" consciousness (or political unconscious) that keeps erupting and that can only be stilled by flight into what is really its inverted double—the fantasized past.

The Brothers Loman

Before setting us loose in that dream kingdom, Miller shifts to the sons and another scene where exposition reveals a complex subtext which completes the picture we need in order to understand what is going on in the grand "regressive" episodes that structure Willy's inner drama. While Willy warms to that activity prior to his reentry downstairs, the brothers engage in a complex *folie à deux* which in many ways repeats and extends the husband-wife drama just ended. The condition driving both scenes is the conflicted unity of the familial psyche—and the role each "individual" performs in its sustenance.

The play was once appropriately titled *The Inside of His Head*. This is one of its rooms—the one where the sons, as extensions of the father and failed attempts to mediate his contradictions, strive to find a solution by distinguishing themselves from one another, only to find that they have been set in predetermined roles, as in concrete, by the attributions whereby the parents fixed their identity. Biff is the favored son idealized by both parents. Happy is the neglected one humiliated by both. His mother criticizes him at any opportunity; his father ignores him or introduces the invidious comparison that drives him against his brother. Three structures are thus joined, defining the position of the siblings in the family neurosis.

Each son is a split personality with the split derived from an identification with one side of the split in the father. Biff is Willy the dreamer trying to find himself and thereby establish his father's essential value on another stage. But his inwardness is no more than a drifter's fantasy, because he is split between that dream and the unresolved conflict that keeps bringing him back home every time he realizes he's never left. Happy is Willy's dream repeated on native grounds, with the father's refusal of inwardness channeled into sexual conquest as displaced aggression toward those men whom he knows defeat him, as they did his father, in the competitive world of business. A deeper subtext in both projects will shortly return us to the mother, but we begin appropriately with the burden she has deftly placed on both—the father's weakness as the "flaw" that must be exorcised, since both sons cannot fail to see the ways they mirror it.

To banish it, they employ the favored familial device—the externalization of inner disorder. Biff locates the fault in his father's eyes; Happy, in his "mind," suitably recast in pragmatic terms. The latter reference then comically cancels the physical defect. If Willy would focus on the pragmatic, the defect that concerns Biff would also disappear. "Why he's got the finest eye for color in the business. You know that" (20). Disagreeing with that assessment leaves one in isolation with the psychological threat Happy will now exorcise by playing Linda to Biff's Willy. Biff complies by identifying the mind as a field of dreams in which the son's dreams repeat, in a new historical situation, the father's primary function, as the creator of illusions. Happy takes up the other side of the split, showing what happens when dreams fail yet must be sustained. Aggression toward their familial source is displaced onto an object, women, which gives the pseudovictory needed to sustain the illusions about oneself that keep the son, like his father, in the game. And Happy doesn't miss the opportunity to reinforce the game's hegemony by noting that he has replaced Biff both as seducer of women and as representative of the familial quest. Any chance Biff may have to sustain the position of critical consciousness is thereby cut off: "You taught me everything I know about women. Don't forget that" (21). Biff becomes instead the site of the flaw that must be purged.

If scene i staged the question What's wrong with Willy? scene ii takes up the corollary, What's wrong with Biff? For Biff, like Willy, has come home "a moody man," beset by doubts. Lest his doubts disrupt the home, Happy exploits Biff's confusion (as Linda did Willy's) and becomes his Iago by identifying Biff as the source of Willy's problems. When Willy talks to himself, Happy tells Biff, "You know something? Most of the time he's talking to you." Willy and Happy thus work in tandem to put Biff on the hook. Everything Willy says directly to Biff has "a twist of mockery" (21). But everything he says alone is, Happy notes, a silent appeal.

Biff sees the trap—"Don't lay it all to me"—but he can't escape because his inwardness is in a greater state of disarray than his father's. If Willy is inwardness troubled by the bill, *die Rechnung,* from the past, Biff is inwardness fixated in paralysis before the future: "I don't know—what I'm supposed to want" (22). Though this line contains a displacement—"supposed to," implying that the answer comes from someone else—the threat Biff poses of inwardness as questioning, unhinged from the pragmatic world, activates Happy's greatest fear. And like Linda, he exorcises it by blaming Biff for having it.

In response, Biff presents a monologue worth careful attention in identifying the terms of Biff's contradiction—and the rather preposterous function Miller will ask Biff to perform in the play. Biff's monologue follows the basic familial pattern: regression, repetition, then flight into abstractions that cannot be dramatized yet must be asserted as the deus ex machina that brings deliverance from the psyche. We must pause over the third stage, since it undercuts the ideological function Miller will later try to derive from the storehouse of humanistic commonplaces he here first puts in Biff's mouth. As in our treatment of Linda, it is important at the start to note the psychological function ideas play in Biff's character so that we can later spot the far different function Miller tries to give those ideas when he puts them in ideological hyperspace.[8]

Biff's monologue shows why he will always, despite Miller, be a parody of inwardness. His real purpose is to deliver himself from alienation and from the inner voice—of the Father as capitalist conscience—that persecutes him, by a flight into romantic sentiments. Biff thus announces his alienation only to deprive it of meaning. He is a "drifter" and has found no satisfaction in his otherness because the "voice of conscience" always recalls him to the home he's never left. But he can't come home to settle accounts because each thought process ends in self-undoing: "I've always made a point of not wasting my life, and everytime I come back here I know that all I've done is to waste my life" (22–23). Nothing important could happen on the road, because the search itself was defined as a waste of time.

Biff's position is similar to Willy's. The one thing he knows for sure is that he must expunge the disorder alive in the question What should I want? by deflecting the issue through a new externalization. Once a searching drifter, he has returned home feeling "like a boy" who must seek refuge in a new form of magical thinking: "Maybe I oughta get married." Self-questioning has led him to the escapist question he asks his brother, who is now installed in the position Ben plays in his father's psyche. In effect he asks Happy the question Willy repeatedly asks everyone: What's the secret? Biff (to Happy): "Are you content?" (23).

But Happy is no Ben. He can only restore his own confidence by showing his brother the proper way to externalize pain. Happy is Patrick Bateman in the making, Willy's dream brought up to date historically. While Willy does "it" for the family, Happy reflects the emptiness of the dream, its devolution to a narcissism that collapses back on itself in a generalized dissatisfaction with the system as a whole. Those above him build houses they can't enjoy once finished. Happy in turn has gotten all he ever wanted, only to experience a loneliness that seeks out women not for support but to make sex the means of expressing his discontent.

Talk has emptied both brothers. They are thus ready to enact together the illusion that has delivered their parents from a similar recognition. With a neat historical twist, Willy and Linda were able to sustain the dream by saying they were living for their children: the future now returns the gift by showing what it has done to them. Two texts meet in the net of the familial psychodrama. The sons together act out a dream of escape in which they repeat the father's founding act, with the mother unmentioned but far from absent. She occupies, in fact, the place of greatest presence, for both sons displace their aggression through a splitting mechanism that paralyzes them: the idealized mother who can't be criticized, and all other women who can only be treated with contempt.

Mom is the deepest subtext because she appears only to disappear. Her power controls, however, and its force is attested at scene's end, when Biff states the source of his greatest anger at his father's reveries: "Doesn't he know Mom can hear that?" (26). Just as Linda is the force keeping Willy on the treadmill, she is the dominant presence in her sons' inner worlds. The father in shame before the idealized mother is the ultimate court of judgment which haunts sons who have failed to live up to their mother's expectations.[9] Because that is so, all three men share an identical split that is fraught with a resentment that can only be displaced and denied. The idealized mother makes all other women whores. You express your anger toward her through your treatment of them. But the pattern only completes itself when you come back home in guilt, ready for a new round of debasement. When young, Biff and Happy shared the dominant male response. Having now split it, each tries to drive the split to its extreme. Happy as an American Giovanni ruins women. Biff no longer has "the taste for it" because he wants to get back to his "pal." Such is the equipment for living and for mature object-choice this mother has given her sons. Her formative work done, she can watch, from the superior position of grieving madonna, as they act out the familial disorders. Biff never has "an abrupt" conversation with her, and both sons always wither before her moralistic attacks, which grow in intensity as the play proceeds.

The First Regression: Denial, or Regression in the Service of the Ego

While everyone else in the family struggles to escape "responsibility" for the ties that bind, Willy, the willing and created scapegoat, takes it all fully upon himself. He does so in four great regressive episodes that dramatize the deep psychological structure of the play by situating the familial complex "inside his head." That structure is dialectical and lays bare, through progressive descent, the truth of Willy's psyche and the denials that will produce its self-unraveling.

In his solitude Willy is never alone. His regressions are really shared regressions, since in them Willy enacts the pull of the underlying lure that binds all members of the family to the shared disorder. He produces this text, of course, by attempting the opposite. Regression for Willy attempts to undo the family's condition and contradictions by recovering in memory the "place" where all once were and will again be "saved."

Though he will consistently violate it from within, Miller's use of expressionist dramaturgy engenders a complex process of self-revelation. As in Williams' *Glass Menagerie*, "the play is memory," because memory is the act whereby in the present one re-creates the past. Its function is always analytically revelatory in unintended ways. Memory is the flawed reconstruction in which the conflicts of the present reemerge as one tells a story about the past which is meant to deliver one from them. Memory flows from free associations which serve defenses and denials. We remember what we want to remember in order to banish what we don't want to face. And when this works, we achieve our end: nostalgia toward the past as denial of the present.

Analytic interpretation strives to disrupt this process by identifying the gaps, the blind spots, and especially the places where memory touches on a text that must be marginalized. Like other slips of the repressed, that text invariably contains the truth which one wants to deny, not simply about the past but also about its connection with the disorders of the present. This is the beauty of memory. It gives forth the truth which it is fabricated in order to deny.

For expressionist drama, this circumstance presents a most productive possibility. Willy flees far into the past yet remains haunted therein by all that has happened since. The best example of this in his first regression is the momentary eruption: the woman laughing is an intrusion that would be unintelligible were memory the recovery of a pristine script, but it is densely revelatory once we see memory as an effort to deny a truth that keeps surfacing, turning memory into a flight that brings forth, with renewed force, the conflicts one wants to deny.

Freud noted that neurotics seek the past because they were happy in the past. What he should have added—since it is the deeper, dramatistic insight psychoanalysis made possible—is that they remain in the past because they can't see how sick it was. Neurotic happiness derives from the blind return to the scenes of one's illness. What neurotic recollection memorializes is one's soul on ice, caught and represented in the scenes that froze and fixated it. This is also the interpretation which the neurotic must deny. Otherwise the ice ax will shatter those scenes, and one will reawaken to existence in rage. Once deprived of the illusions of lying nostalgia, one must confront truths about the past that put one on the rack. The only way to prevent that event is to make memory "regression in the service of the ego," so that one's consciousness, silenced by the dreamlike operations of memory, can perform a double trick on itself.

Such is Willy's quest. But it no longer works. Memory is now disrupted from within by a subtext that keeps surfacing, though he does his best to marginalize it. What he now learns, however, is that it is what remains— and what he brings back from each voyage of memory. Memory as flight thus activates the very conflict that will form the next stage of an inescapable and irreversible drama.

I will now show how this drama develops in Willy's first extended regression. Memory here flows in two great waves that are dialectically connected: the relationship to the sons and to Ben, the surrogate father and would-be mentor.

As Willy drifts into reverie, he returns to a scene of instruction in which he puffs up the fatherly role for reasons that are transparently narcissistic. Fathers tell their sons how to become real men in order to hide their own failure to achieve that status. The first lesson, naturally, is how to be a success with girls. The only thing that can top that is a round of "polishing the car," the paternal penis. The advice this Polonius gives his sons is loaded with tongs, its real function being to force them to become copies of his fantasized self-image. Or one son, that is. For Willy's allegiance, like his self-perception, must be split, with one son becoming the idealized object of projective identification and the other the object on whom Willy dumps the scorn he swallows every workday. Willy never relates to Happy except to belittle him, make invidious comparisons to his brother, and turn a deaf ear whenever the lapdog seeks attention through a desperate refrain, "I'm losing weight, Pop."

The center holds, however, because the three form a circle of cheerleaders pimping for the common pursuit, the American Dream. As in all good cheerleading, everything must be overstated, the real function of the act being to produce group solidification in a manic state. Only then can we dream of hanging a hammock in the yard, as prelude to the father's finer gift—a punching bag.

In such a situation, what can the son do to express his confused sense of a stolen identity except to tell the father he's become a thief? But he does this to no avail, for whenever the negative rears its head, it must be denied. Rather than show concern, Pop applauds the deed as further evidence of the unique Loman identity: Biff didn't steal; he "showed initiative." This is the gaiety of language: through it we transform reality.

The family can now wash itself in the balm of love through what is finally a homoerotic game. "Gee we were lonesome for you," Biff tells Willy (30). Pop then plays Odysseus to their Penelope with heroic tales of his travels, capped by the future spectacle of the boys traveling with Pop, carrying his "bags." To prove they're prepared for such an honor and to give himself something to celebrate in the interim, Willy asks for a report on Biff's progress: "What do they say about you in school, now that they made you captain?" (31). Primed, Biff tries to top Pop's lines by promising him a touchdown. The paternal unit is complete, full of itself, a perfect circle of narcissistic reflections. The most remarkable thing about it is the joy and relief its memory brings to Willy.

But the psyche always gives itself away. It is always disrupted anew within the scene of its deliverance, partly by its own design: memory must find within itself the disruptive, all the better to exorcise it. Enter Bernard, bearing the reality principle in its weakest form. Mockery here suffices, and Willy leads the attack, oblivious to the message it conveys: the father imprints his psyche on the sons by passing on his defects as mandatory attacks they must make on anyone who represents the qualities he lacks. The crowning bad advice is shared self-idealization through contrast with the despised other. After vanquishing Bernard and dismissing him from the stage, Willy belittles him as prologue to the representation of self and sons as Adonises destined for greatness in the world that is now invoked as capstone to the psychological meaning of the lesson. (We here note a split that we'll discuss later. Miller always needs to state a truth, then deflect it: from below, by putting it in Willy's mouth; and from above, by offering the audience Bernard and Charley as representatives whereby they sustain the belief that there are good, honest capitalists who make it because they're moral fathers raising moral sons. Willy is the exception, not the rule.) The business world, for Willy, is an utterly solipsistic game in which men try to exalt themselves by destroying one another. This is the interpellation needed to keep the system going: the power of its revelation here derives from the fact that the statement comes from one who is at the bottom of the ladder, not from Gordon Gekko. Biff provides the perfect choral complement: "Did you knock them dead, Pop?" (33).

Willy's memory of familial bliss can now add the missing element, with all three "boys" ready to present themselves for inspection. Enter Linda, bearing her stigmata, "a basket of washing" (33). So arrayed, she is prepared to join the chorus in further adulation of Biff's superiority over the other boys. Linda is so moved by Biff's phallic power, in fact, that she momentarily drops the mask and lets the Spartan mother shine through: "The way they obey him!" (34). Ripe in that motive, she performs her true maternal duty and inspects the husband, as to his success or failure, under the oedipal shadow that here falls across his ego.

A nice irony underscores the shift, undermining memory from within. Just as Willy never hears Happy, Linda is deaf to Willy's attempt to counter Biff's ascendence with a success story in which "I'm tellin' you, I was sellin' thousands and thousands." Linda: "Did you sell anything?" (34). Willy must lie to himself in order to regain her favor. And to advance that process, she resumes her proper role: that of the stern taskmaster who punctures the lies of "little boys" in order to reestablish the dominance of a reality principle which can only serve to confirm Willy's inadequacy. This Penelope offers no rest. Instead she presents a list of grievances, suitably externalized in appliances and bills. Rather than support, Willy gets *die Rechnung,* and the new bill: "Next week you'll do better" (36). Sparta was generous. You can't come back on your shield; you must take it up again.

To enforce that rule, Linda must teach denial by resuming the cheerleader role. Willy's doubts become the new ledger, checked off and banished by a series of vastly overstated clichés. For every doubt Willy expresses, Linda counters with an overstatement: in the process Willy becomes the most liked, most charming, most witty, and "handsomest" man in the world (37). To send Willy back out to battle, the fractured self must become a narcissistic mirror without blemish.

So "solidified" by another memory in which he was supposedly happy, Willy's reverie is troubled by a new surfacing of the unconscious. Willy knows that everything Linda says is a lie which rubs raw a need. That is why it is always associated with the painful memory of the woman from whom Willy received everything Linda denies by asserting. The other woman is not an intrusion but the activation within memory of a repressed subtext. In exorcising it, Willy descends a further step in his unconscious, revealing the commanding position Linda occupies in his inner world. Linda's action in the scene Willy is here remembering had and has two affects: in humiliating Willy she activates the secret. The other woman thus enters the drama as the displacement which secretes the truth of the scene. Willy's deepest need, the thing in the suitcase he's always trying to sell, is love. The only mirror in which that is reflected, however, is the cracked mirror of a shameful transgression. Willy's anger toward Linda is transformed into guilt, and he overcompensates by idealizing the object of his anger. The rationalization—"I was lonely"—merely holds judgment at bay, depriving Willy of any way to understand the motives for his "adultery." The mirror thereby becomes a laugh at his expense. The small pleasure Willy took is ground to pieces on Linda's treadmill. The stockings he gave in tribute to Eros become the very ones he now sees a saint mending. The erotic fetish becomes a sacrificial fetish that can't be disposed of. He grabs the stockings to throw them away, only to have Linda reclaim them and put them safely in her pocket.

When deep memory then gives way to surface memory, however, everything is inverted. Willy's unconscious moves along a chain of association in which guilt undoes awareness, leaving Willy instead with a new anger that must be projected onto a displaced representative of the self-image Linda's internal power has implanted in his psyche. Willy was a bad boy who must now punish the transgressive son. But in the memory to which he returns, Linda overplays her role. Since her need on the homefront is to attack whatever troubles her, she calms her fear by whipping up his anger. In going too far, however, she activates Willy's need to deny the shared defect of father and son: "There's nothing the matter with him!" (40). Denial thus carries the day, past and present, as Willy asserts two statements that have been completely undercut by the scene: Biff never actually stole anything, since he's "giving it back," and I never "told him anything but decent things" (41).

Thus ends the first half of Willy's first regression. It is punctuated by Happy's appearance, urging sleep. But like Macbeth, Willy can sleep no more, because everything he looks on awakens association which reactivate both his guilt and the need for a new and deeper regression. The suitable object is the kitchen floor and the one reflection that shines forth from its polished surface—Linda. "Everytime she waxes the floors she keels over" (41). One suspects both rituals are performed frequently. In that image, denial faces its impossibility and the need for a new journey into the past.

The familial scene in tatters, this voyage must be a purely ideological one. Reassurance must come from the Big Other, the internalized father. In the previous regression, Willy tried to reestablish his ego through the narcissistic mirror of his sons. He will now call forth the ego-ideal, seeking an explanation of what he must call an "accident." The flaw for Willy must be a mistake that can be externalized and then used as a blank check to cover all other contingencies. Hamartia, to paraphrase Pinter, must lie in "a kind of Alaska," because it must undo vast stretches of time. "Why didn't I go to Alaska with my brother Ben that time! . . . What a mistake! He begged me to go." For regression to work, Willy must be able to use this magical exit to wage an attack on the real causes of his distress. Only then can he assert the clichés that get everyone off the hook, because he will have successfully shifted his identity from the cracked narcissistic mirror to the ego-ideal. So ensconced, his defects can then become the son's burden—"You'll retire me"—while the father sits on the sidelines, succoring his privileged connection to the ego-ideal and its secrets. "I couldn't get past Yonkers today. Where are you guys, where are you? The woods are burning! I can't drive a car!" (41). Willy thus moves toward Ben through a shifting projection of aggression toward the present and flight into the ego-ideal, now identified as a sphinx bearing the secret Willy alone is privileged to hear.

In the intervening scene, as Willy's psyche heats up with this need, Charley enters to perform two of his three functions. He is the reentry of the reality principle, and he plays a fairly good fool, saying, "Cry to it nuncle," to his diminished Lear's need for denial. As reality principle, he is also the force that shifts Willy's memory into ideological hyperspace. (His third function will align him later with Miller in an irony neither escapes: as the good representative of the system, Charley has no drama, only a success story.) Charley's attitude to the past is pragmatically the correct one. Though it isn't easy, he knows that its pull is the primary cause of illusions. Willy can only respond to such advice by belittling its source, making Charley an object of disgust. With "reality" thus banished, he turns to hyperreality for cleansing.

In Ben, Willy seeks to confess his weakness and gain absolution by appealing to an ego-ideal. Unbeknownst to Willy, the chilling scene that ensues reveals that the ego-ideal is really the internal saboteur. In remembering Ben, Willy can't recognize Ben's desertion of everyone, his severance of all connections to the past, and his callous disregard of any concern for those mired in the present. Nor can he see that Ben offers no comfort but uses the question What's the secret? to rub superiority in everyone's face. That's the only activity Ben really has time for. Even Willy's pathetic plea to learn about his father and thereby salvage some story that will help him deny the truth about his parental models becomes an occasion for derision. "Father was a very great and a very wild-hearted man. . . . With one gadget he made more in a week than a man like you could in a lifetime" (49).

The same derision undercuts Willy's attempt to use his sons to win Ben's favor. The boxing match becomes a scene of betrayal and deliberate cruelty engineered by Ben so that he can give precisely the advice Willy refuses to heed: Never trust a man, boy. But so peremptory is Willy's need that in response he sends his sons off to steal in order to show Ben that they are worthy of the terms of respect Ben has just established.

By this point, however, things have gone too far, not for Willy but for Miller. Ben is indeed giving out the secret, but lest we apply it, Miller reintroduces Charley and his third function, to offer deflecting instructions. Charley tells Willy "the jails are full of fearless characters" like Willy's sons (50). But Ben speaks the greater truth: "And the stock exchange, friend!" (51). Willy and Ben have finally found a common theme: Applaud Biff's theft in order to mock Charley's ethics. Willy's aggression can now be safely and freely projected. Naturally he wants Ben to stay and dish out more of same, and his need is such that he takes the empty platitudes Ben offers ("you're being first-rate with your boys. . . . manly chaps") and the tautological proof he proffers ("William, when I walked into the jungle, I was seventeen. When I walked out I was twenty-one. And, by God, I was rich") as the veritable keys to the kingdom because they give him what he wants, the magical assurance that banishes everything disruptive in both the present and the past: "I was right! I was right! I was right!" (52). Thus endeth the first major regression, a remarkable example of Willy's ability to exploit regression for the sake of denial. He has indeed employed "regression in the service of the ego." His defenses work. They banish anxiety and restore his "place" in the world. The cost of such operations can be gauged by the ensuing scene.

What Does a Mother Want? Linda's Mousetrap

While Willy wanders alone in the night, Linda prepares the hit list of details she must discharge by shifting them onto Willy's shoulders. Her problem is to avoid blame for Willy's failure while getting her bets placed on a new horse. Her way is ethics, that is, the maternal guilt trip as the way of discounting complicity in Willy's psyche while activating the maternal superego in her new victim, the son. Approached in such a context, her famous speech about "attention" reveals a message quite different from its choral call to both the sons and the audience.

The topic of talk is the father's "exhaustion," but Linda's task is to make it the son's problem. She is taking leave of Willy while making "attention" to him imperative. Three deft operations carry the day: a guilt trip, the flight into pathos, and then a play of attributions. She hands each son his identity—a philandering bum and an ingrate. The cause of Willy's "problem" is then squarely laid on Biff's return. Linda claims that everything goes well until Biff writes announcing his return. Hope then gives way to anxiety, which turns into "hateful" behavior once Biff arrives. Linda's question, "Why?" thereby becomes Biff's burden.

The half-truth Linda tells conceals the deeper reality. Biff's return only exacerbates what is going on all the time in the house, because it activates memory of the "event" that supposedly caused the family's downfall and that Willy and Biff have been using ever since as a blank check to deny confronting the truth of their relationship. Once the excuse is brought back into play, it contains the dynamic that can unravel everything. For what really happened in Boston is that Willy and Biff saw each other's weakness, and they cannot now look at one another without seeing themselves in that cracked mirror. Biff's spite resembles that of those disappointed lovers who ruin their lives to rub their betrayal in the other's face. Willy's mockery, in turn, is an attempt to resume the position of "awe" befitting the loved one.

Biff's desire to unmask his father thus falls prey to a double-bind which his mother reinforces: he must deny his knowledge, and he must restore the fake. Linda plays the scene magnificently to transmit this burden. Willy has put his whole life into you. You've turned your back on him. He's suicidal. And it's up to you to save him. One thing is needed to complete the trap. Happy supplies it by noting that Biff's failure in the business world derived from his tendency to act out the wrong "aspect" of his father's identity. Biff's trouble is that he "never tried to please people." He whistled in the elevator (as did his dad) and deliberately got caught goofing off. With that defect now identified as the fault, Linda and Happy can work together to cleanse the home by scapegoating Biff. Biff is Willy's double, who fails because he aggressively uses the very behaviors Willy thinks are the keys to success. And as Biff knows, he does it all, in a sense, for his father. "Screw the business world. . . . They've laughed at Dad for years" (61).

In Delusional Chorus: The Family Neurosis Genuflects

Enter Willy at precisely the moment when this testimony of the son's "love" can only be heard as an insult. Everything is now in place for the exorcism needed to restore the collective illusion so that everyone can get some sleep. That process will, however, require a complex drama. The deepest conflict—the look of the other as the dynamic that can tear the familial illusion to shreds—must be made present so that it can be denied. When Willy enters, he sees in Biff what Biff sees in him, not knowing that Biff is ready to make amends.

But Biff and Willy are at the point married couples get to when there is enough blood under the bridge that even the most innocent comment drips with "insult." The deferred subtext of the relationship is now fully present, constantly externalized. The only way to restore things when you reach this point is to shift to an external source of shared frustration which can become a scene of shared illusion. By that act, "insult" is relocated outside the home, and deliverance is provided by finding favor from the same external agency. Such is Bill Oliver's function. Biff invokes the Big Other through the Big Lie. "He [Oliver] always said he'd stake me" (62). The symbolic order thereby reveals the truth of the family. That truth is that they avoid destroying one another by getting on their collective knees before what is destroying them.

The truth of the grand illusion is that it keeps the family from knowing the truth about itself by binding its members together in a single group psychology, united by hatred disguised as mutual reinforcement. That is why the possibility Oliver introduces brings not peace but mania, the need for overstatement, as Willy and Happy play out their version of Lear's desire for one hundred knights, topping each grandiose idea with one more fantastic. It is worth noting that this is the first time Willy hears anything Happy says. A crack-pated delusion thereby becomes "a one-million-dollar idea" (63). If Biff is to save Willy, no small measures will do, because Willy's need has grown in proportion to his sense of defeat. Any attempt Biff makes to play Cordelia can only be viewed as an insult. Yet Biff must be set upon his task reminded of his previous failures: "You're counting your chickens," "Don't pick up anything you drop," "Wear this," and so on. It's Willy's game, and he exploits it to set his house in order, reasserting his role as the son's instructor and also using the occasion to restore his position with the mother. Whenever Linda interrupts, even to applaud, Willy lashes out, because he is simultaneously licking three wounds here: reclaiming his position as head of the family, putting the woman in her place, and striking at the perceived shift in her favors.

To work, the illusion must be shared by the entire family. Willy will now direct that chorus and assign each member its voice in order to reserve what he previously experienced as a dispossession of authority. He remains angry at everyone, especially himself, and misses no chance to project the wound festering in his unconscious. In goading Biff he utters in mockery the ques-

tion he harbors as feared truth: "What're you, takin' over this house?" (65).
But he collapses before the obvious answer and quickly retires.

Threatened with that spectacle, Linda must fill the breach and restore the
dream through the utterly inappropriate act of attacking Biff for defending
her. She knows the litany hasn't worked yet: for symbolic reassurance the
entire family must join in one hosanna which she invokes in perhaps the
single most preposterous line in the play. "Just say good night. It takes so
little to make him happy" (65). The "coda," the good night "kiss," must
then repeat everything in just the right way to solidify the operation. Alone,
Biff and Happy must go through their roles one more time so that Biff can
show he is now as delusional as his brother, ready to give Dad a "whirl" and
send him off to dreamland with the fantasy of what Biff will do to Oliver
tomorrow.

Awaiting that moment, Willy and Linda touch upon their sores. Perhaps
the nicest thing one can say about Linda is that she's an anal obessional who
can't rest until everything in the house, her externalized womb, is in spotless
working order. But the shower drips, and that specter reintroduces Willy's
anger and Linda's fear: Will Oliver remember Biff? The question now is
raised, however, only to be dismissed. Memory is the privileged space of the
shared illusion, and Willy is now ready to use it as the prologue to his sleep.
Enter Cordelia prepared to tell Lear what he wants to hear and then to
receive superfluous instruction without this time losing control of the role.
Lest Linda gear up for a new round of mania, Willy halts things on the
proper note: "You got a greatness in you, Biff" (67). Happy adds his voice
with this howler, "I'm gonna get married, Mom." The chorus of delusion is
complete. Linda can now sing Willy off to sleep, where he will dream of
Hercules/Loman striding forth onto an Ebbets Field transplanted to Wall
Street. All losses will be restored and sorrows ended—if everyone can only
stop talking. Willy to Linda: "Don't talk any more" (68).

Biff alone is left below, with the repressed truth a object in his hand. The
mother and father are at peace, because they have shifted the father's possible suicide and his aggression toward the family onto the son. Biff is finally
home again, the scapegoat in waiting, never more at odds with himself.

Act II: Inside the Head

Rise and Shine—Let's Get Humping

Willy "slept like a dead one" because the burden was shifted to other
shoulders. For the first time in memory, Willy can sleep in and can rise to

play the inadvertent clown: "Wonderful coffee. Meal in itself" (71). Linda can happily busy herself with her wifely tasks because the illusion has already gone forth. Willy and Linda are here momentarily without conflict, because he has already played the Spartan woman to Biff. The reprieve for both characters is, however, necessarily brief. Linda must resume her Spartan role and place new bets on the old warhorse, because with consciousness her obsession with facts returns, now pinned to the precise amount of money Willy must get from Howard. Willy gladly meets her halfway, because a happy consciousness for him necessarily projects an unreal future.

Their mutual need then transforms the scene. From bliss, Willy's anger erupts anew. He sees that Linda's dream is prior to his and defeats both of them. The mortgage that preoccupies Linda will be cancelled just about the time the house and everything in it break down. Willy knows this. He sees what Linda needs to deny: that there is a defect built into the system. He is, in fact, one of the parts that will break down right on time, and with his collapse everything solid in their phantom "substance " will be reclaimed. Linda counters with her characteristic operation: just as life is a leave-taking, the house has "served its purpose" (74). The line is no sooner uttered than it takes on claws.

Shared relief from the anxiety resurfacing requires reinvesting their capital in the illusion that now bears the name Biff. Only now he'll have to marry and have children. The ante always goes up—and with it the reactivation of Willy's own quest. Two knights will now go forth, with Linda as both Spartan chorus ("That's the spirit") and suffering superego about to be redeemed: "It's changing, Willy, I can feel it changing!" (74). Willy needs but a final gentle reminder of his "defects," and he's off.

Linda, left behind, responds in complex self-revelation to a most interesting telephone call from Biff. The Spartan woman here shows her courage as a posture designed to deny her cowardice. Once she found the rubber pipe missing from the gas heater in the cellar, she could claim that she intended to remove it this very day, because its absence proved to her that Willy was back in shape. This belief informed her behavior in the previous scene. Biff tells the truth, and her fear returns. To deny reality, she claims that Willy did in effect remove the pipe: "This morning he left in such high spirits." She then hedges her bets by putting her money on both men. Any remaining anxiety about Willy is thereby exorcised by reminding Biff of his "moral" duty: "You'll save his life." A last twitch of the obsession—"You got your comb?"—and she is free of both men (76). We won't see her again until they return from their respective agons. One suspects she has a good day.

The Split Self: Father and Son

At the end of Act I, the family was put on Biff's shoulders. Miller must now put it back on Willy's. Two subtexts which he can't dramatize but needs for ideological reasons are thereby served. Willy's defeat is paralleled offstage in act II by Biff's, but Biff's ends in recognition and renewal, while his father's ends in death. If the family tries to protect the father by setting up the son, Miller turns the tables, because he knows that hatred of the father is the salvation of the son. Only he won't let us see that. Instead he will give us, at the end of the act, a feast of humanistic commonplaces. To find them plausible, however, one must be prepared to violate nearly everything we know about Biff's character and, more important, about how character is represented in this play. Having practiced a consistent and brilliant naturalism— "They behave like apes"—Miller can only redeem Biff by a sleight of hand. Biff's change is believable not as a process that could be dramatized but as a deus ex machina that must be embraced. We will return to this issue when we discuss the great recognition scene between father and son, but I note it here to underscore the contradiction in this play between ideology and dramatic process. One way to discover a playwright's ideological subtext is by paying careful attention to what he can't earn dramatically through a believable representation that follows the "theory" of character he has established in the play. Blind assertion of themes in the face of that condition invariably tips us off to a playwright's needs and to the dark intent he harbors and must deny. In *Death of a Salesman* this connection reveals the play as a massive act of aggression toward the father, capped by the abstractions into which Miller must flee in order to protect himself from that knowledge.

Willy's anger is the heart of the play. In it his unconscious vents itself on targets that appear diffuse and displaced but are really connected. Those connections, which he expresses but will never comprehend, form the nuclear core "inside his head," revealing its meltdown as the explosion which reveals how everything outside it—the American Dream, capitalism, the family—forms part of a vast psychodrama here "in a single man contained."[10] Willy's unconscious drives the play because it is out of control. Unable any longer to repress, it must instead totalize itself. Biff's unconscious, in contrast, surfaces only to be immediately discharged.

Inside the Suitcase: The Business World

Willy passes, as he must, from fantasy to reality, and from there to a renewed drama of regression that now will find no relief. But what is reality? In some ways, act II might be regarded as an education in the reality principle and the various ways agents either deny it or use magical thinking to transcend its clutches. To ask what reality is, the true beginning is to ask where it is, as, for example, in this "businesslike" scene in which one father's familial fantasy meets another's, with the reality principle revealed as the power to bind and to humiliate. Howard, the proud father who succeeds, inflicts his family on the father who failed. And everything Howard does in this scene is vicious, whether intended or not, because he has already decided he is going to fire Willy. He just doesn't know that this is the day.

Willy tries to appeal to the original father—another representative of the Big Other—through the son. In fact, most of Willy's dialogue is aimed at that absent presence who will be reminded of "promises" by a "strong" agent who has finally come to a "decision." If Willy sacrifices every thread of his dignity in act II, he also makes a last-ditch effort to assert each of its collapsing "foundations." Through the process, virtually every illusion we have about the moral bases of character is brutally destroyed. Willy begins with the illusion of choice in a world in which deliberation and decision address a rational other. His attempt throughout act II is to "sell himself." The suitcase is now center stage, its contents brought forth as so many props in a dissolving game. Decision implies power. But it passes rather quickly, when checked, to asking for a "favor," as Willy moves from the assertion of his personal worth to the invocation of a shared identity. Willy tries to sell himself to Howard by selling both an ancestral presence, Dave Singleman. Because that effort makes no impression on Howard, we see that Willy's real audience is himself, the object of the sale being to convince himself he didn't make the wrong "choice." In the process, the terms of that choice surface, becoming ripe for a subsequent regression. Willy was sold on becoming a salesman when he saw Dave Singleman gain the greatest commodity: he was loved.

That image rubs raw the contrast that erupts in an outburst of rage. Singleman was loved, but Willy knows that he is caught in a scene of humiliation, made more maddening by the fact that Howard, a master at policing the rules of this language game, won't let him call it that. The deepest reason why Willy can't sustain his anger, however, is that he's finally found both its proper object and a new motive for self-abasement. However diminished, Howard is in the position of the Big Other. Rage must vanish, lest Willy threaten two illusions that are crumbling: that the Big Other is forgiving and that Willy can save his diminishing self by an appeal to pity, after which he can regain the dignity slipping away by invoking past accomplishments ("Your father—in 1928 I had a big year. I averaged a hundred and seventy dollars a week in commissions" [82]). That claim, addressed to the Father, is rejected by the son, who exits to compose his role for the denouement. Alone, Willy turns in imaginary conversation to the Father, only to confront the Machine. The recorder answers him in babble and baby talk which he is unable to shut off.

A language of similar impenetrability greets him on Howard's return. Howard abruptly fires him, without letting either use that word. The language of the Father that seduced Willy's imagination here reveals its truth: language is used to manipulate, to pervert meaning, and to disguise what is happening from all concerned. The last thread of the dignity Willy postured at the beginning of the scene, in saying he has decided not to travel anymore, has now vanished, and we get his pathetic attempt to save himself by undoing himself: "I'll go to Boston . . ." (83). Howard, like Ben, has little time for such displays. He needs the office in minutes, the samples in a week, and he reduces all claims to the one thing that really matters: "Pull yourself together . . . there's people outside" (84). Image is everything—a truth known in claws long before André Agassi. Faced with the growing distance between the terms he has always wanted to bridge—the image and the real—Willy is reduced to a howl of pain and impotent rage.

The Second Regression

In crying out, Willy regresses to the memory of a figure and scene which he thinks will deliver him from the present but actually mirrors it. "Oh, Ben . . ." (84). Regression now has for Willy two purposes: to sell himself to Ben and to convince both that he once possessed—on the greatest day of his life—what he is so rapidly losing forever. The irony is that the past into which Willy flees presents the scene in which he originally suffered, without realizing it, the experience that has just been replicated.

In his second extended voyage of memory, Willy tries to satisfy his two great presences in order to overcome self-doubt. "Nothing's working out"— such is the problem he posed then and now. But Ben can only respond by inflating himself and invoking the big dream, Alaska. Linda counters by offering a different scene but an equally grandiose goal. Willy accepts the latter only because he thinks he can achieve a truly noble victory by realizing everything Ben represents on Linda's turf. This is Linda's dream also, and significantly it is she, not Willy, who argues that the "values" characterizing her husband's personality are precisely the tickets to success: "You're well liked, and the boys love you, and someday . . . Wagner told him . . ." (85). When Ben punctures that illusion with the harsh truth—the only facts are those you can lay your hand on—Willy, torn, agrees, "That's true, Linda, there's nothing" (86), only to have her respond by introducing the example of

Dave Singleman to "convince" both Ben and Willy that the Big Other also strides across Willy's landscape.

As Ben, unimpressed, begins his exit, Willy struggles to fill the breach and mediate his internal division in a long and important speech which is really a monologue. In it, doing is replaced by "who you know," which is itself somehow determined by "being liked." And because success must be guaranteed now, quickly, before Ben vanishes—and not just in the future—the scene of ratification is transferred to Biff's transfiguration in Ebbets Field, with Biff's audience already magically transformed into doors opening in business offices, falling before the conquering hero "like timber" in Alaska. "We'll do it here, Ben!" (86–87). Biff's identity has been determined. If the fathers slay the sons, Willy has just put his Isaac under the knife in order to take out an insurance policy to prevent recognition of his own failure. Because regression hides the truth it reveals, Willy recrosses the rainbow bridge into Valhalla and the happiest day of his life. That day must banish all doubts through a massive audience approval in which the familial origin triumphant is already one with the inevitability of its end. That guarantee is Willy's deepest drive. As he here repeats it in nostalgia, we are positioned, by the previous scene, to see it as the source of his self-paralysis. The assurance Willy demands prevents any entry of experience into the charmed circle. Ebbets Field becomes more than a field of dreams: it becomes the privileged site of their incarnation, the guarantee of their Parousia. Willy's manic need to deny Ben's reality principle, and his latent aggression toward it, are projected onto the scene, transforming it from the earthly to the heavenly. Pure celebration commences to cheerlead the coming deed, with father and son wedded in Biff's promised touchdown. Charley's gentle attempt to play Horatio to Willy's mania serves only to enhance Willy's coming pleasure.

But this is precisely the moment when regressive memory gives way abruptly to reality, and a representation of the circumstance that so horrified Arthur Miller that he had to write a play about it: the spectacle of a man talking out loud in public.[11] What was sport then now becomes violent aggression, as Willy rails out loud at Charley while sitting in his outer office waiting to see him. In that rage the restorative purpose regression was supposed to serve is undone. Regression has begun to unloosen the deeper texts it is meant to exorcise. This will henceforth be its through-line.

A Kinder, Gentler Reality Principle

The previous scene with Howard was too disruptive for Miller because it points to political conclusions his drama must deflect. Enter Bernard and

Charley, who parallel that scene with a kinder, gentler reality principle, which restores to capitalism its humanistic illusions. Charley and Bernard are good people, and because that is so they have succeeded beyond exception without losing a humanity they can therefore extend to the fallen. We have another proud father presenting his son to a failed father-son team. The narcissistic proof is also present. It is to him, in fact, that Willy addresses the question that will become his mousetrap. Bernard, like his father, wants to let Willy off the hook on which Howard enjoyed impaling him. He won't crow about where he's going, and he shows genuine solicitude. It is Willy who drives the scene to his own undoing by his compulsive need to lie about Biff's future and his even greater, countervailing need to ask the question he must ask whenever he scents the Big Other: "What's the secret?" (92). Willy's question reactivates Bernard's: What happened to my friend Biff that summer when I saw on his return from Boston that he had "given up his life"? (94).

Bernard's previous question, "Do you want to talk candidly?" (92), introduces the fact—Biff's failure at math—which brings back, as in Miller's mentor Ibsen, the entire past as the haunting complex that has returned, its hour come round at last. Willy tries to escape through what he hopes is a rhetorical question: Was it my fault? . . . maybe I did something, only to bring Bernard to the real question and its true source: what happened in Boston is the key to the secret. Bernard inadvertently plays the agent of the unconscious in this scene. Its power to fashion all other questions into a single noose is here revealed: "I just bring it up because you asked me" (94). The mousetrap has sprung. Willy's unconscious has been trapped by his own devices. When one asks a question of the sphinx, one had better be prepared for an answer that will open the Crypt.

Enter Charley, who engages in some justifiable and long-overdue crowing, which unlike Howard's is hardly vicious once we note that this is the first time he has told Willy about Bernard's accomplishments. Charlie's goal remains what it's always been—to offer Willy a reality principle. But for Willy, reality can only be received as an insult. He can, in fact, only tell Charley he was fired within a context that reasserts the absurd claim that he is closer to the source of power than Charley is. "I named him. I named him Howard" (97). When Charley counters with the truth about every successful businessman from Howard to J. P. Morgan, Willy can only see jealousy, revenge, and unconscious envy lurking in Charley's solicitude.

That's all he can see because these are the actual emotions he has always projected onto all relations. They form the smirk beneath the smile that would emerge had Willy attained his dream. That subtext remains barred, though its presence underlies the grand idea Willy here first hits upon: that through suicide he can magically triumph over all his foes. Thus purged of anger, Willy can drift back into the ozone of a future fantastical tennis match between the two families. The real burden has once again been transferred to Biff. Willy proceeds to the Chop House, where only fantastic success can prevent a deeper regression, now primed.

The Chop House: Guess Who's Coming to Dinner?

We begin with Happy. If there is sympathy for this character, it will dry up by the end of the scene. That said, we can note the ideological purpose Miller's handling of Happy serves. If Biff is to "save" Willy, all the aggression and "spite" must be located in the other son. As prelude to that movement, Happy enacts, in miniature and as prelude to the coming scene, Willy's true relationship to Biff. Biff counters that destructive force by asserting the claims of the three scenes of "recognition" that have structured his day. (He will reserve the third recognition until he finds himself later, at home, truly in need of it.)

The first recognition arose out of the long act of memory and introspection that supposedly marked Biff's day. Sitting alone waiting for Oliver, Biff found himself haunted by the look of the Big Other, utterly devoid of the slightest recognition of him. Trembling before the specter his father refuses to face, Biff made a forced entry into the inner sanctum, where, like his father, he had to try, by theft, to assert the recognition he had been denied. The theft of recognition and identity is now, however, recognized as such. Biff sees that he has no identity. He therefore becomes what he's always been—the running man who will now, however, manage to end that habit with an even deeper recognition which will become the principle of his heroic agency in the present scene. By acting it out he will create a mousetrap that will bring the men in the family to a collective and restorative truth. Resolve enacted as plot will put an end to what Biff knows will "go on forever" without the violence of that process. Happy counters with the alternative that has always forestalled that day; as Linda said earlier, it really takes so little to make Willy happy. Lying to Pop externalizes an indefinite future that will eventually produce forgetting, for Willy "is never so happy as when he's looking forward to something" (105). As it happens, Happy's motive will win out, but only because Biff's attempt to stage a scene of truth will collapse under internal pressures that Biff, who's already had a few drinks, is trying hard to deny.

But drink doesn't work up courage and loosen defenses; it fixates desire and limits awareness. Biff's agency is already tottering through two exclusions. One he carries in his pocket; the other is occupied by the one family member who is not coming to dinner. As he sets his mousetrap, it already starts to snap shut on him. The recognition Biff refuses lies in the pen he conceals in his pocket. He will deliver it only when the true setting for confronting theft as aggression is present later—in the home. There the repressed truth he hopes to avoid through this scene will come back upon him, forcing him to undertake a far more significant attempt to tell the truth. This scene is not a trial run for that one but an attempt to defer it. Biff has always been an expert at acting out. He has now, however, discovered that acting out contains the possibility of self-discovery. The question that remains, however, is this: When does that attempt constitute displacement, resistance, and the attempt to avoid another scene which its failure will force one to confront? This is the dramatistic logic that traps Biff in his own mousetrap. The recognition he wants to withhold in this scene leads him inevitably to the scene where it must be played out.

In fact, Biff's only hope lies in a contradiction: the attempt to play therapist as Joe Friday. Biff's faith is that if they can just stick to the facts and narrate them in the correct story, conflicts will vanish. But any attempt to create narrative from facts cannot fail to reintroduce the grand Loman design. The Lomans have never been anything but a family telling stories to one another, interpreting facts to suit their design. Moreover, whenever facts touch on the past, they rub raw the doubts that Willy can no longer expel. "Tragic irony" and ludicrous comedy thus join in his first reply to Biff: "I'm not interested in stories about the past." To defend against them, Willy will tell a story about the present sure to vanquish the past: "I was fired today." Fact has become rhetorical occasion. Through it Willy says this: How can you, my son, who only a short time ago became the agent of my deliverance, inflict truth on me, in light of recent events? Biff receives the full message. Willy then caps it by introducing the presence sure to unravel Biff's mousetrap. The true object of stories is Mom: "I'm looking for a little good news to tell your mother, because the woman has waited and the woman has suffered. The gist of it is that I haven't got a story left in my head. . . . Now what've you got to say to me?" (107). Nothing will come of nothing, speak again.

Willy's impossible demand gives Biff the mission he deserves. If he is going to tell a true story, he must tell it to the full complex that has generated the disorder he wants to resolve: that audience is composed of the defeated father and the waiting, wailing woman. Because he can't face that task, his attempt to tell his story is shattered from the beginning by his vulnerability to the demands of another story. As the scene builds and unravels, we thus get a truly fantastic process in which Biff tries to get his story on the table, only to face constant interruptions that cue it by asserting the a priori guarantees that must inform it. In effect, Willy tries to tell the story before Biff can tell it, thereby exorcising whatever partial truth could come of it.

Psychological censorship depends on an ideology of narrative form with precise rules of telling. There are, for Willy, only two kinds of stories: those in which the son fulfills his father's dreams and those in which he confesses the spite that lets the father off the hook. Either story is preinterpreted by attributions to which everything in the son's character and behavior can be reduced. Sons are either positive extensions of the father or ingrate bastards. And storytelling is the act whereby the son reveals his identity to the one authoritative audience, the Father.

Neither Willy nor Biff know it, but they are trapped in the logic of the double-bind. That system holds because its overriding injunction is that the bind cannot be transcended. The schizophrenia of the one placed in the victim position is the fulfillment of the law. Biff's effort collapses because he's in that impossible slot.

The bind pushed to excess has a saving grace, however: it turns back on the father. The more Willy insists on the happy story, the more he rubs raw within his psyche the feared story from which he seeks deliverance. All facts thus totter, because externalization has become fraught with associations to everything he has experienced this day. The objects have started to turn back on the subjects. They are indeed symbolic. That's why we move from math to penmanship and then, by way of Boston, to the return with the pen of the entire psychological complex.

Externalizations no longer work because they now bear the full weight of their subtext. Flunking math equals cheating, stealing answers, getting free points. As these associations emerge, the scene becomes a virtual phantasmagoria of shifting positions. They erupt in Willy's mind, but they implicate the entire family. Significantly, Biff's failure at math is dramatized inside Willy's head, yet the actual scene remembered takes place between Biff and Linda. It is she who sends Biff off to Boston. The family is caught in a circle that would forever revolve back upon itself were it not for the pen, which is the call from an unconscious neither character has faced. They know, however, that its privileged site and supposed origin bear the name Boston.

Biff's big recognition withers because it has just been leveled by the chain of associations math introduces, bringing back all he has refused to remember in a day supposedly given over to memory. Being as unable as his father to face the past, he now fabricates stories about Bill Oliver to get both of them out of the mousetrap. He can only halt a drama spinning out of his control by reverting to the mechanism he told Happy he would not use because then "it'll go on forever" (105). But the pen is in his hand, and with it returns the repressed memory of earlier thefts and their tie to the original purpose behind his trip to Boston—to get his dad to perfom a theft for him. His unconscious has reenacted itself, bringing him back to his primal scene.

Happy's mechanism will no longer work, however, because memory has also finally rubbed raw Willy's unconscious. He can only hear spite when Biff, finding himself on the hook ("How'd [Oliver] react to the Florida idea?" [108]), tries to extricate himself from it, only to have his father reintroduce the fact, Biff's latest theft, that makes any return to Oliver impossible. The laugh that erupts from women present and past is now the mockery Willy can't escape. Biff's attempt to steal it by taking the blame— "I'm no good, can't you see what I am?"—is of no avail because the scene has now shifted to its true site, Willy's unconscious: "Someone's at the door, Willy!" (113). Willy was once, in Boston, awakened from sleep by a knock at the door. Try as he might to avoid it, his son has given him another wake-up call. It must be answered alone.

Biff takes his leave in a desperate cop-out—the famous "prince" speech— which really signifies little more than his attempt to shift the burden to Happy. His cry "help me, I can't bear to look at his face!" is more of the same (115). For Biff can't escape the question that he now knows must be brought home. When he there tells the rest of his story, he will claim there's no more spite in it. But that claim raises an unsettling question: Is spite the real motive that has directed the scene just ended? The answer, as Biff now knows, is yes and no, as with all attempts to resolve a problem without facing it. All that Biff's grand project has left him with are conflicts that can no longer be denied and the necessity for a real recognition scene. A double desertion leaves the father likewise alone, in the toilet, with the full burden of the repressed.

In the Toilet: The Third Regression

Memory for Willy is now the scene of the repressed. The suppressed memory he used other memories to keep at bay now comes forth. Doing so, it estab- lished a dialectical connection that transforms regression from its former use, as escape, to its true nobility—the irreversible process that takes the psyche to its Crypts and leaves it there, sans defenses. Boston created the need for the earlier flights of memory Willy undertook to reinforce defenses against it. But the truth that was already present as their subtext now comes forth to drive nails into the coffin those memories have become. Time thereby takes what Walter Benjamin termed "a tiger's leap into the past." Dialectically, Boston emerges as an event that didn't come later to disrupt a prior presence, but the disorder that was already at work there.

The complexity of such a psychological connection prevents the easy interpretations to which this scene has been subjected. Boston functions for many audiences as it functions for Biff and Willy: the reduction of a complex drama to the conditions of a soap opera in which a vast displacement can be used to suppress complex connections. Those who criticize the scene for deflecting the Marxist implications of the drama and those who base their readings of the play upon a reductive psychoanalytic use of the true cause share the ironic fate of missing the connection which joins Marxism and psychoanalysis in an understanding that moves both positions toward a concrete complexity. Just as Biff and Willy deflect everything onto Boston, Miller offers his audience ample opportunity to use it as a deus ex machina. What gets lost in the process is Boston's connection not only with what went before, but with the scene that follows. For the Boston scene, like every other scene, contains a complex subtext which advances rather than arrests a drama in which everything must finally be brought back home to reveal the full horror of its origin. We will now produce that reading.

The scene is full of rather obvious dramatic ironies: the woman won't stop laughing, yet all Willy now hears is the knocking at the gate in Macbeth. Regression now opens the psyche to nothing but self-torture. Though Willy understands little of what happened in Boston, he knows he can't forget it, nor can he transform it—as in other flights into the past—by reworking the materials to restore his illusions.

Miller always writes with an eye to Aristotle. This scene constitutes the reversal, to be followed in the next scene by the recognition. In both cases, however, the correct understanding of how those structures operate go well beyond the characters and, one suspects, the playwright. The power of the scene lies in staging the subtext of what has always been the true relationship between father and son. And that truth is not one of a love they can never quite constitute—though Miller here and in the scene that follows gives way to this humanist sentiment—but of a vampirism in which they live off one another, consistently shifting the burden of both guilt and denial onto the other's shoulders.

In doing so, the scene cuts two ways, exposing both protagonists. It is the "origin" of Biff's spite and of Willy's inability to receive any other communication from his son. But it is also a striking revelation that these are the terms that have always defined their relationship. That truth, however, is staged only to be denied. The subsequent search for reconciliation between father and son is really, as it is in most cases, and contra writers as different as James Joyce and Robert Anderson, an attempt to deny the truth here represented. Nostalgia over lost love and endless search for reconciliation is the mask that covers the real pain: the recognition by father and son that they never loved each other. The motive behind the quest for reconciliation is the desire to find some way to deny the truth. As a result, homecoming can only be, as we'll see shortly, the desperate search for the pseudocommunication that will get both off the hook.

Boston holds the key to that need. An infantile Biff enters, asking forgiveness to an apparent ego-ideal—"I let you down" (117)—only to shift the burden by appealing to the flaw in the father as both the cause and the remedy of the situation. His real statement in effect is You let me down. The aggressive motive behind Biff's failure thereby becomes the weapon he uses against the real target of his repeated failures. Biff failed at math because he acts like his father, studiously following the Loman way to success. The father must now "sell" himself and that mode of behavior to the math teacher to extricate father and son from the bind Biff has deliberately created. In calling on the force of his father's personality to save the day, Biff activates the irresistible attraction of the flaw—its power to cancel present reality. Once that motive clicks, their shared identity is restored, and when that happens, there's always time for a joke at the expense of the other. Biff mimics the math teacher's lisp. Desperate to get Biff out of the room, Willy nonetheless finds the opportunity to share a manly laugh irresistible. Hamartia is here a peremptory principle of behavior. A third laugh joins theirs— that of the Stone Guest.

With the truth now out in the open, Willy reverts to the exit the Lomans have always used—the lie—in what becomes a pretty good imitation, before the fact, of Nixon's logic of the limited hangout. But parental power here expresses itself in the oldest commandment: Biff is forbidden to see the father naked. That becomes the true crime, activating an aggression in which the father would rather destroy the son than allow him to know the truth. Willy here reveals what has always been the core of his relationship to his son: loving solicitude begets the attributions that prop up the father's self-esteem while assuring that his defects will become the son's identity. Thus the lie failed becomes a command which passes to an insult, then a long speech in which Biff is belittled as a child who doesn't understand the world but must learn to follow orders. The great reprieve that tugs at every audience's heart follows:

Biff,   *his weeping breaking from him:* Dad . . .
Willy,   *infected by it:* Oh, my boy . . .
Biff: Dad . . .
Willy: She's nothing to me, Biff. I was lonely, I was terribly lonely. (120)

Such sentiment can only momentarily blind us to the truth. The shared illusion has been shattered: the repressed now assumes the form that will enable it henceforth to structure the relationship. Spite clicks it. Tapping its power, Biff reverses his opening appeal: the math teacher wouldn't listen to a fake like Willy, and his son isn't going to the University of Virginia. The time is now ripe for Mom's presence, since Biff can use it to attribute to his father the lasting identity that supposedly flows from adultery. Willy is a "liar" and a "fake" (121). That may be so, but in the abiding relationship that concerns him, Biff is the betrayed beloved and Mom the symbolic weapon. What Biff can't forgive his father for is a violation which finds him in the position of the woman seduced and abandoned. The homoeroticism characterizing the early scenes between father and son here presents the bill. When Dad was on the road, Biff waited like a lonely spouse for his father's return, bearing the gift of an eternal allegiance. That bond betrayed, jealous rage erupts. Willy can only respond with the excuse that has extricated many an adulterous spouse: It means nothing . . . I was lonely. But Biff is an unforgiving spouse. Mom is also betrayed, of course, but that topic can't be addressed with more than icy piety, lest both characters confront their actions as shared aggression toward that source.

Unlike the previous regressions, this one begets a truth that cannot be displaced and denied. Regression has finally delivered Willy's psyche to itself—its groundlessness, fragmentation, loss of identity. To escape that condition, a new round of magical thinking has already arisen, but it can no longer find its abode in the family. Willy hurries off to "get some seeds" because "nothing's planted. I don't have a thing in the ground" (122).

Staging the Truth: The Family Neurosis Come Home to Roost

Those who have critized Miller for focusing all his works on the family do him wrong, as do those who praise him for his humanistic service to this enclave. Everything finally comes back to the family. But when it does, the truth of the institution emerges.

Linda, the commanding presence, now assumes her true role: she plays the maternal superego to her sons' ids, attributing to them the moral identity that they deserve and that she needs for her own ends. The missing link—the ego—is out back doing "regression in the service . . ." as preparation for his return to what has become the scene of many crimes.

While the superego sets the terms of the ensuing drama, in demanding no more lies, she also begets a pregnant irony which becomes immediately apparent, as she sheds her identity as housewife-maid to assume the voice that sets her above everyone through the claim that she alone loves Willy and sees his torment. But Mom's game isn't working anymore. Biff is on to it. The traditional response of debasement followed by the resolve I'll be a good boy from now on, Mom, is now subjected to movement toward truth that tears at everyone's masks. The first object of Biff's wrath is, in fact, his mother. He tops her criticisms with a litany of his failures, only to throw the whole thing in her face: "How do you like that, heh?" (124). And like George in Albee's *Who's Afraid of Virginia Woolf?* he has one more game to play. The truth suppressed in the Chop House will now be staged in its proper form, told to the Boss, in the mother's presence.

The Fourth Regression: The Ecstasy in the Garden

The regressing ego in the garden is renewing himself for a far different drama. The effort to add up to something devolves to a purely monetary principle without losing its psychological force. Unless Willy can sell himself to the Big Other and also save himself by sacrificing himself for his other internal presence, Linda, he will indeed amount to nothing. It's worth noting that, though it shifts, Linda, not Biff, is the first object of Willy's "remarkable proposition." The cash nexus clicks in as the only term that can compel the two recognitions Willy needs. But selling the proposition must also exorcise the charge of cowardice that has always been the linguistic game par excellence that the Big Other uses to force its subjects to bring their character and their moral worth to the capitalist arena for judgment. The only real men are businessmen, and that is the only stage on which a man can prove whether he has what it takes. Willy's fantasy is that he can in death triumph by getting the Big Other to interpret his deed by the rules of the game. "Let me think about it," says Ben. "Remarkable proposition" (127).

But the term *cowardice* has a broader resonance and ruptures this charmed circle. Cowardice is also the term of Biff's judgment and his spite. Biff must therefore become the new subject of appeal whose approval of Willy's deed will cancel all debts and restore the deeper guarantee Willy is still after—love. The fantasy that bears this burden is the light fantastic: Willy imagines the size of his funeral as the spectacle that will undo spite.

But he knows it may also beget it. This is the dark and magical side of Willy's "plan" and of most suicides. The suicide is a murder, its purpose being to get the ones who will see that they caused it. Biff is indeed "in for a shock" (126), because when that implication clicks, he will have no choice but to carry on his father's mission. The judgment of cowardice will be magically transformed into eternal love. The son will live on permanently condemned to a lying nostalgia that will reach back to imprint itself on his childhood memories. For the first time the site and power of memory is located outside Willy's head—but only to project and assure a larger circle. The father's suicide will awaken the son's nostalgia for the perfect father of childhood, thereby giving the father a new and permanent life. This impossible dream is the real function of the interpretation Willy later imposes on Biff's tears to get from that terrible scene the guarantee he needs.

The circle is complete, but it has a crack in it. For Willy has now installed Biff in the position of conscience. As Ben notes, doing so delivers the question of cowardice over to the ensuing scene.

Inside Out: Staging the Scene of Truth

Both parties want to get off the hook, not knowing that its shared nature makes that impossible. Despite the angry insistence on total honesty thrown at his mother, Biff does not want to tell the whole truth because he doesn't want to reenter the double-bind. Instead, he wants to tell the "simple" story that will give him the quickest exit. His bad faith is compounded by the claim I can't tell the story so you will understand, since the need for avoidance thereby becomes Willy's alone. That operation reveals the true stage Biff has set: he plans a scene of "humiliation" disguised as a leave-taking in which he will tell his father, before his mother, a story aimed primarily at her, since she is the presence that can absolve him from the charge he makes against himself only to shift it to the father. "I'm just not smart enough to make any sense out of it for you. . . . Let's just wrap it up, heh? Come on in, we'll tell Mom" (128). But that shift activates Willy's need to avoid humiliation by giving Biff back to his mother restored in his proper role. The presence to which both are tied is ready, as always, to light the stage with the terms of frustration disguised as solicitude: first with the jab "Did you plant?" then with the retreat into an "ethics" barbed with the judgment of failure: "Cause there's no use drawing it out, you'll just never get along." If Biff leaves, he can't do so as a truth-teller. Yet she won't let him off the hook: "I'm a bum. . . . That clears it," he says (128–29). Not for Linda. She requires the symbolic, the handshake, and she addresses them as if they are no more than bad little boys who have had a fight.

The father, meanwhile, sets the other horn of Biff's dilemma, insisting that Biff humiliate himself before the mother. Like Othello still harping on his handkerchief, Willy reintroduces the object, the pen, that will force Biff to undertake a new act of narrative, now burdened with all he earlier suppressed. Willy will only let Biff leave if his interpretation of Biff's actions dictates the terms of closure. Willy, to Linda: "Spite, see?" (129). That interpretation, however, puts Biff back in the double-bind of spite and blame. Confessing oneself a bum clears nothing. The scene in the restaurant must be resumed, but Biff must now tell the whole story. He introduces it with a new object, more lethal than the pen—the hose he's been carrying all day. That object has the power to unravel Willy's magical design. Suicide will prove the very thing it is meant to exorcise. "What is this supposed to do, make a hero out of you? This supposed to make me sorry for you?" (130).

The competing interpretations of father and son are thus joined in a single story. But that story must, as Biff sees, tell the complicitous truth of the entire Family. This is the scene Biff now sets: "We never told the truth for ten minutes in this house!" Happy's denial—"We always told the truth!"—makes him fittingly the first object of unmasking. But Biff nails Happy only to nail himself: "You know why I had no address for three months? I stole a suit in Kansas City and I was in jail." And to nail Linda: "*To Linda, who is sobbing:* Stop crying. I'm through with it" (131).

Biff knows that to tell the truth about himself he must tell the truth about everyone else by forcing them to see themselves mirrored in the fault that can no longer be denied. He is no longer simply a "bum." He won't avoid blame, but he also refuses to let anyone else off the hook:

Willy: And whose fault is that?
Biff: . . . you blew me so full of hot air I could never stand taking orders from anybody! That's whose fault it is!(131)

Nor will he let Linda escape. For a second time, he rebukes her attempt to assume a position outside the problem.

Linda: Don't, Biff!
Biff: It's goddamn time you heard that! (131)

The fault is called the Father, but we're all in it together. To the death, for Willy: "Then hang yourself! For spite, hang yourself!" (132). To sever the connections Biff establishes, someone in the family must die. The scapegoat mechanism rises, as always, with the promise of resolving drama by arresting it.

But if Biff won't let anyone off the hook, he also provides himself an exit which they are invited to share. He springs it with the grand recognition he's been withholding until now. In telling them the story of the running man who halts on the stairs, theft in hand, for the privileged insight and deliverance that comes the moment "I can say I know who I am," he enters humanist heaven, finding the abode where the true self and an identity that cleanses the subject of history resides. For a guy who has been dumb for so long, Biff gets smart quick. Emersonianism delivers him from dread. American ideology triumphs over American experience. One just has to stop—midflight, stolen pen in hand—and one can put it all together, quickly and totally. You know who you are, and that identity delivers you from everything you've done and are doing. Such are the truths that can't be earned through drama. They can only be repeated as catechism. Repeat them enough times and you become Mickey Rourke at the end of *Angel Heart*.

Drama is always wiser and gives forth the truth ideology denies. The self-knowledge Biff claims is curiously at odds with the self-presentation that follows. In ending, Biff plays the old family game, having things both ways: "I'm a dime a dozen" (132), and I can say it now—to all you—because I know I'm really not. I'm Thoreau. The internal split Biff denies becomes the principle through which he will try to free all of them and thereby extricate himself from the double-bind. Confessing one's weakness confers a redeeming strength and a new pristine identity. The entire family is offered this blessing, if they will abandon one thing—their interpretive scheme.

Willy's reply—I'm not a dime a dozen nor are you—reactivates the deeper instability that haunts Biff's magical resolution. Biff's true "identity" remains familial: his desire is to get Willy to accept and internalize the only condition that will enable him to leave home for good: If I refuse to bring home prizes, you can't wait for me. The family in waiting is the real problem, the specter Biff must vanquish lest all time away from home unravel the effort to leave.

He must claim "There's no spite in it any more" (133), for his own sake more than for his father's, to admit the motive that has ruled him in the past, all the better to deny it now. His tears and the plea for freedom derive from the effort to banish that tension, and not from some great upsurge of abiding love for his father. The kiss is not a sublime moment of shared love finally recognized beneath all the hate, but a plea for deliverance from drama. For all present, that is the real meaning of this tableau, which constitutes Miller's version of the Pietà.

There's magic in it, of course, because it's all Willy needs to become Sally Field: "Biff—he likes me!" The others can then top his line to celebrate collective deliverance. Linda: "He loves you." Happy: "Always did" (133). Everyone then gets a fresh chance, blessed by a superego prepared to resume her maternal role: "You're both good boys" (134). Biff's effort results in precisely what he most feared: the scene can only end when a new "waiting period" has been established for the prodigal son. Willy: "That boy—that boy is going to be magnificent!" (133).

The Final Regression: Transcendance

The truth audiences and interpreters struggle to deny is that nothing has been resolved. Repetition reigneth. Because that is the case, Willy can now regress in peace. The threat of cowardice as interpretation of his project has been vanquished. The positive motives for suicide are thereby set loose in an orgy of magical thinking in which Willy repeats and caps the others' lines: love becomes worship; the father's death confirms the son's identity—and invincible duty. In fact, given the proper money, he can set forth "ahead of Bernard again." Through his death, Willy achieves immortality in a richly endowed son. "Oh, Ben, I always knew one way or another we were gonna make it, Biff and I!" (135).

Love doesn't deliver the family from a sick dream; it roots them to it. Because they love each other, the dream is intact and continues to rule their lives. It also returns a pristine past that is now voided of the conflicts that kept erupting each time Willy regressed to it. We are back at Ebbets Field, and regression is now complete, because the ego it serves is really Thanatos. Lest the audience be left with such a specter, they will be offered, as a surplus, a final consoling "representation" of the values which the play has shown cannot be earned in and through drama.

Requiem: The Scapegoat Mechanism Takes a Bow

The noise of a crashing car frees everyone from the inside of Willy's head, propelling them toward the audience. There they offer a final tableau of mourning designed to loosen the ties that bind us to the great and unresolved conflicts developed in the play.

Don't speak ill of the dead, because if you do, you'll have to understand yourself and your relationship to them. Grief is a public, staged spectacle designed to gain "audience" approval by presenting yourself in the image the group needs to prevent self-knowledge. Appeals to piety do wonders here, and if you can find the right author—divine or secular—to pump up the volume through naked sentimentality, everyone can join cleansed hands in an orgy of deliverance.

Such is the function of the Requiem, in which the characters face the audience united in a shared need that can send everyone into the night "calm of mind, all passion spent," discharged onto a single figure.

In the process, the scapegoat mechanism stands in high relief, showing its claws. Contra Kenneth Burke, we aren't "cleansed" thanks to Willy's "overstating of our case."[12] We are collectively deluded. By words: When is the last time you heard the word *dast*? And by a vow full of denial, since even Happy might suspect that his actions in the Chop House contributed to his father's suicide. Characteristically, he banishes that possibility by saying that his father isn't really dead: "It's the only dream you can have— to come out number-one man," and I'm going to do it for Dad as his living representative (139).

Even the "wise" audience must be sucked in: Biff again presents himself in his newfound role. Willy never knew who he was, and that is why he destroyed himself. But I, like the audience, know who I am, and I am magically delivered by a knowledge that is finally easy to attain, since all one has to do is stop and embrace one's a priori and essential identity. The audience will shortly be offered the possibility of discharging the play through a similar yet superior guarantee that will give intellectual content to the vacuity we might otherwise discern in Biff's insistence. That wisdom arrives thanks to Arthur Miller, who begins churning out interpretive essays on the play the day after it opens. They constitute a school of instruction in the commonplaces of humanism and bourgeois tragedy that are required in order to make the proper flights of interpretive abstraction needed to keep the psychological complex that keeps erupting in *Death of a Salesman* permanently on ice.

But on this occasion, Linda gets the last word. After sneaking in an obsessional fact or two about a "free and clear" house about to collapse with no one there to share her joy in tending it (139), Linda moves center stage. There her inability to cry, confessed, becomes icon and curtain call through which she receives the audience's heartfelt approval. Willy, the reservoir of a great collective disorder, carried through in radical commitment to the self-deluding mechanisms that define it, shines and perishes alone.

Saving the Audience: Mass Delusion as the Space Inside the Head

Miller's drama activates regression the better to deliver us from it. We might call his a drama of regression in the service of the superego. Each time an illusion collapses, Willy regresses to the conflict underlying it. But rather than assume the burden there revealed, he reinvests his money in the ideological interpretation that bars the possibility of insight. He thus presents a striking picture of the frozen sea inside us as a realm in which the inside of our head is packed in a huge cake of ideological ice. The true direction and possibility of regression is violated from within, as the ideological superimposes itself on the disruptive subtext regression uncovers in order to discharge all tension, thereby restoring us to a reality in which nothing has changed. The possibility of using regression to project the tragic insights found there back onto the "real" scene is barred. Repetition thereby becomes the force through which ideology polices the unconscious.

This is the great discovery which Miller cannot face, because his dramatic art constitutes a vast superstructural complicity with it. The name of that game is the scapegoat mechanism, and Miller employs all the devices of bourgeois tragedy to perfect its operations. Willy's drama is thereby structured from outside by principles that serve to deliver us from it. None of them are earned dramatically, as we've seen, but that doesn't alter their success—for over forty years now—in providing audiences with a dishonesty they readily embrace. The unsettling truth thereby revealed is this: the superstructural reassurance Miller offers his audience is a mirror image of the ideological repetitions Willy uses to discharge the possibility of insight. Willy is a willing scapegoat because he repeatedly delivers his inwardness to the ideology that colonizes and controls it.

The humanistic Miller is not a critic of the American Dream but its defender. That defense is constituted by the structure of guarantees he superimposes on Willy's drama so that the audience will remain blind to its implications. The audience is offered the opportunity to "identify" with Willy, then to celebrate their difference. Willy becomes the scapegoat who bears the punishment for every illusion of which they are thus collectively "cleansed."

A great mystery thereby yields its subtext. Virtually every audience—especially businessmen—say they are deeply moved by this play. "That's my father to a T," and so on. Yet this is a play of unrelieved suffering for its protagonist. Miller must make Willy suffer in order to extricate the other agents from the net in which the family is trapped. He offers us a superfluity of guarantees and exits so that the play's secret may remain hidden. *Death of a Salesman* is a murderous attack on the Father. We are "cleansed" thanks to Willy's overstating of our case because we have loaded all our aggressions upon him. The secret we and Miller thereby deny is that we hate Willy because he represents everything we want to deny about ourselves. The scapegoat mechanism protects culture not because it halts a spreading violence, as René Girard says, but because it displaces and extends it. A sick society is cleansed only when it can embrace the big lie: it is always in need of the "outsider." The only change here is that Isaac shifts roles and kills Abraham.

Returning the Ticket: The Other Audience

When conflict is activated, drama unleashes the pull of regression. But regression moves in one of two directions: either toward repetition and discharge, the act and perfection of resentment, or toward an opening of the crypt, which is already fully present on the surface had we the courage to see it. The latter possibility, however, requires sustaining the terms of conflict that regression unlocks by projecting them back onto the "domestic" scene so that the ensuing drama can shatter defenses and drive festering conflicts to their dramatic issue. The anxiety that attends this process derives from the fact that one doesn't know the extent to which it will go in revealing the good, normal world as a vast cover-up. Once awaken the repressed, and one may find everything in the normal deracinated by it.

Willy is the ideal scapegoat because he prevents this process. This is the function of his persistent, ideologically based misinterpretation of his condition. Rather than moving through regression toward new insight that is then projected onto the "domestic" scene, ideology provides the interpretive closure or glue that condemns everyone to repetition. In so doing, it reveals its true reason for being. The primary work of ideology is not to provide superstructural celebration, à la Desert Storm, or general anesthesia, à la the mindless babble whereby, beneath the cathode rays, we produce the determined meaning of the day's news. Ideology does its true work whenever we are stirred by the deeper unconscious conflicts that could rupture the continuum. Ideology then puts Jack back together again by defining the terms and operations whereby we extinguish a nascent inwardness. Inwardness is the space ideology must conquer; its one way is by establishing the terms whereby we police ourselves to discharge whatever puts us at odds with it. A being in conflict with itself over its "identification" with the *socius* is the true object on which ideology operates. Alienation is the privileged moment ideology awaits, because only then can it secure its reign by enforcing the interpretations whereby we criticize and undo ourselves in order to restore the Big Other.

In refusing this operation, great drama goes into the dark and necessarily takes the audience with it. Aggression toward shared illusions is the space of such a theatre. This is precisely the space Miller's drama refuses to let the audience enter. It offers instead a revealing picture of the abstractions to which resistance is drawn in order to save itself from drama: the flight into clichés (Biff and Linda) reinforced by a further flight to a thematics of humanism and its guarantees. The need underlying the process is exposed, however, by the primitive mechanism of defense Miller uses to make it work: splitting. Ideology is exposed in Willy's regression; flight into humanistic abstractions can restore illusions only by removing them from the field of what can be dramatized. In the process, the play presents its great and inadvertent revelation: humanism is precisely that view of human conflict that cannot issue in drama. Drama always begins and proceeds on the other side of the essentialistic guarantees it requires to prevent the ego-identity on which it is based from suffering destruction from within.

Because the task of criticism is to produce what the text conceals, our reading of *Death of a Salesman* has established two audiences: the audience which Miller reifies and the collective psychodrama that one must go through to free oneself from it. The hermeneutic of the latter engagement is the understanding of the family neurosis our interpretation has wrested from Miller's attempts to conceal it. The result of that act: it restores the proper target of aggression. The audience is a family, and that is the source of its inauthenticity and the most secret place of its group psychology. We thus move, thanks to Miller, to plays which confront the family—and get the guests—without submitting immanent critique to any transcendental court of appeal.

Drug of Choice:
Long Day's Journey into Night

Act I: Blame and the Circle of Displacements

The Family and/as Drama

If Miller exposes the family only to protect it, O'Neill goes after the lower layer: the family as a torture chamber with the individual self the slot one rushes to fill in a shared neurosis. Willy brings the comforts of the scapegoat, and his family loves him for it. *Long Day's Journey* shows that we're all in it together in a mutual scapegoating with no exit. In O'Neill the individual psyche is an interfamilial construct that can be understood only when one grasps the interactions that constitute and drive the psychology of the whole. Drama is an attempt to discover the structures that shape this process. O'Neill's goal is to trace a disease from its initial manifestation to its inevitable end so that we'll never again lose sight of all the ways it operates.

As in *The Iceman Cometh*, revealing the structure of a collective psychology is the goal in *Long Day's Journey;* naturalism, the means. They work together because there is one constant of behavior that is omnipresent from the beginning as the subtext of everyday life—blame. Everything said and done in this family, from the opening lines, diffuses an aura of blame. Blame or be blamed is the need at the center of each psyche, shifting the blame the basis of interpersonal activity.

Blame is a shared consciousness that has to be discharged—and can't be. As in *Iceman*, to be conscious is to be traumatized by a shared past that one can obliterate only by projecting it onto the other. The frenzy to avoid blame is such that all members of the family project it freely onto whichever member poses a threat or appears to be momentarily off the hook. Blame thus becomes a cesspool that grows in direct proportion to the efforts made to displace it. Everyone slashes away at everyone else and then rushes to deny the fact. Each makes sure the others can't miss the obvious implications of remarks while denying them that awareness. Everyday life in the family thereby becomes a process of projection and denial in which free reign is given to unconscious motives. I didn't mean that . . . Why did you take my remark that way?—such is the logic of torture, since no "analytic" intervention is tolerated. Everybody gets the message and then denies it was sent. Each is driven crazy by an awareness that cannot be recognized, admitted, or shared. Everyone conspires against everyone else, sustained by the main conspiracy—that what's going on can never be confronted forthrightly. When one member tries, the others immediately band together to attack. Aggression becomes the constant that must be constantly denied.

On the surface, much in the early parts of *Long Day's Journey* could be taken as a contribution to the psychopathology of everyday life. When families get together, they necessarily make small talk. O'Neill's insight is that they make it with claws. Everyday life is the effort through conversation to discharge the psychic pain haunting one's consciousness by projecting it onto others. Drama is the necessary result. What we want to avoid we necessarily engender by structuring interrelationships in such a way that aggression always escalates. Denial grows as defenses become progressively more extreme and insistent: cumulative internal panic rises, craving any release.

Two exits are barred: simple repetition and the scapegoat mechanism. With each repetition the psychological conflict deepens, with no way to discharge the accumulated tension onto a single figure. Drama is the process whereby the psychological roots of ordinary behavior come to light.

Rejecting the appeal of the scapegoat mechanism is the Magna Carta for understanding that process. In this family, no one gets off the hook because everyone spends their time putting the others on it. If the scapegoat ritual worked, one member of the family could be loaded with the collective guilt, and the others could bathe themselves in that blood, as in Lethe. When no one is willing to take on the scapegoat role, its real function—shifting and extending blame—comes into the open.

This process operates from the beginning of *Long Day's Journey*. Everyone feels blameworthy, but no one is willing to take on personal responsibility. Blame is a metonymy that circles back on each agent only to diffuse itself in a general atmosphere of brooding. Because there are no cheerleaders here to deflect the brooding into ideological commonplaces, as there are in *Death of a Salesman*, no relief is offered. The family experiences itself, instead, as a depressive entanglement that can't be relieved through discourse. While discourse offers the bliss of pseudotranscendence in *Death of a Salesman,* discourse in *Long Day's Journey* only increases psychic discontent.

Folie à la famille

The psychic pain at the center of each consciousness becomes the common burden that can be "discharged" only by creating what I will term a *folie à la famille.* Psychic pain is so central and inescapable that the only way to relieve it is by enmeshing the others in it. Many families play this game and get the requisite relief because they manage to establish, however dishonestly, discrete origins and causes.

Early on O'Neill lets this logocentric motive surface, only to undercut it by showing how each member exploits a history that can never be established "empirically," since it exists only in the uses to which it is put. Every attempt to tunnel into the past, seeking a way to find the origin of one's distress or to fix blame on the other as cause, only further ties each character to a common burden that has already outstripped every self-serving search for origins. The best example: everyone gets blamed for Eugene's death, which is exploited as the origin of virtually everyone's "guilt." Whereas most plays expend all their energy fixing the blame or finding the primary psychological cause, O'Neill reveals such efforts as the main way in which the *folie à la famille* operates to extend a psychological net, rather than to resolve it. Mark this as the first lure whereby he snares the audience. We are sick together, not because x once did y or heard z say whatever, but because we use such mechanisms to conceal the prior disorder: projection and denial function as the dynamic whereby the interfamilial psyche is generated.

A properly hermeneutical understanding thus replaces a logocentric logic of origins and causes. The family is a psychological drama that always begins in media res. Parents choose one another out of unconscious motives. In denying these motives, while enacting them, they pass their shared disorder onto their progeny, only to get it thrown back in their faces by their children/victims. As O'Neill shows, the main thing to avoid in analyzing this structure is any attempt to simplify its operations or to give one member in the system undue power or undue blame. Every time one does so, one arrests the possibility of knowing the whole. Those arrests constitute theories of family therapy. This is the second lure: it clicks in whenever we use one of those theories to simplify and interpret O'Neill's drama.[1]

To carry out a dialectical investigation, one must immerse oneself in the circle without taking sides or superimposing a privileged explanatory framework to simplify the data. For it is in the minute particulars, the language games and behavioral rituals, that the inseparable psyches of family members are forged. To understand that system, one must be willing to see it as a structure of mutual cruelty, in which the deep wound in each psyche determines the way members relate to one another. That perspective also offers the deepest insight into the conditions of object-choice in which the complex found its origins. It is said that married couples come to resemble each other. What really happens is that all differences that aren't functional to the shared disorder evaporate with time as the interaction comes to express nothing but the frustrations of the relationship; which is, of course, the knowledge both parties resist. That's what relating is all about. Children, in turn, are inserted into the interaction, as the parents use them to further their conflicts. Finding themselves so situated, siblings relate to one another not as free individuals but as terms of dispute and discontent within that larger context in which the battle between the parents completes itself by pitting their offspring against one another.

It takes a long time to get the structure in place, but once it clicks, the family has become a pure psychodrama ready for its repressed conflicts to be activated. This is where O'Neill begins, with every line and every prop advancing the drama, because there's no longer anything that can fail to signify and exacerbate a systemic disorder. From the opening lines, the movement is from day to night, with the journey both arduous and inescapable, because there is nothing said in the daytime that does not point to an unconscious subtext as the truth that is always in some way present, inflicted. Once the family is in place, there are no innocent remarks.

Blame's Metonymy

Tyrone tells Mary that she is "a fine armful . . . with those twenty pounds you've gained," and Mary takes it as an insult. She retaliates, "You expect everyone to eat the enormous breakfast you do" (14).[2] By the time he says, "Keep up the good work, Mary" (17), no remark can fail to wound. The appeal to intentionality—I didn't mean that, and so on—can't halt this process, because blame giving reveals a density of agency and a complex history that each day renews its progress. Any remark can get the process going, thanks to two principles which are dialectically one: one agent can spot the other's subtext or claim its presence. Blame clicks in because a remark that might not intend harm is so received because on other occasions that was its function. Once couples have achieved a certain history in their relationship, "idle talk" constantly shimmers with its subtext. It's not important who starts any particular round of blame, because the shared reality is an intersubjectivity that must issue in drama. Such is the nature of marriage. Tyrone and

Mary are not separate individuals but a single psychological complex defined by a conflict which each tries to discharge by displacing it onto the other.

When blame has assumed this status, everyday life becomes a drama of shifters. The apparent dissymmetry of the initial situation is misleading. If, at the start, Mary appears to be more on the attack than Tyrone, she is also the one most concerned to shift the burden of blame, since she knows she is always under inspection. She seeks relief by shifting criticism onto the sons: "It's Edmund you ought to scold for not eating enough" (16). But displacement always advances the burden it would repress. Tyrone deftly exploits the new topic to identify Mary's relationship to Edmund as the cause of defects that move from diet to character: "You'd find excuses for him no matter what he did" (18).

The sons enter the drama as sites of displaced aggressions that will develop through the alignments in which each parent tries to enlist them. The easiest way to do so is by using the defense mechanism known as splitting. Tyrone criticizes Edmund to get at Mary—and to protect himself. To do so he splits his son's psyche. Edmund's disorder is tied to his relationship to his mother. His potential health is a function of a yet-to-be-formed relationship to his "strong" father. Mary retaliates in kind by identifying Jamie as the son most like the father in order to charge both with insensitivity: "You're like him. As soon as your head touches the pillow you're off and ten foghorns couldn't wake you" (20).

But in shifting the blame she has awakened another observer: "Why are you staring, Jamie?" (20)—and the possibility of new alignments. This shifting play of alignments gives the beginning of the play a distinctly structuralist flavor. With all the characters in place, O'Neill's first concern seems to be to develop all the possible permutations, of dual and triangular relations. Each alignment, however, bears a dialectic whereby its necessary collapse produces the net that will enmesh them all.

The couple can attempt to relieve blame by shifting it onto the sons, but this act inaugurates a new instability. Mary's attribution of blame to Tyrone and Jamie creates the possibility of the two men forming a group, casting blame at her. Each subsequent attempt to regroup for support creates the possibility of a countermovement. With Edmund's entrance, we get a play of triangular alignments, with each triangle having as its telos a primitive scapegoat mechanism.

That process gives us a unique insight into the way the family dynamic operates. The sons enter allied in a potential two-versus-two relationship. But two versus two is a stalemate destined to collapse. Since blame is the threat that must be displaced, every two-versus-two relationship turns into a triangular alignment against an excluded and targeted other. To avoid that slot, each individual must activate a group alignment. The excluded individual must react by activating a competing triangle. Dramatic conflict thus blossoms with each effort to arrest it by isolating a single target of blame. Before the fact, O'Neill shows René Girard why the scapegoat mechanisms will not halt the sacrificial crisis.[3] In doing so he generates a drama that is neither naturalist nor structuralist, but something deeper: a phenomenological psychopathology of the family which traces the basic operations in everyday life whereby the disorder at the core develops from its initial manifestation to its full horror. As in *Iceman,* he thereby tracks a group psychology to its foundations.

Peace is unattainable. No remark can fail to drop acid on someone's nerves. Even a moment of comic relief ends up being at someone's expense. The tendentious nature of the joke, as Freud taught, is the hearing together at the expense of someone else who is present.[4] The boys band together to tell a joke at the old man's expense, and Mary provides an almost girllike chorus applauding the mischief. Jamie uses the Shaughnessy story to get at his father and to save his alignment with his brother. But the second purpose necessarily fails, for he cannot anticipate the delight Mary will take in the joke to establish a triangular alignment against Tyrone. His first purpose, however, could not be better designed to advance the drama. The joke works only too well, because it gets at Tyrone's core disorder, his desire to identify with the upper classes in order to purge his class origins and find in money a safety he can never find within. The joke opens up this hole in himself. In projective reaction, Jamie becomes the object in which Tyrone locates everything that threatens in himself. In counterattack he seeks to purge all his disorders by opening up the wound at the center of Jamie's psyche—his feeling of worthlessness: "You've a fine talent for that [for scorn], if for nothing else" (26).

With each alignment, a deeper disorder surfaces and is made the object of a counterattack. In the joke, Tyrone's character is made a shared object of ridicule and humiliation. His reply mounts a similar attack on the being of the jokester, whose nihilistic psyche is identified as the motive underlying his activity. But all attempts to arrest the drama on a single target are only way stations proceeding toward a deeper eruption. With Edmund's exit, a shift in the direction of blame brings the entire complex to a new condition, and to an unavoidable question: Can any alignment of three versus one hold, or is blame such that it will always rise up and seek a new object?

This issue is activated by Edmund's unique position in the "system." Is he the sibling counterexample to Jamie? The threatened illness all three must purge? Or the audience each alignment of two agents must play to in order to attack a third? As we'll see, his impossible position is that he occupies all three slots. The opportunity offered by such a position becomes evident when, in his absence, what initially looks like a movement of shared solicitude engenders a new circle of blame which advances the drama to the point where it cuts directly into the core disorders of each character.

The key to repetition in O'Neill is that each time a structure repeats itself, a deeper disorder surfaces in a new subtext which drives the drama to its next stage. Structure is the progressive revelation of a psychological complex in which "unconscious" motives proceed apace, as the clash of agents brings them slowly to light. Premature conclusions, especially about character, blind one to the dramatic process. For what appears to explain things at one moment will later be driven by the drama to a disclosure which recontextualizes it. Understanding the character of each agent and his or her contribution to the familial complex requires, for O'Neill, this slow, meticulous attention to dialectical progression. For the dark truth is that everything which looks like repetition is avid with direction. That is why the circle of blame that breaks with Edmund's departure expands, in the second half of act I, as a direct result of the agents' efforts to limit it. That movement is composed of three scenes of apparent solicitude. It is as if each character wants to halt the spiral of blame by introducing humane considerations. The question, of course, is whether this is possible or whether every tie of affection will be drawn into the net, so that each effort to halt blame will only expand and deepen a drama in which love, invoked, will succumb to forces it is powerless to contain.

In the typical American family drama, love always wins out, especially when the situation ends unhappily. In a fairly typical example, such as *I Never Sang for My Father,* we all come to recognize on some deep level that love, however blocked, was the deepest thing between father and son. And so the word *father* still matters, and the audience can leave the theatre knowing that, though it was never communicated, love was the deepest bond in the family. That sentiment is profoundly consoling, for it retrospectively redeems all that the agents did to one another.

O'Neill's greatness is that he submits this a priori guarantee to drama. When drama is genuine, nothing can be held in reserve; everything must be submitted to the situation. The discovery we must be willing to make is that love may be the grand illusion. Love, concern, solicitude, are not a priori guarantees that reside in some essential interfamilial humanity ready to provide the deus ex machina that can save the family from itself. Drama is dangerous because ethical values and essentialized "identities" are submitted to a concrete realm which measures them by this existential imperative: Every value is what it has become and is now, through drama, becoming. The family's present condition gives us the deepest insight into its past. Even if there was "love" at some "mythical" beginning, its appeal can be no more than nostalgic. Love can't deliver us from drama; it can only deliver us over to it. We are always ready to situate—and purge—hate. We must do the same with love if we are to reclaim Aristotle's insight that the family is the most tragic site for drama because the greatest horror arises when cruelty is done where the presence of love is assumed. Then the drama cuts into the a priori guarantee hidden in essentialistic affirmations of love. Love may still become a motive, but only after all the lies have been faced, not before, since constituting that possibility requires knowing all the ways in which the assertion of love serves to advance a way of relating antithetical to it. Solicitude is wonderful, but when it has been used and abused over time for other ends, its assertion can only serve to extend the web of conflict in which everyone is enmeshed. This is the circle traced in the second half of act I. It is also the final lure, for as it closes we will find that O'Neill has committed both himself and the audience to a radical immanence.

The Play of Solicitude

One fear controls Tyrone and Jamie—that Mary will go back on drugs. Another fear reinforces it—that Edmund's condition will precipitate her collapse. Both fears activate a deeper subtext, since Edmund's birth is the pseudo-origin everyone is fixated on as the cause of Mary's addiction, a fixation necessary to both Tyrone and Jamie, because it displaces the blame they might otherwise receive. Fear generates the need for an insurance policy. If Mary lapses, an immediate cause must be located, and Edmund is the readiest target. Thus, while solicitude appears ascendent, both Tyrone and Jamie are hedging bets and preparing for their exits.

Fear is also a source of immense power, and Mary knows how to exploit it to tyrannize all of them. Everyone supports her need to deny reality, and she attacks anyone who violates that contract. An honest discussion of Edmund's illness is the first casualty: "You always imagine things!" (27). The shared solicitude of father and son becomes the need to calm the mother by lying to her. And her need is such that Tyrone's attempt at a limited disclosure of Edmund's condition makes him the target of her aggression. Mary is an expert at exploiting fear to reinsert the proper barbs in her opponents. The issue of doctors has for a long time been a perfect way to establish Tyrone's guilt for her addiction. Playing that card activates their suspicions, of course, but that only increases the need for shared mutual denial in compliments to her beauty, which can only quicken the power of other memories. Edmund is again the casualty: "It wasn't until after Edmund was born that I had a single grey hair" (28).

What remains of Edmund's claim to solicitude dissolves in the first of what I'll term Mary's public monologues. They are the key to her character and enact a complex, contradictory purpose. In a sense, Mary is, from the beginning, in the position Blanche attains in scene x of *Streetcar*. She is always slipping away from herself, yet desiring that release, as she fights a simultaneous battle on two fronts. Externally, she is engaged in an aggressive effort to project her conflicts. Internally, regression pulls her toward psychic dissolution. The first effort constitutes a secondary gain from illness; the second taps the deeper disorder which that practice tries to hold at bay. At this point in the play, the first is ascendant. Mary knows that the best way to hurt them, in taking leave of them, is to do it in slow stages right before their eyes. The only hitch is that each success produces a further internal regression.

Mary wants to deflect attention and blame while leaving Tyrone and Jamie with the burden of both specters deftly shifted onto Edmund. But her face and gestures have already begun to betray her. "Girlishness fades from her face," and laughter gives way to "a brisk businesslike air" that becomes exaggerated as she deliberately caps her first leave-taking by presenting them with a deeply worried face (28–29). It is a passive-aggressive masterpiece and drives home their deepest fear: it's all over already; all that's left for them is the long, slow, passive suffering as they watch the drug do its work. Addiction is the weapon she uses to control and eventually destroy them. Their solicitude empowers her ability to use fear to paralyze them. Thus, by scene's end, an inescapable fact—Edmund's illness—has given way to a more horrifying possibility, and Tyrone and Jamie are left alone, with the specter of blame.

The scene that follows exposes the shared need underlying their solicitude. As the two try to band together over the two externalized illnesses that threaten them, the deeper psychological disorder that binds all four agents erupts in a new circle of blame which, by scene's end, moves the entire drama into a purely psychological space.

Jamie attacks Tyrone. Tyrone counters with a deeper attack on Jamie. Both then go for the jugular: Jamie by focusing on his father's fixation on money, Tyrone by reversing the charge with the attribution that the son is a bum who failed as an actor. Jamie's weak counter (that he never wanted to act) and Tyrone's honest complaint (that Jamie failed to spite him) can't arrest the process. Nor can a moment of exemplary honesty.

Tyrone: You . . . sneer at every damned thing in the world—except yourself.
Jamie: That's not true, Papa. You can't hear me talking to myself, that's
          all. (32)

Jamie introduces the possibility that blame giving abhors—honest psychological probing. To deflect it, Tyrone recasts blame by using the doctor issue
to put both Edmund and Mary on the hook: "He's always been a bundle of
nerves like his mother" (33). No one in this family ever forgets anything
previously said. Remarks fester until they can be expelled by identifying
another—in this case Jamie—as the primary object of blame: "You're more
responsible than anyone!" (34).

Jamie must respond in kind, because he agrees with the judgment. He has
already opened his Crypt—"You can't hear me talking to myself"—and his
father has now driven the knife in. The key to Jamie's exemplary character is
that he is in touch with his unconscious. He has organized his life, in fact, to
punish himself for the knowledge. He knows that unconscious envy is at the
core, and he suspects that he shares this disorder with everyone in the family.
As a partly willing victim, he has internalized that knowledge as endless,
low-level depression. That effort is about to be tested, because blame has
deepened its hold. Each began by blaming the other for making Mary uneasy. Now the psychological core of the other's character is identified as the
"cause" of a much larger disorder in the family.

Like Hickey in *Iceman,* Jamie wants to be the conscience of the unconscious, but there is one connection he must deny, and his father has just
identified it. Jamie needs to deny responsibility for Edmund's psyche: "All I
did was make a pal of him and be absolutely frank so he'd learn from my
mistakes that—" (34). The suppressed motive that erupts late in Hickey's
narrative is constantly present in Jamie's consciousness. Unless he can distin-
guish his brother from himself, he will have to face his Frankenstein monster.

That necessity clashes with his father's desire to lump the brothers together in order to get himself off the hook. Jamie's effort to establish a
separate identity and agency for Edmund is far truer than he realizes, but his
underlying motive undercuts the assertion by hitting on an association that
drives blame deeper into both himself and his father. The neon lights of
Broadway haunt both of them, and the slightest allusion to that setting
reawakens Tyrone's deepest fear—"You and Broadway! It's made you what
you are!" (35)—for he suspects that Broadway is what has made all of them
what they are, with his agency the cause. To avoid that implication, he uses
the younger brother to attack the older. This goads Jamie into an attack on
Edmund. In it the otherness he just struggled to establish in order to protect

his brother becomes an attack on Edmund which he must immediately retract in order to halt the skid into his unconscious.

Jamie is trapped in ambivalence and must use splitting to preserve the "loved" object against the unconscious envy that attacks it. In the process, the object progressively shrinks. Tyrone's praise of Edmund—to further the attack on Jamie—forces Jamie to diminish him. He must plead, "Can't you lay off me!" (36), because he knows he must redirect every criticism thrown at him onto Edmund. His unconsciousness erupts, torn between jealousy, shame, and a desperate effort to repress his deepest fear—that hatred may be the one secret he's keeping from himself.

Tyrone, in contrast, uses magical thinking to banish disorders. Nostalgia defines him as it does his wife, making all trouble "damnable luck" that can be exorcised by the invocation of his defining fantasy: "This home has been a home again" (36). Jamie momentarily shares that dream. Only one word is needed to undo this bond of feeling, however, the little word that reintroduces the shared need for denial which can only operate through a new attack on one another. Mary "seems" to be all right (37).

The Lomans use hyperaffirmation to banish such words, while for the Tyrones, language, however evasive, reestablishes the primacy of blame, which now expands to its largest circle. Tyrone takes out a new insurance policy by reworking Edmund into the conversation. Edmund carries the seeds of Tyrone's defeat because illness evokes the entire past. Since the past can no longer be avoided, Tyrone must make it the focus of an elaborate and self-defeating attempt to fix the blame. It is a marvelous sequence. First Mary is to blame. Then Edmund: "It would be like a curse she can't escape if worry over Edmund—" Then no one. Then "the bastard of a doctor." The circle then implodes on the inventor's head. Tyrone is to blame: "So I'm to blame! That's what you're driving at, is it?" If so, an escape hatch beckons. Jamie's nihilism is to blame: "You evil-minded loafer!" (39). Jamie need not reply; he has already included himself in the catalog aria. The stalemate that results is the full hermeneutic circle that emerges whenever, through interpretation, anyone tries for an exit. Blame is inexorable.

Mary times her reentry perfectly. Her venom has done its work. Offstage, however, the aggression has produced its corresponding regression. Mary's long unraveling has commenced. To halt it, she needs to deliver a new blow. Action always involves this dialectic for Mary, because psychic disintegration is her means of aggression. In staging before them a monologue characterized by the flight of ideas and the drift to symptomatic fixations—her hands—both purposes are served. Suspicions confirmed, Tyrone and Jamie make a quick exit.

The following scene, between mother and son, parallels the previous one, exposing a similar process in which apparent solicitude only activates a destructive subtext. In doing so, it completes the circle of blame by establishing the unique contribution the other two agents in the play will make to it.

The scene is subtle and brilliant. It offers a parody of maternity and a complex picture of the contradictions implicit in the effort of the oedipalized son to become the analytic agent. Edmund's desire to communicate honestly with his mother runs up against a solicitude full of projective aggression: "You're such a baby. You like to get us worried so we'll make a fuss over you" (42). The options offered Edmund are to deny his illness or admit that he uses it as a weapon. The stakes of leveling with Mom have just gone up a few pegs on the psychic register. Having so positioned him, Mary can now play mother—"Big as you are, you're still the baby of the family to me, you know" (43)—and oedipalize Edmund in order to turn him against her two antagonists by establishing the exclusive nature of their bond of poetic isolation, refinement, and suffering.

But for this process to work, blame must again reveal its power to bind and loose. As it goes forth to claim Tyrone and Jamie, Edmund is offered a chance to join Mary and get off the hook, but only if he'll renounce any identification with his father and brother: "No respectable parents will let their daughters be seen with you" (44). In this remark, which caps a process in which Mary has carefully positioned Edmund, love shows its claws. Edmund is left with the psychological implication clear: You'd be different, and closer to me, if you weren't a child ruled by your father and brother. Edmund's option, in a sense, is what kind of baby he wants to be.

The hook planted, Mary can put her need center stage, seductively reinforced and protected from attack. In an attempt to preserve a countervailing purpose, Edmund makes his strongest attempt to direct that topic in the right analytic direction by getting Mary to see that she shares blame for her condition. This is the role he wants to assume. But the attempt runs up against the maternal presence, which as internal regulator activates an inhibiting guilt. And guilt is precisely the force Mary knows how to exploit to set up a double-bind with an impossible option. Her demand, "Don't . . . remind me," runs up against his analytic recognition that forgetting is her greatest danger—and his too. For Edmund the bind is one of nostalgia, the dream of "home," the place he keeps returning to because he fears it never existed. That fear leads him to violate the analytic position that he's just tried to assume. Mary will now instruct him in forgetfulness: "I don't understand why you should suddenly say such things" (45). Edmund's analytic effort only raises for Mary the specter of six eyes in concert staring at her.

She can exorcise that specter only by shifting the blame and expanding its scope.

The request "Trust me" thus becomes a parody of that concept, since trust requires that Edmund not only forget the past but also regard his attempt to bring it up as evidence of a shameful lack of trust. Analytic agency has met its match. Mary's panic is genuine; her operations are a neat mechanism for psychological displacement and projected aggression. The mere thought that something may be wrong with her has been stigmatized. Edmund now repudiates that thought and, with it, his project to oppose forgetting. He then gets his proper reward for having introduced it: he is reduced to another "spy" as Mary's accumulated aggression erupts in an attack in which all men are blamed for the position they force on women. Her goal is thereby achieved. Mary cannot bear to be alone with her psyche or with another consciousness that reminds her of it. The charge that it would serve them right if their suspicions were true reveals the complex motives behind her addiction. "Drugs" are her way of acting out aggression toward them, blaming them for her condition, and then enforcing the injunction that they extinguish the consciousness she cannot bear.

Edmund complies in order to escape the trap that will spring if, seeking proof of her love, he tells her of his illness. To avoid blame for her condition, he must deny his own. "It's only a bad cold" (48). His insight, undone by the fear through which she controls him, becomes the appeal that if it's more, she must not exploit the fact. Mary seals her victory with a demand: forgetting becomes the duty she enforces as the price of proving one's love. Having been manipulated into a bind in which he's aligned with Tyrone and Jamie, Edmund is now charged with the duty to inflict forgetfulness upon them. Mary can exit to "lie down" (49), secure in the knowledge that suspicion has now become guilt.

Thus ends the first grand movement of the familial circle. In playing itself out, blame has unleashed the underlying force it struggles to displace—guilt. That power will structure the ensuing drama of act II.

As overture to that examination, act I concludes appropriately with the first tableau in which Mary stands alone in the isolation she desires, fears, and finds intolerable for two contradictory reasons. Alone, she is never alone, for that is when she finds them watching her most intently. Being alone condemns her to the subtext she constantly enacts before them—but without their eyes to displace it into the momentary relief blame giving brings. Alone, hers is a psyche unbound, feeding on itself. Mary has put out their eyes and closed her own, only to be awakened from within by an insight into herself which she cannot contain, even as she desperately tries to

locate it in a hystericized body. The hands she so invests betray her and
remain "driven by an insistent life of their own, without her consent" (49).
Such is the first way in which, as the day deepens, the Unconscious announces itself as that which must rise to the surface.

Act II: Guilt and the System of Defenses

Scene i

Masks

The question of act I, Who's to blame and for what? becomes in act II the
question Who's guilty, and at what psychic level? With the advance, the
drama moves from displacements and delays to defenses and fixations. The
characters now strike at one another's masks. Repetition operates under the
strain of regressions that must be projected, because as defenses crumble,
close, pent-up guilts stream forth. Denying and projecting guilt emerges as
the primary motive behind defenses. This is the through-line of act II. In
dramatizing it O'Neill submits the ego to a shattering critique.[5]

As O'Neill shows, we organize elaborate patterns of interaction, such as
blame, in order to displace the deeper threat of guilt. We also develop
elaborate defenses to escape detection. This system of masks constitutes
what we call our character.[6] It is composed of that habitual set of defense
mechanisms which confer a coherent sense of identity by giving us semiautomatic ways to escape situations of anxiety. The whole thing works because
the social process is a contract in which we agree, by and large, to respect
one another's masks. Each of us prepares a face to meet the faces that we
meet, and we become such good actors that we are taken in by our roles.
Human interaction becomes dangerous—and significant—only when the
masks begin to slip or are challenged.

This process is the focus of act II. O'Neill's goal here is to go after the
psyche beneath the behaviors. As a consummate dramatist, he knows that
the only way to do so is to show how actors, in playing out the roles that
protect and defend their "character" from the threat of discovery, give
themselves away. Character is revealed as masks crack, strain, and break
under the pressure of their clash with the masks other actors have fashioned
to "master" similar conflicts. If act I constitutes a psychopathology of everyday life, the first half of act II constitutes a psychopathology of acting styles.
The appropriateness of a theatrical focus when dealing with this particular
family should not blind us to the broader implication: perhaps all families

are theatres in which acting is not only the primary process but also the deepest necessity.

One way to conceptualize the family is as a theatre in which all actors con their parts to deceive the others and avoid drama. But when the masks begin to slip, something interesting happens. The actors start to catch on to one another. Rather than feeding the appropriate cue, each directs attention to the poor quality of the other's performance: You're a bad actor, and I'm an audience who's no longer taken in. Ensemble acting—And what is a happy family but such a troupe?—has become psychological probing.[7] The ensemble no longer feed one another the emotional reactions needed to bring off a collective attempt to dazzle one another. Instead, habitual emotional processes are blocked. Each actor tries to frustrate the other's need for emotional release in order to get at the "anxiety" hiding beneath the mask. The actors have entered the situation De Niro speaks of in noting that in life as well as onstage we don't express our emotions; we conceal them, and in the process of concealing them, our true emotions seep through. The three episodes composing act II, scene i, trace what must happen to masks for this process to become irreversible.[8]

The family reaches a particularly pregnant stage in its drama when the question becomes Who's acting and who isn't? Jamie introduces this issue at the beginning of act II, when he tells Edmund that he can't bluff him and claim he hasn't snuck a drink: "You're a rottener actor than I am" (53). The literal topic carries as resonance the deeper question: What is done to avoid reality (Mary's condition) after reality has made avoidance impossible? That question activates the drama of masks.

When one actor calls another a rotten actor and the latter needs to hold on to the role, a peculiar kind of contract is possible. Jamie offers it: "Why kid me? We're pals, aren't we?" (53). That is, I'll play along with you, even though I'm on to you. Edmund has an alternative. He can turn Jamie's original assertion back against him and raise the ante: You're as bad an actor as I am, and I'm on to you, too. The two could then proceed to hack away at each other's masks. But Edmund can't play this option, because his mask rests on the defense mechanism known as denial, which he will cling to desperately until it collapses at the end of the act.

That need leaves Jamie empowered to assert a series of attributions—I'm wise, and you're just a scared kid; we're pals, but I'm the one who knows human nature—without activating the unconscious fear that his love for his brother conceals and projects ambivalence and hate. Masks unchallenged are powerful weapons whereby unconscious motives proceed unchecked and undetected. Edmund's mask is another matter. No one has to tell him he's a bad actor, because he has already begun to suspect it. He must, however, deny the knowledge, lest its implications land him on the psychic stage where the others await him, once he realizes that he must confront the nature of his relationship to his mother.

When the topic shifts to Mama, sustaining masks takes on a deeper urgency. Jamie now needs to attack Edmund. And Edmund can't withdraw, because Jamie strikes at the illusion about Mary that Edmund must sustain in order for denial to serve its intrapsychic purpose. Drawn into battle, Edmund attacks Jamie's superior knowledge as a cynical pose, invoking the old refrain everyone constantly uses against Jamie: "Can't you think anything but—?" (56). Like his father earlier, he need not complete the sentence, because Jamie already has done so within.

Aggressive action now produces an equal and opposite reaction. Jamie exploits the charge to shift the theatrical space to the place where everyone must finally play out their roles—and where he thinks he has found the role that holds a particular demystifying power. All acting is finally in the head. Cynical knowledge provides the only antidote to reality—and the perfect mechanism of defense. But once you strip away all roles, what role do you play? That of the instructor who goes after the need for denial underlying Edmund's role. Edmund is not only a bad actor; he's taken in, Jamie now tells him, by another bad actor—his mother—because he refuses to see that her word is a piece of deliberate acting. But when Jamie says her promise "doesn't mean anything," Edmund must say "it does this time" (57), for being her helpmate is the one mask he must sustain to preserve denial.

But denial of reality is one thing; denial of the blame that resurfaces once the topic turns to Mary is another. With that shift, a new drama of masks commences, with Jamie both taking the lead and defending himself by asserting a "truth" Edmund dare not call cynicism: "You never knew . . . until you were in prep school. Papa and I kept it from you. But I was wise ten years or more before we had to tell you. I know the game backwards" (57).

Guilt resurgent and reality impending, Edmund can reply only with a doubled reassertion of his defense mechanism: "She didn't! You're crazy!" (57). Though Edmund could hardly make the latter charge stick, its threat is such that Jamie must join Edmund in assuming the mask of shared denial: "I guess I'm a damned suspicious louse" (58), because if his suspicions prove correct, his psyche will descend to the self-torture beneath the cynical pose. Cynicism is the perfect intellectual defense against the unconscious motives cynicism seeks to transcend by mimicry. At the end of the scene, both wish they'd grabbed another drink, because they will soon find their roles severely tested.

The Addition of the Third Actor

When Mary enters, acting out that role of "peculiar detachment" both have learned to read, each seeks a new defense to hide what has been going on behind the masks. When denial is no longer possible, Edmund resorts to repression. "He believes what he wants to believe for the moment" because, with her tender kiss, his mother dons the role sure to activate his guilt, both as the proximate cause of her condition and, intrapsychically, for having just been suspicious of such a loving mother. Knowing the truth, Jamie also resorts to a new defense—open aggression. But the "defensive cynicism" into which he retreats becomes, in the course of the scene, an extended pout (58). Infantile regression quickens beneath the masks both sons now try to sustain. Defenses have a layered structure; with the collapse of one, a descent begins. Both brothers have begun that journey.

Mary, trapped between adolescent needs, tries to deflect attention from the role that has begun to claim her, by playing up the erotic/motherly connection with Edmund, thereby offering him a victory of sorts over the brother who recently castigated his "youth." Alignment resurgent, Jamie's cynical pose becomes the object of a joint attack: "What a big baby you are! Isn't he, Edmund?" (59).

When one is first working to achieve it, repression is a strenuous, intermittent activity. Bearing the strain of an awareness that won't vanish, Edmund counterattacks with a line that forces Mary to resume her dominant role of detachment.

> Edmund: He's [Jamie's] certainly a fool to care what anyone thinks.
> Mary: Yes, the only way is to make yourself not care. (59–60)

But solidifying the mask activates their need to strip it away, since her detachment is the behavior they most fear. They know that when it clicks she will have taken leave of them—and their needs.

To get another person's mask, however, you must be willing to put your own on the line. Neither son is up to this effort. Instead, realignments circle, awaiting deliverance through repetition of a prior structure—blame—projected onto a favorite target, the father, who, Jamie notes, remains outside, gabbing to the neighbors about his troubles.

Left with the interim, Mary tries to regain control by assigning each agent a role for the ensuing drama. She moves, as always, in a double direction: each disruptive interchange produces a further regression in her inner world, which she acts out by deepening the attack on their internal worlds. The first part of the long speech she makes here thus generates the second as its necessary sequel. What begins as a fairly deep self-revelation really amounts to a weapon directed at many potential targets. Mary's topic is the loss of one's "true self," caused by what was done to you before you realized it (61). Past and present form a closed circle which completes itself in the impersonal recognition that there is nothing anyone can do, or ever could. That text enters directly into the soul of both sons, because it delivers a double message: Your mother is a lost soul who knows that you are too. Mary here gives both sons a glimpse into the true nature of her mothering in order to reopen a wound so deep in their psyches that both sons will rush to displace it by forming a triangle dedicated to exposing their father's cherished illusions about hearth and home. It is a brilliant move.

But at this point in the speech, her mask begins to slip. Resentment, not detachment, surfaces, and though it has the automatic, habitual quality of a long-established defense mechanism, it also shimmers with Mary's unconscious need to attack her husband's masks. The thing that happened long ago that ruined one's life must be given a local habitation and a name. In rehearsing her tribulations in trying to fashion a home for one who says he wants it more than anything but continually subverts her efforts, she primes both sons for the coming attack. By the end of the speech, home has become a travesty of that concept, and Tyrone a target of ridicule, though hardly its primary object. The sons know she has played the speech to mock an illusion they share with their father—and to again take leave of them right before their eyes. Aggressive triangulation is not enough. Everyone must be given a dose of venom.

To counter that blow, Edmund must momentarily let her see that he sees the visage beneath the mask: "What makes you ramble on like that, Mama?" But unable "to look up in her eyes," he beats a quick retreat (62). The only way to strip a mask is by acting out one's conflict with another actor, not by simply commenting on the role he or she is playing. But to do that, one must engage in a genuine give and take, risking, as actor, one's own mask. Edmund instead jumps at the quickest excuse to go get Pop, the surrogate target. When knowledge generates repression, one necessarily flees conflict by seeking a scapegoat, an external object onto which all can discharge accumulated tension.

Jamie's defense produces a different result. If, like Jamie, one knows and rages, anger can be displaced, but it cannot be denied. Edmund gone, Jamie casts on Mary's mask the look she can't face, because it has the power to make guilt the term of disclosure.

There are only two things one can do with guilt: one can either project it or turn it back against oneself. Both Mary and Jamie fear the latter process, but Mary has fashioned the role that displaces the threat. When Edmund returns, she uses her "nervous excitement" to enlist his aid to silence Jamie: "Your brother ought to be ashamed of himself. He's been insinuating I don't know what." Edmund is offered precisely the alliance he needs—one of denial. But he can no longer use the mechanism to discharge tension, because the anger he turns on his brother—"God damn you!"—violates the detachment which his mother's use of that defense mandates (63). For Mary, denial only works if blame is transformed into resignation before inevitable facts that doom and excuse everyone. Denial for Edmund, in contrast, requires the lie. Repression is Edmund's goal, while Mary's is the obliteration of consciousness. Mary leaves him with that difference as a gap he can't bridge except by attacking Jamie as the intruding force of reality testing: "You're a liar" (64). He has regressed from one infantile mechanism to another: Mama, say it ain't so! has become How dare you say such things about my mother? Everything we need to know about Edmund's psyche is revealed: beneath the masks, his is an infantile psychology. He had better hang on to the role of consumptive poet as long as he can, because the disorders it hides threaten a regression as archaic as the one his mother seeks.

"The Player-King"

The ensuing scene brings back on the stage the actor whose masks have the power to drive the drama to a new state. Picking up where she left off, Mary uses her new theme—"Oh, I'm so sick and tired of pretending this is a home!"—to reverse the "logical" order of the self-presentation she's just acted out in order to target Tyrone as the cause. Six successive complaints beginning with the word *you* identify Tyrone as the object of communal attack. She need only remind her sons that she remains the primary object of their concern to indicate that they can best show that love by loading all guilt on Tyrone. Had he not done all the things just listed, "then nothing would ever have happened." The line carries a double message: she has made the past their burden while telling them that nothing can be done about it. And to make sure they get the message, she treats them to another spectacle of her vanishing presence: a flight from reality into vast generalizations which place her condition and its roots in a realm they can never touch while offering their father as the displacement they can dig their teeth into. Anything that could trouble her in the present, such as the drinks she notes they've had, now only serves to enlist their service in delivering a single charge: "You're to blame, James" (67). For detachment to reign, past and

present must unite in that charge. But it is precisely with that end in sight
that Mary's unconscious betrays her, with the free association to a burden
she has not yet exorcised: "Don't you remember my father? He wouldn't
stop after he was stricken. He said doctors were fools! He thought, like you,
that whiskey is a good tonic! But, of course, there's no comparison at all. I
don't know why I—" (67–68). The dash is the Unconscious threatening an
awareness of connections that will open up a past that extends much further
than Mary wants to go.

The Lethe of forgiveness must reign. It's time to eat, and the sons rush
off to that ritual. But a new pair of eyes has been awakened. Mary is
confronted with the Look of a master actor who knows how to read her
roles, and where to take them. The Sartrean Look of this other isn't guilty
and afraid (Edmund) or guilty and angry (Jamie) but "sad and condemning" (Tyrone). Her defenses are powerless before this look. She sees it
staring at her through the back of her head, unraveling all her roles.
Undeterred by the plea that she used so adroitly on her sons—"You don't
understand!"—its accusation stands (68). Counterattack and excuses both
fail. She can ramble on in "her strange detachment," but this audience
refuses to be sucked into the flight of ideas. He checks it instead with the
question he won't renounce: "Why couldn't you have the strength to keep
on?" (69). Her only defense is to assert denial in its most primitive and
automatic form: "I don't know what you're talking about." But in disdain,
he refuses to be drawn into a conversation that can only delay a foregone
conclusion: "Never mind. It's no use now" (70). He's made a bold beginning, but he's done so by wearing the mask of an actor who has concen-
trated his entire role into the power of the look. The question is, can he
sustain it as a deed?

Scene ii

Crumbling Defenses: The Catholic Hour

In such a family, someone must assume the position of the ego, the mask of
substantial identity. It's a powerful position, especially if backed by a mighty
fortress and a lot of income properties. Tyrone's ego is based on three props
which are necessarily connected—the home, Catholicism, and money. Their
exposure, in sequence, makes up the first movement of scene ii. The second
movement brings forth the psychic burden they are meant to exorcise. The
first movement reveals the truth of James Tyrone's ego-identity: the contradictory, self-defeating project which constitutes what we may term the obses-

sional system of defenses. With its collapse, the principle rises which will claim him and the others. It is what all obsessionalism struggles to deny: the presence of the past. To get to the roots of the neurotic totality that is the family, the position of substance must be unmasked. For if the ego is also hollow at the core, then nothing can prevent collective descent into the maelstrom. This is the development we will now trace.

Through the issue of home Mary again illustrates her great ability to take responsibility for a disorder, only to switch the burden of guilt onto others in a way that annihilates their illusion and strips away their mask. Tyrone fights to prevent that outcome by claiming that substance existed before she destroyed it: it may no longer be a home, "but it was once, before you—" She masterfully reverses the blow and drives the knife directly into his psyche by reminding him that she, not he, knows the meaning of home. She sacrificed it in marrying him: "In a real home one is never lonely. . . . I gave up one to marry you—my father's home" (72).

The key wounds in Tyrone's psyche are reopened. He never had the identity he tried to locate in the home, and that is why all his efforts to deny that fact by building a home are foreordained to crumble away. Mary provides a litany of supporting evidence. Instead of making a home, he buys junk properties. Rather than getting a real doctor for Edmund, he uses a cheap quack, as he always did, especially when he sold Mary's "soul" to his own need to get a bargain. All Tyrone provides is cheap substitutes for the values he claims to represent. He sells out everyone to his insatiable need to deny his emptiness. The home has crumbled because the ego that constructed it lacks any foundation. The panic anger that spills over when Mary delivers the final blow, by identifying the home as the place where "one day you find yourself in hell" (74), can be withdrawn once it's done its work. "Forgive me, dear. . . . It's useless to be angry now" (75).

The forgiveness motif here introduced is one each character will resort to often as the play proceeds. From the start, O'Neill shows its function as a projective defense mechanism that operates within the orbit of what Freud calls negation. Through negation, one says something and then denies it because one really means it. In this play, forgiveness is always an ambiguous request—with claws. What one really asks is that others deny or not respond to the blow just inflicted on them. Forgiveness is that call for a halt to aggression which really amounts to an indirect way of advancing it. One can forgive only by denying that a wound has just been opened in one's psyche. "Forgive me" is really the command to engage in an act of repression. But it is also an offer Tyrone can't refuse. He must comply in order to sustain his own illusion: "This isn't a prison." He's fallen into the trap, and Mary exits the scene, delivering the crowning blow: "No. I know you can't help thinking it's a home" (75).

Ideology Takes Command: God—and Mammon

Intellectualization works best as a defense mechanism when one is able to identify one's position within an existing ideological system. Jamie and Edmund have given themselves powerfully to this motive, but as we learn in this scene, their father is its grand exemplar. He has invested his ego in the grandest substantiality yet constructed—the holy Roman Catholic Church, Irish style. Ideology is always a defense against knowing. But its greatest appeal arises when it offers a way to take the very thing one doesn't want to know and to know it in a way that prevents the knowledge from disrupting one's sense of "self."

In this scene, three ideologies battle it out before the common threat of the reality they don't want to know. Jamie's cynicism reduces Edmund's identification with Nietzsche to an intellectual pose constructed to defend against internalizing the very feelings it enables him to mimic. Edmund's attempt to parody and then scorn Jamie's cynicism thus lands him in a trap: "Christ, if I felt the way you do—!" Jamie responds, "I thought you did" (76). But cynicism is the great threat to Tyrone's worldview, and to vanquish it he wages a battle that extends from the neon lights on Broadway to the Upper Engadine. All "modern" ideologies signify nothing but sick psyches caught in the consequences of a theological denial that "has brought nothing but self-destruction." Sanity resides solely in "the one true faith of the Catholic Church" (77). Because the sons can respond to their father's faith only with dismissive scorn, Tyrone is free to evoke the substantial benefits it provides.

Tyrone is the best kind of Catholic—a lapsed Catholic. None better testifies to the faith's power to fulfill the deep function that is easily lost sight of when one is dazzled by the glitter of its rituals. Faith is the great protection against any reality testing that might lead to cynical, depressive recognitions. Knights of the faith know that the one unshakable task by which they prove their allegiance is to oppose the negative whenever it rears its head. In the face of hopelessness, a ray of hope must dawn. The grand theatre in which Tyrone gives his final performance every night, as he gets down on his knees and prays, is a theatre of magical deliverance. It provides an impregnable mask, for if one has the true faith, one has a true self, and though one can lapse, one can never lose it.

The residual benefit he receives confirms the difference between him and his wife: "If your mother had prayed, too—She hasn't denied her faith, but she's forgotten it, until now there's no strength of the spirit left in her to fight against her curse" (78). It's a nice piece of reasoning, faithful unto its source. Tyrone's strength of spirit is assured, his wife's addiction confined to a demonic force. Mary's curse cannot be laid on Tyrone's head. It exists instead to test a faith that can still provide deliverance.

Tyrone can face the inevitable because what's about to be repeated in his home is just another cycle in which hope disappointed by worldly agents—"Only I wish she hadn't led me to hope this time" (78)—lives on, bringing succor from above. As a first benefit, it restores the illusion Mary previously attacked. Tyrone takes the strength of spirit his faith provides and confers it on his family roots. Mary's illness begat Edmund's, and Tyrone is cleansed of both: "I never thought a child of mine—It doesn't come from my side of the family. There wasn't one of us that didn't have lungs as strong as an ox" (79). Catholicism has done its work: all losses have now been restored, and sorrows ended. Tyrone's ego is again secure, reinforced with a new character-armor.

If God protects Tyrone from knowledge from on high, Mammon delivers him from below. But in doing so, it too makes it impossible for him to attend to reality, especially within the home. The issue of money paralyzes him, because he has fixated the obsessional bases of his character on its operations. The topic of money need only be mentioned for Tyrone to be seized by an anxiety so peremptory that every effort he makes to check it proves powerless. He cannot halt a process which only stops when money reasserts its total claim over him. The comic side of his dilemma is that he always begins by trying to open his wallet, only to find a new reason why he can't.

Jamie is so aware of this mechanism that he knows any effort to persuade his father to tap the mother lode and send Edmund to a decent hospital is doomed. He also knows that medical science is powerless to challenge a further line of defense: those peculiar beliefs ("bog-trotter ideas" [80]) the Irish have developed about disease, its etiology and inevitable course, that really amount to an elaborate phobic mechanism. All this has its comic aspect, but the tragic side of Tyrone's dilemma concerns what's in the wallet. It is as empty and as full of need as Willy's suitcase, because it contains his actual ego-identity. Money functions for Tyrone as a mechanism for denying the loss and emptiness that defines his psyche. Poverty may have been his instructor, but Tyrone, like his wife, has learned to exploit the origin, to get "a secondary gain from illness." His obsessional fixation on investing money derives from an unending effort to deny a sense of psychic bankruptcy. Of necessity, all of his purchases end up being bad ones, because the unconscious always contrives the proper revenge. He must invest his money unwisely because hoarding is based on a loss that must repeat itself in order to sustain itself. Even if he got lucky and attained financial stability, the process would continue. There can never be enough money, because one must always use it to try to purchase from without the security one can never find within. As defense mechanism, however, the obsessional process indefinitely forestalls the day of reckoning by establishing a praxis that keeps all the masks rigidly in place and the total system running at whatever cost. The system of which we speak is capitalism, and though Tyrone is not one of its giants, he is a perfect representative of the phantom substantiality that drives the system as a whole in what remains a logic of implosion.

Earlier, Tyrone possessed the power of the look. Conflict has now forced him to articulate the ideological bases of his role as the familial ego. On one level it looks like a solid set of defenses, for O'Neill here represents the semiautomatic and habitual means whereby Tyrone banishes conflicts before they can gain a real footing. But once defenses have been activated, the process of their collapse has also commenced. Forced to assert themselves under strain, they no longer function as discharge mechanisms but move toward a direct confrontation with the reality they were invented to contain. That reality is the past, and with her reentry Mary first starts to bring it to fruition.

The Presence of the Past—And Its Future

Tyrone and Mary are locked in a perfect battle, because each agent's defense system is perfectly designed to drive the other person crazy. Magical denial of reality through obsessional mentation is Tyrone's defense. Projection is Mary's. His greatest fear is the collapse of the obsessional process. Hers is the return of the projections. His requires that "facts" be reworked until they are properly reinterpreted. Hers requires inflicting her anxieties on others. Guilt is their common burden. His need is to banish it by asserting the pragmatic claims of the present—and thus the pastness of the past. Her need is to secure its talons by making the entire past present, the better to inflict it on the other.

This conflict, focused on the issue of home, will be driven to drama with her reentry. In the process, the past, rather than either character, will reveal itself as the agent directing the scene. At the beginning of the scene, Mary and Tyrone repeat the old games in an effort to forestall the rising force of the past. Mutual leave-taking is commencing, with final excuses sought as defenses for what each will do with an isolation that is both desired and feared. Negation renews its work as each barbs the other, then withdraws the remark. But the claim that one has not taken offense builds to the point where the past erupts, and from this point nothing will stop it. The catalyst is the junk car and corrupt chauffeur Tyrone provided to keep Mary occu-

pied: "You mustn't be offended, dear. I wasn't offended when you gave me
the automobile. I knew you didn't mean to humiliate me. I knew that was
the way you had to do everything. I was grateful and touched. I knew buying
the car was a hard thing for you to do, and it proved how much you loved
me, in your way, especially when you couldn't really believe it would do me
any good." Such disclaimers make the deepest attacks and are received as
such. In reaction Tyrone strikes out at her entire system of lies. Mary's
trump card, the plea for forgetfulness and resignation, made nostalgic by
reference to "a romanticized" past which she wants to claim as an eternal
presence—"James! We've loved each other! We always will! Let's remember
only that"—now signifies for him the real truth: "You won't even try?"
(85). Reference to the past will now only serve to make its conflicts present.

Mary invokes the convent and plays it off against the mistress who sued
Tyrone shortly after his and Mary's marriage. He counters by recalling the
night when, without drugs, she "screamed for it, and ran out of the house in
your nightdress half crazy, to try and throw yourself off the dock!" (86). But
negation, "You mustn't remember," and barbed appeal, "You mustn't humiliate me so," followed by outright denial, "It doesn't matter. Nothing like
that ever happened. You must have dreamed it," will no longer work (86–
87). The past has now broken loose from all defenses. Attempts to shift the
blame—to Edmund and through him to Tyrone—only spread an evolving
pool of guilt. Tyrone's repeated plea to "forget the past" is thus brought
before a truth that will shortly ensnare the one who asserts it: "Why? How
can I? The past is the present, isn't it? It's the future, too" (87). The mutual
effort to teach repression has brought about the return of the repressed.

Enter Eugene, the dead child who has haunted the drama as the representative of the failure to mourn properly that has, over time, enmeshed the entire
family in guilt. Through his agency, blame becomes the token for attributing a
guilt that now reaches directly into the unconscious. Mary: "I blame only
myself. I swore after Eugene died I would never have another baby. I was to
blame for his death. If I hadn't left him with my mother to join you on the
road, because you wrote telling me you missed me and were so lonely, Jamie
would never have been allowed, when he still had measles, to go in the baby's
room. I've always believed Jamie did it on purpose. He was jealous of the
baby. He hated him. Oh, I know Jamie was only seven, but he was never
stupid. He'd been warned it might kill the baby. He knew. I've never been able
to forgive him for that." No one need ask who "warned" Jamie. The past
erupted returns envenomed. Mary's need to project the past is met by Tyrone's need to deny it, because failure to mourn is also the price he has paid in
order to repress the guilt: "Are you back with Eugene now? Can't you let our
dead baby rest in peace?" (87).

From one who claimed she couldn't remember the past, Mary has become its guardian. Her duty is to activate one past as revenge against the men's effort to force her to remember another. Her earlier plea against bringing up the past was really a threat, and she now delivers its subtext. Those who humiliate her with the past get their just deserts: she drives the blow back into their own Unconscious to set loose the guilt festering there. In shifting to that deeper register, it now becomes her holy duty to locate the true fault. Characteristically, she begins by assuming responsibility only to discharge it in a widening circle of guilt that now includes Edmund: "It [Eugene's death] was my fault. I should have insisted on staying with Eugene. . . . I shouldn't have let you insist I have another baby to take Eugene's place." Her only mistake, in short, was supporting her husband's failure to mourn. "I knew from experience by then that children should have homes to be born in. . . . I was afraid all the time I carried Edmund." Actually, she was addicted. "I knew something terrible would happen. . . . I never should have borne Edmund." Fleeing the guilty burden of this subtext, Tyrone activates another: "Be careful with your talk. If he heard you he might think you never wanted him" (88). But Mary is well tuned now. Denial has unleashed a rage that targets the other's unconscious.

Whenever one does so, however, one's own unconscious streams forth. This is a tide Mary may be unable to stem: "It's a lie! I did want him! More than anything in the world! You don't understand! I meant, for his sake. He has never been happy. He never will be" (88). Mary's use of mothering to produce the attribution which, as internal saboteur, controls Edmund's psyche is finally out in the open. The message she's been giving him all along—which he's received but refused to recognize—is this: Your death to atone for my guilt is the unalterable determination of your psychic being.

When one so nakedly expresses one's unconscious motives, the attendant regression always produces the return of something even more deeply repressed: "And now, ever since he's been so sick I've kept remembering Eugene and my father and I've been so frightened and guilty—" (88). Mary's psyche is unbound. Everything that comes after this dash can no longer be suppressed. When Edmund reenters, Mary panics, because he has now become a walking symbol of her unconscious guilt. The moment of comic relief O'Neill provides—as Tyrone tries to buy his way out of the situation by giving Edmund a ten spot—can't arrest the pressure that breaks as Mary tries to vanquish the Stone Quest: "I won't have it!" (90). What she won't have is any further talk about Edmund's condition, because death is the one reality that no one in this family has ever been able to face. As this scene develops, the drama begins to move toward the recognition that the denial of death, and of loss in general, may be the deepest force organizing each agent's Unconscious, with failure to mourn the operation that solidifies its power. The imperative—"I won't have it!"—derives its necessity as a last line of defense from the anxiety crypted in the psychic conflicts it would banish.

Edmund's illness must become "morbid nonsense," a pose derived from his books and mimicked in his poems, so that denial can now flourish as attack: "You're not really sick at all!" (90). The true purpose behind Mary's careful oedipalization of her youngest son is about to be revealed. Edmund faces a double dilemma. Denial of his mother's true feelings toward him is no longer possible. Her seductive behavior now reveals itself as play-acting, evidence of a fundamental lack of concern. "Don't, mother." In a sense, Edmund's dilemma is that he can't die but must lay dying. Exiting, Tyrone deftly exploits the situation, using the closeness between mother and son to lay his burdens on his son's shoulders: "Maybe if you asked your mother now what you said you were going to—" (91). The dash leaves Edmund with a contradictory task: to ask Mary to give up drugs and to ask her to face his illness. Edmund is caught in "the parent trap." What he doesn't know yet is that it's a system in which his illness is the weapon both parents use to deny and project guilt. His father does so by leaving him to bear that collective burden; his mother, by playing the guilt out to a more destructive end.

Mary has just "admitted" the real purpose behind her mothering. She will now reenact that role grandly to allay guilt and, in full regression, to salvage mothering's deeper purpose, autoaffection. Edmund activates that regressive necessity by resisting the appeals that previously snared him. The two characters stand at cross-purposes at the deepest psychic register. Edmund now knows that he must find some way to reverse the attribution that paralyzes his psyche. Mary, desperate to reestablish it, regresses to the unconscious motive that first led to its creation. In doing so, she moves herself irreversibly onto the psychic stage she will henceforth occupy. By act's end, she is indeed abandoned by all of them, but she has driven them away in order to liberate an internal drama. Deprived of worldly consolation, she can now seek heavenly deliverance, knowing that the greatest joy in heaven is over a sinner who repents, especially one who does so masochistically.

The soul is a great deliverer from the psyche. Proclaiming it lost conveniently abolishes the reality of one's situation. Redemption is what matters, not endless mucking about in the past. The Blessed Virgin Mary cometh not to bring truth but to deliver one from existential guilt. Her forgiveness then restores a pristine past in which you were once united with her before woeful experiences, whatever they were, estranged you. And when the Blessed Mother comes to rescue you, the more abject and alone she finds you, the better. Mary fits herself perfectly to that role by donning the perfect mask—that of a martyr who "scream[s] with agony" and "laugh[s]" at the same time because a true self has been restored (94).

Ripe in that purpose, Mary banishes Edmund and gets ready to go to the "drugstore" (94). Euphemisms are no longer needed. She may need drugs to get there, but the BVM is the mainliner that will deliver her psyche from itself and from her family. In a parting shot, she consigns her sons to the company of the other kind of woman. Exit Edmund to join two offstage voices bidding their rapid adieus.

Left alone, the dream of deliverance collapses. Why? Mary cites dishonesty as the cause, but on the deeper psychic register a far greater disruption has taken place. I call it the return of the projections. Without external pegs to sustain projection, guilt streams back into the psyche, unraveling all mechanisms of denial. "You're lying to yourself again. You wanted to get rid of them. Their contempt and disgust aren't pleasant company. You're glad they're gone. Then Mother of God, why do I feel so lonely?" (95). The BVM has her work cut out for her. Mary's struggle to escape consciousness has barely begun. She has, however, moved onto the proper stage, as have the others. With the collapse of defenses, all attain that inner stage where the core conflicts they hoped to escape lie in readiness for the great psychological examinations that will constitute the second half of the play.

The adage Once a Catholic, always a Catholic usually refers to the inability to overcome guilt. In this act O'Neill shows that its deeper function is as a mechanism of denial and transcendence. The permanent appeal of their religion for Tyrone and Mary is the fog it introduces into their consciousness, such that nothing in the real world or the past can be attended to forthrightly. Catholicism creates a particular kind of inwardness, one that prevents genuine psychological probing by mimicking that process. The pseudodrama of sin and deliverance is a drama of abstractions and theological generalities (forgiveness, redemption, mercy) that absolve agents of concrete responsibility for the actual psychological wounds they inflict on one another by making it impossible for them to attend to those realities in any meaningful or honest way. Dissolving in a pool of guilt (i.e., the old Church) or shedding the bag of guilt we all carry (the new dispensation) are opposite sides of the same coin and amount to the same thing: protecting the psyche from the only responsibility worthy of the name—the responsibility to know oneself in depth without hiding behind abstractions, especially those which introduce the labor of the negative—guilt—all the better to deprive it of its concrete power to expose the hidden places of one's experience and one's psyche.

In seeing Catholic guilt for what it is, O'Neill perhaps becomes the first ex-Catholic. The convenient joke Catholics make about their guilt is thereby turned back against that audience. Real guilt awaits them at the other end of their pseudodrama. Mary is correct in this: in one sense Catholicism is, indeed, to blame, because it has created the internal regulators that hold in place a process that prevents self-knowledge. It must do so, of course, to bar the kind of psychological probing that produces psyches with the power to reverse the reign of the internal saboteur. But lest we become sanguine, O'Neill will now show us that as inner presence the saboteur regulates the psyche in ways we have scarcely begun to fathom.

Act III: The Return of the Projections: or, Mary's Narratives

Act III, dominated by Mary, is composed of two long scenes of self-revelation played out before two radically different audiences. In the first, Mary thinks she's found, in the servant girl Cathleen, the perfect audience for restoring her illusions. The collapse of that effort drives her to the self-revelation she then inflicts on her proper audience, the three men, in order to bring them to the same psychological state that affects her.

O'Neill's stage is now one of extended self-revelation. Two choral voices define its competing pressures. The first, the fog, defines the collective project. The second, the foghorn, is the intruding voice from within that must be silenced for consciousness to extinguish itself.

The Uncanny Audience

When one's projections start to return, one seeks an audience. Flooded with a past that terrifies, one must replace it with a past that delivers. Memory must be diverted into innocent channels of association, as when the foghorn here recalls Tyrone's snoring, recounted with the requisite nostalgia. If we must remember the past, let's remember the trivial facts that can be exploited for idle talk with someone who will offer only reassurance. Mary is looking for the kind of audience we find when we join a support group or choose to tell our troubles to that friend whom we know will never probe beneath the surface. In Cathleen, Mary has apparently found such an audience in the Irish "folk," ready on cue with the archaic beliefs. On snoring: "It's a sign of sanity, they say" (99).

But if Cathleen is the perfect audience for reassurance, she's the least useful for the deeper motives behind projection. To keep projections from returning, one must get the other to bear them. But when Mary presents her litany of the men's failing with the detached air that terrifies them, Cathleen, charmed by the performance, raises the question that cuts through the mask: "Speaking of acting, Ma'am, how is it you never went on the stage?" (101). Sometimes the most innocent audience asks the uncanniest question. The need to deny she's acting drives a wedge right into the core split that defines Mary's psyche. Acting is both Mary's fear and her desire. The dialectical connection between those motives is the instability she must deny to sustain her role. "I was a very pious girl. I even dreamed of becoming a nun. I've never had the slightest desire to be an actress" (102).

With no one to carry the projections, the pent-up guilts projection was meant to relieve stream back into the subject. Acting now requires a narrative presentation of oneself. But in telling one's story, one must attempt through narrative to halt a process that can easily slip out of control. Each episode is, in effect, a limited exposure, meant to put an end to narrative. Doing so, it produces the opposite. For each story Mary tells exacerbates the split in her psyche, which can only be displaced by a further story. We thus get a chronological series of collapsing illusions which lay bare, with perfect logic, the psychic disorders they were meant to conceal. Mary recounts what looks like the chronology of her successive dreams, only to reveal an underlying structure that makes the process a ceaseless repetition of a single fixation. The neurotic's desire—to find that past in which one was happy—is thus progressively undermined and exposed. Narrative, in fleeing into the future, circles inward toward the buried past, eventually producing a full return of the repressed.

Mary begins by playing up the split between the "morally questionable" claims of the theatre and the ethical superiority of a more exalted stage. Brought up in a respectable home and educated in the convent, one hardly knows there is such a thing as the theatre. And one hasn't "the slightest desire to be an actress." If you are a pious girl, your first dream is to become a nun. The irony, of course, is that one appeal of that vocation is the power of the costume, complete with cross in front and the gold ring signifying your marriage to Christ. Mary is always a dreamer, but her first dream is one of sequestered transcendence in a realm where conflict can't touch her. As we'll soon learn, that dream exists because conflict has already scarred her: Mary's first dream is her mother's and bears the contradiction defining her parents' relationship.

Cathleen again punctures the illusion with a comment that calls attention to the effect Mary has on any audience that sees her in action: "Well, I can't imagine you a holy nun." The straightforwardness of the remark demands further narrative. Mary must strive to reinforce the split that has become its theme by drawing out the effects of the negative term. Theatre now becomes the force that deprived her of two homes and that "has always stood between me and—" (102). She can't complete the sentence, because her theme has now become loss. To avoid that specter she must turn back and delve deeper into the past, seeking a presence prior to loss. That motive takes her back in longing to her original scene—the parental home—where surprises await her. All she knows is that the pain she experienced in losing it has never left her. The secret she will soon reveal is that the pain was actually created there.

Cathleen, by literalizing all topics, functions as Lear's fool to Mary's flight into the fog. In recounting her experience earlier in the day with the druggist, Cathleen inadvertently puts the topic of drugs in the proper perspective. A drug is a great way of denying psychic pain, but until the drug clicks, the pain must be externalized. The principle of association no longer brings relief, however. Locating the "fault" in her hands, Mary flees into memories that are meant to displace loss but only succeed in exposing its origins. In evoking the dream that was supposed to replace the loss of her original dream, Mary reveals familial conflict as the source of both dreams—and their hidden connection. Though it is nurtured in the convent, Mary's second dream, of becoming a great concert pianist, bears the conflicts of her relationship with her father, just as her first dream, we now learn, carries the weight of her mother's psyche. The second, in replacing the first, is meant to be a substitute which restores its loss. Instead, it exposes the subtext that reveals both dreams as flights from the disclosure of suppressed familial conflict. Mary's mother created the guilt for which the convent offered the only exit. Her father gave her a different identity in offering her the role of a pampered child, a part she plays for all it's worth.

Mary speaks of her second dream as if it were a natural outgrowth of the first, in order to suppress the "oedipal" connection that is its true foundation. But its imaginary sequel delivers that truth: the grand European tour with Daddy is interrupted by the emergence of James Tyrone, because he's the object-choice perfectly designed to bring the contradiction at the center of Mary's psyche out into the world while making it impossible for her to live there. "I might have gone—if I hadn't fallen in love with Mr. Tyrone. Or I might have become a nun. I had two dreams. To be a nun, that was the more beautiful one. To become a concert pianist, that was the other." The second appears to be only a slight fall from grace. But when Mary now looks at her hands, the association brings a third dream and the need to find, in narrating it, the accident needed to deliver her psyche from the accumulating pains of a lost past. It will, however, unleash the subtext that collapses all temporalities by revealing the identical function all dreams play in Mary's psyche. Drugs are but a conduit to the real process: "You go back until at last . . . Only the past when you were happy is real" (104).

To get there you have to pass through the past where you weren't happy but thought you were. Mary's third dream is about that momentary resting place. She must now tell that story so that its collapse will enable her, unencumbered, to renew the search for that prior past where she was really happy. The truth thereby revealed will expose that haven as the breeding ground of a psyche shaped to provide a perfect representation of the repressed sexual conflicts between her parents.

Mary's third narrative develops through two long monologues. The first is spoken in the presence of Cathleen. The second is enacted under the shadow of the BVM. Their connection will emerge, and with it the contradiction that Mary will act out in the second half of act III. Mary's narratives enact a dialectic that always moves in two directions. The first occupies her "conscious" effort: to replace one past with another which restores loss. The second is the voice of the unconscious: the revelation of the hidden connections that make the entire process a vast circle of self-deception and self-unraveling—endless, convoluted loss.

As Mary narrates the story of Tyrone's appearance in her cloistered world, the subtext active in the first two dreams rushes forth to reap its buried treasure. As Cathleen notes, Mary indeed was not destined to be a nun. "If you think Mr. Tyrone is handsome now, Cathleen, you should have seen him when I first met him" (105). Tyrone then strides forth in romantic readiness to fulfull every sexual dream the convent fosters by repressing. Mary becomes the maiden, rescued from the tower by the dashing knight whom she loves at first glance and who carries her off. That fantasy fulfilled, a deeper desire can surface. Mary proves victorious over all women who stand in waiting, whether in convents or at stage doors. Preparing for the victory, she primes the envy of the other convent girls with the letter from her father telling her she will meet the matinee idol at Easter. Recounting that event, she gushes in language meant to diffuse, for Cathleen, the proper randy atmosphere into the afternoon's drinks.

In the process, a new subtext tumbles forth, this one shared by father and daughter. If a father must eventually give away the daughter he's eroticized in reaction to the overpowering guilt his wife tried to give both of them over things physical, what better palliative to his self-esteem than James Tyrone? Priming the match that will fulfill his fantasy, he gives Mary and Tyrone just the right facts about each other, then carefully brings them together. Tyrone struts his hour on the stage. Mary, drawing on the books she, like a similar agent, Emma Bovary, read when immured in the convent, weeps for joy and then, afraid her "eyes and nose would be red," cons the perfect part as she goes backstage to meet a man who is "different from all ordinary men, like someone from another world" (105). In recounting the moment, Mary makes no effort to hide her coquettishness from Cathleen. In pure and blushing teary-eyed girlhood, sans makeup, Mary presented herself, a master performer, to another great actor, who also fell in love at first sight.

Mary has always been acting, and in finding the stage that becomes her, she gives herself over fully to her greatest role: "I forgot all about becoming a nun or a concert pianist. All I wanted was to be his wife." The proper psychic register has now been primed in Mary's audience; the true appeal of the dream can now be revealed. Though none dare call it so, Mary's victory confirms an erotic power so great that other women remain powerless to tamper with it. Thirty-six years of marriage and not a "breath of scandal about him. I mean, with any other woman. Never since he met me" (105), the added pleasure being the memory of the scandal concerning a rejected woman that surfaced shortly after the marriage.

Mary's dream always was an erotic one, and in fulfilling it Tyrone seems to cancel the split Mary's mother worked so hard to enforce. Audience applause is no longer needed to sustain that illusion. Having served her purpose, Cathleen is dismissed with the appropriate words: "Yes, yes, go. I don't need you now" (106).

The Ideal Audience

As we all note whenever it suits our purpose, those who don't understand the past are condemned to repeat it. In Mary's case, that connection is about to reveal how the split that defines her psyche weds her to an impossible project in which each dream of deliverance produces a regression which activates the claims of a disorder which drives her even further into the past, because her unconscious is ruled by the effort to make an impossible reparation. If the sexual has finally arisen in Mary's third narrative, it must now be banished.

With the loss of a vicarious external audience, another audience resumes its place in Mary's inner stage and claims its pound of flesh. Mary's dream of happiness with Tyrone is destroyed by the pull of a prior dream. In reasserting its power to provide the only past in which she could be happy, it reveals itself as the neurotic source that shaped the past which she has just evoked and must now destroy. That deeper attachment now rises as a voice that takes its revenge by tearing her sentimental romanticism to shreds. The pristine past must cancel the other, lest their sexual connection rise to consciousness. In marrying Tyrone, Mary has violated her tie to the BVM—and on the deepest level the tie of guilt that binds her to her mother. To restore it she must get back to a time "before you knew he existed" (107), a time before the fall into sexual experience and a loss that can never be repaired, yet must be—that of virginity.

To regain union with the BVM, she must eradicate everything that connects her to her husband—and to her children—in a regression so complete that it wipes them from her consciousness. That impossibility must here "grow to event," because "the eternal feminine" that draws Mary on presides internally in a relationship she can never escape. She can only placate it, while awaiting the chance eventually to merge with it, in a dissolution of identity.

The BVM invoked at the end of act II to deliver Mary from loneliness here presents the bill. As purification ritual, the BVM imposes on her devotees the duty of an unremitting self-criticism. In carrying out that categorical imperative, one must undo everything that has happened since one first strayed from her. If, as Freud claims, finding the inner "object" is always refinding it, Mary can do so only by confessing the nullity of everything else.

Distinct inner voices collapse, revealing their true identity. The voice that cynically attacks Mary—"You're a sentimental fool. What is so wonderful about that first meeting between a silly romantic schoolgirl and a matinee idol? You were much happier before you knew he existed, in the Convent when you used to pray to the Blessed Virgin"—is the person to whom she prays her "Hail, Mary, full of grace!" It is also the voice that immediately replies, "You expect the Blessed Virgin to be fooled by a lying dope fiend reciting words! You can't hide from her!" (107). Arisen in its true venom, this is the voice that condemns Mary to the impossible project she must now attempt. Cleansing her psyche by self-undoing has become the duty to shed the ties that bind her to the agents shortly to return. To do so, she must deny her role in their conflicts in such a way that the burdens she thereby projects and discharges will be borne by them at a deeper level of their psyches than she has thus far addressed. Mary may tremble at their return, but she is also "horribly lonely" (108), because the inner voice feeding on her craves other blood. She must find some way to bring everyone to the state she's reached so that all will be left with the same burden and the same need.

The Real Audience

Returning home, Tyrone and Edmund face a problem that makes them ripe for Mary's work. What does one do when the necessary illusion is dead and the struggle to deny the facts over? Mechanisms of defense are running down. In repeating themselves, they now start to reverse themselves, bringing forth the results they were meant to hold at bay. A general unbinding of the psyche is in progress, and it will catch up with each agent in act IV. Mary provides the necessary catalyst. What begins as another ritual of inter-familial alignment thus produces a strikingly new result. Mary revives the game of alignment and exclusion—"Jamie has been lost to us for a long time" (109)—to load collective ills on a single scapegoat, only to play it out so that by the end of the act all three men are united under that sign as a single agent with a single malevolent purpose. Mary has not yet achieved the past of bliss. Too much of the other past is lurking about. The causes of her fall from grace must be identified and loaded with responsibility before deliverance can spread its bright wings and claim her for itself.

Good-Enough Mothering

The first thing that must go is the mother's connection to her babies. The attack on Jamie's childhood begins as a story of Mary's attempt to save Edmund. In the course of the tale all three children are abandoned—of necessity, since that is the only way to deny psychological responsibility for what happened to them in infancy. Nostalgia creates an unreal past—they were perfect, happy infants—in order to repudiate responsibility for their present condition by making it impossible to locate its cause in the original mother-infant dyad. Jamie's childhood is thus split between the perfect child she created and the jealous brat he became.

Denial is a magnificent mechanism up to a point, but that point is now quickly reached and spills over into what can no longer be denied. Eugene was happy like Jamie "before I let him die through my neglect" (109). Childhood is becoming a scene of multiple disruptions. As they intrude to shatter Mary's story, each must be exorcised by being shifted onto a substitute son who, in infancy, becomes everything his siblings were not, with the cause now located in his "nature," not in his mother's actions. The infant Edmund gets "frightened about nothing at all" and cries "at the drop of a hat." The repressed truth of her own neglect thereby becomes the fault of nature laid solely on the substitute son's shoulders. The good-enough mother never had a good-enough child. So identified, Edmund returns the ticket: "Maybe I guessed there was a good reason not to laugh" (110).

To discharge that blow, Mary must repeat the entire process, with the fault now shifted back to Jamie. But the maternal home can no longer be the scene: "Who would have thought Jamie would grow up to disgrace us." Disorder must come from an outside that intrudes inside the home. Jamie becomes a brilliant schoolboy, only to fall apart through drink. The only hitch in this story is the extremity of the contrast: "It's hard to understand—" Another gap. Projection intervenes to get the fault located in Tyrone's example: "You brought him up to be a boozer." The cause thus located is then read back into childhood: Tyrone always gave Jamie "a teaspoonful of whiskey" for a nightmare or a stomachache (110).

Projection as denial can now do double duty. Edmund's nightmares can be admitted as proof that he was born with a "flawed" nature, but that fault can now be shifted onto the father. A great concern is thereby exorcised. Mary is well aware that her anxiety is the probable cause of Edmund's nervousness. And where your fear of detection is greatest, your mechanism of denial must be foolproof. Seeking double assurance, Mary returns to narrative in order to play up the split between Tyrone's family origins and hers. That theme is richly overdetermined with the conflicts Mary suppressed in earlier telling Cathleen the romantic version of her marriage to James Tyrone. In now telling the rest of the story, she releases the subtext she previously repressed. What begins as a story about Tyrone's family ends up revealing the sexual disorders present from the beginning of a relationship Mary previously staged as one of sexual bliss.

Man and Wife, Therefore My Mother

The story we now get is one of a drunkard carried home by his friends while still on his honeymoon. Memory locates the fault in the spouse, not in the blushing bride, who claims such knowledge would have saved her from marriage. Mary's memory, as always, is carefully selective. One might well ask why Tyrone needed to vacate the marriage bed. To keep that text repressed, Mary recounts the countless subsequent times when she waited alone in "ugly hotel rooms" while Tyrone got drunk (113).

In response, Tyrone could activate the subtext he will turn to in act IV when sexual conflict becomes the meat of his tale. But at this point his need for denial is so desperate that the look of authority which terrified Mary in act II has now become the mask of a comic clown who invents one preposterous avoidance after another. Early in the scene, blinding himself to the obvious, he tells her he's glad to be home "when you act like your real self" again (112). When she ends the present attack by asking rhetorically whether she's been a good wife, he quickly reassures her: "I'm not complaining, Mary" (114). And he remains powerless when Edmund seizes on his mother's story to make his father responsible for whatever ills he wants to project: "Christ! No wonder—" (113).

Tyrone has retreated to his last line of defense. All he can do is label everything Mary says as drug-induced behavior not really intended to cause harm. Mary is free to remember "out loud" while claiming she's sorry for whatever offense unimpeded memory begets. Under that dispensation, she completes the banishment of Tyrone by telling the story of her wedding day.

The carefully selected details she presents about the circumstances surrounding that event, however, give forth the subtext neither wants to confront. Memory for Mary has become an act of deliberate cruelty that cuts
deeply into Tyrone's psyche. But the past has become a place loaded with
traps that will rebound on the inventor's head. She cannot recall it without
reexperiencing the loss that came to define it—and without being driven
further toward a past that will not replace the loss but will reveal loss as the
origin of both projection and repression. In telling the story of her wedding
day, everything kept from Cathleen rushes forth. Arrayed for the bridal,
Mary's psychic energies are focused then and now on all she has invested in
her wedding gown. In the process the husband virtually disappears. Mary's
parents, however, emerge in a new light as determining agents in her psyche.
The mother, who wanted a nun, now turns guilt into a judgment which
projects resentment into the future: Mary is destined to be a lousy wife. To
complete the blow, her father is identified as cause: " 'You've spoiled that
girl so, I pity her husband if she ever marries. She'll expect him to give her
the moon. She'll never make a good wife' " (114). The father, in full prodi-
gality, enacts revenge and his oedipal role by dressing his daughter in the
best garments money can buy. Tyrone doesn't know it, but he's been cast in a
role similar to the one in which Scottie finds himself in *Vertigo*. The other
man dresses Mary, and she is an apt pupil whose pampered vanity is perfectly matched to the miserliness of the husband her father chooses for her.
The perfect match, in short, is a stark contradiction sure to fester.

The conflicts Mary will bring to the relationship are all present in the
gown. "That wedding gown was nearly the death of me and the dressmaker,
too!" (114). Endlessly fashioned, it is "never quite good enough." Once
done, a touch threatens to "spoil it." The dressmaker must leave. Mary
alone is permitted "to examine" herself "in the mirror." The narcissistic
perfection thereby attained completes Mary's triumph over other women:
"You're just as pretty as any actress he's ever met, and you don't have to use
paint" (115). The mirror on the wall confirms who's the fairest of them all.

But the object that embodied the perfection of that mirroring is no sooner
refound in memory than it is again lost—forever, it seems—and with that
fact comes the duty to seek it to the exclusion of all other concerns. The
gown has now taken on a double function. It is the Lacanian *objet petit a*
that invests Mary's narcissism in the lure sure to capture the desire of the
other, and it is the lost object that compels Mary to repeat the magical effort
of the *fort/da* game in a regression that will drive her ever further backward
toward that past which made her marriage the foreordained disaster it has
become.[9] Thus, as she speaks, both present and future vanish. The gown,
evoked in memory as something Mary hoped to pass on to her daughter,

becomes, as she speaks, a mausoleum which she fits herself into by becoming "as small as possible," a toy doll. Her father, welcoming that adornment, lets her "have duchesse lace on my white satin slippers, and lace with the orange blossoms in my veil." After marriage she takes the gown out whenever she is "lonely," but then it only makes her cry because it has become the grand symbol of the loss that has haunted her since marriage (115). That loss is not the loss of her vanity but of her virginity. Having lost it, Mary must bury the symbol so that someday she can find it again and reclaim her innocence. She has created a Crypt for herself so that she will never have to give herself over to experience.

That Crypt now torments her. Its logic has begun to take its revenge. Because that is so, by the end of the monologue all her projections have returned. But they now become a burden that cannot be re-repressed. Mary must find the lost gown, both to expel the sexual conflicts that have broken loose in her psyche and to return to the haven that will enable her to forget them by assuring herself that they never existed. She's on a main line to the BVM, in full regression, but she can't complete that movement yet. To secure her desire, further banishments are required.

The Arrival of Hate

To achieve her goal, all intruding realities must be subjected to a withdrawal of concern that reduces them to the status of nonentities. Edmund is the first thing that must go. In the ensuing scene between Edmund and his mother, the question he asked earlier—Do you love me, Mother?—is answered with the arrival of the force that will dominate the rest of the play—hatred. As it moves center stage, each will be confronted by it with the knowledge they most want to deny. As overture to that process, this scene, in repeating the earlier scene between mother and son, drives forth its subtext with a vengeance.

Edmund's attempt to tell his mother of his illness becomes a process in which the two of them take leave of each other by delivering the message each previously suppressed. All of Mary's attempts to enlist Edmund's sympathy now confirm for Edmund only one thing: his mother does not love him. Her need supersedes all other claims. Though he listens, in bemused sympathy, as she spins out yet another story mocking Tyrone's origins, he is no longer taken in. Her attempt to turn that fact against him blows up in her face: "Yes, dear, you've had to listen, but I don't think you've ever tried to understand" (117). Edmund receives the subtext—the charge that he's an ingrate—and returns it, upping the ante: "You haven't asked me what I found out this afternoon. Don't you care a damn?" Mary's need to deny responsibility for his condition by shifting the blame now produces the opposite effect, as Edmund locates the cause of disease not in his father's boozing but in his mother's psyche, a blow he reinforces by making Mary's addiction the origin of his own disorder: "God, it made everything in life seem rotten!" (118).

The real terms of their relationship are now out in the open. In communicating the details of his illness—"I'm going to tell you whether you want to hear or not"—Edmund now aims directly at the deepest psychic register, driving Mary into a paranoid panic over the prospect of a jealous Tyrone sending her son to the sanatorium to deprive her of "every one of" her babies, especially the one she loves most. (119). Come full circle, Mary clings to her last son in a desperate effort to deny her cruelty toward him. Mary's psyche is laid bare. All her operations and defenses now expose the core.

Edmund deliberately advances that process. Her lack of concern is no longer the issue. The issue is now love and hate. Making the latter explicit, Edmund now admits, for the first time, that if he left home to get her attention, he also did so in order to hurt her: "And why are you so against my going away now? I've been away a lot, and I've never noticed it broke your heart!" (119). The cycle of fleeing home in anger only to return seeking love has again collapsed, but Mary's attempt to turn Edmund's absences to advantage—"After I knew you knew—about me—I had to be glad whenever you were where you couldn't see me"— now only reinforces Edmund's charge: "All this talk about loving me—and you won't even listen when I try to tell you how sick—" (119–20).

A new connection has begun to stalk the stage. All surface mechanisms now shimmer with a subtext that connects hate with the drive toward death. Mary's need to deny death is such that she can only respond to Edmund's illness by calling it a piece of acting: "You're so like your father, dear. You love to make a scene out of nothing so you can be dramatic and tragic." In response, Edmund throws the repressed in her face: "People do die of it. Your own father—" That blow activates, as a last defense, the voice through which the mother polices the son's unconscious, the imperative, barring the introduction of reality. "I forbid . . . do you hear me?" Edmund submits, but only after delivering two final blows: "I hear you, Mama. I wish to God I didn't! It's pretty hard to take at times, having a dope fiend for a mother!" (120). The son's submission is now full of resentment and a refusal to deny reality. "Forgive me" is a defense mechanism that will no longer work. They have no way of renewing contact. All they can do is leave each other to an isolation that has become a space dominated by the other person's hate.

Confined to that space, Mary momentarily gives herself over to death and the possibility of a suicide which must be accidental if it is to achieve its purpose—a merger of her cleansed consciousness with the BVM. As we'll see, this is precisely what she will achieve at the end of act IV.

The Isolation Ward

Hate rises up in a different way in the scene that ends the act. In mutual isolation, Tyrone and Mary face each other, unable to bridge the gap between them. Instead, they go through the motions of concern for Edmund, so that, in retiring, they can give their exit line the twist of a new dispensation. Tyrone gives himself permission to say he hates her: "Up to take more of that God-damned poison, is that it? You'll be like a mad ghost before the night's over." Mary seizes the opportunity to identify all three men as a group united by that hatred: "You say such mean, bitter things when you've drunk too much. You're as bad as Jamie or Edmund" (123).

Hatred is now out in the open as the truth of the family. It is a truth that has been produced by the repeated efforts to deny it. As such, it is the origin, the process, and the end of all the interactions that have been in progress since the play began. It is what relationships become when defense mechanisms make attention to conflict impossible. Hate may not have been the only thing that was present in the beginning, but it is what happens to the origin when its conflicts are repeatedly displaced and delayed. Hate is what the repression of conflict produces through and as time. And when it finally announces itself, its results are irreversible. The patient labor of acts I–III has produced this inestimable gain. O'Neill has taken the sentimental notion that the force of love is somehow always present in the family, struggling for rebirth, and delivered it over to the just verdict of experience. Once upon a time love may have been present, but it is no longer. Only the counterfeit gestures remain, now seen by all as tokens in the working of hate. The family has finally moved onto a tragic stage. What they do when they find themselves there generates what is perhaps the greatest drama—the attempt to confront hate as the truth one must face about oneself and one's family. This is the drama of act IV.

Act IV: Self-Revelation as Self-Unraveling

Toward the Crypt: The Dialectic of Regression and Projection

Long Day's Journey dramatizes regression as the process that leads the psyche to the truth about itself. Once intellectualizing defenses have collapsed and "regression in the service of the ego" has failed, the regressing psyche is progressively stripped bare, as its more "advanced" states reveal that they have no being apart from their defensive function. The only way to prevent descent into one's hidden conflicts is to project them onto others. Once this process is blocked, consciousness becomes a rising anxiety that can only deepen as all the disorders we've externalized stream back inward, infecting the psyche with itself.

When one projects and discharges one's aggression, one has found a great release but no solution to the burden of one's psyche. That burden remains the truth one must continue to flee, because projective aggression is ultimately rage over a relationship controlling one's inner world that one refuses to face. That is why it is only when aggression meets a reciprocal or greater aggression that the psyche first attains that Hegelian struggle to the death that creates the possibility of self-overcoming.[10] Each agent strikes at the core of the other's inwardness, with no way to halt that process by latching on to some available object of projective blame.

We have attained the truth of our condition. When our projections are blocked, we are first given over to ourselves in a privileged way. It is now possible to spot the hidden motives we've been acting on and become properly frustrated with their abiding control over our lives, developing a frustration that can only grow as we discover we still have to find some way to project them, since aggression undischarged festers and, raging within, turns on the inventor's head. The only real alternative is self-overcoming, and for once the psychological context and requirements for that act are on the table. Regression has brought the psyche to the dialectical core of its being. It can now move only in one of two directions—toward dissolution or toward active reversal.

Regression, in shattering the rational ego, delivers us over to the psyche. The regressed self is not a subject who has lost identity but one who has regained contact with the passions and motives that have shaped its experience. The drama of regression derives its power from the possibility that its logic is neither repetition nor the restoration of the rational function, but a descent into the Crypt, toward a recovery of those conflicts and principles of psychic self-mediation that forever shatters the system of lies we have set up to escape their demands. For once all escapes are blocked, the psyche is gnawed inwardly toward recognitions it can no longer evade.

Another way to formulate this idea is as a dramatistic logic of projection. If you want to know someone, study what they inflict on others. This aphorism attempts to formulate the tragic possibility contained in Harry Stack Sullivan's great insight that the attitude we manifest to others must faithfully reflect the true attitude we have toward ourselves. It takes that idea and makes it raw, dangerous—a principle that necessarily issues in drama. Projection is the need to be rid of the self-consciousness that haunts you by inflicting it on others. It is also the act that brings that truth to light. For projection is essentially this: We take what nailed us, and we pass it on.

The crypt from which projection derives is the realm of the basic wound and its correlate, the threat of psychic disintegration.[11] This is a realm presided over by those primordial others who exist as internal sabo-teurs, inflicting the judgment that turns all our efforts to escape their power into acts of self-unraveling. That situation maintains, because the wound is always tied to any underlying conception of self—as worthless, bad, shameful, humiliated, guilty—that is so terrifying that we will do most anything to escape it. In doing so we invariably project it, because, to be safe, we must drive it out into the world; and the only way to keep it securely anchored there is by investing it in someone else. But all es-capes remain haunted castles built on sand. Once the ego and its defenses are stripped away, we return to the gaping wound we must assume as our innermost being because the elaborate structures we have designed to es-cape it are nothing but evasions and delays, no matter how solid they may seem or how reinforced they are by consensual validations and reflected appraisals.

It is often said today that we must reinvent love.[12] Here's one thing that need might mean. When we finally meet that other who throws our projec-tions back at us—initially, in most cases, through the reciprocal projections we have activated—the possibility of a drama that will take us to the core of our being has finally been engaged. As conflict develops, one regressed psyche projects its core, which activates the countermovement of another psyche that is driven, in reaction and reply, to a deeper delving into its own crypt. Relating has become the act of mutual self-discovery.

A process similar to this overtakes the agents in the final act of *Long Day's Journey*. With the crypt fully opened, the real motives stream forth. All the characters reveal the deepest truths about themselves and their rela-tionships. In saying this, I'm not suggesting that the characters attain self-understanding. As we'll see, they remain in many ways blind, because the movement of self-revelation for them is also a movement of self-unraveling. The truth is available only to an interpretation that articulates both sides of the dialectical connection. This is the possibility that a drama which enters the Crypt creates for the audience. As the characters onstage grope toward the core of a psychic disorder which they know only insofar as they suffer from it, the structural dynamic of the interfamilial psyche is revealed. For the authentic audience, articulating and internalizing that understanding becomes the task of interpretation.

Act IV is composed of two great recognition scenes, one between a father and son, the other between two brothers, followed by Mary's coda. The two recognition scenes are built on a series of circles drawn by the characters in an attempt to contain the reality that has risen up to claim them—hate. Each circle breaks apart at the end, forcing the need to draw a larger circle. In the

(149), now carries the force of his own desire—which is not for knowledge but for a release from the consciousness that arises when stories go too far. He will shortly be forced to confront that consciousness, driven to it by his father's need to move into the heart of his own ulcer.

As that second wave breaks, Tyrone confronts the paradox that has never ceased to unnerve him. Unlike the other members of his family, he found the thing he loved—and with it the promise of an artistic integrity that could replace everything previously suffered and lost—only to sell out his talent for money. Because he knows where the cause of that fault lies, his character has now become a genuine problem to him. As he probes it, the past in which he was once "happy," and all the subsequent pasts in which he snatched a momentary respite, become scenes of a loss that can't be replaced or denied. It is a great moment, for though he doesn't understand the psychological truth of what he is about to reveal, the circle of denial has for once been shattered. For the first time in the play, loss is accepted. Though the cause must remain a mystery, the mystery is located squarely in the self: "What the hell was it I wanted to buy, I wonder, that was worth—" (150).

Edmund intervenes with understanding, forgiveness, and the desire to put a halt to knowledge. But those mechanisms cannot halt the third wave, because Tyrone is now fixated on the right relationship to money: "I don't know what the hell it was I wanted to buy" (151).

He does know what he sold, however, and remembering it he now inflicts upon himself the shame he earlier tried to discharge. Mary has misplaced a gown. We now learn that Tyrone has also lost an object, a paper with some words of praise from Edwin Booth he carried in his wallet until he could no longer bear all that it came to signify. Edmund's poetic poses are abhorrent, because they are but intellectualized parodies of a fault that tumbles forth as Tyrone for once hits on the right Shakespearean allusion: " 'The fault, dear Brutus, is not in our stars, but in ourselves that we are underlings' " (152). That fault is buried in a crypt he now opens. It contains the truth of Tyrone's character: a tragic suffering one can never escape, over a lost object— oneself—that one can never reclaim.

Edmund: Nostalgia before the Fact

Edmund finally has the cue for real poetry. The impact of his father's narrative draws forth an attempt to recognize their consubstantiality so that he too can accept a knowledge he can no longer escape. His moment of self-revelation is at hand, but the narrative that contains it unleashes a subtext that will drive the drama to a psychological space deeper than the one his father has attained.[14]

The labor of memory for Edmund is connected with the sea. Turning to it, he unlocks the meaning concealed in the long romantic speech in which he earlier evoked it. The sea is now the refuge from a prior homelessness in which time is abolished, no human context remains, and freedom is experienced purely—and for the first time—as an unbound pursuit of death. Edmund at sea experiences that moment of awareness Schopenhauer defines and the proof of genius. He thus achieves the secret beyond willing, followed by the inevitable plunge back into a world in which one is no longer mystified, because one now knows that resignation is the only praxis. A profound theory of tragedy, no doubt; it is also, as Edmund reveals, a vast displacement. Edmund has practiced what he here preaches, with disastrous results. The sea has not delivered him from home; it has mandated the necessity and terms of his return. At sea Edmund is like Melville's water-gazer, but Edmund's suicidal impulses return him to death's original scene. Death is the reality that breathes through Edmund's poem. The appeal of the sea is the escape from individuation. The poem begins and ends with the theme of homelessness; however, because bringing the anxiety of that condition home is the act that closes and completes the circle. Edmund has come home to die because all his wandering has only served to exemplify his failure to mourn a corpse. This is the abiding experience he has of himself: death-in-life returned to the place of its entombment. Haunted, like his mother, by psychic unraveling, he must return home in order to stage his contribution to the family system.

If Edmund now begins to move toward such knowledge, he does so through a narrative that lacks the experiential complexity of his father's. The substitute, a Joycean language of lyric transcendence, that of the artist as a young man, yearns toward that order of knowledge while holding it at bay. For the moment, that praxis works because Edmund has not yet been brought before the experience that will expose the limits of lyric apprehension by forcing Edmund to confront a language of truth more devastating than his father's. In that process, the circle of hate will be redrawn and deepened, as Jamie submits Edmund's "knowledge" to a real test.

Jamie: Doubling, Revenge, and Self-Consuming Love

The question Who's acting? is again the way in, but the drama moves quickly to the hate dynamic because Jamie is deeply in touch with it and desperately in need of denial. The others come to their Unconscious only slowly. Jamie lives with his, and it rages within. It is the voice beneath a cynicism that is authentic, because he has made dredging up hidden motives a principle he unremittingly directs upon himself. Others flee their unconscious motives; Jamie seeks his out. As he earlier told his father, "You can't hear me talking to myself" (32). We now enter that interiority. In its depths, what Jamie incessantly hears is self-hatred undoing every effort he makes to arrest it. Projection for Jamie only momentarily halts a process in which aggression is turned back against the self. Thus the statement "No one else gives a damn if you die, but I do," becomes, without real provocation, "You don't believe I care, eh?" (156–57). Throughout the scene, such contradictions repeatedly erupt, as the unconscious streams forth in a language Jamie can no longer control.[15]

Attempts, through mimicry, to shift the burden onto his father only provide momentary theatrical relief. Jamie's unconscious again intrudes. If Edmund accepts the sanatorium, "It's your funeral—I mean, I hope it won't be" (158). Panic denial is upon him, because Jamie knows that the desire for his brother's death is the date with his unconscious he can no longer escape. What he doesn't know is that the desire derives its force from the pain of a lovelessness he must endlessly repeat, even when parodying it, to prevent the underlying hatred from directing itself upon the internal object who controls the entire process.

The story of Fat Violet is hardly a match for his father's and brother's narratives, yet it unleashes that deeper subtext. Jamie sees Fat Violet as his objective correlative, and the farcical drama with her as his equivalent of Edmund's walk in the fog. By parodying the emotions his mother's actions have reactivated, he hopes to transfer them onto another. But deliberate cruelty toward a pathetic subject is not his key; it's his mother's. He ends up feeling sorry for Violet because she reminds him too much of himself.

The effort to allay rage through this comic love match is destined to almost immediate collapse. While Violet may have gained the hope of love, Jamie acted out of hopelessness. His attempt to deliver himself from his condition by mocking it has only driven him back to the line that marked the tale's beginning: "What is a man without a good woman's love? A Goddamned hollow shell" (158). If Jamie finds momentary relief in turning a whore into a beloved, he'll now reverse the metaphor by finding terms appropriate to the one who taught him whores were the only women with whom he could find love. Unleashing his hate, the shell asks the appropriate question—"Where's the hophead?" (161)—propelling both brothers into endgame.

Edmund's desire to limit the scope of knowledge now reverts to an angry insistence on denial. But hate now stalks the scene in an agent who will redraw all the circles in order to rend them forever. His method is the Catholic one, confession, but sans priest, sans absolution—and sans cynicism. Jamie's last hope is that confession will cleanse everyone's soul through his assumption of the scapegoat role. Hate will be isolated and bound to a death-work he will drive into the innermost places of his unconscious. The truth found there will set the others free. But the process in which he is engaged moves to a different end, because the scapegoat is both his desire and the role the family has assigned him. The latter connection has created a reservoir of rage. Therefore each effort Jamie makes to isolate the rottenness in his unconscious becomes an act which exposes a deeper unconscious that is familial and must be shared.

Jamie's first confession goes about as deep as most people ever care to go. He admits that his unbreakable tie to his mother means that he can overcome his addiction and despair only if she can "lick" hers. On that great day the psychological identification played out as anger will transform itself, revealing the underlying love. Such confessions are finally good for the soul. But Jamie no sooner tries on this explanation than a deeper text surfaces in an eruption of unconscious rage: "I'd never dreamed before that any women but whores took dope!" (163). Jamie's flaw wasn't belief in his mother but his failure to see her hated of them—her use of addiction as the passive-aggressive means whereby she gains their trust, all the better to shatter it. He still thinks only whores take dope. The apparent disavowal in the line is actually an attribution. Seeing his mother's hatred, Jamie sees his own and now knows what he was really doing when he acted out a parody of their relationship with Fat Violet.

The issue of brotherhood is the inescapable corollary of that confession. Jamie is tortured by the question of whether he can reverse hate by finding a new object to love or whether hate begets unconscious envy and an unremitting effort to poison the very springs of life in that new object. In Edmund's illness, the latter motive smells victory and, with the death of the favored sibling, a chance to repeat Eugene's death rightly and gain a new and exclusive relationship to the mother.[16]

In affirming his love for Edmund, Jamie tries to exorcise this desire before the fact: "We've been more than brothers. You're the only pal I've ever had. I love your guts. I'd do anything for you." Edmund's readiness to put that proposition beyond doubt only activates Jamie's need to state the opposite in what amounts to a legal brief: "Yet I'll bet you've heard Mama and old Gaspard spill so much bunk about my hoping for the worst, you suspect right now I'm thinking to myself that Papa is old and can't last much longer, and if you were to die, Mama and I would get all he's got, and so I'm probably hoping—" (163). Confession has taken on a radically new purpose: the probing of one unconscious in an effort to deracinate its force within the other's unconscious.

Though he only gets the first half of that message, Edmund responds in kind. He will no longer limit knowledge: he now insists that the Unconscious be exposed: "Shut up, you damned fool! What the hell put that in your nut? Yes, that's what I'd like to know. What put that in your mind?" (163). Jamie has deliberately put himself in a mousetrap. Any attempt to re-repress hate will now be played out in a context sure to claw at both of them. Jamie has always been conveniently cast by the others in the role of one suspected of hoping for the worst. His relationship to his brother has been an attempt to displace that accusation and create an enclave within the family. In that effort he has been only too successful. Brotherhood has become the mirroring of a deep psychological identity. Jamie will now bring forth the results by revealing that the whole game has been an act of hate.

He delivers the blow in two stages. First, he deprives Edmund of his achievements, saying they merely reflect credit on him. He then debunks the achievements, expressing disgust with them as further evidence of a role he has forced his brother to mimic. In confessing his unconscious envy, the insult he goaded his brother with at the beginning of this speech—"You're only an overgrown kid! Mama's baby and Papa's pet! The family White Hope!"—is inserted with surgical precision straight into Edmund's psychic identity: "Hell, you're more than my brother. I made you! You're my Frankenstein!" (163–64). Jamie's self-disgust has created in Edmund its mirror and mechanical puppet. The identity beneath Jamie's masks is revealed to Edmund as the prediction of a future he can never outstrip. Seldom has the Lacanian message, The I is the other, been delivered with as much clarity and vehemence.

"All right, I'm your Frankenstein. So let's have a drink" (164). Edmund now desperately needs repression and drink, because the dialectic of hate is about to instruct him in the two things he does not want to know. First, that Jamie set him up for the romanticized death drive he's been acting out. Second, that genuine death-work is a much deeper psychological process, in which he's but a rank amateur. Edmund is in love with easeful death. Jamie is about to instruct him in the process one has to go through in order to kill oneself. To do so, he focuses death-work on the one thing that has sustained his contact with life. To kill oneself, one has to rid oneself of love. In teaching his brother this lesson, Jamie gives him an ambiguous gift. Death-work requires that one deracinate the last ties of love that bind you to the world. Hate must strike inward at the beloved object by inflicting hate externally on that object. Both lines of renewal are thereby severed.

Delivering that message is also a tragic act, because it constitutes a last desperate effort to love. Jamie's true purpose is to articulate the circle of hate that binds the brothers, in order to extricate Frankenstein from it. To do so, he uses the most archaic mechanism of defense—splitting—in order to reverse the effects that the original split underlying his ambivalence has produced. The contract he offers his brother takes this form: I'll take the bad side of the relationship and "live" with it; you remember the good side and use it to banish me from your psyche. The ambivalence that has ruled both partners must be made explicit so that it can be driven to the breaking point. Jamie's through-line in this great act of self-revelation and self-unraveling is the effort to reverse the displaced cause-effect relationship in Wilde's aphorism with the proper genealogy: "The man was dead and so he had to kill the thing he loved" (166). In the process, Jamie exposes Catholic confession, moving it into a new psychological space wherein its sentimental guarantees about love are submitted to a tragic imperative: "Greater love hath no man than this, that he saveth his brother from himself" (167). Death-work here has an end. For once, hate, completing itself, severs the circle. Jamie's tragic effort in this great scene is to enact the psychological process of intrinsic death.

As such, his confession places the principle that has operated from the beginning of the play under the proper category: deliberate hate is the unconscious force underlying all the behaviors through which the family inflicts their shared disorder upon one another. In asking his brother to "absolve" him and then to avoid any further relationship, Jamie forces Edmund to see that any further company between them will manifest Edmund's attachment to death-work. Edmund's psyche will only be free when he has purged the internal tie that informs the external behavior.

Jamie knows one more thing which he doesn't state: that the logic of death-work he has articulated derives its power from his identification with his mother. But that is a tie that Edmund cannot break. Nor can Tyrone. Together again, with talk now the enemy because it can only renew circles of hate, they can only wait, in frozen tableau, before the final spectacle, each providing a chorus that only rubs raw the common discontent—and fixation. The final exercise in acting is reserved for Mary. In it she fulfills her greatest role and curtain—death-work completed, the collective psyche unraveled and unbound, free at last to pursue its true pleasure.

Mary, Conceived without Sin, Pray For . . .

Mary plays the piano, touching the keys of a solipsism achieved. The return to girlhood and daddy completes the first movement of her long sonata for the dead. Jamie provides the right line: "The Mad Scene. Enter Ophelia!" (170). As Mary drifts from one past to another—from Sister Theresa to Sister Martha to the BVM—time is stripped, then and now, of all but "dreaming and forgetting" (171). She has come to recover something and brings with her another lost object, recently refound. But it is an object found only to be abandoned, since it connects her to the wrong past. Earlier, in magical thought, putting her wedding dress on again enabled her to regain that state just prior to marriage and the loss of virginity. But that state bears a contradiction that holds her psyche in perpetual tension. She must get back further: "I'm going to be a nun—that is, if I can only find—" (172). The position she reaches here parallels Tyrone's recognition scene, in which he found himself forever looking for the piece of paper he lost. But Mary can't suffer the knowledge of loss attained. That which is lost is "something I miss terribly. It can't be altogether lost." From not being altogether lost it must be magically reclaimed—and the relationship be-tween the two sentences must be reversed—because for Mary, need always supersedes the possibility of loss: "Something I need terribly. I remember when I had it I was never lonely nor afraid. I can't have lost it forever" (173). Infantile psychic fixations thus cancel every appeal of a reality princi-ple. The inability to mourn requires the annihilation of everything that intrudes on flight into the perfect past. Edmund could not have timed his last attempt to intervene with the fact of his illness at a more futile point. "I've got consumption!" "No!" (174). Mary hears, when she needs to, and passes the judgment of her unconscious. The negative, which is the origin of the unconscious, here reveals itself as both the first and last mechanism of defense against the inability to face death.

Those who cannot mourn cannot be touched: "You must not try to touch me. . . . It isn't right, when I am hoping to be a nun" (174). The hope is metaphysical, in that it confers an order of being prior to those experiences that would give one an identity. Perhaps the most striking thing about Mary's last act is its severely logical nature: the logic of psychotic bliss.

To complete that process, Mary must pass to Mother Elizabeth and the visionary experience in which she first discovered her "vocation." It is an ideally contradictory perfect double text, because Mother Elizabeth sees what few who live in the hothouse atmosphere of the convent let themselves know: Mary's vision is sexuality a-bloomin', in flight from itself and the world. The irony of the situation is that Mary can't understand why Mother Elizabeth, who was previously the reservoir of understanding, won't share her belief but insists she prove "it wasn't simply my imagination" by submit-ting herself to a test (175). The test has two foregone conclusions. The first Mother Elizabeth already foresees. The second is the one Mary must submit that result to in order to undo it. Mary knows what Mother Elizabeth is implying, but she "never dreamed Holy Mother would give . . . such ad-vice." Shocked but obedient, yet knowing the test "was simply a waste of time," she complies, but not without another visit to the BVM to gain the best kind of absolution, absolution before the fact—and with it the promise of later refuge from the "harm" to which Mother Elizabeth has just condemned her (176).

After such devotions, what is experience? Nothing but the fall into time which can now be remembered, because, on the deepest register, Mary has assured herself it never was. Mary's final lines are among the coldest in literature. She fell in love and was "so happy for a time" (176), but that time is here remembered only to be labeled a false happiness that is now obliterated, as she completes her retreat into that past in which she was once, and is once again, neurotically happy. Standing before them, she no longer needs to inflict that past upon them. For she is no longer present. They are left staring, paralyzed by the knowledge that she never was.

The Ties That Bind: The Family as System

The family is a system of interlocking chains with no single point of origin or agent of control. Reciprocity inhabits it from every point in time. If our children never get free of our psychic wounds, it is also the case that we are never free from what they may do to return the favor. The only summing up that does justice to any of the agents in a family must formulate the way in which each individual disorder contributes to the development of the system as a whole. Only so can each agent receive his or her due, caught, by the dramatic evolution of the whole, in the net of one's own devices.

The absences that haunt Tyrone are his gift to the family. In Tyrone's account of himself, the founding act was his desertion by his father and his self-sacrifice for his mother. Later sellouts are seen, even when he finally admits them, as necessary outgrowths of that harsh baptism.

The knot which that core situation begets is, however, a good deal more complex. Tyrone remains the father who has failed and who inflicts his failure on the rest of the family. His sons can never be the actor he was, yet it is the only occupation he allows. The identity he attributes to his wife is equally convoluted. She must become the Mother whose sole vocation is housewifery. Tyrone claims that everything he does is to create a home for the family. But his relationship to home is essentially the same as his father's: he deserts the family for long periods of time, but unlike his father he doesn't have the decency to stay away. He come back to study the effects. His desire is to keep everyone in the family in a state of suspended animation. He can thus do unto them what his mother did unto him, enact his revenge, and study the consequences. The home is the only value, yet the home must be a fraud; absences must haunt it in order to reveal all that was never present in his mother's house. Tyrone pictures his mother and himself as martyrs, yet his effort in making Mary become like his mother is to strip away support. In effect, he wants to reverse his earlier self-sacrifice by putting the woman in the identical position, then refusing to give what he was forced to give before. Thereby he can do unto the substitute mother what his father did to both of them.

Projection creates systematic fraud. In looking at his family, Tyrone sees nothing but himself mirrored. Because his life was sacrificed to his mother and his siblings, he creates a family in which everyone is sacrificed to his needs. But if the family is the mirror of one's Unconscious projections, it is a cracked mirror that constantly reminds him of all he's failed to overcome. This master actor is haunted, in all his roles, by a line from Yeats he has probably never read: "Mirror on mirror mirrored is all the show."

The family is that hall of mirrors in which one's projections meet an equal and opposite violence. Tyrone and Mary are another perfect couple. Her family romance is an inverted mirror image of his. Mary's enabling pain is her desertion by her mother and by the nuns and her sacrifice by the father who passes her on to another man. She is haunted by rejection. No one will let her remain in the havens she seeks. She is always betrayed to experience, driven from one world to another. She must accordingly make the home a place where she expresses her sense of loss and her rage over what she need must feel as a violation. Because home is Tyrone's illusion, it becomes the constant target of her remarks. If the home is Tyrone's way of building a powerful male identity, it becomes for Mary the scene of his recurrent castration. He must be constantly reminded that he has failed and that his failure has produced her ruination. Wanting a wife who will become a substitute mother, he gets a hysteric who acts the part to perfection.

As mother, she enacts a similar revenge on her sons. She rejects one son and smothers the other, thereby producing a sibling rivalry ruled by maternal excess and destructive mothering. Like Tyrone, Mary creates mirrors of herself. The son she smothers becomes a projection of the "purity" she claims was wrested from her and a claustrophobic reenactment of the sexual and narcissistic needs that shaped her "vocation." The other son, relegated to whores for affection, becomes an expression of her disgust with female sexuality. The fact that both are, in effect, dying of consumption is an appropriate objective correlative: mothering as infanticide. Mary's power is her ability to keep all three men fixated on her. They form a group, a single male psyche, defined by a shared and inescapable frustration: the inability to satisfy, help, or reach her. This lure locks them in endless battle. As rivals for her love, they believe that male identity comes only to he who understands and fulfills Mary's need.

The knot of that need condemns them to perpetual failure. For Mary's pain is individuation. Her deepest desire is to undo her consciousness. Experience is a violation of the virginity and loss of consciousness she endlessly seeks to regain through the effort to merge with her image of the perfect mother, the BVM. Only before that mirror can she undo the guilt her own mother carefully planted in her so that when she entered the world of men she would find herself endlessly violated. But because she can't get back to the BVM, she must become the object they in turn cannot reach. They want her to be Mary, the Mother; she will show them that Mary is a *deus absconditus*. She becomes to them what the BVM is to her: the object that fascinates and fixates in unending frustration. They cannot reach her, and yet they cannot stop trying to reach her. She pays them back for violating her by trapping them in the home. In undoing her psyche before their eyes, she repeatedly undoes theirs. She is as adept as Blanche DuBois at playing roles, but the one that informs all others is that of the vampire. Mary's is an Unconscious ruled by vampirism.

Jamie lives the family disease as an unalterable determination of his being. Nothing he does can alter the sense of guilt both parents saddle him with. His oedipalization is unique: he is the murderer of the sibling whose action has destroyed his mother. He can accordingly only escape endless self-punishment by healing her. This is the knot she uses to torture him. In return, he stays in the home in order to rub the spectacle of his degeneration in their faces. When parents successfully pass something on, they always deepen it. Jamie has taken the guilt in which they are all trapped and internalized it as an unconscious envy that strives to poison the very springs of life, in order to turn that pain back on himself. He thus becomes the conscience of the family. He annihilates the efforts each makes to avoid the shared truth he would bring them to, so that each can derive succor from his internalization of their disorder. His agony is deeper than that of Donald Winnicott's ideal depressive. Jamie is not afraid that hate will prove stronger than love. He already knows that. His only hope is that his destructiveness can be held at bay.

His is the negative consciousness unable to negate the situation and thus condemned, despite his anguished awareness, to passing it on. Edmund has a daily beauty in his life, and a daily smile from his mother, that makes Jamie ugly. Despite Jamie's efforts, brotherhood becomes sham. The only real relationship he can have to the sibling is the Salieri-like effort to do to his brother what his mother has done to him. This is the real source of the Frankenstein doubling. The power his mother had to destroy him is the power he will have over her favorite. Two desires thus lock, with one goal. Jamie strives to present his suicided self to his mother under the refrain, Look what you've done to me. That effort failed, he will rephrase the statement by presenting her favorite under the same guise: Now that I've done it to your beloved, do you finally see what you did to me?

The horror of Jamie's consciousness is that such an action confirms a prior badness he is powerless to change. His self-hatred thus circles back onto each member of the family in an effort to destroy the illusion that anything can be rescued from the familial disorder. In destroying illusions, his desire is to usher them all into the bitterest truth. If deliverance from consciousness is what the other characters seek, Jamie lives out the recognition that there is no exit. Consciousness is hell. The home is Svidrigailov's bathhouse. While the others can fool themselves, Jamie performs the extraordinary act of both internalizing and projecting their collective unconscious so that he may suffer it—and in that suffering gain no relief. His is an unconscious ruled by self-hate.

With all this going on, it's not surprising that Edmund has been given a lot of sympathy. Some critics have even argued that his liberation is the through-line of the play. He is, after all, the future author of *Long Day's Journey,* here seen undergoing the events that will be memorialized in the play this experience eventually enabled him to write. But if Edmund is O'Neill's portrait of the artist as a young man, it is a chilling one, which reveals that the difference between the young aesthete and a true artist derives from a fundamental transformation in the nature and direction of aggression.

If Edmund is a victim, he is hardly blameless or passive. He lives out a drama of passive-aggressive homecoming. All his efforts to leave the family take the form of a flight from consciousness that completes itself with a suicidal return to the controlling presence who nurtures his attraction to death. Edmund can't commit suicide on the road, for the act would lack its proper setting. His need is to do it slowly, at home, in front of all of them. His project, in short, is identical to his mother's. Art fits that disorder rather than offering a way out of it. By playing the aesthete, he produces nothing but pale imitations of imitations, because his life is the imitation of another's. Edmund wants not to separate from his mother but to merge with her. Individuation terrifies both of them.

Edmund perpetually returns to his origins not out of guilt—as is the case with Stephen Dedalus—but to inflict his sufferings upon the source. The play O'Neill wrote after a lifetime of struggle is not a celebration of that motive but its exposure. O'Neill actively reverses Edmund's aggression by directing aggression upon him. The shift from lyric to drama is the method of that transformation. True art is creative aggression, an attempt to break into and reverse the frozen sea inside us by exposing our complicity in our paralysis. Edmund has barely begun to discern the terms of such an artistry.

This does not gainsay the fact that Edmund has a good deal to be angry about. His lot is perhaps harder than Jamie's. While Jamie pays the family debt through self-destructive behavior, Edmund is set up as the child who will heal everyone's wounds through his achievements. Formed in the image of artistic grandiosity, he is trapped in a narcissistic dilemma in which identity forever eludes him. The only solution he sees is oceanic deliverance from the burden. He is caught in the projection his mother has imposed upon him: he must become the perfect child in order to heal her guilt over the lost child. As he suspects, this puts him in the position of the dead and dying child. He inflicts his illness on everyone, because his deepest agony is that no one can care for him as an individual. As he sees, he came too late. The family set was complete, all the parts assigned, with his predetermined by the lost child he has to replace. That child's death condemned him to a condition in which he could never exist in his own right. Edmund will do virtually anything to get their attention, but he is always a token rather than a person. If Jamie is scapegoat, Edmund is tabula rasa, deprived by each of them of individual being. All he can be is this sick, suffering body, wasting away, virtually mute.

In that role, his underlying anger finds its method. Direct confrontation could produce change; he wants instead to give them another occasion to show that they can't hear or help him. He is an expert at denying what he knows and then playing his victimage so that the others take on responsibility for keeping him ignorant. He repeatedly says that he doesn't want to hear what he already knows. Edmund's desire is to watch everyone wallow in it. He will sustain the system of lies, not because he loves the family, but because he knows that denial is the long, drawn-out suffering they have imposed on him, which he will deliberately throw back in their faces. He wants pity, but he knows it's the wrong kind of pity. Edmund's is an unconscious ruled by death.

O'Neill's psychological greatness lies in his systematic understanding of the interrelationships that define the neurotic activity of each member of the family. He isn't interested in characters as individuals, because he knows that the only reality is the system as a frozen whole. To break into that ice, he must dramatize the totality, while showing that it has no single cause or temporal order. When the characters finally tell the core stories of what ruined their lives, what they reveal is the event they seized on and exploited because it offered them the excuse needed to solidify the rule of a deeper unconscious desire. Such desires, biting into one another, are the source of generational begetting and the key to a correct understanding of the psyche of each member of the family. Just as that system has no origin, it produces results in which the future drives back into the past, producing psychological consequences in each of the agents that none of them can arrest or control. The family moves in only one direction—toward each member's crypt and the discovery that mutual cruelty is the bond that sustains the system, bringing its just deserts to each participant. O'Neill's greatest insight is that cruelty isn't an occasional lapse, but the through-line, avid in the behaviors that make everyday life a ceaseless effort to discharge our burdens by inflicting them on those who do likewise. The truth of desire is that you always get what you want and reap what you sow. If, as Miller argues, every great play is a jurisprudence, the court in which subjects deliver their verdicts upon one another is a wholly self-contained *Prozess*.

One can argue, of course, that O'Neill's characters are deeply Catholic and his play no more than an indication of how internalized guilt, controlling all interactions, constitutes true baptism into that religion. But this escape hatch conveniently evades O'Neill's secular insight. Catholicism is no more than a particularly clear example of the power of projective guilt to bind our psyches. Catholicism's rituals nurture that process, but its roots—and family ties—lie far deeper in the psyche. O'Neill's hook is thus doubly barbed. He gets the Catholic guests, but he also gets those guests who want to discharge what he reveals by limiting its scope to that religion. In doing so, those guests merely illustrate another way in which we use projection and denial whenever the shoe fits.

Casting the Audience

What are the implications of O'Neill's understanding of the family for dramatic form? O'Neill has written a drama where no one gets off the hook, and it is within this purpose that he casts the audience. Sympathy shifts often throughout the play, but this is the way O'Neill sets the mousetrap. As the play develops, our need to extricate ourselves—or some concept of "health"—from the maelstrom in which the family is trapped repeatedly rises, only to be frustrated. In so engaging us, the play shows that the frameworks of explanation we use to limit the impact of that recognition are defenses which have their true significance in revealing the particular kind of cruelty they need to cover up. This is the wound the play drives into our psyche—a wound that goes right to the foundations of our mendacity. In constructing theories of the family, we are primarily engaged in creating intellectual defenses that reveal, with their collapse, the underlying motives they are designed to repress.

The beauty of *Long Day's Journey* is that it springs this trap on virtually every pathos about the family by representing the ways its agents exploit familial ties for destructive ends. This is why a premature commitment to any one interpretive paradigm prevents entry into the psychological richness of the play. If, for example, one sees Mary as a victim in a "feminist" reading or as a cannibal in a psychological reading of a different sort, one is barred from seeing the larger complex in which such frameworks of explanation are revealed as defenses against knowing a more primary fact—that of mutual cruelty. The reason we hang on to partial views is not hard to fathom: the alternative is to internalize an understanding of cruelty by seeing how we enact and reinforce it in interpretation. In the space thereby cleared, O'Neill offers a profound understanding of the ideology of form and the neurotic needs it serves.

Whenever one exposes a dramatic structure (the scapegoat, victimage, familial piety) and the psychological need that informs it, drama becomes the opening of a crypt. It must evolve new forms suited to that discovery. The movement from day to night, from the conscious to the unconscious, from everyday life to dreamlike and drunken states, are hardly new tropes. But it is one thing to celebrate such commonplaces—as in Baudelaire's oft-quoted poem—another to find the dramatic form that will draw out their psychological implications in order to get at a psychic register that traditional dramatic forms—and current critical theories—have been constructed to repress.

The issue is one of regression as a source of psychological insight and a principle of dramatic form. To replace one psychology with another, one dramatic ritual with a more authentic one, one must expose the former by showing how the latter forms its unconscious subtext. To constitute and preserve that insight, the destruction must generate a dramatic structure that will not revert to prior forms of their underlying assumptions. Regression produces illumination only when it shows that the archaic is the truth of "higher" functions and rules them in such a manner that the most rational operations conceal the avidity of the most archaic motives and drives. Unless that dialectical connection is maintained, regression will invariably become "regression in the service of the ego." To unlock the more radical possibility, O'Neill must therefore begin by dramatizing the true condition of the surface, everyday life as a vast system of projection and denial, in which "innocent" and "purely rational" statements often function to discharge an underlying conflict by putting the burden of disorder on the other, who is thereby "neuroticized."

The operations of projection and denial are, of course, virtually limitless. There is no gainsaying the fecundity of human mendacity. The point of each operation, however, is always the same: to ward off the archaic by projecting it. One person so acts. Another responds in kind. And through little dramas of attribution, both psyches are set on edge. The result is further use of the means of denial to project at a deeper level the "message" that has come back at us from the other.

Such processes can produce endless "comedy" which we can always arrest and transcend by identifying ourselves with rational functions, so that the split-off self on which we've acted can continue to fester with all that reason confidently expels. A study of behavior along such lines may be the best that naturalism and realism can offer toward resituating the ego in terms of the actual motives it serves and the self-awareness it denies. This is the informing principle behind O'Neill's painstaking effort to track down the actual truth and function of everything that gives everyday life its irreversible movement from surface to depth. Even when his characters seem trapped in endless repetition, the play's effort is to position us for a rereading that will articulate how a series of apparently identical phenomena reveal the meticulous movement of an inexorable process.

In so doing, O'Neill shows that the movement from the apparent absence of conflict to psychic eruption, from the "highest" mental operations or most sophisticated defenses to the most archaic drives, is really a movement toward the truth of the former. Dialectic exposes the binary operations we create to protect ourselves from detection in order to put us, as reexistentialized beings, on the rack.

That is the opportunity O'Neill offers his audience. Everything we bring to the play to prevent such a regression is deracinated by it. The guests are cast by this play in a situation more radical than any we have seen thus far. As the frameworks of explanation we use to prevent facing the reality of interfamilial cruelty collapse, we are forced to regress, along with the characters, toward psychodynamic explorations that we can scarcely comprehend, since the psychological theory that would articulate them has not yet been developed. Much has been made of O'Neill's supposed dependence on psychoanalytic theory; the secret thereby concealed is the deep challenge his work poses to psychoanalysis by exploring dimensions of the psyche that it has chosen to repress. Freud's maxim that the poets knew "it" first is once again here confirmed in its deepest meaning: they continue to know it best.

Long Day's Journey regresses into the crypt in search of fundamentally new insights into the psyche. It is empowered to do so because O'Neill has made dramatic form an inaugural and independent way of knowing. He sees that quite literally there is nothing but drama. Drama thus becomes a principle of exploration and discovery in a way it never can be for a thematic and "humanistic" writer like Miller. O'Neill commits himself to a radical immanence. There is no content, no commonplace, no dramatic form or relationship to the audience that isn't put in process and on trial in his work. Exploration into the hidden places of the psyche is the source both of dramatic form and of psychological theory, because there is nothing prior to or outside the process of sifting through the debris of everyday life in search of the underlying psychodynamics. There is no ideology that can be superimposed upon that process without becoming a component that is tested and exposed by it. When one commits oneself to such immanence and stops playing at drama with hidden essentialistic guarantees, dramatic form has become a primordial way of understanding the psyche. Few writers are capable of such regression, however, because there is no way to undertake it without risking one's psyche. The one assurance the process offers is that it will invariably expose the untested guarantees we didn't think to exclude from its impact because we were unaware of how deeply we had invested in their appeal. When writing as creative regression remains genuine, all guarantees are already submitted to their destruction. Such is a labor of the negative worthy of the name. Dramatic form has become, in its *logos,* a structure of irreversible discoveries that blasts the continuum of everyday life. O'Neill awaits those who undertake that task with unexampled insights.

The Academic Festival Overture:
Who's Afraid of Virginia Woolf?

Albee's Dramatic *Prozess:* Getting to the Marrow

Drama, Death-Work, and Phylogenetic Regression

Who's Afraid of Virginia Wolf? deracinates every neurotic fixation in order to expose the underlying psychotic anxieties which neurotic behavior displaces and denies. Albee's goal is to get to the marrow, to expose the deepest layer of human conflict and show how it drives the play by undercutting each game the characters play in an effort to escape or limit it. My goal is to show that the through-line of that drive is the movement to death, self-fragmentation, and the descent into psychotic anxieties. Everything we proclaim about the self and identity is thereby put in question. "Solid" intrapsychic positions—and the games whereby they are maintained—are concretely referred to the deep disorder from which they derive. Once activated, it stalks all the displacements which merely delay its work. The structure that evolves is thus a virtually pure psychodrama of aggression as the power that rules the psyche. As it strips away the language games and roles that couples play in sustaining the great institution of marriage, the audience is exposed to a recurrent eruption of anxiety. This is the process whereby the play gets the guests—and not just the two who find themselves onstage.

George and Martha are a true match—of mighty opposites—because aggression has for each a distinct dialectical telos. The goal of aggression for Martha is to strike through masks in the belief that through this process she and George can regain human contact. Such, at any rate, is her claim. Aggression for George, in contrast, is the perfection of death-work, the attempt to strip away everything that protects us from the void. The difference between George and Martha is the difference between one who oedipalizes conflicts in order to defend against a deeper regression and one who dramatizes the deeper psychotic anxieties which oedipalization displaces and denies. Martha stays at the meat of things; George goes for the crypt. In the process, the issue of psychosexual identity is placed in a context even more radical than the one Tennessee Williams developed in *Streetcar*. Violence, for Martha, is a turn-on, and twice early in the first act she seems willing to let it all dissolve in love play: but George refuses to kiss her and later says she just wants "blue games for the guests" (59).[1] His desire inverts hers: aggression doesn't prime sex; sex collapses before the greater pleasure of aggression.

If renewal demands the surfacing of the greatest disorders, George is its inadvertent priest. That agency is also the source of his most disruptive relationship to the audience: George's goal is to show that devolution is the only way to psychic honesty—and its irreversible result. George knows that all the games people play are attempts to displace death-work and the threat of regression to the crypt. Activating that movement is the through-line of his engagement. In going after the marrow, his desire is to expose the "inadequacy" of roles, in order to activate their repressed.

As his autobiographical narrative shows, George is keenly aware that on the deepest psychic register we are all perhaps already dead. Our oedipal games are attempts to hide that fact. But if the psyche is to know the truth about itself, it must be exposed to the psychotic anxieties that constitute "fear of Virginia Woolf." For George, the purpose of aggression is to bring about a regression which is not ruled by the ego. This thrust gives George his dual role: his power as truth-teller and his identity as "embassy of death." My attempt in discussing his agency is not to empower George as hero but to show his agency as the force that drives the play toward an awareness that deracinates all illusions. The attempt of interpreters to undo George's work and discharge the anxiety he unleashes by reducing his agency to a neurotic motive is not a solution to the threat he poses but a defense mechanism which itself collapses within the play beneath the withering critique he directs upon it. He may perform the right act for the wrong reason, but that does not cancel the psychologically revelatory status of the results. George is that psychological power which enforces "psychosis" as the necessary preliminary to any knowledge or reconstruction of the "self." As death-work, he produces a phylogenetic regression that strips away every intrapsychic structure that "saves" us from Munch's howl.[2]

For George, however, that process does not produce the possibility of active reversal. His concern with devolution is with the impossibility of reversing oneself. Regression into psychotic anxieties aims, for George, at the void, the prior death, into which everything dissolves when the fight to keep up life has bottomed out. As such, George may not be the last word on phylogenetic regression, but he is the first, since he exposes the psychic register into which active reversal must reach and the necessary direction it must take. One can achieve change in depth, in the basic structure of the psyche, only by actively reversing the wound or "basic fault" at the "core," that is, by assuming the actual self-reference that makes the "self" the unsubstantial shadow that it is.[3] To do that, one must know that wound intimately. Progression only becomes possible after one regresses and descends, step by step, into the basement of the psyche. Works like *Virginia Woolf* are uniquely salutary because they dramatize psychic dissolution as the necessary prelude to that possibility. Self-identity is achieved only through a systematic understanding and outstripping of its counterfeits.

The drama in which George and Martha are engaged is a progressive uncovering and regression into the crypt. One does it wrong to see it simply as a repetitive thrust and counterthrust of oedipalizations, for each attempt Martha makes to repeat that process uncovers deeper disorders. It is as if the oedipal were a vast disguise, a hoped-for closure. Its collapse, through its own machinations, is the true source of drama.

To grasp this process, it is important not to overinterpret the initial form that conflicts take, for one then misses Albee's skill at dramatizing the unconscious of his characters. This is especially the case with George. George generates plot instabilities in act I which he and the play only slowly catch up with. One of the subtle beauties in this play is that George and Martha use every available prop to introduce new games which will alter the terms of the preceding drama. Each keeps redefining the theatrical space, yet in a continuous way, because each redefinition picks up and makes an explicit term of conflict what was subtext—often by strong denial—in the previous movement. As the transformation of the theatrical space proceeds, a scene of insult becomes a scene of seduction, which then becomes a scene of mutual betrayal, and so on, until we finally reach a scene of ritual murder with the identity of the victim richly overdetermined. To grasp the psychodynamics of the play, it is crucial to avoid premature interpretation of character and motives, since the depth psychology of each agent is precisely what the play's movement will reveal.

The dynamic that drives the play is the movement from one text to the irreversible emergence of its subtext. This is the key to analyzing the games these people play. Games are psychodramas that delay and displace deeper psychodramas. When you analyze a game properly, you know the desire it was meant to satisfy and the deeper disorder it strove to displace. The inability to achieve "satisfaction" (*Begierde*) is the underlying circumstance that dialectically connects both structures. This is the way drama develops. We play a game for a cheap psychological payoff; we fail to get it, or we taste real blood. Either way, the ante goes up, for a deeper disorder surfaces which must seek satisfaction through a more dangerous game. Albee is the dark deconstructor of Eric Berne.

Get the Guests is the game of games, the true space of this theatre. George and Martha hack at each other in order to bring the other, the audience, into the web. Their combined action is similar to Hickey's singular effort—the goal being to implicate the audience in a discovery of their complicity in the disorder staged by depriving them of their hiding place. Nick's greatest need is to say I'm not like you. George and Martha's combined effort is to show him that he is. Through such process, *Virginia Woolf* puts the audience onstage, then strips away whatever illusions they use to flee the drama.

The Groves of Academe

Given that purpose, why the academic setting? It is far from universally acknowledged, but a play about unconscious envy and the anxiety it displaces could hardly find a better locale. Academe is the privileged site of that drama and of its strenuous denial. Here people are, as the saying goes, so petty because the stakes are so small. The positive side of this circumstance is that small stakes can become the Hegelian battle for pure prestige. In one sense we are fortunate to be the underpaid aristocrats of pure mind. Thanks to this circumstance, the smallest stakes can become scenes for staging the greatest disorders, with the only possible payoff being the one so often lost when real money is at stake: the assumption of the position of the Hegelian Master, seated on the throne, in infinite condescension toward those who lack "his" phantom substantiality. The unspoken "I'm better than you" endlessly transferred to the predicate of one's newest title, publication, or grant is a visible text that reveals the insistent need to exorcise the subtext: the knowledge of one's emptiness and the failure to put anything meaningful there. Academe is primarily a battleground of pure psychic needs and disorders waged through an endless play of surface texts (editorial boards on which one has served, conferences one has attended, the reputation of one's publisher, the length of one's vitae, and so on).

From Hitler's favorite song, "Who's Afraid of the Big Bad Wolf?" to its academic parody is but a small step with a phantom difference. Hitler loved the violent subtext of the fairy tale. Academics characteristically turn it into their favorite parlor game—the hollow joke that has no humor except for those who need to be witty to prove their superiority and thereby give their community the group cohesion proper to it. Intellectualized wit banishes anxiety. The fear of Virginia Woolf is one of the most incisive definitions of the academic mind: the flight into poses of intellectual transcendence, always exceedingly au courant, to allay an underlying anxiety. The need to laugh more uproariously each time the stale joke is repeated reveals the collective desire for the big discharge. Academics are already like the group at the end of *The Iceman Cometh,* only they'll never know it.

In her early review of the play, Diana Trilling asserted that in thirty years in academe she never met anyone like George and Martha.[4] The complaint betrays the obvious. And so it goes: "Albee's play is really about how homosexuals relate," and so on. One should never underestimate the automatic, albeit desperate, measures audiences will take to discharge works that threaten them. The simplest defenses are the ones that get you most quickly to the nearest exit—where Sartre awaits with the concept of bad faith.

Structure and Psychodrama: To Speak of the Woe That Is in Marriage

Structure, as Aristotle teaches, is the soul of tragedy. Albee takes this insight and makes method of it. *Virginia Woolf* comprehends the dialectical interrelationship of the four structures and two options that constitute "modern marriage" and then dramatizes the movement through which these structures pass in their long night's journey into the void.

Four relationships constitute the psychological bond of a married couple. One psychodynamic underlies the relationship of the couple to each other. There are no individuals in Albee; I am my relationship to an other. This is the primary scene and focus of conflict. Couples enact the truth of the disorder they share by adopting competing roles. The roles make no sense apart from their function in a core conflict. A second psychodynamic derives from the relationship of both partners to their parents. This is the source of the original pairing, the seed of discontent, and the subtext that inevitably surfaces as the conflict between the couple develops. A married couple bears the history of their conflicts with their original object-relations as the underlying condition of object-choice. This is the subtext that comes a cropper through time. A third psychodynamic is engaged whenever a couple relates to other couples. This factor dynamizes the first two and becomes their target: the look of the other couple (i.e., "We're happy, while Joe and Jane are . . .") as source of Sartrean battle. A final psychodynamic surfaces out of the relationship of couples to the "child," both their own and those of others. Here the fantasy/possibility of making it different for your children and thereby perhaps even renewing (salvaging) the relationship is submitted to the truth of repetition: the child as savior becomes the child as victim.

Thus whenever a couple is present, their conflict contains both the force of the past (the parents) and the possibility of the future (the child) caught in the staging of their (unconscious) conflicts, which are exacerbated the moment another couple appears. *Virginia Woolf* takes these four structures and brings them to a head by dramatizing the two options whereby couples can relate to their conflicts—actively, aggressively, as with George and Martha, or passively and by avoidance as with Nick and Honey. The secret thereby revealed is the absence of difference. The plot of the play is the submission of these structures and options to the drama of aggression/regression as an "irreversible" process through which the truth outs, leaving the dramatis personae stripped of all illusions about themselves and their roles.

As a group psychology, the play thus offers us a single psyche which we can know as a whole only by annihilating all the defenses whereby we try to extricate ourselves from it. For in this play, the needs defining all four structures lock the protagonist in a battle in which everything unravels. We can gain an initial entry into that complex by defining the need or desire that "characterizes" each participant. Nick's need, that of the narcissistic pragmatist, is to think he's better than others, especially castrated men. Honey's need is avoidance and the anesthetization of consciousness. George's need as "embassy of death"—group analyst as aggressive demystifier—is to show everybody they are just like him, only they don't know it yet. Martha's need is to displace psychotic anxieties into oedipalized roles. It is worth noting that in this alignment genders are matched as mirror doubles. Honey hides without consciousness in the place that Martha fears to find herself conscious. George strips Nick's narcissism to reveal his unconscious envy as defense against self-loathing.

The Rites/Rights of Aggression

Aggression is the force that structures the play by ripping through all masks and roles. Anger here expresses its nobility by exposing the great lie of the Berne generation: the belief that when couples honestly express their resentments, they gain renewal. Renewal of love is the guarantee, anger the method. *Virginia Woolf* takes this pathos and tears it to shreds. The trouble with most "domestic quarrels" is that they never get to the real discontents. The "angry" couple may be on the way to a psychoanalysis of the relationship, but as long as they stop short of the unconscious motives that bind them, they're just making wind, exercising, playing a comedy.

If anger is to have any chance, it must touch on real discontents and then draw out the dialectic of the entire complex. But once begin this process, and Pandora's box is open. Moreover, as genuine psychoanalysis shows, you never open the box correctly as long as you preserve a guarantee—such as in sentimental practices of aggression which assume that real love was once there and stays as the substance that is regained by clearing away the detritus.

George and Martha take two steps beyond such commonplaces, Albee a third. The first, their basic contract, is an exemplary and lacerating honesty: aggression must aim at unconscious motives, and nothing can be withheld. In effect, they follow the basic analytic rule. Only by bringing out all discontents can we meet. Implicit in this contract is the possibility that the couple may discover that there is no core of love that was present at the beginning and that survives the process. That romantic guarantee simply disguises the real conditions of object-choice—the conditions of an ideal frustration that it takes "time" to plant and sow the terms of mutual cruelty and soul-murder.

The big lie of "marital counseling" rests on the myth that love and marriage derive from a healthy, conflict-free dimension of object-choice. By clearing away the destructiveness that has arisen, one regains the core. Even when divorce results, one leaves with the illusion that one made a mistake but is now "OK," free to go forth with illusions about one's newfound "freedom and identity" in the confidence that one can (now) build "good object-relations" or at least the recognition that the next marriage had better be a safe one with someone who will show equal care not to disrupt the shared commitment to diminished existence.

Freud formulates the basics simply, yet profoundly: in every relationship there are, at least, four parties—the man and his mother, the woman and her father. A free relationship is possible only after both parties have annihilated the hold of the parents, not before. Before, you either marry someone like the parent or someone unlike the parent whom you turn into or treat like the parent. The ironic truth is this: the marriage "contract" is attained only when the couple has re-created the conditions of their original frustration.

George and Martha strive to bring this condition to light through an exercise of aggression strikingly different from the usual sort (where the same things are said repeatedly without ever being said clearly). And as we watch the drama in which George and Martha lay bare the true terms of their relationship, we also see the disappearance of the guarantees that ego psychologists use to control aggression and communication in order to sustain a social engineering and ideology whereby relationships, even those beyond repair, are protected from their truth.

The alternative to the big lie is of course the petty one: Nick and Honey, the marriage contract as avoidance through false solicitude. If George and Martha do everything to shatter illusions, Nick and Honey do everything to sustain them. Death occurs behind the couple's back. As Albee shows, their solicitude is actually a feast of passive-aggressive behavior used to distance the couple from each other. The ordinary end of such marriages, of course, is the pathetic spectacle of a couple who have never exchanged a harsh word discovering that there is absolutely nothing between them. Putting this audience onstage, Albee offers them a radically different "lesson."

Nick and Honey's desire is to proclaim their difference from George and Martha. This is the reason why they are such an "attentive" audience, so easily drawn into the play so that, in reaction and ideological celebration, they can affirm and represent the "proper balance" and health of the normal couple. As stand-ins, they serve as perfect representations for those who will later leave the theatre proud to assert that their marriage is not like George and Martha's. Nick and Honey are, at the beginning, what that audience must become when the revels are all ended if they are to discharge the play by denial. Once home, they thereby renew the solicitous talk dedicated to resuming the roles they had prior to the play. Denial is, for them, the task of interpretation. But it is trapped in an irony: they can perform it only by giving themselves over to psychological operations which plunge them back into the disorder that the play has carried to the end of the line. They are thus left with the depth charge it has imploded in their psyche as a gaping wound certain to haunt them, but behind their backs. They may even discover that, thanks to Albee's insinuation, there are no longer any innocent remarks.

In striving to deny that condition, Nick and Honey advance it while depriving themselves of any chance to attend to it. The means are avoidance, denial, anesthetization, and, above all, solicitude. Honey only speaks to prop up Nick's narcissism; Nick only speaks to keep her tranquilized. And they give every indication that these are not just the masks they wear in public but also the way they relate in private. Privacy for them is the acting out of the social roles assigned by the Big Other. It is the arena in which subjects try to prove to the *socius* that they have the kind of normal, healthy relationship it holds up as the "ideal" all must mirror. Nick and Honey are the same in public and in private because for them there is no difference. George and Martha are uneasy in public, given to acting out behaviors, because they see social space (academic evenings, etc.) as a vast theatre of lies. Their desire is to bring the truth of privacy onto the public stage, which is precisely what they will do in the play.

Albee's masterful dialogue lays bare the subtext of everyday speech. Idle talk is not what Heidegger assumes: the attempt to be relieved together.[5]

Instead, its purpose is to relieve our anxiety by creating anxiety in the other. Idle talk is barbed speech. It works best when we are able to confuse the other while we secrete an aggression that can't be attended to directly. Speech is verbal aggression, and because it is indirect it works best through ambiguity.

Act I: Games Couples Play

"What a Dump": Language—and Forms of Life

The dreary work of exposition become the spectacle of an unbound aggression: such is one way of defining the work of act I. In many ways the opening is the most fluid yet complex scene in the play. All subtexts are in play, but a general unburdening of conflict, a Thanatos preparatory to sleep, is in process.[6] Conflicts are touched gently, one final time. George and Martha try to unburden themselves of aggression by a play of aggression. But working off what's left of one's wits is a dangerous game, and by the end of the scene each character will have made an irreversible choice, with the movement of devolution thereby engaged. Even when energies have run down, motives remain at work, stirring the unconscious back into action.

The evening has stirred up many discontents—as any academic gathering is sure to do—which the characters here try to discharge through a drift, toward sleep for George, toward "reconciliation" and lovemaking for Martha. No remark is innocent of aggression, but here it's a tired game of thrust and counterthrust the couple play together in weary recognition of "truths" they've learned to live with. Neither can resist the chance to deliver a blow, but the blows fall on shoulders already prepared to receive and deflect them. Martha's opening line "What a dump" (3) names the home and underscores George's failure while deflecting the blow toward what he can take as an innocent allusion and question. Basic conflicts are stirring, but both characters want to slide away from their deeper resonance. All of Martha's remarks call attention to George's failures; all of his replies stress her vulgarity as cause. But both here play the game as a sort of foreplay which yields the distinct pleasure each needs in order to discharge psychic tension.

A possible objection to this reading yields the subtext both want to escape but can't. Martha knows the guests are coming and is setting George up. But as the scene plays, she almost forgets this fact as her private game of insult-as-foreplay moves to the point where she wants George to make love to her. It is only when George rejects her sexually that Martha remembers and seizes this safety valve. Had George responded "properly," they could simply have let the bell ring. The implied picture of how they resolve conflict when alone is evoked only to be sundered. Tonight there will be no exit. Playful aggression always holds in reserve a deeper aggression which it primes. The Unconscious is catching up with both characters. Whenever they play one game, another rises to claim it. Aggression as foreplay can't end in sexual release, for Martha's subtext activates the deeper subtext in George it is designed to hold at bay.

The collapse of the initial game in fact reveals a fundamental difference in motives. Aggression for Martha is de Sade's knife held forth "to intensify the love play."[7] George's insults turn her on. She readily regresses to baby talk and is willing to end the game with a simple appeal: Kiss me. At this point, however, the real drama begins, for with George's refusal, Martha's fear of Virginia Woolf surfaces. George now has her where he wants her. Her aggression has awakened another psychodynamic of aggression. She's played the game to its "erotic" end. He abruptly reawakens her with a dose of Thanatos. Recoiling, Martha senses, for the first time, that there may be a death of the soul at work in George. The place where he lives may be one she can't reach. The moment at the party, which she will later recount, of looking at George and seeing him disappear, has returned to haunt her. Her fear is that she's sleeping with the iceman, that the real purpose of games for George is to suck on death.

Martha has one through-line, George another. Martha plays all games so that Eros, however twisted, will win out over death, whereas George wants death-work to cut to the marrow so that the void, not renewal, will emerge. George has played his part in order to frustrate Eros, to create panic in that motive by presenting the passive-aggressive splendor of an unreachable other who has chosen the greater delights of death. When he refers to her two heads and she calls him a "zero," both have hit on the truth they fear. The structuring principle that will drive the drama is now engaged. Each subtext will drive the prior subtext to destruction. The relationship of Eros and Thanatos is, indeed, as Freud feared, dialectical.[8]

One could of course argue that George refuses to kiss Martha simply because the guests are coming and he knows from Martha's description of Nick that he's in for another castration. He thus responds in kind, before the fact, with a prior desexualization of her. On this level, George's problem is that he simply cannot trust any affection from Martha because she has so often used it to set him up. But on a deeper level, George's reaction derives from his knowledge that Martha is herself acting out a deeper subtext which she must compulsively renew. Eros for Martha is aggression aimed at either sexualizing or castrating the other. The one subtext invariably bears the other as threat, and George chooses to focus on the deeper motive because it activates his desire to bring both texts to zero-degree. Hydra-headed, Martha is trapped in her own game. Realizing that, she will play it brilliantly to stage a counter action.

Another way to look at the opening scene is as preliminary instruction in language as the force that will drive the play. At the start, George and Martha use language to jab at one another in an effort to pin down in words the attributions needed to arrest and discharge conflicts. Verbal aggression is the modus operandi of desire-in-language: the necessary detour through and fixation on speech as the way to rid ourselves of anxiety.[9] But language betrays them, here first revealing its power to destabilize every attempt to bring the process it unleashes to a halt. Language continually slips away, bringing the characters back to what they use it to escape. Thoroughly conditioned to aggressive connotation, George and Martha hear the call of battle even when it's not intended. As we will shortly see, a similar fate awaits characters who use language to avoid same. Language bears a history which comes a cropper when all speech drips with results that can no longer be avoided. Martha will later talk about there no longer being any way she and George can touch each other. The fact of the matter—made painful by how close they momentarily come in the opening scene—is that this possibility is no longer present, because, to use currently fashionable terms, language is now speaking them. When that happens, it is because language is now presenting the bill for what has been spoken through it over time.

Ambiguities don't just happen. They are sought and exploited and then, usually, denied, because we use speech to express and conceal our motives. The ambiguity that comes to seize the couple so that nothing said fails to rub raw the sores is not an inadvertent linguistic infelicity but the end product of a complex history. Such are the language games, unknown to Wittgenstein, that will drive this play to the marrow. Language serves this purpose through its collapse. Speech cannot stay safely on the surface, fixated on certainties, because its practice constantly reintroduces the very subtexts it tries to abolish. Language games thereby eventually reveal the true grammar of the "form of life" they reify, which is why linguistic foreplay is the right starting point for a drama in which naturalism and realism will constantly erupt in psychodrama.[10]

George and Martha are never far away from fairy tales and childhood games. One purpose of the games they play at the beginning of act I is to strip away the veneer of "culture" so that they can indulge in deliberate bouts of childishness. Two kinds of talk are juxtaposed repeatedly: intellectual wit aimed at injury, and baby talk aimed at letting go. The secret is their identity along the lines of a regression which is never in the service of the ego. The fact that one regresses to childhood fantasy only to erupt again in naked aggression undercuts the protective function of the imaginary child before his appearance. Fantasy may be the Emerald City of love play, but aggression is the yellow brick road. Baby talk gives George and Martha only a momentary pause, until the deeper structure again exposes its claws.

We've Got an Audience

Their conflicts in place, the ante is raised immeasurably for George and Martha by the entry of the "force" that will dynamize everything—the presence of an audience. For Albee the psyche is interpersonal; the true Sartrean drama of the *pour soi* is that of couples looking at and being looked at by other couples. The look that turns us into a thing—compelling the struggle for recognition by inverting the terms—is the look of the other couple. With that threat and invitation present, George and Martha's joint task is no longer to insult each other but to draw the audience into the net. As creatures with a taste for metatheatre, George and Martha know that the best way to do so is to make the audience uncomfortable while using their voyeurism to put them off guard and draw them in. The audience's pose— We are civilized, normal human beings who are politely shocked by your behavior—is what most arouses an actor's aggression. George and Martha now hack at each other to bait and probe Nick and Honey. Working together, they use their relationship to implicate the guests by activating a complex subtext focused on male authority. Martha invokes her father to shame George and to prime Nick's male competitiveness. She baits Nick and George simultaneously: the spectacle of the man who failed activates the other man's need to assume the mask of phallic superiority. George then stirs up the doubts that must underlie that role by calling attention to Honey, the huge hole in Nick's mask, present for all to see.

This is not to say that George and Martha aren't still after each other. But the play of aggression they stage before their audience has as its deeper motive the arousal in that audience of the very disorders Nick and Honey try to repress by positioning themselves as objective observers of the spectacle before them. But aesthetic distance is always a reaction formation derived from a prior involvement that is denied. George and Martha are fascinating lures for both operations, because they display, with such relish, the aggression we all on occasion find in ourselves yet need to deny. The duplicity of that reaction engages two motives: the possibility that normalcy is a sham and that the chance to get a look at the bitter truth about human beings—at a safe remove—is an irresistible theatrical opportunity. Lest the bad faith lurking in both motives retard our pleasure, we displace it onto Nick and Honey. We are now comfortably seated for a safe pleasure: in Nick and

Honey we can allow ourselves to indulge the belief that the normal life in which nothing is faced is one in which slow death merely accumulates with no possibility of demanding our attention.

Much has been said about Nick and Honey as surrogate children whom George and Martha want to help by getting them to face their problems. But this sentimental reading, apparently endorsed at play's end, conceals a purpose George and Martha can't control even if they wanted to. Once you start stripping away masks, you can't just stop at some predetermined point and reassert a humanistic core that will deliver you from the game. The darker possibility present the moment one begins is that the real core may be the void and that humanistic guarantees are merely the illusion that survives as proof of little more than exhaustion and the refusal of humanism to dramatize its discontents.

Male Bonding I

Martha dominates the early stages of the play because she attributes the identities that force both men into phallic competition. Everything Martha says makes one statement which both men recieve: George failed because he wasn't like what you, Nick, appear to be. By goading the two men into phallic competition, Martha introduces what will become her master plot, only to exit the scene.

In the ensuing scene, George's redoubtable task is to draw Nick into that game by tapping his aggression while getting the goods on him. George isn't after information but a reaction, and he brilliantly uses his own vulnerabilities to draw out his opponent. The game is his version of Twenty Questions. The goal is to find the vulnerabilites that cluster around the three topics men use to measure one another—job, wife, and children. These topics entail a single dialectic, because they are the three contexts through which the male presents his narcissized phallus through the external evidence certain to compel recognition. The scene thus constitutes a parody of male bonding which reveals its subtext. The drama here proceeds like so many early rounds of a boxing match: jabs, feints, light blows, retreats, all meant to get the opponent confused and off balance. Conversation probes for weak spots that will enable one to gauge the true extent of the other's "organ." George is here like Ali against Foreman: he offers his body for a number of heavy blows to tire the opponent, and he exults when Nick gets angry—over his declension game—because he knows he now has the other on the ropes.

George's agency is always grounded in a version of the Sartrean game "loser wins," and he deftly plays it here to undermine each assurance upon which the other's narcissism depends. He grants Nick's superior pragmatism only to suggest that careerism is the pursuit of shallow beings who know nothing about history. Nick provides the perfect response by indicating that he couldn't care less. But George knows that history always carries the larger resonance of knowledge about one's personal history. The narcissistic reassurance he offers Nick thus puts the other so off guard that Nick blurts out the basics about the main impediment in his personal history, his wife. This has been George's target all along because he knows (as he puts it later) that the "way to a man's heart is through his wife's belly" (113), especially when the discrepancy between that man's narcissism and the cracked mirror reflecting it is so apparent.

Opposed motives thus drive both agents to the second topic that invariably attends certain forms of male bonding. After comparing ourselves "career-wise," we "share" complaints about our spouses, the better to prevent their defects from casting a reflection on our substance. (We do so unless, that is, we possess "the beautiful object" which provides the perfect narcissistic complement which activates the other man's envy.) In Honey, Nick has something to hide, but he knows how to distance himself from it. In the Unconscious, however, the conflicts stirred up by the discussion of wives have a direct issue, and in displacement Nick blurts it out: "Do you have any other kids?" (97).

The opening round is a superb illustration of George's ability to deprive the other of the illusion of difference in order to activate his aggression. To win, he must show Nick that he already occupies the position he resists by projecting it onto George. George plays with language to reveal its hollowness, to make speech stop dead in its tracks: "What were the things that motivated me?" (31). He knows Nick believes that the best conversation is one that says nothing, but he turns that principle of avoidance back against Nick. Nick's only out—and George counts on it—is aggression ("You can play that damn little game" [33], and so on). But once Nick ends the first game this way, he's landed himself in the second. Aggression recognized can now become the explicit target of speech—and action.

Beneath the surface, George and Nick have engaged in a complex drama which reveals the fundamental difference of their psyches. George is a man who can no longer be castrated, but he can be humilated. He also knows that humilation is the greater threat, because it reactivates regression to the "basic fault." When he is humiliated, his self-loathing becomes unbound. It can gain relief only by getting at the same psychic register in the other. Nick, in contrast, is a man whose psyche is ruled by unconscious envy. That is the instability behind the voyeurism that draws him into George and Martha's net: Nick wants to see the weakness in other men in order to prop up his narcissistic mask. George taps a deeper discontent. Self-loathing, not envy, is the true basis of action. George can be unmasked only when one gets at the experience envy displaces—the catastrophe of humiliation that reduces the psyche to a gaping wound.[11] Envy, in contrast, girds the false self of narcissism in order to exorcise that threat. It aims accordingly at the other's self-worth. And it will attack the very springs of life, if necessary, in order to sustain the narcissistic illusion. Narcissism feeds on the spectacle of the other's failure.

George, in contrast, is curiously without envy because he sees that the other is as unsubstantial as he is. Self-loathing lives on, however, as that will-to-truth which will put an end to all illusions.[12] Just as that power enables George to get at the psychotic anxiety beneath Martha's oedipalizing, it quickly puts him in touch with the disorder beneath Nick's narcissism. He knows that he and Nick are the same, only Nick hasn't realized it yet. Nick desperately clings to his difference and needs to identify the weak spot in the other to reinforce his narcissism. That is why he's such a naive player of the game. He can't see that his insistence on keeping everything on the surface and the Image conceals as it reveals the drama that commences once such roles are referred to their repressed.

For now, George deflects that topic by renewing the attack on Martha's father, but his actions at the beginning of the scene show that his unconscious is already racing ahead toward the plotting of a greater drama in which all the guests—present and absent—will be caught. Just before Martha left, he in effect dared her to talk about "you know what" (29). That topic capped the foregoing drama between them by introducing the instability capable of transforming all its terms. George plays Martha's game up to a point because he knows how to exploit it: to claim that his castrated status is the result of the combined action of Martha's bitchiness and her father's power over her. His self-loathing is thereby held at bay. But if "the bit" (18) comes up, George will be put in the slot of the Father, and the whole drama will shift to another stage.

In the scene between George and Nick, an interesting psychodynamic of audience participation comes into play. We are happy to participate when, to invert Aristotle, we are assured that we are better than the characters on the stage. And this works best when their inferiority lies in the realms that most concern us. This is why Nick's statement roughly midway through the scene—"I don't like to become involved in other people's affairs"—rings hollow, and resounds, slumbering in a "foolish ear."

The men end the scene wondering what women talk about when alone. They will shortly learn, and when they do a curious thing about the scene offstage will surface. While changing clothes, Martha in effect does to

Honey what George does to Nick. She shows Honey the costume she will use to "seduce" Honey's husband. And while doing so, she invokes the beauty of her son. When alone women talk about their husbands and their children, and this conversation, like that of the men, has a competitive subtext. Offstage Martha adds, before the fact, the missing link to the scene she will now stage—castration of the other woman.

Martha's Sunday Chapel Dress

When George hears Martha is changing, he knows they have now moved toward a major staging of the two grand games they are always playing: Humiliate the Host and Hump the Hostess. Martha previously set the terms for what she's after in this drama by casting the husband as castrated male before the other man as oedipalized rival. The next step is to phallicize the other man in George's presence while belittling George's "organ." Career will again be the focus: it is an offer the two men can't refuse, given the fact that they have just activated its phallic subtext.

Martha's purpose in positioning both men for a drama she will control is to trap them in reified roles in order to foreclose the deeper drama she fears George is after. Its expulsion is her deepest subtext. For while Martha's target is George's body, George's target is Martha's mind, which he has already identified, in commenting on the painting on the wall, as the unity of surrealism and psychosis. Martha thus knows that George has already sounded his later threat to have her committed. The game in which they are both engaged is properly called "driving the other person crazy."[13]

But Martha's dilemma is that she can win only by endlessly castrating George. Her self-contradictory project is to stir him into an action that will prove his affection for her and thereby allay her fear that his only target is her psychic "integrity." Martha wants George to move from one oedipalized role to another, whereas George wants to strip away all roles. She wants him castrated so that he'll get on his feet fighting. He wants her dead, defeated, humiliated, and rejected—refused once again the kiss she's after.

Nick's role in this drama is a good deal more complex than it appears, because he has been placed in a complex slot. The mousetrap Martha here sets entails the following conditions. Martha will recount, with glee, before a younger man, the story of her husband's castration by an older man, her father, in order to cap the process by using the story to seduce the younger man. Martha enacts a double castration of George by telling Nick, the surrogate son, the story of George's defeat by her Daddy. George is thereby cut off at both ends, as it were. This movement is crucial to the psychological structure of act I, because diffuse aggression now focuses on a potential scapegoat which Martha and Nick can both exploit for different ends. As we'll see, the slot this puts George in leaves him with no option but to go after both "sons."

For one who claims he doesn't like to get involved, Nick shows little resistance to Martha's come-on because his narcissism is such that it feeds on the other's castration. Nick, in fact, loves aggression when the other is its object; it only becomes unfair, as we'll see, when he becomes its object and the defect in his image its target.

Career and being "at the meat of things" (63) are now one. In responding to that fact, George chooses to activate one of Martha's subtexts, which he will keep alive until he reverses it in act III. For in refusing to light Martha's cigarette, George declares that he is not a houseboy. Martha retaliates with the first extended narrative in the play: the scene in which that attribution was first solidified. In doing so she reintroduces one of the two absent presences, Daddy, whose specter will drive the act to the point where all subtexts and its complex psychodrama will fully emerge.

Daddy and Martha cast George in Daddy's phallic boxing match, and Martha, following her trainer's directions, threw a sucker punch. George's retaliation—with the fake gun—reveals the rage smoldering beneath his passive-aggressive stance, but Martha misses the point because she's still playing the scene to get from George the kiss he earlier refused. She will not quickly renounce the claims of Eros to another dynamic of aggression. Martha's belief is that if she can drive George into rage, that means he loves her: "You? . . . Kill me? . . . That's a laugh." George's stated belief is somewhat different: "Well, now, I might . . . someday" (60). And this is the force that now drives the drama as George redefines Martha's desire for a kiss as "blue games for the guests" (59), thus putting Nick back center stage. Martha was playing the game for one end, in which Nick, as displaced foreplay, was really peripheral, but George now insists that it be played out for another. Martha's hope to arrest the drama by reawakening the erotic bond is already effectively dead, because the presence of the third has inserted Eros into another drama which it cannot contain. The pathetic side of Martha's character is that she keeps trying to reassert it. George knows that this desperate hope is the key to getting at her marrow.

That drive is now introduced, as George replaces the image of "loving" Martha with the reductive picture sure to drive her up the wall: Martha, the drunk bitch with hot pants whose vulgarity knows no bounds because she is defined by one uncontrollable need—to get at "the meat of things." The erotic game ended, the oedipal one will now drive the drama by creating a context in which all the participants, two of whom aren't present, will find themselves fully engaged.

Humanism, According to George

This is the day George will kill her, and the attack begins with her body, now pictured in images of disgust—excessive, rutting. The prize thereby defined, he ups the ante by characterizing the mental endowment of her academic "suitors." Since this is one of the spots where Diana Trilling must have squirmed, it is worth noting that dismissing George as a mocking inversion of the humanist ideals he has failed to fulfill conveniently displaces the possibility that George has a deep understanding of what has happened to humanism—especially in the university. The humanist audience must, of course, externalize the threat by attacking George, lest they internalize his point: that humanism perhaps survives as little more than an exhausted defense mechanism, out of touch with its own basement and thus an easy prey to the "wave-of-the-future" (107) boys bound to replace it.[14] George knows that Nick *will* take over the History Department. We know he has triumphed throughout the humanities. If George is bitter toward humanism, it is because his is a humanism that has always been open to the tragic and that put that imperative before career. He knows that the only humanism worthy of the name is one that is willing to descend, without reserve, into the Crypt of the psyche.

Humanism is for George what it was for Nietzsche: an attempt to restore psychology to its position as the queen science through a critique of the essentialistic rationales humanism uses to hide its psychological disorders and appeal. Contra the thematic abstractions that have gathered around Albee's use of the humanism-science opposition, George grounds that issue in the psychological meat cleaver that cuts both ways. Humanism brings forth the full measure of his despair while goading Nick to an assertion of the resentment behind his pragmatism—"I'm going to be a personal screwing machine" (69)—with the object of that act being to top "you ineffectual sons of bitches" (111) who got sidetracked from pragmatism by inwardness. "The meat of things" may be a real presence for Martha. For George and Nick it's the symbolic object whereby they wage, in a battle for pure prestige over the possession of the phallus, the deeper Hegelian drama of Recognition and Unhappy Consciousness.

While this drama has been heating up, much to Martha's delight, Honey has not, appearances to the contrary, been in the ozone. In fact she never is. She always knows when to intervene, and careful attention to her interventions shows she isn't a cipher or spectator but an acutely engaged audience who hears everything because she listens with an Unconscious that is always right out on the surface, verging on hysteric collapse unless she can banish the conflicts that threaten her by displacing everything onto a new scene that will enable her to slip back into the privileged space of her self-anesthetization. The irony is that, in running from itself, such a consciousness invariably introduces the terms that will later trap it. She thus tries to reclaim Nick, and escape sexual conflict, by shifting to the new topic—Tell us about your son—which will drive the drama to its next stage.

Fathers and Sons

The fantasy child is the safety valve that has always limited George and Martha's destructiveness and restored their illusions. Once it is mentioned before the Other, however, it becomes a term in the game. Both its functions are thereby unhinged: they will collapse together because they are actually mirror images of each other.

A child for any couple holds the irresistible appeal of magical thinking. By making the child imaginary, Albee is able to highlight the psychological functions actual children perform. A child conceived to heal a couple becomes the psyche produced by the parents to project their conflicts—the battleground in which they act out what amounts to soul-murder, even though they often do it in the terms of idealization and sacrificial love. As a Brechtian device, the imaginary child with one stroke clears away the "empirical" details that can so easily distract our attention from these psychological facts. Naturalistic and realistic dramas about the family spend most of their time cutting away the details so that they can finally get to the place where Albee begins. The story of the imaginary child is perhaps the true story of every real child—the story of the binds the child's psyche finds itself in thanks to the desires of the parents.

The deepest resonance that is touched whenever the child comes into play is the shared illusion of the loveless couple, the "what if" which reawakens the founding illusion about what has become a nightmare—that there was "love" in the beginning and it must therefore still be present somewhere beneath all the crap. But that myth begins to totter the moment the topic of the child comes up. The child is the repetition in fantasy sustaining the myth of origins, and the mirror which eventually shows the truth both agents refuse to face about the original terms of their relationship. The latter begins to surface the moment the "little bugger" is mentioned. George and Martha want to keep the child free of their conflict, but Martha can't resist using him to further the attack on George: "Deep down in the private-most pit of his gut, he's not completely sure it's his own kid" (71). Even the attempt to retreat into lyricism over the son's "deep, pure green eyes . . . like mine" is barbed with castrations soon to be recounted: "Daddy has green eyes, too" (75). Martha wants to protect the child and shift to the topic sure to "get"

George. Questioning George's paternity serves both ends. George's counter-attack, though muted, is already in progress, as he tries to unhinge Martha by contravening her lyricized descriptions of the son. The child is never shared; it is a weapon used by each for furthering what has become a sexual battle, oedipalized in all directions, from beginning to end.

From the moment George dares Martha to mention the child, he is, in his Unconscious, in the process of killing it because his master plot requires using this force to get at the vulnerabilities in Martha that will lead to the marrow. Martha's most cherished role has not yet appeared onstage—that of the loving mother who only "plays" the bitch because her spouse forces that role upon her. George will now play up to that contrast to force Martha into a bind. With her two roles simultaneously engaged, Martha is caught: she must strive to keep the fantasized child free of the oedipal game she is playing with Nick at the very moment George keeps suggesting that Martha is now doing to Nick what she already did to their son. It is a brilliant counterattack, but it doesn't work precisely because it introduces the missing link Martha will use to spring her own mousetrap. The absent Father has always been present. He will now stride center stage, revealing the "wheels within wheels" that establish a far more complex psychodrama than either George or Martha bargain on. Untangling its shifting positions and exposing its core will require the rest of the play.

The question Who is the Father? deepens the instabilities of George's present situation, for the essential definition he offers of fatherhood is re-venge. In doing so, he reveals his present purpose: to repeat, with the surro-gate son, roles reversed, what Martha's father did to him. Nick is the immedi-ate object of that attack, but Sonny's head has already been put on the block. Do unto others what was done unto you: it seems an inescapable temptation, an ineluctable process. The initial staging of Sonny thus develops through a play of unhinged pronouns that circle around what may be his truest defini-tion: "When's the little bugger coming home?" (70). Such, at any rate, is what he becomes in the course of the play as George and Martha try to place him at that point in the other's anatomy. Sonny is the "little bugger" because he's actually the stand-in and agent of the other absent presence—Daddy. When George and Martha later posit faults in the son—to get at each other—they take care to ground those faults in the partner's neurotic tie to his or her parent. Doing so, they activate the subtext that will undercut every illusion about the protective space they could create through the son by showing that his true function is every cruelty he can be used to inflict. The son's identity derives, George claims, from Martha's perverse relationship to her father. Tyrannical fathers produce bitches who can't keep their hands off innocent kids. Withholding the grand story of George's family romance for later use,

Martha replies in kind by reducing George's charge to that of an "S.O.B." who projects his failures onto the son because he "hates my father" (76). George's parenting derives from a double disorder.

To make the accusation stick, however, she must tell the story of George's relationship to her father. It is a dangerous but necessary gambit, because, as all four agents know, everything from the beginning has revolved around Daddy as the unavoidable question everyone asks in trying to account for Martha and George. It now erupts in a context certain to activate all its subtexts. Martha will tell her story in order to castrate George, as father, before the substitute son, as her culminating act in a seduction aimed at tapping Nick's transgressive oedipal desire. The question *When is Sonny coming home?* haunts the drama, because the home is the one place he has never been. On the psychic register, however, he's finally made his entry.

Daddy: Martha's Master Plot

We must pause here to consider a way of interpreting the conflict between George and Martha that is both true and false, partial and deliberately misleading. George and Martha draw on a romantic myth of origins like a blank check to limit the scope of destructiveness. In one sense, George and Martha are good old romantics at heart, as they were, according to their accounts, when they first met seeking mutual deliverance—she from Daddy and an oedipal attachment, he from oedipal guilt. It's a good story and a convenient one. Each wanted to be healed by the other. Each let the other down, betraying the initial bond of love. All that's happened since is the long, drawn-out revenge and protest over the violation of that initial contract. Martha claims that her true desire was always to be freed from her father. George claims that his desire was to win recognition from a woman who would see that his courage in writing a work of psychological confession made him a man far superior to the blustering assertiveness of men like her father, men devoid of inwardness.

It's a nice story, but as Freud taught us, the conditions of object-choice are subtle. It is not merely that one often chooses a person unlike the parent of the opposite sex in order to repeat one's frustrations with that parent by turning the partner into a replica. The deeper truth is that the depth charge sounded in the psyche when one meets the right other is the recognition that one has finally found the person perfectly suited to this process. George is perfect precisely because he never will stand up to Martha's father. Martha is perfect precisely because she will use George's psychological wounds to destroy him. Love is the myth that hides the truth the couple refuses to face: love was not there *in illo tempore*, but hate diffused and displaced into a net sure to entangle everything as the couple lives out over time the subtext active from the beginning.

All the better to conceal this connection, the play here first turns to extended narrative as the best way to get an opponent. This, the first in a dialectical series of narratives, is also the first big lie and the first big lure to trap the audience.

Martha's story is supposed to show why George hates Daddy—because of his superior power—but it really reveals how George functions as a term in Martha's hatred and frustration. George, like Martha's first husband, is cast as the oedipal criminal, because Martha's desire is to commit the transgressive crime. Her first attempt, however, was a dream of magical release from her psyche, predestined accordingly to run up against a "No Exit" sign. Martha's quest for erotic escape with an other (her Mellors), totally unlike her father and outside his world, was actually a game played (as this game usually is) to get Daddy's attention—and intervention. It thus served its purpose: to bring her back to the home as the scene where her frustration and her desire are fixated. The dubious battle she must wage there is the situation that meets its necessary condition of object-choice in George. Finding and inserting the other man in Daddy's world is the act needed for the true beginning of Martha's drama. Martha's only chance to free herself from Daddy is to use the other man to triumph over Daddy, but on Daddy's turf and in the terms Daddy dictates. The husband must become the rival of the Father for the daughter's love, and he can triumph (as he must) only by besting the Father at his own game. Martha must marry a faculty member— an "heir apparent"—who must be assigned a predetermined role. Whatever makes the object different from Daddy makes him unfit for battle and thus becomes a target of ridicule. The courtship is almost a blank spot, an insignificant moment in Martha's narrative, because it is only when she shifts to the career issue that the psychodrama is engaged.

The air of defeat and of a darker purpose is already present, however. As Martha notes, George is virtually the only object available. The fact that he is thoroughly unsuited for his role adds to his deeper appropriateness. For through George Martha can reexperience the initial conditions of her frustration, while shifting the burden. Martha and Daddy thus conspire to wage their relationship through the Other. The father's humiliations of George (the key one deliberately withheld for now) are aimed at reestablishing his exclusive possession of his daughter, whose oedipal status has by now been enhanced by a fantasy twice fulfilled—her mother's death and her stepmother's. Martha is on the throne with Daddy, presiding over New Carthage: caught in that toil of desire, she imposes it on George. She can use him both to rub raw her frustration and to reestablish her bond. What she can't do is extricate either of them from the conflict. Instead, she loads the whole thing on George's back—by breaking it.

George's claim to attention for his distinctive qualities can't gain a hearing. He receives instead rejection, played out by Martha and Daddy when they cast him in the role of "oedipal son" with the career game made competition for phallic possession of the daughter/mother. When Martha now reenacts that story, while recasting George in the part of an impotent father humiliated before Nick, the phallic son, she hits the marrow. In implosion, George's psyche momentarily collapses in sheer noise: his chanting of the Virginia Woolf rhyme drowns all voices in endless repetition. All dramas collapse as they rush into that void. Psychotic panic ends the act.

In that eruption of the Unconscious, George is, however, far ahead of himself. Unable to turn the oedipal drama to any advantage, George must activate the deeper psychic disorders it represses. George has always had one foot in that psychic space; he must now make it the boot that will kick them all into a frenzy.

The deepest psychic disorder in George has been pried open and rages within, unbound. He can reverse its force only by becoming its agent. But death-work requires careful plotting, because one must get at the internal structure that keeps the opponent alive. George will shortly begin that process by carrying out the threat he earlier used to delay Martha's attack: If you humiliate me, I'll destroy the son, and I'll do it systematically—first, by exposing the oedipal son, Nick, and then through a direct attack on the fantasized child. George does not yet know he will kill the child, but he does know that its function in the drama must be totally reversed. The safeguard that kept Martha from the fear of Virginia Woolf must now be used to "drive her crazy" so that she can feel what he's now feeling and, her equal again, he can say, Now how do you like it? In its collapse, George's mind races *entr'acte* to the plotting of a truly systematic mousetrap. The conflicts developed through the psychodramas of act I will now be subjected to the "embassy of death." It will drive them to a deeper psychic register by forcing all the agents to produce a dialectical series of self destructive narratives. There are two kinds: the stories we tell to prevent psychotic regression and the true ones we suppress lest their telling unhinge us utterly. Two kinds of stories, but they will come to the same end—the opening of each psyche to its Crypt.

If that possibility is the implicit danger in all storytelling, it enables us to locate the lure act I has dangled to hook the audience in a process they won't be able to avoid. Martha's story is a first attempt at psychoanalytic interpretation through totalizing narrative. If that interpretation collapses, another supply can be found. We can even take delight in teasing out its subtext (as I have done above), sure that eventually a story and an explanation that works will be found. That confidence introduces the audience to a process in which interpretations collapse, only to be replaced by the need for a deeper and richer framework of interpretation. Interpretation isn't relativized; it is made dialectical. Following that process, act II will take us into a vast labyrinth of oedipalizations in order to produce an understanding that collapses all analytic frameworks (Freud, Lacan) grounded in the primacy of the oedipus. The result will take us, with George, to the darker places of interpretation and a theatrical space where oedipus is but a poor player.

Act I may be defined as the movement from Fun and Games to authentic cruelty, that is, the drive to subject the other psyche to catastrophe through the exposure of the basic fault. Fun and Games has served its purpose by using the free play of aggression to seek out basic wounds. *Walpurgisnacht* will now dramatize the irreversible movement of the subtexts that are engaged once that process has drawn the right kind of blood. In doing so, it will redefine both the threatre event and its psychic space.

Act II: *Walpurgisnacht* as *Kadavergehorsamkeit*

Since nothing is slain in absentia or *in effigie* the through-line of act II is a progressive descent in which everything that protects the psyche from the exposure of its crypt is stripped away. That movement has a six-part structure which renews each of the dramas set up in act I in order to expose their repressed.

Male Bonding II

In renewing the parody of male bonding, George stokes Nick's desire to assert his difference. Nick complies, with the perfect non sequitur—I try not to get involved in other people's business—since, as George knows, he's just shown he's quite willing to get involved when the game is helping a woman humiliate her husband. To turn the tables, George must lull Nick into a secure objective stance while playing upon the fascination Nick can't resist. George notes that it must be pathetic to see two old types hacking away at each other, missing most blows. Nick quickly corrects him: he's "impressed" by the fact that George and Martha "don't miss." George knows that the bait has been taken. If he can now get the goods on Nick, he can set a trap that will not only destroy the surface difference Nick claims but will also get at the deeper difference George wants to deprive him of. Nick's discomfort doesn't prevent him from accepting a series of drinks, because he needs to hear more—both to find out precisely what he must disclaim and because the need to do so has begun surfacing and will shortly erupt in narrative.

To get at what Nick's concealing, George provides a long reflective interlude, spoken as much to himself or to no one as to Nick and as much to reopen his own wounds as to prime them for their labor. George's "bergin" story is the still point in the turning world, the zero-degree of the psyche containing the insight that George will enforce on all of them. It is also the first extended example of what will be the key strategy of act II—narrative as self-revelation and entrapment. And in many ways it is the deepest one, because, as we'll see, it questions beforehand the status of the other stories. George's oft-noted preoccupation with history derives from his insight that narrative alone is sufficient to explain—and to expose—the psyche. The story George here offers thus provides a possible paradigm for reinterpreting the others.

Based on an absurd contingency, the accidental murder of both parents, Geoge's story nevertheless sets forth a theory of the core psychological trauma. The denial of unconscious motivation is a perfect case of the lady protesting too much, and one suspects he knows it. The bergin cherub has done in reality what every child wants to do in fantasy and perhaps must do in inner reality: he has killed the parents.[15] And he suffers the consequence—silence. The function of George's unexampled linguistic power is here revealed: to use words to say nothing, to deprive words of their ability to point to anything but the void. This is the place from which George proceeds, and the painful honesty of his story is in direct proportion to the violence of its sequel. The lack of difference George pursues is far more radical than the surface one Nick wants to assert. George's insight is that death hides behind all roles and masks. The basis of his relationship to others is the effort to force them to attain or refute a similar awareness. Nothing less will satisfy him. Nick thinks George is after the abolition of a superficial difference (I'm not like you—in marriage, career, etc.), whereas George's goal is to abolish the deeper differences on which the identity of the ego depends in order to defend itself from a regression into psychotic anxieties.

Nick's response presents us with the curious paradox of one who insists, "Don't try to put me in the same class with you" (102), offering a story that does precisely that. As Honey did earlier, to displace his anxiety Nick blurts out the facts about children, pregnancy, that puts it on the table. As George learns, without much probing, Nick's is a story of an arranged marriage, without passion, orchestrated through a hysterical pregnancy and entered into for money. If, as many critics claim, *Virginia Woolf* is a study of sterility in marriage, Nick and Honey have covered all the bases. To underscore their essential similarity, George "invents" a story about Martha's money, which he later says probably isn't true. Its truth doesn't matter, because activating a subtext is its raison d'être: George has been drawing Nick out to get the goods on him, and he now has everything needed to spring the mousetrap.

When Nick sees the mousetrap about to spring, he struggles to reassert his narcissistic *moi*. The fantasy of self-identity and the game plan of career success thus come together in the "plowing" of "pertinent wives" (113). The drama suspended at the end of act I is thereby renewed, with the "unwilling" participant in Martha's game now unable to resist becoming "a personal screwing machine" in order to gain possession of far more than her body. George has drawn Nick from his narcissistic mask to his underlying conflict, and he won't let him disown it—"No, baby, . . . you're serious, and it scares the hell out of you" (443)—because it shatters Nick's desire to claim he's not in George's psychological world.

The seeds planted in their first conversation have now ripened, and George can complete this second parody of male bonding by claiming he wants to warn the younger man. He knows there is no way his advice can be taken, since doing so would require, from Nick, a recognition of the similarity he needs to deny. We pause here to note once again that many interpreters have claimed that George and Martha's real desire is to help the youngsters.

Nick's movement from his opening discomfort to "Up yours" (116) is a psychological progression he can't escape. The vulgarity cues George's greatest speech, which does not mourn the loss of civilization but celebrates it. Language has gotten down to basics: "Up yours." "The principles of . . . principle" have given way to anal metaphors. George is exhilarated because he knows he has activated the unconscious conflicts that will draw Nick fully into the game.

The Fantasy Child and/is the Oedipal Child

The renewal of that game produces the clash between fantasy and oedipalization. When Martha inadvertently reintroduces the son, George seizes on the topic to spring the trap he baited in act I. Both have now dropped all pretense of the child as a shared haven and must use it to attack the other. Call this the first murder, since, by the end of this scene, one function the son performed is no longer possible. Nick is the term that galvanizes this instability, because he has been cast in the role of the oedipal rival—the apparent contrast to Sonny who will ironically bring out the actual relationship George and Martha would have to any child. As George and Martha attack each other, through the imaginary son, in order to wage battle over Nick, the oedipalized son, Albee collapses the two poles of the developmental process to give us a unified concept of the psychological function of parents in forming the identity of children.

Both now use the son to attack the other's sexuality. But they can do so only by sexualizing the son. His psyche, the inner world thereby created, is regulated by the intrusion of two competing presences, both fixated on his genitals. The imaginary stories George and Martha now tell reveal what would be the actual result of their parenting: the sexual "confusion" of the son. Furthering that process, they now repeat the "original" crime to further the attack on each other. The imaginary son matures, like real ones, to discover the impossible position the parents have put him in so that they can use his "sexual identity" to get at each other.

The suppressed truth of parenting emerges. The formation and development of psychosexual identity is a process in which the psyches of most children are ravaged so that the parents can use their illness to attack and blame each other. As psychoanalysis has shown, this formation, erupting in adolescence, is the true "identity" one brings, as a system of core conflicts, into every subsequent relationship. The bitter knowledge contained in the psychoanalytic recognition that parents act out and reproduce their sexual conflicts in and through their relationship to the child is that we are all, in effect, fantasy children. The real child is as absent as the fantasy child, since to be a child is to be the clash and paralysis of parental projections.

George exploits this insight to spring the trap he set in act I. George can concede the mother's psychological closeness to the child because he can use it to transform the battle with Nick. The infant child becomes a scene of sexual strife won, as must be the case, by the mother. The adult child thus becomes the oedipal rival whom the father must use to punish the woman for the original crime. The adult male child, phallusized in infancy by the shift of the mother's desire from the father to the child, is the rival the father must defeat for the good of all concerned. George uses Martha's relationship to the child to establish the justice of his revenge. The mother sexualized the child. The father protested by withdrawing from both. Now, in a reenactment of that true primal scene, the mother parades the surrogate son before the father to reenact his castration. The father justifiably goes for the jugular to restore the proper order of things.

George is a student of Lacan *avant la lettre,* and with an ironic twist.[16] Everyone remains mired in oedipal rivalries, unless or until the father intervenes. The adult male child is the object onto which the mother has shifted her desire—by producing either the son's sexual confusion and paralysis, as with Sonny, or his phallic grandiosity, as with Nick. She did so, however, George argues, because of the prior relationship with her own father. The mother's tie to her original oedipal object is what produces the oedipal relationship to her son. Contra Lacan, fatherhood is not the way out but the original source of the problem. George, as father, can't intervene and put the mother in her place because her father already trapped all of them in a bind that has no exit. George reintroduces Daddy to show that his real effect was not George's destruction but the destruction of George and Martha's son. George's weakness is thereby expunged, his revenge long overdue.

Humiliate the Host

In retaliation, Martha takes the oedipal drama beyond the somewhat conventional point it reached in act I toward the deeper psychic register. Her new game: I will now seduce the other man while telling him your deepest secret. Castration now drives toward the marrow of humiliation, as Martha makes public the privacy she and George shared before that privacy was betrayed.

George puts on the right record, the slow second movement of the Beethoven Seventh Symphony, which Wagner called "the apotheosis of the dance." Martha grinds to a somewhat different tune, however, and accompanies her movements with an aria of sorts, a "sad" story, in two verses of doggerel and forced rhyme, which completes the saga of George and Daddy begun in act I with the suppressed tale that tears away George's attempt both to save himself from humiliation and to preserve a necessary illusion. The first verse trivializes his effort to understand himself: "Well, Georgie-boy had lots of big ambitions / In spite of something funny in his past. . . . / Which Georgie-boy here turned into a novel. . . . / His first attempt and also his last" (133). George's attempt to heal himself and to win Martha from her father by writing a fiction which is psychologically true is subjected to travesty. The clincher is true in a double sense: his first attempt at actively reversing his life was indeed his last.

The second verse identifies the source of his capitulation in order to lay the blame solely on his shoulders: "But daddy took a look at Georgie's novel. . . . / And he was very shocked by what he read. / A novel all about a naughty boy-child. . . . / Who killed his mother and his father dead" (134). Martha excludes herself from George's defeat; the game of recognition is played out solely between the two men. George's weakness, not Martha's bitchery or betrayal, is the cause of his defeat. "And Daddy said . . ." Daddy assumes the voice of institutional authority, the commanding and impregnable superego: "Look here, I will not let you publish such a thing . . . kid . . . whippersnapper, you'll just withdraw that manuscript" (134–35). This, the sequel to Martha's poem, draws out the groveling lengths to which George will go to preserve a sliver of his integrity, only to capitulate totally. In a last-ditch effort, he proclaims the truth—"Sir, this isn't a *novel* at all . . . this is the truth . . . this really happened . . . TO ME!" (136–37)—only to be met with the father's disavowal of anything but officially sanctioned images. Academe exacts its pound of flesh. (Note: The issue of publication isn't whether the book is good enough but whether George will have the courage to defy the institution's injunction.) George is doubly deprived of identity: the look of the Other ravages the object in which he risked and revealed himself, a novel about "the silence" condemns him to silence. Memory can only be mockery, which is precisely the key Martha has been sounding. Humiliations past and present become one. This is the power of narrative: it is the privileged way to "get" someone.

Humiliate the Host is the first of the three grand narrative games played in *Virginia Woolf.* Their function in developing the drama is to sublate— with all the force of a genuine dialectical *Aufhebung*—all previous games. A narrative retold takes the existential being of the Other—the *Da-sein* as a whole—and makes it an object of ridicule. It can do so because narrative is the attempt to totalize the connections which explain one's life. In narrative, one tries to find the connections that will reveal the truth of one's condition in order to establish the possibility of active reversal. Once we can make sense of our life as a narrative, we have a complete picture of the burden we must assume in order to reverse death-work and recover our existential being. The pity of George's lost novel is that it was a pretty good beginning. But if someone else can take the narrative in which a psyche articulates its truth and turn the story into a humiliating game, the possibility of active reversal is cut off. George's novel is read, but it communicates nothing. He is, instead, seen as a whole, found wanting, and condemned again to silence. George's existence, with the basic fault exposed, is cast into the void, with mocking voices presiding over his subsequent self-mockery. His paralysis is complete: the present scene merely reinflicts a wound which is not castrating but humiliating.

Martha has had a field day, but in achieving such a victory she has upped the ante. The game is now the production of narratives that will reveal the root paralysis of subjects in order to humiliate them. George's preoccupation with history will serve him well as he plots the response in kind needed to invert the situation.

Get the Guests

Betrayal of trust was the possibility Martha excluded in her account of George's failure. George will restore this connection by making it the theme of his "second novel." We aren't ready to play Hump the Hostess yet because the proper terms aren't in place, nor is the audience properly positioned. Nick is still too frightened for that game, while Martha is too eager for it. She becomes an anxiously intrigued auditor, however, alive to deeper possibilities and excited by uncertainty about what George is planning, when he introduces an intermediate game, Get the Guests.

The return to the plural is crucial, because George knows that the real object of any humiliation must be the couple. Otherwise there's always an exit, some way to wiggle off the hook, as Martha has just shown. To make his second novel work, George must position each member of his audience so that each is exposed and betrayed by the other. He does so by playing the first half of it so that the agents present each reach the point where he or she wants him to stop. The story then sprung will enmesh them all. George's story thus falls into two parts, with the first half deliberately filled with gaps and questions that will cut the ground out from under everyone's feet when the second half—a flashback—brings out the missing link that forces a devastating rereading of the prior text.

On the surface, the first half seems to be primarily about opportunism. Intimate details are rehearsed in "public" space, but they seem to touch primarily on pragmatic issues. All this can be somewhat embarrassing, but none of it cuts to the quick. Even Honey likes this "familiar" story (143) up to a point, for she reaps its fruits. Since the story exemplifies "historical inevitability" (144) it is a context Nick can't disallow. It is indeed the source of his distinctly pragmatic pride, since historical inevitability is the pragmatic justification that covers many contingencies. It is only when the story starts to turn on the overwhelming question haunting it that everyone starts to squirm. For there's one big hole in the story—present in the form of the "mouse" (142), of whom Nick is "solicitous to a point that faileth human understanding" (144)—and that hole leads directly to the question of how far Nick will go. Where are his loyalties? Is Honey a partner or a prop he will dispose of once it's served its purpose?

Once that question is in place, George can spring the flashback with Nick impaled ("NO!" [145]) on the stake that now stands forth for all to see. The issue is one of trust and betrayal as a question that existentially unites present and past. When do you know someone loved you and wasn't just using you? The only way you can know, George shows, is by finding out what secrets are inviolable. The story he thus tells the anxious audience, Honey, is about the mirth and spite her partner derived in telling the one secret which she believed he would never reveal.

George goes Martha's violation of his secret one better. The basic wound he inflicts is this: Your husband told me, a stranger, the most humiliating secret about you, for no apparent reason other than contempt. Nick's revelation, unlike Martha's, was not part of a seduction but was told, from pure spite, to gain a maximum distance from any connection to the embarrassment called his spouse. Nick's pragmatism knows no bounds and is more careless in its cruelty than anything George and Martha do.

Nick's defense, repeated four times, "I didn't mean to," provides no protection, because intention is no longer the issue, nor the psychological space of the drama. It is also of little avail in calming Honey, who shows she has always been fully present at the place where reality transpires: "You told them!" (147). George's mousetrap sprung undercuts both sides of Nick's "identity." His narcissism is wounded and his pragmatism threatened. The deeper disorder underlying both motives is laid bare by the meaning Nick himself assigns to the event. It is damaging, "damaging!! to me!!" (149). Concern for his wife's feelings is a nonexistent context. Relationships have no meaning except as pragmatic career moves. His solicitude extends no further: he now openly admits what he previously concealed when he told the false pregnancy story to George. George dismisses him with the only appropriate metaphor: "By God, you gotta have a swine to show you where the truffles are." Then George goads his pragmatic "sensibilities" to the battle he's been preparing: "Well, you just rearrange your alliances, boy" (149). Aggression primed and unbound, Nick vows: "I'll play in your language . . . I'll be what you say I am." To this George replies, "You are already . . . you just don't know it" (150). Difference abolished, George now has Nick where he wants him. The real battle, which will have Hump the Hostess as its ineluctable focus, can now commence. Martha is, after all, the ultimate audience the scene has been staged for, and she is quick to celebrate it as such by demanding he move on to the real thing. "You did a good job. . . . It's the most . . . life you've shown in a long time," but it's just "pigmy hunting" (151).

Total War

Everyone's aggression has now been sufficiently primed, but the real work of aggression has scarcely begun. George and Martha will now draw up the terms of that contract. Hump the Hostess now has its phallic prop, Nick, the "quarterback," and George flashes it, as with Sonny, daring Martha to pick it up. But to bring things to the condition of total war, George must destabilize the entire previous context of eroticizations. He does so by suggesting that "I did it all for you" (152), Martha, thereby bestowing the kiss Martha has been after since the beginning of the play. To deflect the blow, Martha is driven to invoke the master justification for her aggression: "You married me for it" (152). There is a dissymmetry here, however, and George will use it to redefine the work of aggression. George's aggression has functioned as foreplay to sexualize the environment for Martha, whereas Martha uses aggression to castrate, to desexualize George. The battle has been unfair because it has been waged within a context of oedipalization, which Martha controls. To sustain that context, she adds a codicil whenever a deeper play of aggression threatens. That codicil is the claim "It's not what I've wanted" (153) and on it rests the self-conception she will do anything to defend, since it is her defense against the threat of psychotic anxiety. Martha can persist in her role because she has convinced herself that George's need is the cause of her aggression and that she's always been more than willing to drop it for a loving relationship. George knows, in contrast, that this romantic fantasy is precisely what saves her from recognizing that her action springs from a deeper disorder which uses George as an occasion rather than a cause. Insanity is the threat that arises should this illusion collapse. This is the possibility—and context—George must activate for the drama of aggression to drive toward the marrow, from her ballpark to his.

The battle between George and Martha has always been a battle over the proper use and target of aggression. But the dissymmetry controlling its practice will now be reversed. Martha uses aggression to protect her enabling illusion, whereas for George aggression is directed against all illusions. Martha's fear is that she is in fact a bitch, for deeply buried reasons she dare not face. Her defense is to play it fulsomely, while asserting the interpretation that will protect her from the attribution: She's a bitch because George forces her to be one, not because the role serves a psychic disorder she must impose on him. Martha takes great care to place her greatest fear—hysterization, of becoming like Honey—offstage. Aggression for her projects the feared self-image (weakness, psychic disorder) onto the other and then attacks its externalized presence, the notion being that if one can destroy it externally, one exorcises it internally. Projection and attack are thus grounded in and serve denial. Bitchiness is play-acting in the service of the ego-illusion that one is really a loving being. That illusion and the incessant practice of aggression are dialectically interdependent: their reversal—with aggression directed back inward—thereby becomes the only possible road to psychic self-knowledge. In redefining the context of aggression, this is the tranformation George prepares.

For George, aggression can do its work only if each partner is willing to turn it back against him- or herself in an attempt to uncover and destroy the illusion that protects each from the truth about the psyche. This has always been George's drive, but thus far he has primarily inflicted it on himself, because he too is protecting an illusion. His is a subtler illusion, but it derives from Martha's. Martha claims she gives George what he married her for.

George can accordingly regard his defect as his repeated willingness to get sucked into this illusion. If she gives him what he wants, his fault is that he keeps taking it in order to protect her from herself. The fantasy child, twenty-three years of false battle, and the refusal to go after her marrow have blinded him to the fact that he too shares the illusion that, through it all, his love has also been struggling to somehow be born. George is still working on his first novel. But he works not for recognition or to regain Martha's love, but to exorcise the depressive's greatest fear—that hate will prove stronger than love. That suspicion has for a long time been the working principle of his activity. He is about to learn the true nature of the claim it has upon him.

Because the psyche's core defense is at stake, charge and countercharge now aim at the underlying anxiety: Who's the sick one? Though George and Martha play this game the way most children do—charging the other with what the other has just charged you with—George's attack sounds the deeper chord because it identifies Martha's self-conception as the proof of her mental instability. With that in place, he reintroduces the quarterback, and the son, to focus the threat. Everything Martha says about herself proves that she has moved "bag and baggage" into her "fantasy world" and is now just playing "variations" on her "own distortions" in a solipsism that will implode once he has her committed. Institutionalization is merely a pseudothreat: the deeper threat, and Martha knows it, is George's total withdrawal. When she recounts the moment when, during the party, she looked at George and he vanished, anxiety, not counterattack, is uppermost in her mind. What "snaps" (157), then and now, is not the attempt to "get through to" George, but the belief that there's anything there to get through to. In destroying the self-conception that will prevent that recognition from doing its work, George leaves Martha alone with her greatest fear—that she must play on without illusion and bereft of an audience.

George doesn't have to mention the quarterback a third time. For in reintroducing the castration game, pitting George against younger men, Martha knows she's clutching at a straw. Her threat to "howl it out" is precisely what George wants, because he has now deprived her of the ratio-nale that protected her from seeing her real motives. Martha's claim that she will do "it" for her own pleasure, and not to either win George back or break his back, is an attempt to forestall the recognition she will be driven to when she finds, in the next scene, that she can't carry out this project. She will then find herself in Honey's position, hysterical and ripe for the reduc-tions of the third act, in which the "sad" adult of the evening's beginning regresses to the dependent child of its end.

When "It" snaps, the illusions and interpretations sustaining the "whole arrangement" (156) collapse. That collapse leads Martha into an ever more desperate attempt to reassert them. This will be her through-line for the rest of the play. For George, in contrast, it requires the annihilation of the defenses that sustain both of them. Martha will have to castrate George again to see if he cares. George will have to kill the child. He thus applauds the choice of the quarterback as object for retaliation and all but begs Martha to "do it" because he needs that act to position everyone for the final drama—the only humping of the hostess that counts, the violent penetration of her mind.

"Total war" (159) is the call for an unbound aggression that attacks the self-interpretation on which the other's sanity depends. The psychic space that each agent previously held in reserve—in order to control the practice of aggression and to preserve a saving illusion from attack—now becomes the explicit target of aggression. The most disruptive possibility is thereby brought into play. Unbound aggression either annihilates the other or turns back against the self. In unleashing that dynamic, the act of aggression takes a quantum leap, making what has happened thus far seem like child's play. To wage total war, a couple must come to the point where they are willing to go after the Other's unconscious and to put themselves totally at risk in that act. Existentially and psychoanalytically, nothing can any longer be held in reserve. The self-conceptions and illusions that have protected each from the threat of psychic dissolution must be engaged. Previously, aggression nibbled. Now it sees its true target as the self-interpretation that sustains the other's neurosis as a defense against psychosis. For Martha, aggression works only if it produces an endless repetition of the same; for George, it works only by applying a scorched-earth policy to the fixations that prevent a descent into the deepest psychic disorders. The latter possibility is about to assert its claims.

We pause here to note a possibility that positions the right audience for the drama that follows. In declaring total war, George and Martha perhaps first enter into the only marriage contract worthy of the name. The declaration of love is only as good as the truth-value it commits both persons to: the contract to root out everything sick and inauthentic in each other's psyche so that, as couple, we can turn aggression back against ourselves in an effort to strip away the defenses that hide each psyche from the self-knowledge which, until faced, inevitably gets laid on the other's shoulders. The crisis point in a loving relationship, usually passed long before the contract has been given a chance, is reached when one party refuses that contract and projects the whole burden of analytic scrutiny and change onto the other's psyche. This moment occurs whenever either in effect says, I will go this far about myself and no further, and I refuse to internalize anything you say that would destroy my self-delusions.

Given the conditions of object-choice, this is, of course, the point all couples must get to, marriage being perhaps a possibility that occurs only after the "fact."[17] But once one agent refuses to go there, the other must perforce attack the illusion that protects them, because they have violated the implicit "rule" of the one game worth playing. They have, in effect, become passive-aggressive agents habituated to acts that prevent aggression from doing its analytic work. In a perverted way, George will restore its rights and dignity.

Hump the Hostess: Foreplay and Positions

In this scene, it is almost as if Martha acts out George's unconscious as he drives her to take the actions that will undercut each of her subtexts. George can exit the scene once Martha says that she and Nick "want to be alone" (161), because George knows he's now the absent presence in control. In deeply ironic compliance, Martha plays the ensuing scene to get from Nick everything George refused earlier. Nick lights her cigarette. He gives "mommy" the "great big kiss" George wouldn't. He then tries to become "a personal screwing machine" in the game George has already inverted. As Martha says, "It's all in the faculty. We're a close-knit family here" (163–64). Nick is then inserted in his proper position as Martha invokes Daddy as the presiding genius who primes, commands, and defeats transgressive desire. Martha adds one personal appeal to prime Nick: he can betray Honey and return, pragmatically refreshed, with a good experience for a change, sure that she'll never know the difference—nor will anyone else. Martha's only problem, once Nick bites into his assigned role, is to retard his "pulsion" until she can insert it into the proper register of the psychological game she's playing, with herself: "Take it easy, boy. Down, baby. Don't rush it, hunh?" (165). For many this would be a real turn-off, but Nick's adolescent sexuality is pure drive-discharge mechanism.

George reenters, singing what has become his favorite tune. He is cheerful, a fact duly noted, with suspicion, by Martha: "What are you so cheerful about?" (166). All the pawns are scurrying into place: Honey, asleep, rolled up like a fetus, sucking her thumb; Nick and Martha ready to goad George with another round of the oedipal game in which Martha assures George, that "it's never your turn." When Martha says, "You're in a straight line, buddy-boy, and it doesn't lead anywhere . . . except maybe the grave," he tells her to "hold that thought" (168), because he'll soon show her that death is the space their theatre has now entered. Her attempt to use sex as an "acting-out" behavior to escape death and his use of that deed to further the death-work is the difference he will now turn back against her, annihilating the last flickering claims of Eros. George has her in a no-win situation. The passive-aggressive method he used to prompt her responses in act I is now certain to achieve its desired affect. All he need do is sit, reading a book, as she tries, with rising anxiety, to catch his attention by telling him she doesn't want or need it. She claims, "I'm going to entertain myself, too" (170), but she can't stop giving him a running account. She thus acts out a desperate sexuality in the face of his cold assertion of its insignificance. Martha: "I'm necking with one of the guests." George: "Oh, that's nice. Which one?" (170). All sexual differences are abolished in his general indifference. The attempt to use the act to show him—"I'll show *you*" (170)—is subjected to an even more devastating reduction, which transforms Martha's sexuality from a place of desire to one of loathing: "No . . . show him, Martha . . . he hasn't seen it" (172). Hump the Hostess thereby becomes the game in which Martha and Nick act out the disgust George wants everyone to internalize as the sole and shared truth. His unconscious, not theirs, presides over this scene, as well as the one shortly to occur offstage.

Nick's attempt to reassert his difference—"I have no respect for you"—is leveled with a stroke: "Because *you're* going to hump Martha, *I'm* disgusting?" (172). The most important blow is, however, reserved for Martha's last attempt to get George to either prevent the act or accept her interpretation of it. Martha: "You come off this kick you're on, or I swear to God [this time] I'll do it." To which George merely avers that for once she should do the right thing for the right reason, by putting her own motives up front. "Lord, Martha, if you want the boy that much . . . have him . . . but do it honestly, will you? Don't cover it over with all this . . . all this . . . footwork." Departing, she can only reply with a blind repetition of the ancient story, the tired, exposed motive and self-interpretation reiterated as in a catechism: "I'll make you sorry you made me want to marry you. I'll make you regret the day you ever decided to come to this college. I'll make you sorry you ever let yourself down" (173).

When, after her exit, George throws his volume of Spengler at the chimes, he shows that he does not exclude himself from the psychologically destructive process he will direct on all of them. Spengler's intellectualized pessimism (George has been reading from *The Decline of the West*), George's favorite mask, now hits upon its proper object. The striking of the chimes is the call to the destruction of all illusions.

Returned from her fetal nap, Honey spills the beans about her "little murders" (177). If George wanted assurance that Nick is no threat, he now has it: the young couple's marriage is even more sterile than George and Martha's. If he wanted another round of Get the Guests, Honey has just provided the ammunition he needs to spring that game and reverse the advantage Nick hopes to attain offstage with a final, definitive castration. But George never will reveal Honey's secret because he has already moved to a much deeper game, in which such possibilities are no more than amusing asides. The temptation to screw Honey, thereby doing unto the other what you can spring on them when they shortly proclaim their delight in having done it unto you, is an idea that surfaces only to be brushed aside. George is only concerned with one person, whom he addresses as if she were in the room: "I'm going to get you . . . Martha" (175). As always, George's unconscious rushes ahead of his awareness—plotting toward, while the others only plot from.

Martha has no idea how little ammunition is left in her arsenal, but George knows that he has repeatedly warned her that her actions entail a hidden connection: if you screw Nick, I'll go after Sonny. With the substitute rival virtually defeated, George's proper target surfaces. The plan he hits on is not really all that surprising. He has been destroying the son since the topic first came up. But if the child is already dead, he has not yet been slain. Nor has the psychic yield of that process been reaped. Unless the death is staged, there is no way it can do its work on Martha's psyche. But if the coming murder is an exorcism, we must ask, What is being exorcised—and what will remain? This is the question we carry into act III.

Act III: The Exorcist Cometh

What is an exorcism? Is it a process in which devils are cast out so that their innocent victim—usually an adolescent child—can regain a cleansed psyche? Or is it a process in which one slays the last protection in inner reality that keeps the devil from coming forth? This question relates to a dramatistic one: in what ways is Sonny a scapegoat—for all four characters and the audience—and in what ways is Albee exposing the scapegoat mechanism as pseudo-catharsis in order to drive the play to the darker conclusion that constitutes his mousetrap?

Though briefer, this act, like the second, has a six-part structure.

Clink: The Fractured Mirrors

The hysteria beneath Martha's oedipal games and the romantic fantasies she requires to sustain them have both become unbound. In this scene, in three magnificent and internally contradictory asides, she exposes the core George will shortly work upon.

The solitary space Martha inhabits is defined by fear, sadness, and the horror of isolation. To exorcise the double that haunts her—Honey on the bathroom floor, fetally isolated, sucking her thumb, regressed to the nadir of autoaffection—Martha must conjure up an audience or, if that fails, parody the condition of the actor bereft of the essential prop: "Deserted! Abandoned! Left out in the cold like an old pussy-cat." But deliverance through wit, the methodology of act I, is a game that no longer works. Martha's psyche is unraveling. To prevent further regression, she must restore autoaffection through imaginary conversation. The first calls on George and a return to earlier games which they can repeat now that they see they've misjudged each other. But "WHERE IS EVERYBODY!!! Hump the Hostess!" (185) is a plea that only forces a deeper regression, to a second imaginary conversation, this time with Daddy, the deliverer, who now makes no reply because he cries all the time too.

Martha finds herself caught in a hall of mirrors: everything gives her back only her own fractured image. She is reduced, accordingly, to a displaced *fort/da,* the child's game of hide and seek. Children play this game so that it can end happily, allaying its underlying anxiety, when the others reappear. "I'LL GIVE ALL YOU BASTARDS FIVE TO COME OUT FROM WHERE YOU'RE HIDING!!" (185). Martha's command is really an outcry for deliverance from self-dissolution into tears. She fights them back through wit, forced laughter, literary allusion (the first of two in this act to *Streetcar*), and, finally, vaudeville: "I've got windshield wipers on my eyes, because I married you . . . baby! . . . Martha, you'll be a song-writer yet," (186). But the face that emerges is the visage of Picasso's "Weeping Woman," fragmented and frozen, its tears chilled to the ice cubes George and Martha put in their drinks. Albee's fascination with *The Iceman Cometh* here achieves its Kafkan correlative: the psyche is frozen in ice; every aggression that drink liberates is really an attempt to anesthetize a deeper disorder. Only drunken self-obliteration can prevent aggression from turning inward and becoming the Kafkan "ice ax" that chops at the "frozen sea inside us."

After such knowledge, what activity? Unable to bear much reality, Martha can avoid psychic dissolution only by seizing on a new object of aggression—Nick. Having "seduced" him, her need is to complete his castration. But to avoid landing back in the subtexts which the previous oedipal drama has revealed, she must proceed under the aegis of the illusion that she really loves George. In the process, George will, for the first time, become the sexual male—and later the rescuing Father. But whether this attribution is a red flag meant to enrage the gored bull or a fantasy-illusion meant to calm Martha is by this point an undecidable in the best sense of that term because the exposed reality that stands forth as the motor of all such operations is Martha's psyche.[18]

Characteristically, Nick has learned nothing from his experience. He is left merely with the blind reiteration of the two illusions needed to restore his narcissism: They've all gone crazy, and he's not like them. The narcissist can't learn from experience because there is no place in the psyche where experience can be internalized.[19] Martha punctures Nick's defense mechanisms with a double debunking: "Relax; sink into it; you're no better than anybody else." Nick: "I think I am." Martha: "You're certainly a flop in some departments" (188). Nick's treasure, the noble complement to the narcissistic *moi*, is reduced to the status of a dangling and misplaced modifier.

The tension between Martha's deep disorder and the role that she plays to relieve it is now such, however, that rather than enjoying the game, Martha can only express contempt for the role it traps her in. The dimension of her inwardness explodes in her second great speech. Martha as "Earth Mother," readied for *Le Sacre du printemps*, sees all men as flops. But her disgust has for once the right direction: "I disgust me" (189). This is the first time George's constant refrain is used by anyone else in the play. The great description which follows of the "comic" dance endlessly repeated at the cocktail parties is drawn out in slow naturalistic detail to underscore its infantile absurdity. The "seduction" game males incessantly play to prove their phallic power is a parody of courage. But in that game Martha reserves the worst position—and the greatest insight—for herself. Again alone, waiting, her dress up over her head, she sits, a paralyzed primitive, "suffocating." A great one-liner clinches the annihilating connection between her role and its *situs:* "But that's how it is in a civilized society." The discontent of the erstwhile Earth Mother is self-disgust, because pointless (would-be) infidelities really do no more than insert her as pawn in the male fixation on phallic combat, the object of which is never Martha's pleasure or her psychic needs, but the castrating victory over other men. As Lacan would put it, woman's position does not ex-ist.[20]

After such knowledge, what escape? Having seen the truth, Martha must undo the entire speech by finding an escape hatch. Only lying nostalgia can deliver her. "There is only one man in my life who has ever . . . made me happy. Do you know that? One!" (189). Martha hangs on by the most delicate of threads—soon to be broken—the belief that George was and is different. The "sadness" of it all is the blind effort to affirm a bond of love that can still somehow turn all this pointless mayhem into a game of renewal. But the monologue in which Martha evokes it is really an extended wish list in which the recently sexualized George also becomes the "good" Daddy who "can hold me, at night, so that it's warm."

There is much self-lacerating truth in the speech and many an enabling lie. But the through-line and the context in which she places everything contains the true self-revelation. That context is one in which Martha's favorite song is still "Rescue Me" and her greatest fear that of being left alone. Her self-criticisms thus carry a self-canceling subtext, her continued search for magical deliverance. Martha, in effect, tries to live up to George's "contract"—that total war go to the marrow—so that she can remain both the author and the director of that drama. George's role is that of the respondent "who keeps learning the games we play as quickly as I can change the rules." A shift of pronouns at the end of the monologue completes the drift to magical thinking: "Some stupid, liquor-ridden night . . . I will go too far . . . and I'll either break the man's back . . . or push him off for good . . . which is what I deserve" (191). By identifying with the aggressor and then shifting the roles, the fear of isolation is allayed. Even if she gets what she deserves, she will have controlled the process and brought it on herself. Loss of control is the fear that the psyche will do virtually anything to itself to allay.

While a bout of self-criticism may be great for the soul, Nick need but join in for Martha to resume the sexual attack on Nick and reduce him to the houseboy who must jump at her command. He gave her the "kiss" George refused, yet he still gets told to "go answer the door" (193). But all roles are shifting quickly now, and Martha repeats the language of insult George previously used to get at Nick: "You're ambitious, aren't you, boy? You didn't chase me around the kitchen and up the gaddamn stairs out of mad, driven passion, did you now? You were thinking a little bit about your career, weren't you? Well, you can just houseboy your way up the ladder for a while" (194). Her hope is that she and George in tandem can play a game of Get the Guests. But George reenters bearing "gifts" from another kingdom: "Flores; flores para los muertos. Flores" (195). The allusion to Blanche gives us the best designation of the psychic state Martha has acted out in the previous scene. But if she is Blanche DuBois, what Stanley, his hour come round at last, slouches home for a birthday party?

The Beloved Returns

George comes bearing death to the sadness Martha clings to in renewing an old game she hopes will pluck a responsive chord. Having reversed the roles, she will now castrate Nick before George in order to give George a chance to reclaim the phallus and thereby offer "proof" of his undying love. But while George and Martha delight in drawing out the vaudeville possibility of "houseboy or stud" to mock Nick, George only plays the game as a diversion leading into the game he introduced, on reentering, when he called Nick "Sonny." The flowers are for him, too, and come from "Daddy's greenhouse" (198). To position Nick and Martha for the game he has come to play, George proceeds to confuse both of them with the seemingly pointless insistence that the moon went down, then came back up. Nick is so confused by now that he admits, "I don't know when you people are lying, or what." But when George adds the story of his father and mother taking him to the Mediterranean as a college graduation present, Nick makes a last attempt to halt the dizzying play of stories by sarcastically asserting the rights of the literal—"Was this after you killed them?"—only to be met with George's defiant "Maybe" (200), as he springs the trap he's been preparing: "Truth and illusion. Who knows the difference, eh, toots? Eh?" (201). It is an offer Martha can't refuse, because her psyche depends on a final, however momentary, fixing of that game with the interpretation that will allow for another round.

George has finally driven things to the question on which everything turns and has played it to catch two audiences. The first, Nick, is a perfect stand-in for the theatre audience, many of whom find themselves in a position of confusion similar to his, no longer knowing what is true, what false, yet needing some principle of difference, however literal, to begin sorting things out toward a clarifying interpretation that will limit the psychological space that threatens to engulf everything in a whirlpool of free-floating anxiety. The question of "Truth and illusion?" must be answered, or some principle for answering it established. But a formalistic deconstruction that would leave it in the safe realm of the epistemologically undecidable simply won't do, because the anxiety, by now unleashed dialectically, sublates the weight of the entire drama. The audience is finally in place for the most dangerous game: the abolition of all epistemological games before the primacy of a psychological reality in which they are necessarily implicated, since they can never establish the distinctions needed to extricate themselves from it.

Martha, the immediate audience, is also perfectly positioned as the agent who must strive to find that difference which will reestablish the possibility of Eros. So positioned, she is ripe for the death-work that will obliterate all games and with them the intrapsychic structures that conceal its ruling presence.

Truth and/or Illusion?

Truth and illusion is the dialectic whereby the collapse of every logic of objective reality takes us to the marrow. For Martha, truth or illusion is the question of whether George cares. For Nick it's the question of whether he can eventually get the "facts" he needs to get free of George and Martha and reassert the claim necessary to his narcissism—that he is different. George will now use that need to force Nick into the role George was given in act I.

Martha apparently gives Nick the defense he needs when she says, "No; you're not a houseboy" (202), but the testament provides no relief because Nick sees that he's no more than a token in a game where all her dialogue is really addressed to George. But what is the game? Oedipal rivalry, truth and illusion, or Snap the dragons? George lets Martha play it one way so that he can replay it to another end.

The drama of truth and illusion falls into two parts. The first, apparently controlled by Martha, brings forth an uncharacteristic question from George: "Who's lying?" George, who has always known how to throw that question back in the questioner's face, most recently when he dismissed Nick's question about his "dead" parents, now sets it forth with apparent urgency. Martha bites, playing it to the closure she needs in saying Nick isn't a houseboy so that she can spring on George a statement that is really a question: "Truth and illusion, George; you don't know the difference." The unspoken: If you did, you'd know that in some way, offstage, I told Nick you are the only man I've ever loved, and you'd see that the game has all been played for your benefit. George's reply inverts that possibility: "No; but we must carry on as though we did" (202). The language of games, of appearances, is all we have, and we must play it out without taking flight into the privileged interpretation we've always held in reserve as guarantee.

We must, instead, repeat the game to rupture its charmed circle. To turn Martha's question back against her, George replays the game with a new through-line. Snap, the game that initiated the contract of Total War and was then put on hold for future use, here returns with the anxiety proper to it unleashed. George replays "houseboy or stud" to force Martha to repeat her closing statement as an anxious question, capped with a significant change of preposition: "Truth or illusion, George. Doesn't it matter to you . . . at all?" The implicit either/or on which Martha sustains herself is subjected to George's brutal reduction of everything to appearances and the abolition of difference: "SNAP! You got your answer, baby?" (204). She does and must let that be an end, because the oedipal space to which she wants to confine drama has been brought to the point of implosion.

As George is quick to point out, that does not mean the end of games but the true beginning. In putting an end to the oedipal space, George has moved everything irreversibly into "psychotic" space. Difference is abolished, but that is not an end; it is a movement of descent into the "reality" that all plays of difference defend against, displace, and deny. All that George now requires is to get everyone back onstage, properly positioned, for the game that will reverse every psychic disorder (and its attendant role) that has been activated since the beginning of the play, with him alone now in the slot of power, driving everything to a single "conclusion."

George thus resets the scene of act I with the roles switched. Martha is now the tired one. She doesn't "like what's going to happen" (206), but her emotions are so exhausted that she can only plead, "No more games . . . please" (207). In that plea, Martha drops the illusion she clutched earlier in act III, when she claimed that George kept learning the games as quickly as she changed the rules. His job is to do unto her what she did to him in act I, by getting her back on her feet, angry for battle, so that he can tell her, "We're going to play this one to the death," for "this is a civilized game" (209–10). Honey provides the missing link that identifies its target. She has "decided I don't remember anything." Prompted by George, she reiterates that logic: "*Don't* remember; not *can't*" (211). Repression is the most civilized, advanced defense mechanism, and George knows it's the one he must get at because it unites all three of them. As the song goes, "What's too painful to remember we simply choose to forget," which is why the way we were is the way we will be. Martha is past master of this mechanism because every game she plays repeats itself in an endless cycle of the same. But repression operates on many levels, ranging from Honey's deliberate obliteration of consciousness and Nick's refusal to internalize experience to Martha's elaborate use of acting out behaviors for the purpose of undoing and denial. All three are about to be brought to a lesson in the tragic claims of insight (*Einsicht*) and working through (*Durcharbeit*).

Honey again inadvertently blurts out the principle of their undoing: "I peel labels." Martha cannot resist the momentary call of a new game: "Label. Peel the label," but George articulates its ruling principle: "We all peel labels, sweetie; and when you get through the skin, all three layers, through the muscle, slosh aside the organs [an oedipal aside to Nick] them which is still sloshable—and get down to bone . . . you know what you do then? . . . When you get down to bone, you haven't got all the way, yet. There's something inside the bone . . . the marrow . . . and that's what you gotta get at" (212–13).

Bringing Up Baby

To get at the marrow, the most advanced defense, repression, must be brought back to the archaic operations underlying it—the defense mechanism known as splitting—and the dialectical connection between the two exposed. Splitting is the original defense against knowledge that creates the subsequent logic of binaries required to provide the psyche with the rationalizations that will save it from self-knowledge. Splitting is thus the marrow that must be exposed so that the entire edifice can be brought down. The fantasy child must be brought back on the stage and seen as a product of the original act of splitting that underlies all the games people play in sustaining the grand illusion that is marriage.

To deracinate the split, that illusion must be fully activated and then destroyed. In Bringing Up Baby, George must rend from Martha's very heart all of her "love" for the fantasy child in order to make its murder strike the marrow. The intrapsychic illusion that protects Martha from the depressive's anxiety is the belief that love always somehow proves stronger than hate. The fantasy child is the final stand and resting place of that illusion. To get that patient on the table, George provides the choral cues that prompt Martha to express, with aching love, the core illusion she has projected onto the child. That illusion is as much about herself as it is about the child or, better, about the identity that binds them as symbiotic sides of a single psyche. For the child Martha evokes is a "restless child" (219), driven by fear, who is made perfect because he has more than "good-enough mothering." He is the lamb and she the maternal presence who delivers him, as infant, from fear and rescues him whenever, as toddler, he strays and falls and breaks a bone. Symbiosis is always waiting to deliver him from individuation, because the child is the double, the mirror in which Martha rescues herself from the fears ruling her psyche by bestowing on the child's "presence" a constant loving care.

As such a child matures in wisdom, age, and grace before God and man, he thus becomes the protector who walks between, a hand held out to both parents, to receive what is best from both of them, and to bind the family in "mutual protection . . . from George's . . . weakness" (221–22). Like George, we let the end of the exordium pass for now. The child returns Martha's blessing and delivers her and her marriage from fear. But "this perfection . . . couldn't last." To exorcise fear, fear must be externalized. Someone must become the big bad wolf in sheep's clothing, and that disorder must again threaten the child if Martha is to rescue it and complete the symbiotic circle. As George says: "I knew she'd shift" (223), because she has to. The fear projected into the child is Martha's fear about herself, and she can exorcise it only by attaching it to an intruding, and necessarily male, presence.

George has already prepared the reply that will reverse Martha's projection once he reveals the mother as the woman who uses the son to castrate the father. But to play that card, he knows he must throw himself fully into the game. To kill the child, he must be willing to also kill himself. Unlike Martha, he won't preserve a saving illusion. Instead, when she appears ready to stop, he supplements her criticism of him by dredging up the excuses he previously used both as explanations and as weapons to get at her, thereby forcing her to repeat her grounding justification—"I have tried . . . the one thing I've tried to carry pure and unscathed . . . above the mire of this vile, crushing marriage . . . our SON" (227)—so that it will neatly cascade with his reading from the introit of the *Dies Irae*.

Honey's moment of "recognition" midway through this process ("I want a child") and her protest that now erupts ("JUST STOP IT!!") cannot stop this drama. All they can do is initiate the minor movement that will live out a desperate existence for the rest of the play: the desire for deliverance through sentimental recognitions. We note that appeal here in its inception so that we can drive the proper coffin nails as we proceed. In the process, a sizable audience of critics will find their *tombeau*. George's reply to Honey is a question addressed to every audience member who is alive, engaged, and resisting, at the deepest psychic register, what is about to happen: "Why, baby? Don't you like it?" (228).

Exorcism: Inwardness as Sein-zum-Tod

Honey's protest ("You . . . can't," "Please . . . don't") and Martha's protest ("YOU CAN'T DECIDE THAT FOR YOURSELF!" [232]) are parallel labors, which, like both women's efforts to give birth, will go "pouf." Like Hamlet, George has always loved to draw out murder, delaying the final end, because he knows that the one thing you can't do once you've murdered someone is—murder that person. Psychological cruelty, making the paralyzed victim live on, suffering, is the act proper to the psychic stage. But eventually the mousetrap must be sprung, and in doing so George is careful to put his head in it: the reported death of the imaginary son is a deliberate plagiarism from George's first murder: "He was . . . killed . . . on a country road, with his learner's permit in his pocket, he swerved, to avoid a porcupine, and drove straight into a . . ." (231).

Martha's protest, that George cannot decide such things, lays bare the a priori rules Martha insists must ground and limit play. Martha's claim that the son's life must remain a mutual decision is her last attempt to cling to the illusion that play is a shared reality. George, in contrast, demonstrates that nothing between them was ever really shared. All games can be played any way any given player wants to play them. Play is dangerous game, not safe space, for the rules are always changing and nothing limits what can happen. The only rule, like the contract of total war, is that one is always potentially at risk because one agent can always introduce a dynamic that will expose the illusions on which the other depends. George's game was always death; he just didn't play it until now. Or, to put it in terms closer to its immediate impact on Martha, in killing the child George shows her that they were each always alone, projecting their isolation into the conditions of a mutual frustration. One is reminded of Edna's statement in *A Delicate*

Balance: "To realize that the only skin you will ever touch is your own." Any other possibility is now annihilated—"POUF! Just like that!"

George clinches the blow by leaving Martha isolated with the line she earlier directed at him—a line that reactivates all previous games, since it is the taunt that requires a response in kind ("a new game") but is now left to fester as she has no one to return it to: "Now, how do you like it?" Martha can only respond with the howl "NOOOOOOoooooo" (233) because George has just delivered her over to her deepest fear. Language collapses before an aggression that cannibalizes all relations. Martha's last-ditch effort to find a fact or loophole that will force George back into some language game is subjected to mockery—"I ate it [the telegram]"—followed shortly, with Honey's help, by a final regression to infantile "speech." Honey: "You ate it all down." George: "Like a good boy." Honey: "Like a . . . g-g-g-good . . . boy" (234–35). Everything in the psyche that was bound is now unloosed. The two linguistic contracts that sustained games are both collapsed: language as the game of wit and intellectual maneuvers whereby George and Martha try to outsmart each other, and language as the pleasure of baby talk whereby they relieve each other. These were the two ways the game was indefinitely extended. In consuming them both, George finally reveals himself as the big bad wolf.

As George has come to realize, his game always was death, and its rules will now enforce their naked results. Repetition is replaced by an irreversible process in which the successive peeling away of labels or layers brings us not the heart of the onion but the logic of the Crypt. George and Martha are necessarily at cross-purposes in a final quarrel over "the rules of the game," because George has collapsed the nominal subject, the son, into the demonic principle. Martha: "HE IS OUR CHILD!" George: "AND I HAVE KILLED HIM!" Martha: "Why?" George: "You mentioned him" (235–36). Mentioning and killing have become equivalent deeds, part of a process in which anything anyone introduces into the psychological space now cleared becomes the corpse on the table, readied for dissection.

Vertigo: Between the Two Deaths—The Sentimental Fade-Out

George can now let everyone depart, by whatever exit they choose, because he has assured that they can never leave.

Nick characteristically makes the first attempt—the flight via interpretation. The "great" understanding Nick here achieves really amounts to yet another attempt to reassert the literal (even the chromosomological) in the face of the psychological. His statement, "I think I understand this" (236), is the equivalent of Honey's desire for a child. She wants deliverance through magical renewal, with George and Martha's fantasy literalized. Nick wants a reality principle in which the other's tragic condition restores his difference. The "children" George sends home, bursting with sympathy for all concerned, will probably conceive and bear a child, thereby confirming that they have understood nothing, since children have now been revealed as the primary way couples avoid and project their problems. Given the understanding they have achieved, Nick and Honey's real child will have less chance than the imaginary child to escape the destructive effects of the parental relationship. And yet this moment is cited repeatedly in interpretations as evidence that George and Martha have had the good of the young couple at heart throughout the evening and have successfully shown them the dangers they face unless they change their relationship. The desire for escape and renewal will clutch at any straw as the audience struggles, like the representative figures on the stage, to find "meanings" we can live with.

A second operation of sentiment is soon to follow. The dead child has not been used up. He can still provide pseudodeliverance, despite the fact that George has exposed this function as the source of all problems. When George, then Martha, confess, "*We* couldn't" (238) have a child, their open sharing of responsibility for the failure of the marriage strikes sparks waiting to stoke the embers of renewal. Having finally faced the truth—together— George and Martha have supposedly attained a renewed affection on which they can build. That belief in place, we are ready for a final movement of sentiment. It comes when, alone, George and Martha share the recognition that "it will be better" (240) without the child. All protection gone for good, they must—tomorrow at the very latest—face their relationship. As if they hadn't. What they could learn tomorrow that they haven't learned tonight, or how that knowledge could restore *Das Prinzip Hoffnung,* staggers the imagination.[21]

But the scapegoat mechanism is supposed to assure renewal. Rather than endorsing this idea, Albee exposes its underlying sentimentalism by presenting a parody of its founding evidence. It is dawn. Light streams forth from behind the stage. Before a well-justified sleep, George and Martha present a final tableau. Softly, slowly they come together, his hand finally gently on her shoulder, her head cradled. But rather than the dawn of a new beginning, the play ends with the final regression. We end where we began, with Daddy and his little girl, as Daddy sings, for the third time, the song that puts her out. And this time he gets the response he needs. The little girl admits her fear and cradles herself in the arms of her deliverer. But George has the last laugh, at his own expense, and at all males. As he knows, this end is not the fulfillment of desire or the victory achieved over the threat woman poses, but the collapse of everything into the "origin," frozen, reified for good. Daddy isn't the rival you must defeat in order to become the real Other in a woman's inner world. Daddy is the Big Other whose presence controls everything Martha does: she always was and always will remain a dependent child.

The position of the Father is equally confining. In a striking variant on the Lacanian theme, George finds that the real Father is once again the Dead Father. But the "female" variant on the Lacanian theme reveals the darker conclusions Lacan suppresses. The Dead Father is not the guilt empowering the superego but the imploding force that reduces everything to nursery rhymes. George has become Martha's Daddy, but she is about to sleep with the iceman, and George knows what Hickey only slowly came to realize. Fantasy dead, language collapses to the prior state. The death of self, like the silence enforced by George's first novel, is here revealed as the position Martha has also always occupied. The big bad wolf and the fear of Virginia Woolf are one in this psychic economy, because the former's presence, controlling Martha's inner world, empowers the anxiety that rules the manic activities—the roles and games—whereby she incessantly flees it. Fairy tales hide as subtext the dark unconscious. Nursery rhymes stage it. The murderer rocks you off to sleep, singing a song about himself, in and as the question you can never ask.

Unlike Daddy, however, George has an unspoken line which summarizes the psychological knowledge he has brought, as ice ax, to the sea in which they are all frozen. I take it from another equally compelling descent into the ground possibility for a genuine dialectic of Eros and Thanatos. When in *Last Tango in Paris* Jeanne tells Paul she's in love and has found the man who will protect her and take care of her and build a fortress where she will never be lonely again—thus fulfilling the romantic delusion that can only end, Paul notes, with the narcissistic worship of that man's "prick"—he tells her she'll never find such a man: "No, you're alone. You're all alone. And you won't be able to be free of that feeling of being alone until you look death right in the face. I mean, that sounds like bullshit and some romantic crap. Until you go right up into the ass of death—right up his ass—till you find a womb of fear. And then, maybe, maybe then you can—you'll be able to find him."[22] Such a journey has now been completed.

The Audience Crypted

Love, as possibility, only arises after death-work—but not for George and Martha. If it exists as possibility for us, it only does so thanks to the effect works such as Albee's have on us. In opening the crypt and forcing us to seek our psyches at that depth, such works give us the task of phylogenetic regression as the only meaningful response to the process of devolution George has enacted. Our task is no less than to reverse ourselves from the "ground" up by taking the basic wounds and faults of the psyche upon ourselves in an effort to undo the psychological structures (defenses, emotions, and modes of human interaction) which the failure to face them has produced.

But that possibility requires a prior act, a final getting of the guests. The audience that at the end clutches the sentimental text by ignoring its disruptive subtext does so because they have never really been present in this theatre. The bad faith that was their price of admission remains the ticket whereby they reclaim their investment. They prove the fact by seizing, of necessity, on the "interpretation" needed to discharge whatever tensions the play has generated in them.

Sustaining the force of the subtext, in contrast, is the act whereby a far different audience claims its rights by rejecting the "intellectualizing" operations, or defense mechanisms, whereby critics traditionally achieve interpretive closure. The greatest of these mechanisms remains the flight to thematic abstractions, to a discourse of "meaning" that "sublimates" the conflicts the work has opened up by transforming those conflicts into abstract propositions—about life, love, marriage, sex, death, rites of passage, vertiginous possibilities of linguistic aberration, whatever. The search for such escape routes is alert throughout the play, storing "data." It now retrospectively rereads and consecrates whatever details can be used to deliver the audience from the play.

To cite one kind of example: the body of thematic interpretations that have explained the play as an opposition between the old culture and the new, the East and the West, the movement from night to day, and as a study of homosexual behaviors masquerading as a study of heterosexual experience. A seemingly more sophisticated but equally subsumptive procedure—the superimposition on the play of ahistorical universals about ritual and myth—views the play as yet another example of ritual slaying and the scapegoat mechanism, or of life in the wasteland awaiting the arrival of Godot and the inevitable movement from winter to spring.

"Deconstructive" procedures claim less self-mystification but finally produce similar results. Thus, the snapping of the truth-illusion binary and, retrospectively, its elaborate construction deliver us from conflict to the haven of an epistemologically sophisticated relativism. Albee has crafted a plot of undecidables, thus demonstrating the by now familiar but psychologically convenient dogma that makes the skeptical play of wit in interpretation the highest act of critical intelligence.[23] So ensconced, one can easily slide over the fact that Albee does no such thing. Wit is one of the first games targeted in the play, and Albee's purpose in doing so is not to build for it a grander, safer fortress but to identify its defensive functions so that he can clear the space for a descent into a psychic crypt where it will be of little avail, since the difference between truth and illusion doesn't matter once psychological reality has announced its primacy.

For it is decidable. One of its powers, in fact, is the ability to reveal sophisticated epistemological games as a defense mechanism grounded in deliberate bad faith. Entering that psychological space—and sustaining the anxiety attendant to it—is the work of dialectics or concrete "deconstruction," which is not yet another intellectual operation but a use of intellect to enter a space where greater powers in the psyche will control and determine mental operations. In learning to live humbly there, intellect achieves its authenticity as the cutting edge of a passion to do more with one's experience than merely knowing, since intellect is only as good as the anxious discipline of psychological deracination it serves.

In playing either of the dominant interpretive games, we protect ourselves from this possibility by banishing all the ways in which a work like Albee's is designed to get both his immediate and his interpretive guests. Our concern here is with the latter, though the connection is worth noting, since critics by and large make foolproof the operations audiences perform by moving the game into a safer hyperintellectual space.

As Albee's mousetrap closes, each search for an origin, each interpretive framework (for explaining character, motives, causes, etc.), and each attempt to arrest the descent into the Crypt are undercut, and their psychological foundations exposed. In the process, available frameworks of explanation that could be imposed upon the play are revealed as moments within the psychological critique that is its subject. We note, in passing, a conspicuous one. Our reading can be labeled psychoanalytic, and yet it is based on none of the theories that have been developed in the history of psychoanalysis.[24] Its function, rather, is to challenge current psychoanalytic theories by articulating precisely what those frameworks cannot see—or, better, what they must cover up. Such a practice deliberately reverses the way the game of interpretation is usually played. The common practice is to get a fixed set of psychoanalytic concepts—whether from Freud, Lacan, Kohut, object-relations, Erikson, or whomever—and then impose them on literary works, the assumption being that Albee, say, either consciously used them to construct his work or, for unconscious reasons, wrote an illustration of their universal truth. The possibility Freud granted the artist is thus cut off: the possibility that art knows things psychoanalysis doesn't and provides an original source of insights with the power to refute some of its most cherished assumptions. The main one, of course, is the question of how far one must go in seeing the ways in which psychoanalysis protects itself from a radical knowledge of the psyche.

In moving beyond what the conventional analytic wisdom offers, Albee invites it to enter the most dangerous game. For his purpose throughout is not simply to debunk interpretive frameworks but also to expose the motives beneath them so that the psyche will be driven to descend into the depths to confront what interpretive frameworks are designed to protect it from. It is not the interpretations alone that are wrong, but the psyche that clings to them in order to escape a self-knowledge it cannot bear.

Albee springs a similar trap on the emotional confidence of a far different theoretical audience. As the play progresses, far more than interpretations collapse. The greater collapse is of the patterning of desires and expectations audiences use to control the emotional impact of such a work and the subsequent effort of affective critics to make the act of interpretation an articulation of the emotional response the work is designed to produce. The conspicuous example here, since they have done it rigorously by trying to specify emotional form through close structural reading, is the movement that used to be called the Chicago neo-Aristotelians and is now simply termed rhetorical criticism.[25] Based on a theory of emotion left for the most part implicit, the grand assumption of the approach is the claim to understand the emotions—and specifically the emotions created by those works that are finally of greatest interest and concern to us: serious, tragic works that often stir up emotional turmoil and even threaten our emotional well-being. Not the least of such a critic's tasks is to protect and restore our emotional health and to identify and domesticate artistic excess. Comedy tomorrow, tragedy tonight, for if one can use interpretation to save the identity of an audience confronted by such works, our other emotions will take care of themselves.

Confronted with a work like *Virginia Woolf*, however, another possibility arises. The emotions that rhetorical criticism claims as basic to human character and that it uses to control our emotional response to literary works are precisely the emotions that Albee exposes as defenses developed to conceal deeper, more disruptive emotions. As Spinoza noted, an emotion can only be replaced by another emotion. Emotions exist and take on value because they protect us from other emotions while giving us the sense of ego-identity and of command over our emotional life and over those experiences that threaten it.

Because it goes to the marrow, Albee's play hacks at the greatest of these, pity and fear, in order to bring to the surface the deeper emotions which they exist to conceal—and repress.[26] Our emotional life is a layered structure which has as its basic truth the proposition that we don't know how we "really" feel because our emotions are, for the most part, defenses operating to discharge the threat of experiences that produce anxiety. Only when one enters such experiences, with anxiety unbound and sustained, does one's buried emotional life come forth. Moreover, once one does so, the emotions we use to control our responses reveal themselves as the petty and self-protective things they are. We can always say that Albee has gone too far, but we should not at the same time claim to produce an interpretation that honors the emotional structure present as the *dynamis* of his work. This either/or really signals a double defeat for this approach, since it reveals the need to assert, at the level of a philosophic theory of the universal principles of human response, the emotions necessary to sustain the ego-identity on which the theory is based. The irony here is similar to the one at the expense of psychoanalysis discussed above. Albee has gone where rhetorical criticism fears to tread. It can only defend itself against the threat by misinterpreting his work, either by violently yoking it to the emotional responses the normal audience requires or by asserting that Albee has produced a work that is aesthetically unsatisfying, since it lacks the closure we demand. The old warhorse catharsis thus strides forth again, revealed in an ironically modern equivalent of its original medical meaning.

If we are alive to Albee's gift to the audience, the process the work forces us to undergo is finally similar to that of the characters on stage. The only difference, and by now one hopes it has collapsed, is that most of us contrive to play out this process in a purely intellectual—and thus inauthentic—space, the space we call interpretation. The plot of *Virginia Woolf*—as the getting of the guests—is the necessary and irreversible march of a dialectical structure in which interpretive frameworks, psychological needs, and emotional safeguards collapse together, as subtexts arise to activate the conflicts and feelings these structures repress. We are thereby entangled in a process of regression in which our defenses are destroyed as we are brought before an Unconscious we can only face in dread, since death-work emerges as its presiding agency.

Albee's play dramatizes the basic operations whereby the psyche either resists or moves toward self-knowledge. Its attempt is to strip away all defenses and hiding places so that a genuine movement of descent can commence. One suspects that at some level every audience knows this. That "knowledge" generates the two broad movements of participation in the play. If we respond defensively, we must, like Nick, find some way to assert our difference. Diana Trilling did, as did those in other professions who simply inverted her point; so did those who rush in to tell us that the play has no relevance to heterosexual relationships because . . . and so on. If we refuse such easy exists, we become agents, rather than spectators, engaged in a process roughly analogous to that of the psyches laid bare on that stage. They, in turn, are no longer "pathological characters" but have become internalized presences who shock us with recognitions we initially welcome, only to squirm when we find ourselves, like them, caught in mousetraps that make urgent our desire to deny the psychological probing we previously welcomed. In becoming such agents, we enter the space that must be cleared before any actual psychoanalysis can begin.

The first audience knows that fun and games is the reason most people go to the theatre. But theatre remains fun and games only as long as we are reassured that things won't get out of hand or that a "useful" purpose will be served. The through-line of act I is the destruction of this guarantee; acts II and III offer a rigorous exploration of what emerges once it no longer rules the stage. The end of act III is a wake-up call for Eric Berne and friends, who have been nodding off for several hours now. Albee restores the illusions needed to get their applause, but he does so by parodying them: the need for illusions is thus revealed as the deus ex machina that will spasm forth at the slightest textual prompting. "Catharsis" is thereby offered and withdrawn at one and the same moment. The needs of the typical theatregoer and the space of the theatre are split. The latter remains a space of anxiety and psychological effort only for those who do not need to take their leave, because they know that no one really can.

When does the audience leave the theatre? We can now say that they do so whenever they reach the spot where the drama shows they were never really there—as *Da-sein*. When a play uncovers psychic conflicts that must remain closed and delivers the audience over to an anxiety they cannot attend to, they take their leave, even though most politely remain in their seats, as they must, since the guarantees they use to limit drama must find some way to reassert themselves. What we call interpretation is a storehouse of such operations.

The audience that remains present, experiencing the inadequacy of their interpretations as blessing rather than loss, enters the hermeneutic of engagement. Interpretation as defense gives way to an authentic regression that takes the entire psyche with it. Unconscious motives, now unmoored, have become the targets of a drama that occurs in the seats as well as on the stage—or, better, between the two, since the "casting of the audience" has now become the innermost necessity of the audience. To use and abuse a currently popular term, this is the act that is required in order to become a member of Albee's authorial audience.[27] In radically opening the Crypt, Albee may, of course, give us no more than a beginning. But there is no way we can know that unless and until we descend into the crypt without reserve, to find through phylogenetic regression and the effort of active reversal whether love can reverse death and all that we earlier thought was safely outside its power but which is now seen as its domain.

Nothing less will do, because all the psychological theories that would save us from such an effort have been exposed as flights from it. In letting death-work triumph, Albee has given us the great gift of a scorched-earth policy toward all our illusions and avoidances. It is an offer we can't refuse because, even if we attend the play alone, as inter- and intrapsychic beings we are the couple who must return home, after the performance, not with the promise of dawn but with a long night before us. The play's greatness is its refusal to restore any illusions. In doing so, it leaves us with the barest and richest of possibilites. Like George and Martha, we can't go back to the old games. If we are to escape their "fate," we must begin with a descent that looks irreversible but that actually gives the possibility of active reversal the only marrow that can nourish it.

Like O'Neill and Williams, Albee has practiced the best game in town: get the guests. And as our study has shown, the guests are gotten best when they know it least or deny it most strenuously. Great plays aim to take up residence in the Unconscious, the place where nothing sits still. When the conscious mind resists that internalization, it merely reifies the nondialectical side of its agency, thereby generating by reflex an Unconscious that is more avid in its operations, as a result of the refusal to recognize all the ways in which we dance to its tune. The dead audience lives on. The greatest play and the most exacting analytic practice cannot alter that fact. Habit, as Beckett wrote, is a great deadener. But if the dead live on, banishing the theatres in which we perform their autopsy, we now know how they do so— and at what cost.

Epilogue: Entering the Crypt— Beyond Reparation and the Symbolic Order

The attempt here has been to initiate a new direction for psychoanalytic theory; to liberate the truth of depression and get it out into the world; to expose and reverse the reparative bind; to reveal the hollowness of the Symbolic Order and the implosiveness of its reified logic; to liberate psychotic anxiety so that we can enter the Crypt, know the power death-work and soul-murder have in the constitution and regulation of the psyche, and begin to seek out the possibility of the dialectic that could attempt their reversal—

to show that what theatre offers is not yet another safe space in which we enact the rituals needed to restore our guarantees, but the place where the secrets we hide from one another are made public so that we may enter that space, deracinated, all exits barred, brought face to face with the existential imperative which drama inserts directly into the deepest places of our psyche.

. . . And when he returned, dismembered, the gods of the underworld told Orpheus that he had finally attained the conditions of song.

Notes

Index

Notes

Introduction

1. A *hermeneutics of engagement* is the general label I offer to identify the dialectical theory of interpretation I am developing. I provided the philosophic bases for this approach in *Inwardness and Existence: Subjectivity in/and Hegel, Heidegger, Marx, and Freud* (Madison: University of Wisconsin Press, 1989). The present book is the example constructed to illustrate how that position applies to the interpretation of literary texts. A hermeneutics of engagement is intended as an alternative to other hermeneutic theories, among them those of Heidegger, Ricoeur, Gadamer, and Habermas. It also refers current literary theories and approaches to a framework of problems which they necessarily both illustrate and repress. The possibility of an immanent critique of the practices currently dominant in the profession is thereby offered.

2. New theories have come and gone since I wrote *The Act of Interpretation* (Chicago: University of Chicago Press, 1978). Little has changed, however, in the way most critics apply theories and concepts to texts. The dialectical epistemology attempted here tries to show the ways in which authentic engagement opens up an understanding which frees us and the literary work from the convenient way in which the Kantian turn has been appropriated by critics who are happy to acquiesce in self-imposed epistemological limits. Interpretation thereby becomes merely an occasion to demonstrate mastery of a technique and its dogmatic imposition. Literature in this context has nothing to teach us, because there is no way, epistemologically, we can learn anything from the encounter. All we can know is the self-reference of our categories in the a priori closure of their circularity—the infinite fascination of Narcissus with the impossibility of ever seeing anything but his own image.

3. In this sense Albee's play completes the process, but only because the previous examinations have created the context through which we view and engage it. Often in the text I will use the word *Aufhebung*—which carries the simultaneous connotations of "to cancel" "to preserve," and "to raise to a new level"—to call attention to the larger argument—or phenomenology of the psyche—enacted in the book. That process can also be thought of as a drama which has as its five acts the five interpretations needed to constitute its agon. In so doing, this work generates the content that concretizes the dialectical concept of subjectivity that I formulated in *Inwardness and Existence.*

4. The present study thereby renews the project of *The Act of Interpretation* by making the audience, or what is now generally called reader-response criticism, the explicit focus of critique. Moreover, the critique is radically destabilizing, because it

shows that extant theories of reading, audience, and interpretation are set up in order to repress the psychological conflicts and anxieties which the critique liberates. In this connection it is worth noting that in conversation Wayne Booth once suggested that *Get the Guests* could appropriately be subtitled "The Rhetoric of Drama." That designation fits, but with this proviso: my effort is to assert the claims of an order of existential-psychoanalytic conflict which overturns the essentialistic and humanistic assumptions upon which the implied audience of works such as *The Rhetoric of Fiction* depend in order to safeguard their "identity" and deprive the literary experience of its most authentic possibility.

5.   In developing a new theory of the affective charge on the audience embodied in the dramatic structure of a literary work, I attempt, in effect, to wed Freud and Aristotle in an interdisciplinary marriage that transforms both parties. Drama catches us up in a uniquely revelatory experience because the psyche is a dramatic structure and exists forever given over to that inescapable self-mediation. Thus, I join Aristotle's idea of reversal and recognition as the structuring principles of tragic drama with Freud's understanding of how the repressed, in actively structuring our experience, gives our life the continuity of a drama that grows apace, however disguised or deferred. Such is our fate because reversal and recognition, the movement to crisis and trauma, are the innermost principles that constitute the dialectic of the psyche, giving experience a structure—and a justice—that cannot be escaped, even though one may never become consciously aware of the sad affair one has made of one's life.

To prevent misunderstanding, I note here that, as with Freud, my relationship to the *Poetics* is critical—not only with respect to pity, fear, and catharsis but also with regard to the metaphysical guarantees and the theory of human nature that Aristotle used to impose ethical and humanistic limitations on the exploratory power of art— because my goal is to historicize the *Poetics* through the (tragically) illuminating reflection of dramas that bear the conflicts of a world that has little in common with Aristotle's golden moment. In taking up R. S. Crane's great question—"What would Aristotle have had to change in his theory of tragedy had he known *Macbeth?*"—I will respond, "Virtually everything."

Chapter 1: Souls on Ice

1.   For an overview of current conceptions of group psychology, see Saul Scheid-linger, ed., *Psycho-Analytic Group Dynamics: Basic Readings* (New York: International Universities Press, 1980). For more promising directions, suggested more than developed, see W. R. Bion, *Experiences in Groups* (New York: Basic Books, 1959). My goal in this chapter is to offer *The Iceman Cometh* as the example which radically undercuts the protective assumptions that have controlled the theory and practice of group psychology.

2.   This is the position Freud develops in *Group Psychology and the Analysis of the Ego*, in the standard edition of *The Complete Psychological Works*, ed. and trans. James Strachey et al., 24 vols. (London: Hogarth, 1953–74), 18:65–144.

3.   Martin Heidegger, *Being and Time* (New York: Harper, 1962), 154–63.

4. The concept of death-work, which I introduce here, is the central idea which requires the entire book for development. The difference between this concept and Freud's thought on Thanatos and the death instinct is considerable; nor can anything comparable to the concept of death-work I am developing be found in current psychoanalytic theory. For modern theorists, with the exception of Lacan, who finally sticks close to Freud's position, death is a drive that psychoanalysis has vanquished. Thus the concept here advanced of death as a work active within the innermost constitution of the psyche—and therefore a primary motive behind the operations that inform the ego and shape the quotidian—is an attempt to formulate the terms for the date psychoanalysis refuses to keep with the unconscious. For a careful reconstruction of the death drive in Freud and Lacan, see Richard Boothby, *Death and Desire: Psychoanalytic Theory in Lacan's Return to Freud* (New York: Routledge, 1991). Though her reifying framework confuses the issue, Melanie Klein offers invaluable insights on death as drive.

5. Eugene O'Neill, *The Iceman Cometh* (New York: Vintage, 1946). All page references in the text are to this edition.

6. This concept both of reading and of the identity on which it depends is implicit throughout Wayne Booth's work. He comes closest to an explicit discussion of it in *Critical Understanding: The Powers and Limits of Pluralism* (Berkeley: University of California Press, 1978).

7. One of the best guides to the concepts of transference and countertrans-ference is Robert Langs, *The Technique of Psychoanalytic Psychotherapy*, vols. 1 and 2 (New York: Jacob Aronson, 1974). For the richest, deepest probing of the topic, one must turn to Enrique Racker, *Transference and Counter-Transference* (London: International Universities Press, 1968), and to Donald W. Winnicott's seminal essay, "Hate in the Counter-Transference," in his *Collected Papers* (London: Tavistock, 1958), 194–203.

8. Freud, "Some Character-Types Met with in Psycho-Analytic Work," in *Works* 14:311–33. Freud's work remains a gold mine of radical thought about art, but his official position is for the most part conservative and ironically achieves perhaps its standard formulation in Norman Holland, *The Dynamics of Literary Response* (New York: Columbia University Press, 1975). Holland's position still typifies what most psychoanalytic literary critics do today, though in far more ornate post-structural language.

9. Freud, *The Problem of Anxiety*, in *Works* 20:11–121. See also Roy Schafer, "Danger Situations," *Journal of the American Psychoanalytic Association* 24 (1960): 1–32.

10. See Jacques Derrida, *Dissemination* (Chicago: University of Chicago Press, 1981), 95–117.

11. The contrast here and in subsequent disagreement is with Jessica Benjamin's recent book *The Bonds of Love* (New York: Pantheon, 1988). Benjamin's book is representative of the new wave of American ego psychology. Interestingly, a severely truncated understanding of Hegel's great theory of Self-Consciousness (*The Phenomenology of Mind*, translated by J. Baillie, 2d ed. [New York: Humanities Press

Inc., 1931], section B) is used to ground the project. For me the significance of the book is that it provides a perfect contrast to the theory of psyche I am developing. In effect, it constitutes an attempt by denial to purge the crypt from the psyche.

12.   On the concept of the internal saboteur, see W. R. D. Fairbairn, *An Object-Relations Theory of the Personality* (New York: Routledge, 1952). By grounding the concept of the internal saboteur in a metapsychology of death-work, I make an effort to radicalize Fairbairn's framework by destabilizing the ego-syntonic assumptions on which it is based. The concept of death-work thereby reverses and radicalizes Fairbairn's framework.

13.   The great psychotic Dr. Shreber first coined the term *soul-murder* to describe his state. Leonard Shengold reintroduces it in his recent *Soul Murder: The Effects of Child Abuse and Deprivation* (New Haven, Conn.: Yale University Press, 1987). Unfortunately, few of the disruptive implications of the idea are developed. Nor does Shengold go into the implications of this experience for metapsychology. Bion's work on psychotic anxiety—especially in "Differentiation of the Psychotic from the Non-Psychotic Personalities," *International Journal of Psycho-Analysis* 38 (1957): 266–75, and "Attacks on Linking," *International Journal of Psycho-Analysis* 40 (1959): 308–15—strikes the deeper chord and gets at the kind of experiences where the concept of soul-murder must be taken in order for its radical possibilities to be realized.

14.   Basic trust is thus perhaps the regimen that creates the basic fault, that core and most deeply repressed site of the psyche's founding disorder. Michael Balint introduced this term in *The Basic Fault* (London: Tavistock, 1968). The most significant developments of the concept, largely sans the term, are in the works of Winnicott and Bion.

15.   Gregory Bateson, *Steps to an Ecology of Mind* (New York: Chandler, 1972), esp. 201–79, 309–37.

16.   On sexuality as identity, see my *Inwardness and Existence,* 296–307.

17.   Donald W. Winnicott, "Psychoanalysis and the Sense of Guilt," in *The Maturational Processes and the Facilitating Environment* (London: International Universities Press, 1965), 15–28. Repeatedly in the brilliant essays collected in this volume, Winnicott attains tragic insights which exceed the reassuring framework, or holding environment, in which he couches them.

18.   Elias Canetti, *Crowds and Power* (New York: Viking, 1962).

19.   One conceptual through-line of *Get the Guests* is an attempt to overturn the ritual theory of theatre by showing precisely where it must violate the text in order to superimpose its ideological need. The two most powerful statements of the dominant view of ritual's social function and its formative power as a principle of structure in literature are the works of Kenneth Burke, and René Girard, *Violence and the Sacred* (Baltimore: Johns Hopkins University Press, 1977). Mention should also be made of Victor Turner, *The Ritual Process* (Chicago: Aldine, 1969), and the work of Mircea Eliade and Joseph Campbell. For the completion of the counterargument I am constructing, see below, chap. 4, n. 3.

20.   For patient, accurate, and critically reflective descriptions of these assump-

tions, see Hans Loewald, *Papers on Psychoanalysis* (New Haven, Conn.: Yale University Press, 1982), esp. 16–33, and Roy Schafer, "The Psychoanalytic Version of Reality," in *A New Language for Psychoanalysis* (New Haven, Conn.: Yale University Press, 1976), 22–56.

21. For Lacan's view, see especially Jacques Lacan, *Écrits: A Selection* (New York: Tavistock, 1977), 292–325. Because both Lacan and I want to sustain the disorder that is the psyche, Lacan's work and mine have many points of similarity, including the use of Hegelian and existential sources. From my perspective, however, Lacan's "Cartesian" concern to formulate the pure logic of the psyche's positions bars genuine engagement with the experiences and passions that are crypted therein. We get instead the schematization of structures in which the psyche is frozen in endless displaced repetition. Since that is the case, irony is therapy.

22. Paul Ricoeur discusses Freud's Spinozism in *Freud and Philosophy* (New Haven, Conn.: Yale University Press, 1970).

23. Heidegger, *Being and Time*, 315–41. Never is the Kantian formalism of Heidegger's analytic more distressing in its ability to arrest powerful insights into existence. In the course of Heidegger's discussion, guilt, refined out of real existence, becomes abstract and a priori.

24. Freud, "On Negation," in *Works* 19:235–41. Negativity as determinate negation—which is the structuring principle of Hegel's *Phenomenology*—offers this alternative: a systematic understanding of what one denies as the reality that overturns what one affirms. In making that principle the totalizing and innermost imperative of his book, Hegel in effect takes the concepts of reversal and recognition, which Aristotle confined to tragic drama, and makes them the ontological bases of thought and experience.

25. On undoing, blowing away, and other primitive defense mechanisms, see V. Volkan, *Primitive Internalized Object Relations* (New York: International Universities Press, 1976), and P. Giovacchini, *Treatment of Primitive Mental States* (New York: Jason Aronson, 1979).

26. On the manic triad and its defensive function, see Melanie Klein, "Mourning and Its Relationship to Manic-Depressive States," *International Journal of Psycho-Analysis* 21 (1940): 211–18, and idem, "A Contribution to the Theory of Anxiety and Guilt," *International Journal of Psycho-Analysis* 29 (1948): 63–79. See also Winnicott, "The Manic Defence," in *Collected Papers*, 129–43.

27. On this concept, see Melanie Klein, especially *Love, Guilt and Reparation and Other Works, 1921–1945* (London: Free Press, 1984). The concept of reparation is currently being celebrated in many circles as the grand therapeutic solution. My goal in the course of this book is to reverse its claims by exposing the guarantees it superimposes in order to deliver Kleinian psychoanalysis from its great, dark investigations of the psyche. Closing the circle, it offers a mirror image of the blindness at the beginning, that is, Melanie Klein's refusal to see the mother's part in forming the terrors of the unconscious. Reparation seals that fault.

28. On the mass psychology of fascism, see T. W. Adorno et al, *The Authoritarian Personality* (New York: Norton, 1975), and Georges Bataille, "The Psychologi-

cal Structure of Fascism," in *Visions of Excess* (Minneapolis: University of Minnesota Press, 1985), 137–60.

29. For the formulation of this concept of how regression works within ego psychology, see Ernst Kris, "Regression in the Service of the Ego," in *Psychoanalytic Explorations in Art* (New York: International Universities Press, 1952), 186–212.

30. For Hegel's understanding of death-work as the ground of dialectics, see *Phenomenology*, 93ff. My attempt here and subsequently is to use this concept in a way that concretely reverses the rationalistic march of Hegel's *Bildung* by opening up those tragic dimensions of the psyche which cannot be sublated. They point instead toward a Nietzschean, tragic reconstitution of dialectical thinking. That goal is the through-line of my overarching project.

Chapter 2: The Perfect Couple

1. The structure of this chapter is dialectical. Thus each section constitutes the *Aufhebung* of the previous one. Tennessee Williams, *A Streetcar Named Desire* (New York: New Directions, 1980). All page references in the text are to this edition.

2. The grounding of psychology in gender and the reduction of sources of conflict to this focus is so widespread within feminist criticism that it would be inappropriate to cite a single source. It is also unnecessary to endorse the power and cogency of these argument. My hope in this chapter, however, is to suggest the claims of "mutual cruelty" to get at a prior and deeper source of psychological conflict/disorder which has the ability to sustain itself irrespective of gender.

3. Drawing freely on Hegel, its parent text, George Lukacs' *History and Class Consciousness* (Cambridge, Mass.: MIT Press, 1971) offers the paradigmatic modern formulation of this position. It has been widely adapted, often without reference to Lukacs, by a number of feminist theoreticians. For an early example, see Jean Baker Miller, *Toward a New Psychology of Women* (Boston: Beacon Press, 1976).

4. My attempt is thus to refer both the Lacan of *Feminine Sexuality* (New York: Norton, 1983) and those feminist theorists who constitute their position by simply inverting Lacan—the most noteworthy example being Irigaray—to a problematic of mutual cruelty which gets at a psychodynamic that is prior to their starting point. It thereby challenges both sides of the opposition and the theories of male and female psychology derived from them.

5. On the *fort/da*, see Freud, *Beyond the Pleasure Principle*, in *Works* 18:1–64.

6. In what follows I illustrate the dialectical movement of this logic of contradictions in order to provide a contrast with Derrida's deconstructive methodology.

7. On the concept of active reversal, see my *Inwardness and Existence*, 260–65, 300–313.

8. See my *Inwardness and Existence*, 98–106, 151–56, 234–39, 282–96.

9. This paragraph echoes Williams' epigraph for the play taken from Hart Crane's great poem "The Broken Tower."

10. The finest formulation of this interpretive method remains R. S. Crane, *The*

Languages of Criticism and the Structure of Poetry (Toronto: University of Toronto Press, 1953).

11. Elia Kazan, "Notebook for *A Streetcar Named Desire*," in *Twentieth Century Interpretations of "A Streetcar Named Desire*," ed. Jordan Y. Miller (Englewood Cliffs, N.J.: Prentice-Hall, 1971), 21–27.

12. On unconscious envy, see Klein, *Love, Guilt and Reparation.*

13. See Harold F. Searles, *Collected Papers on Schizophrenia and Related Subjects* (New York: International Universities Press, 1965), pp. 254ff., for a striking development of this concept.

14. Lacan, *Feminine Sexuality,* 138–161.

Chapter 3: All in the Family

1. Although I develop the ideas differently, I am indebted to Lois Tyson's "The Psychological Politics of the American Dream: *Death of a Salesman* and the Case for an Existential Dialectics," *Essays in Literature* 19, no. 2 (1992): 260–78, for the understanding of Willy's flashbacks as psychological regressions. Tyson shows how the play answers the questions "How?" and "Why?" in a way that illustrates the explanatory power of Althusser's theory concerning the reproduction of ideology in the individual subject. I am also indebted to Gretchen Cline's not-yet-published work on this play.

2. Arthur Miller, *The Theatre Essays of Arthur Miller* (New York: Viking 1978). These essays are an invaluable summary of the assumptions humanism brings to theatre and to the concept of tragedy. The critique of Miller developed in this chapter constitutes the Marxist moment of the present inquiry and a concrete exemplification of the necessary dialectical connection of Marxist and psychoanalytic categories argued in my *Inwardness and Existence,* chaps. 3 and 4. The position here taken is also aligned with that of Walter Benjamin and the practice of the Frankfurt school on the interpretation of culture. Arthur Miller, *Death of a Salesman* (New York: Vikings, 1949). All page references in the text are to this edition. Since the theory never changes, the best statement of the rationale behind interpreting literature in terms of themes that can be abstracted from the work remains Gerald Graff, *Poetic Statement and Critical Dogma* (Chicago: University of Chicago Press, 1970).

3. My attempt here is to show how Althusser on ideology (see especially *Lenin and Philosophy and Other Essays* [New York: Monthly Review Press, 1971]) and the psychoanalytic concept of internalization (which Althusser would condemn as left-wing pre-Marxist Hegelianism) can be related to the dialectical benefit of both frameworks, that is, the development of an understanding of ideology that gets at the deepest places of that power and thereby identifies the site and sources of resistance.

4. With good reason a number of recent cultural critics, most notably Baudrillard, have seen implosion as the concept that may best describe the logic of late capitalist society. In the hollow center it refuses to recognize, *Death of a Salesman* already knows that eventuality.

5. The attempt in this chapter is thus to reverse the neostructuralist nondia-

lectical opposition Fredric Jameson establishes in *The Political Unconscious* (Ithaca, N.Y.: Cornell University Press, 1981) through his deployment of the Lacanian categories, especially the Symbolic. Lacan is, of course, the grand master of their hypostatization. This close reading of Miller prys loose the kind of understanding that is barred as long as interpretation remains concerned primarily with the permutations of abstract categories.

6.   This effort aligns the methodology of this chapter to Hickey's effort in *The Iceman Cometh*. The audience I am after is, of course, far more sophisticated.

7.   On the difference between concrete dialectic and deconstruction, see my *Inwardness and Existence*, 346ff.

8.   Biff will finally put his money on a romantic-naturalist myth of self-presence; Miller as humanist ideologue will later perform an analogous act in his essays through the assertion of an essentialistic humanism that provides the guarantees he needs, both before and after drama, to prevent the Marxist and psychoanalytic implications of the play from getting out of control. Miller uses these frameworks up to a point—as ways of locating character's defenses—but refuses to let them impinge on the humanistic and essentialistic views of identity and character he superimposes upon them.

9.   In *The Price* Miller confronts the biographical basis of this experience.

10.   The ironic allusion is to Wallace Stevens, "The Auroras of Autumn."

11.   Miller, *Theatre Essays*, 138–44.

12.   See Kenneth Burke, *Language as Symbolic Action* (Berkeley: University of California Press, 1966), esp. 81–139.

Chapter 4: Drug of Choice

1.   Two of the better books dealing with the concept of the dysfunctional family are Jay Haley and Lynn Hoffman, *Techniques of Family Therapy* (New York: Basic Books, 1968), and Lynn Hoffman, *Foundations of Family Therapy* (New York: Basic Books, 1981). See also the work of Alice Miller, especially *Prisoners of Childhood* (New York: Basic Books, 1981). In striving to limit the impact and scope of their insight into the disorder that reigns in the normal, ordinary family, these works invoke guarantees reminiscent of Miller. O'Neill, in contrast, dives directly into the disorders Miller strives to repress.

2.   Eugene O'Neill, *Long Day's Journey into Night* (New Haven, Conn.: Yale University Press, 1955). All page references in the text are to this edition.

3.   On the sacrificial crisis and the ritual role of theatre, see Girard, *Violence and the Sacred*. My interpretation endeavors to show that O'Neill's play constitutes the most concrete critique of the guarantees and needs that underlie Girard's definitive statement of the ritual view. Once we overcome the spirit of resentment, we have to undertake a deeper deracination—the desire for sacrifice. In making the throughline of *Get the Guests* a concrete argument against sacrifice and the ritual approach to theatre it celebrates, I am well aware of the long cultural traditions I am bucking. See, for example, Walter Burkert, *Homo Necans* (Berkeley: University of California

Press, 1983), and Nigel Davies, *Human Sacrifice* (New York: Morrow, 1981). My effort is to show, however, that the ontological possibility implicit in the very nature of drama is the critique of ritual. Theatre thereby becomes the space where the death of god is made real through the creation of "rituals" for the godless, the place where ritual structures and needs are submitted to a critique which, in overturning them, exposes the audience to all that such structures cannot contain.

4. Freud discusses the tendentious nature of jokes in *Wit and Its Relationship to the Unconscious*, in *Works* 8:1–236.

5. By delving into guilt, O'Neill's critique of the ego and any psychology based on its maintenance gets at the lower layer that the otherwise brilliant Lacanian critique of its delusional narcissistic functions does not reach. See Lacan, Seminar II, *The Ego in Freud's Theory and in the Technique of Psychoanalysis, 1954–1955* (New York: Norton, 1991).

6. The pioneering study of the topic, and a work of enduring value, is Wilhelm Reich, *Character-Analysis* (New York: Farrar, Straus and Giroux, 1949).

7. Artaud and Grotowski made conspicuous attempts to mandate this process. It remains the innermost and radically destabilizing possibility that is present whenever an ensemble gather to rehearse a play. It is thus in no way opposed to the givens of naturalism and realism, since it constitutes the level to which the great actor descends in building a character and creating a role. This dynamic is also why acting always remains of necessity an existentially dangerous profession. For a superb presentation and sorting out of the major issues surrounding modern theories of acting and performance, see Timothy J. Wiles, *The Theater Event: Modern Theories of Performance* (Chicago: University of Chicago Press, 1980). Mention here should also be made of two theories with which mine can be meaningfully contrasted: see Herbert Blau, *The Audience* (Baltimore: Johns Hopkins University Press, 1990), and Bruce Wilshire, *Role Playing and Identity* (Bloomington: Indiana University Press, 1982).

8. Acting as theme is thus a dramatic structure and not an abstract idea. O'Neill's "themes" are invariably announced with all the subtlety of a sledgehammer. Their development never moves in the direction of abstract "philosophic" ideas, however, but is focused on the discovery of dramatic processes. O'Neill is thus one of the more eloquent critics of what is generally done in "thematic" criticism. For there is no way to transform his "themes" into abstract meanings without deliberately tearing them from their concrete existential locus. Playwrights think by creating dramatic processes and structures, and that is where their thought resides. Literature doesn't employ or illustrate philosophic ideas; it tests and exceeds them. Attempts to relate philosophy and literature through thematizing dissolves "the ancient quarrel." It is only renewed, in contrast, when the unique principles of literature as an independent way of thinking are acknowledged. O'Neill, the supposedly third-rate purveyor of Schopenhauer and Nietzsche, provides a good example.

9. On the connection between narcissism and the *objet petit a,* see Lacan's discussion of schema L in *Écrits,* 1–7, 314–24. For Lacan's thought on the *fort/da,* see also Seminar I, *Freud's Papers on Technique, 1953–54* (New York, 1988). In Kohut's hands the study of narcissistic disorders leads to a far more conservative

theory of the psyche, which fits comfortably within the "social," adaptational designs of American ego psychology. See Heinz Kohut, *The Analysis of the Self* (New York: International Universities Press, 1971). One way to formulate my labor, contra Lacan: The Lacanian system is based on a terror—of the imaginary, the pre-Symbolic, the Mother, the preoedipal—which it won't face. Flight into the oedipus, the Symbolic, is the primary defense; the discussion of narcissism and the impossibility of desire until one ascends to the symbolic, the secondary defense. My effort, in contrast, is to enter the psychic terrain Lacan consigns to silence so that we know and constitute its claims. Attention must finally be paid to such a realm.

10. My effort thus is to join Hegel and Nietzsche, dialectical self-overcoming and *amor fati*, by making the crypt the place into which spirit must repeatedly descend if it is to be what Nietzsche calls it: "The life that itself cuts into life: with its own agony it increases its own knowledge." We are now prepared to see this as the proper role of aggression, and a completion of the rehabilitation of this concept I initiated above. For an understanding of aggression that has many points of similarity to mine, see Winnicott, "Aggression in Relation to Emotional Development," in *Collected Papers*, 204–18.

11. I find Bion on catastrophe the richest attempt to explore such issues. See above, chap. 1, n. 13. Bion argues that catastrophe is the largely unexplored possibility that makes an appearance somewhere in every analytic hour. As Bion discovered, it was not only the most eloquent of his patients who knew that we have never been born properly.

12. Since Julia Kristeva sounded this call in *Tales of Love* (New York: Columbia University Press, 1987), a book that failed to deliver much beyond a rehashing of old ideas, the statement has become a grand iteration, and many have rushed in to fill the bill. Reinventing love has thus become one of the grand commonplaces of current criticism. As far as I can tell, no one has tried to think the issue through along the lines offered in this paragraph.

13. For the standard presentation of this mechanism, see Holland, *Dynamics of Literary Response*, 162–90.

14. Critics have persistently held that Edmund is different and see his liberation as the key to the play. The only way to sustain this view is by wrenching materials, such as his "sea vision," from the context of act IV, where the function of everything Edmund says and does within the familial neurosis is made clear.

15. One such eruption of the unconscious exposed Hickey. In exemplifying this principle, Jamie's story plumbs the darkness Hickey first brought to light. This connection also defines the relationship and the dialectical progression of the two plays.

16. He gets his desire and suffers its truth in the great coda, *A Moon for the Misbegotten*.

Chapter 5: The Academic Festival Overture

1. Edward Albee, *Who's Afraid of Virginia Woolf?* (New York: Atheneum, 1981). All page references in the text are to this edition.

2. On phylogenetic regression, see Harold F. Searles, *The Nonhuman Environment in Normal Development and in Schizophrenia* (New York: International Universities Press, 1960).

3. M. Balint, *Basic Fault*. For a deeper probe into its "origins," see Margaret Little, *Transference Neurosis and Transference Psychosis* (New York: Jacob Aronson, 1981).

4. Diana Trilling, "The Riddle of Albee's Virginia Woolf," in *Edward Albee: A Collection of Critical Essays*, ed. C. W. E. Bigsby (Englewood Cliffs, N.J.: Prentice Hall, 1975).

5. For Heidegger's explanation of idle talk as a structure of everyday life, see *Being and Time*, 211–14.

6. For an understanding within the terms of traditional metapsychology of how Thanatos might function as a principle of form in creating the psychodynamics of narrative structures, see Peter Brooks, *Reading for the Plot* (New York: Knopf, 1984). Fortunately, the human living of the conflict produces concrete dramas that cannot be explained in terms of such abstract forces because human agency is precisely the reality in which they are existentially and psychologically *aufgehoben*. This chapter thus constitutes a critique of Brooks's theory.

7. The allusion is to lines by de Sade in Peter Weiss's great work of metatheatre, *Marat/Sade*.

8. Freud's understanding of Eros and thanatos as dialectically related—and thus as cultural forces that cannot be explained in the reductive terms of drive-discharge metapsychology—is developed in *Civilization and Its Discontents*, in *Works* 21:57–146. On the nature of dialectical categories and the logic of their relationship, see my *Inwardness and Existence*, chap. 5.

9. Lacan gets at a similar understanding of language as aggression in *Écrits*, especially "Aggressivity in Psychoanalysis," 8–29.

10. The contrast here is with Wittgenstein's introduction and masterful development of this concept in *Philosophical Investigations* (New York: Macmillan, 1953). The kinds of games George and Martha play with words get at precisely the kind of psychological realities Wittgenstein must marginalize in order to make his social theory of meaning and of "identity" work.

11. In trying to get at the experience of humiliation prior to envy, my use of the concept of envy departs considerably from the Kleinian framework to which it is indebted. It then tries to take the whole thing in a radically new direction, toward a probe into precisely those psychic disorders Kleinian metapsychology defends against. The closest approximation I find to the direction in which I am moving is in the work of Wilfrid Bion.

12. The comparable developments of this concept are in Nietzsche and Foucault.

13. H. Searles, "The Effort to Drive the Other Person Crazy," in *Collected Papers*, 254–80.

14. For a critique of humanism, its rationalistic assumptions, and its marginalization of psychoanalysis, see my *Inwardness and Existence*.

15. This is the act of murder that constitutes the internal reversal of death-work. It is thus the founding act creating the possibility of psychic liberation.

16. For the Lacanian view outlined and criticized in this paragraph, see *Écrits*, 281–91.

17. The initial scheme from which subsequent psychoanalytic efforts to map the conditions of object-choice—or loving—derive is in Freud, "On Narcissism: An Introduction," in *Works* 14:73–102.

18. This concept of the undecidable and its psychological implications is quite different from Derrida's and De Man's, since it shows their articulation of the formalistic logic of the situation to be an intellectual defense against probing its revelatory psychodynamics.

19. This is the ironic circumstance Kohut keeps running up against, and this is why his attempt to develop a "psychology of the self" that can be neatly attached to a traditional metapsychology is a theoretical flight from deepening the examination of the disorder that is his subject.

20. The idea is not as outlandish as it initially appears once one sees that it derives from little more than abstract wordplay. See Lacan, *Feminine Sexuality*, 86–99, 137–49.

21. The allusion here is to Ernst Bloch's attempt to develop a utopian aesthetic for Marxism. Our effort to deracinate that hope constitutes a regard for the antithetical principle.

22. Bernardo Bertolucci (director), *Last Tango in Paris* (1972). The dialogue in the film, quoted here, is much sharper than in the printed text, thanks no doubt to Marlon Brando's contribution to the script.

23. For development of this critique, see my *Inwardness and Existence*, 52–57.

24. We here complete the through-line that establishes the claim made in the introduction—both that a new psychoanalytic theory is being constructed in this book and that it derives from freeing the "poets' " insights from the psychological frameworks we impose upon them.

25. The rigor with which R. S. Crane set up this problematic remains an unrealized model that measures the looseness of most of what goes on under the banners of reader-response and affective criticism. At the same time, Crane's framework is limited—severely to my mind—by its inability to open itself to the distinctly "modern" emotional exploration that characterizes the kind of tragic works we have discussed.

26. Two fine and rigorous discussions of the topic are Kenneth Telford, *Aristotle's Poetics: Translation and Analysis* (Chicago: University Press of America, 1965), and Gerald F. Else, *Aristotle's Poetics: The Argument* (Cambridge, Mass.: Harvard University Press, 1957).

27. For this outgrowth of the Boothian framework, see Peter Rabinowitz, *Before Reading: Narrative Conventions and the Politics of Interpretation* (Ithaca, N.Y.: Cornell University Press, 1987). My point, of course, is that Albee's "authorial audience"—and mine—is one that the critical tradition Rabinowitz represents cannot join.

Index

The Wisconsin Project on American Writers

Frank Lentricchia, General Editor

Chicano Narrative: The Dialectics of Difference
Ramón Saldívar

The Dickinson Sublime
Gary Lee Stonum

The American Evasion of Philosophy: A Genealogy of Pragmatism
Cornel West

Specifying: Black Women Writing the American Experience
Susan Willis

American Sublime: The Genealogy of a Poetic Genre
Rob Wilson